FROM
Easy
TO
NATIONAL PARKS OF THE AMERICAN WEST

By
Don and Barbara Laine
and Eric Peterson

EasyGuides are ✦ Quick to Read ✦ Light To Carry
✦ For Expert Advice ✦ In All Price Ranges

FrommerMedia LLC

Published by
FROMMER MEDIA LLC

Copyright © 2014 by Frommer Media LLC, New York City, New York. All rights reserved. No part of this publication may be reproduced, stored in a retrieval system, or transmitted in any form or by any means, electronic, mechanical, photocopying, recording, scanning or otherwise, except as permitted under Sections 107 or 108 of the 1976 United States Copyright Act, without the prior written permission of the Publisher. Requests to the Publisher for permission should be addressed to the Permissions Department, Frommer Media LLC at partnerships@frommermedia.com.

Frommer's is a registered trademark of Arthur Frommer. Used under license. All other trademarks are the property of their respective owners. Frommer Media LLC is not associated with any product or vendor mentioned in this book.

ISBN 978-1-62887-066-4 (paper), 978-62887-067-1 (e-book)

Editorial Director: Pauline Frommer
Editor: Pauline Frommer
Production Editor: Donna Wright
Cartographer: Roberta Stockwell

For information on our other products or services, see www.frommers.com.

Frommer Media LLC also publishes its books in a variety of electronic formats. Some content that appears in print may not be available in electronic formats.

Manufactured in the United States of America

5 4 3 2 1

ABOUT THE AUTHORS

Residents of northern New Mexico for more than 40 years, **Don** and **Barbara Laine** have traveled extensively throughout the Rocky Mountains and the Southwest, exploring the mountains and deserts and especially the national parks, with their always-curious dogs. The Laines have authored or contributed to a number of Frommer's travel guides, including all previous editions of this book, and have also written *Little-Known Southwest, New Mexico & Arizona State Parks,* and *Best Short Hikes in Arizona* for The Mountaineers Books.

Eric Peterson has been writing about travel for more than 20 years. Beyond covering the Rockies in numerous Frommer's guidebooks, he's written about skiing, hiking, and other ways to get up and down mountains for such publications as the *New York Daily News, Delta Sky,* and his own *Ramble* series of travel books. When he's not on the road, he covers the arts, technology, and city-building for Confluence Denver, a hyper-local website. Eric lives in Denver with his wife, Jamie, and their trusted canines, Mini and Duncan.

ABOUT THE FROMMER TRAVEL GUIDES

For most of the past 50 years, Frommer's has been the leading series of travel guides in North America, accounting for as many as 24% of all guidebooks sold. I think I know why.

Though we hope our books are entertaining, we nevertheless deal with travel in a serious fashion. Our guidebooks have never looked on such journeys as a mere recreation, but as a far more important human function, a time of learning and introspection, an essential part of a civilized life. We stress the culture, lifestyle, history and beliefs of the destinations we cover, and urge our readers to seek out people and new ideas as the chief rewards of travel.

We have never shied from controversy. We have, from the beginning, encouraged our authors to be intensely judgmental, critical—both pro and con—in their comments, and wholly independent. Our only clients are our readers, and we have triggered the ire of count-less prominent sorts, from a tourist newspaper we called "practically worthless" (it unsuc-cessfully sued us) to the many rip-offs we've condemned.

And because we believe that travel should be available to everyone regardless of their incomes, we have always been cost-conscious at every level of expenditure. Though we have broadened our recommendations beyond the budget category, we insist that every lodging we include be sensibly priced. We use every form of media to assist our readers, and are particularly proud of our feisty daily website, the award-winning Frommers.com.

I have high hopes for the future of Frommer's. May these guidebooks, in all the years ahead, continue to reflect the joy of travel and the freedom that travel represents. May they always pursue a cost-conscious path, so that people of all incomes can enjoy the rewards of travel. And may they create, for both the traveler and the persons among whom we travel, a community of friends, where all human beings live in harmony and peace.

Arthur Frommer

PLANNING YOUR NATIONAL PARK ADVENTURE

The National Parks of the United States are, to put it as subtly as possible, wonderful, stupendous, fabulous, stunning, and some of the most beautiful places in the world. And if you don't believe us, ask the many Europeans, Japanese, Australians, and others who flock to our parks every year.

The national parks—especially those in the American West—have a rugged beauty, but more than that, they offer visitors myriad opportunities for hiking, climbing, rafting, sightseeing, and even learning. They are truly America's National Playground.

The purpose of this book is to help you get the most out of these national treasures, to know when to go, what to see and do, how to avoid the crowds, and all-in-all, to help you have the very best national park experience possible.

FINDING THE BEST NATIONAL PARKS FOR YOU

In planning a national park vacation, one of the first decisions you have to make is which park or parks to visit. The authors have thoroughly explored each and every one of the parks in this book, and we assure you that there are no duds here. It would be pointless to try to rate them, to create a "Best Of" list, because each one is unique and truly the best of the best.

But the real question is, which parks are best for *you*? Each national park has its own personality and opportunities, so to determine which ones you should visit you'll need to do your homework—and maybe a little self-analysis—before heading out the door.

First, think about what kind of experience you're looking for. If you are a **looker,** your main motive in visiting a national park is to see that fantastic scenery first hand. This may involve hiking, or at least walking, which you'll also enjoy, but *seeing* the mountains, rock formations, lakes, streams, and all the rest is why you're really there. On the other hand if you're a **doer,** your primary motivation is to hike the trails, climb rock formations, kayak, and enjoy whatever other activities are available.

The National Park Service has done an admirable job of making every park in this guide wonderful places for both lookers and doers, and at every one there are hiking trails, walking paths, scenic drives, viewpoints, visitor centers, and ranger programs. But some parks are best for sightseeing while others are ideal for hikers and those who enjoy other outdoor

The National Park Service's website, **www.nps.gov,** has general information on national parks, monuments, and historic sites, as well as individual park maps that can be downloaded in a variety of formats. The site also contains a link to every individual park's website, and those often contain links to nearby attractions and other useful tips.

Another useful website is **www. recreation.gov,** a partnership of federal agencies that can link you to information on national parks, national forests, Bureau of Land Management sites, Bureau of Reclamation sites, Army Corps of Engineers sites, and National Wildlife Refuges. You can make reservations at campsites, book tours, and either apply for or purchase various permits.

activities. To give two contrasting examples, Arches National Park near Moab, Utah, is an easy and fun place to see spectacular red rock arches, from the scenic drive or along a trail after a short walk. Right across the road at Canyonlands National Park you'll find a few nice viewpoints, but to really appreciate the park you'll need to hit the hiking trails or backcountry roads. The first therefore is for the gawkers, and the second is best for folks who like a challenge.

While all of the parks in this book offer a variety of opportunities, some may be better for you than others. Here's a compressed list of the top destinations for vacationers with different interests and goals:

CAVES   Carlsbad Caverns, Sequoia and King's Canyon

ESCAPE THE CROWDS   Badlands

FAMILY TRAVEL   See "Taking the Kids" on page 4

GEYSERS AND HOT SPRINGS   Yellowstone, Olympic

HIKING   Grand Canyon, Glacier, Yosemite, Rocky Mountain, Bryce Canyon, Zion

HORSE AND MULE RIDES   Grand Canyon, Bryce Canyon

PREHISTORIC AMERICAN PEOPLE   Mesa Verde

MOUNTAIN SCENERY   Glacier, Grand Teton, Mount Rainier, Rocky Mountain, Sequoia and Kings Canyon

SCENIC ROCK FORMATIONS   Arches, Canyonlands, Bryce Canyon, Grand Canyon, Yosemite, Zion, Badlands

VIEWING THE AWESOME POWER OF WATER   Canyonlands, Glacier, Grand Canyon, Mount Rainier, Zion

WILDLIFE   Glacier, Olympic, Redwood, Rocky Mountain, Yellowstone

Generally, the larger and more popular parks, such as Grand Canyon, Glacier, Olympic, Yellowstone, and Yosemite, offer a greater range of experiences—something for everyone. For instance, at the huge Glacier National Park in northern Montana, you'll have numerous possibilities for hiking and boating, but also wonderful scenery that can be experienced from the scenic drive in your own car or on a guided tour, or even a boat trip on one of the park's crystal clear lakes. On the other hand, the smaller parks, such as Carlsbad Caverns and Mesa Verde are more specialized.

Even though distances seem vast in the western United States, it's possible to visit more than one of the region's national parks in a single trip. In fact, people often combine visits to Yellowstone with Grand Teton, Yosemite with Sequoia and Kings

FINAL CONSIDERATIONS WHEN CHOOSING
the right park

First, decide if you want your park experience to be one of looking or doing, or a combination of both. Then, consider your physical abilities and limitations, remembering that many of these parks are at fairly high elevations that will tax the stamina of even the most gung-ho go-getters from sea level.

In addition to reading this book carefully, check the individual park websites for current conditions such as construction or road or facility closures. Finally, narrow your list down to the number of parks you can practically fit into your schedule, and for trips of two weeks or more we suggest planning a spare afternoon or two to catch your breath.

Now, make your reservations, pack your bags, and hit the road.

Canyon, and Zion with Bryce Canyon and the North Rim of the Grand Canyon. You'll want to check out the map on the inside front cover to see which parks are closest to each other, and we've arranged the parks by region to help with those decisions.

Although it's fun to combine several national parks in your vacation trip, try to not make the all too common mistake of attempting to see everything there is to see in too short a period of time. Be realistic about how much you want to see and do at each park, and create an itinerary that lets you thoroughly enjoy one, two, or possibly three.

Visitor Centers & Maps

Your first stop at any national park should be the **visitor center.** Some large parks have more than one, and we list the location of each. Not only will you learn what there is to see and do there, but you'll also get timely information such as road and trail closures, updates on safety issues, maps, and the schedule for ranger programs. If you plan to do some serious hiking, especially into backcountry and wilderness areas, you'll need detailed topographical maps as well, which are usually available at park bookstores.

Fees & Passes

Though park fees have increased, visiting a national park is still a bargain. Entry fees, ranging from free to $25, are usually charged per private vehicle for up to 1 week. Those arriving on foot, motorcycle, or bicycle usually pay lower per-person fees.

Those who enjoy vacationing at national parks, national forests, and other federal lands can save quite a bit of money by using the federal government's annual passes. The **America the Beautiful—National Parks and Federal Recreational Lands Pass** costs $80 for 1 year, from the date of purchase, for the general public. It provides free admission for the pass holder, and those in his or her vehicle, to recreation sites that charge vehicle entrance fees on lands administered by the National Park Service, U.S. Forest Service, and other federal agencies. At areas that charge per-person fees, the passes are good for the pass holder, plus three additional adults. Children 15 and under are admitted free.

The annual passes are also available free for members of the U.S. **Military** and their dependents. In addition, passes for U.S. citizens and permanent residents age 62 and older—the **Senior Pass**—are available for a lifetime fee of $10. Passes are free for

WHAT should I take?

In packing for your trip, keep in mind that the West is a land of extremes, with an often-unforgiving climate and terrain. Those planning to hike or bike should take more drinking water than they think they'll need—experts recommend at least 1 gallon of water per person per day—as well as good-quality sunblock, hats and other protective clothing, sunglasses with UV protection, and insect repellent.

Summer visitors will want to carry rain gear for the typical afternoon thunderstorms, and jackets or sweaters for cool evenings. Take a first-aid kit, of course, and make sure it contains tweezers—very useful for removing cactus spines from your flesh if you should you get too close.

U.S. residents and permanent residents with disabilities—the **Access Pass.** The Senior and Access passes also provide 50% discounts on some fees, such as camping and ranger-guided tours in some parks, including Carlsbad Caverns.

The Senior and Access passes can be obtained by mail with an application form available online (see below) plus a $10 processing fee, or without the processing fee in person at national parks, U.S. Forest Service offices, and other federal recreation sites.

The Military pass should be obtained in person at national parks, U.S. Forest Service offices, and other federal recreation sites. The general public version (the $80 one) can be purchased in person at any unit of the National Park Service, by phone (© **888/275-8747**; option 3), or online at **http://store.usgs.gov/pass.**

Taking the Kids

One of the greatest family adventures is exploring a national park, and every time we visit a park we bring back images of extended families gathered around a campfire, staring up at a roaring waterfall, or walking a trail. These are the memories your children will carry with them throughout their lives.

Most national parks offer **Junior Ranger** programs that give kids the chance to earn certificates, badges, and patches for completing certain projects, such as tree or animal identification, or answering questions in a workbook. It's a fun way to learn about the national parks and the resources that the Park Service protects. Also, many parks offer special discussions, walks, and other ranger-led activities specifically for children.

The bigger and more popular parks have the most organized children's programs. For instance, **Yosemite** not only has a Junior Ranger program, for kids 7 to 13, but also offers a Little Cubs program for children 3 to 6. In both programs, kids use a booklet to complete projects in the park and receive buttons or patches. At **Yellowstone** there is a Junior Ranger program for children 5 to 12 and those 5 to 9 can become Young Scientists, and receive a patch or key chain, by completing science experiments. **Zion** National Park has a very good Junior Ranger program and also offers a variety of kids' walks and other activities in summer. **Zion** has "Web Rangers," a Junior Ranger program for kids that can be completed from their home computers before visiting the park.

But aside from organized programs, there is plenty for kids to see and do at the parks. **Grand Canyon** and **Bryce Canyon** have plenty of kid-friendly walks, especially along the canyon rims, and at **Zion,** the Emerald Pools Trail, where you'll always get just a little wet, is a winner for children of all ages. Kids love to see the huge moose and elk at **Rocky Mountain** National Park, and you can't beat a jet-boat ride at **Redwood** or **Canyonlands** for family fun. Kids are also fascinated by the huge trees at **Redwood** and **Sequoia.** Another favorite park for children is **Olympic,** with both a sandy beach along the Pacific and a fascinating tropical rainforest—don't step on that yucky banana slug! And at **Yellowstone,** kids are enthralled by the bubbling hot springs, burping mud pots, and geysers shooting out super-hot water.

One word of **caution,** however. National parks are not amusement parks, and while they are certainly family-friendly, those traveling with children need to supervise them carefully, especially in areas with steep drop-offs, and where they might get too close to wild animals.

Tips for Travelers with Disabilities

The National Park Service has come a long way in the past 30 or 40 years in making the parks more accessible. Most parks have accessible restrooms, and many have at least one trail that is wheelchair accessible—the Rim Trail at Bryce Canyon is a prime example. In addition, as campgrounds, boat docks, and other facilities are upgraded, improvements are being made to make them more accessible. Many parks now have campsites designed specifically for travelers in wheelchairs, most in-park lodging offers accessible rooms—some with roll-in showers—and park amphitheaters can usually accommodate wheelchair users.

But perhaps just as important as upgrades in facilities is the prevailing attitude of National Park Service personnel that these parks are for the public—the entire public—and they are going to do whatever it takes to help everyone enjoy his or her park experience. People with special needs are encouraged to talk with park workers, who can usually assist, opening locked gates to get vehicles closer to scenic attractions, or simply by pointing out trails with the lowest grades

One note on service dogs: Seeing Eye and other service dogs are not considered pets and are legally permitted anywhere in the parks. However, because of potential problems with wildlife or terrain (sharp rocks on some trails can cut dogs' paws), it's best for people taking service dogs into the parks to discuss their plans with rangers.

And don't forget your **Access Pass** (see "Fees & Permits," above).

Tips for Travelers with Pets

Most national parks, as well as other federal lands administered by the National Park Service, are not pet-friendly, and those planning to visit the parks should consider leaving their pets at home. Pets are usually prohibited on hiking trails, especially in the more popular parks, in the backcountry, and in buildings, and must always be leashed. Essentially, this means that if you take your dog or cat into the parks, the animal can be with you in the campgrounds and inside your vehicle, and you can walk it in parking areas, but that's about all.

Aside from regulations, you need to be concerned with your pet's well-being. Pets should never be left in closed vehicles, where temperatures can soar to over 120°F (49°C) in minutes, resulting in brain damage or death.

Those who do decide to take pets with them despite these warnings should take the pets' leashes, of course; carry plenty of water (pet shops sell clever little travel water bowls that won't spill in a moving vehicle); and bring proof that the dogs or cats have been vaccinated against rabies. Flea and tick spray or powder is also important, since fleas that may carry bubonic plague have been found on prairie dogs and other rodents in some parks, such as Mesa Verde and Bryce Canyon.

Although pets are not permitted on the trails or backcountry in most national parks, those traveling with their dogs can hike with them over trails administered by the U.S. Forest Service and Bureau of Land Management, as well as some of the state parks that are adjacent to many national parks. If you want to focus on hiking the trails in the parks, however, it is usually best to leave your best friend at home—it's much better than a hot car in a parking lot.

Health & Safety

Bears, rattlesnakes, and lightning can be dangerous, but that driver heading for you on a park road can be even more dangerous. In fact, **motor vehicle accidents** cause more deaths in the parks every year than anything else. Scenic drives are often winding and steep; take them slowly and carefully. And no matter how stunning that snowcapped peak is, keep your eyes on the road.

When out on the trails, even for a day hike, keep safety in mind. The wild, untouched nature of these parks is what makes them so exciting and breathtakingly beautiful—but along with wildness comes risk. The national parks are neither theme parks nor zoos. The animals here are truly wild and sometimes dangerous. This doesn't mean that disaster could strike at any time, but visitors should exercise basic caution and common sense, and follow the rules of the park. Remember, we are guests in these wild animals' home. Respect them.

It's equally important for your safety to know your limitations, to understand the environment, and to take the proper equipment when exploring the park. Always stop at the visitor center before you set out on a hike. Park staff there can offer advice on your hiking plans and supply you with pamphlets, maps, and information on weather conditions or any dangers, such as bear activity or flash flood possibilities on canyon hikes.

Since many park visitors live at or near sea level, one of the most common health hazards is **altitude sickness,** caused by the high elevations of many of the parks in this book. Symptoms include headache, fatigue, nausea, loss of appetite, muscle pain, and lightheadedness. Doctors recommend that until you are acclimated—which can take several days—you should consume light meals and drink lots of liquids, avoiding those with caffeine or alcohol. One proven method of minimizing the effects of high altitudes is to work up to them. For instance, on a visit to southern Utah, go to lower-elevation Zion National Park for a day or two before heading to the higher mountains of Bryce Canyon. Those concerned about altitude sickness might also consult with their doctors before leaving home; there are drugs that can be taken beforehand that may minimize the risk.

Health experts also warn outdoor enthusiasts to take precautions against **hantavirus,** a rare but often fatal respiratory disease, first recognized in 1993. About half of the country's confirmed cases have been reported in the Four Corners states of Colorado, New Mexico, Arizona, and Utah. The droppings and urine of rodents usually spread the disease, and health officials recommend that campers and hikers avoid areas with signs of rodent occupation. Symptoms of hantavirus are similar to flu, and lead to breathing difficulties and shock.

Adventure Tours

A number of nationally recognized companies offer guided trips to many of the parks in this book and surrounding areas. In most cases, you pay, and then the outfitters arrange everything, including lodging, meals, transportation, and equipment such as mountain bikes and rafts. Offerings range from fairly standard biking, hiking, or boating trips to luxury adventure vacations, where you spend your days hiking or biking and your evenings being pampered with gourmet meals, hot tubs, and first-class hotels. You'll want to contact companies as far in advance as possible, as reservations are required and group sizes are limited. Good online source for a variety of outdoor adventure trips are **www.adventurefinder.com** and **www.adventurecenter.com.**

Protecting the Environment

Not long ago, the rule of thumb was to "leave only footprints"; these days, we're trying to do better and not leave even footprints. It's relatively easy to be a good outdoor citizen—just use common sense. Pack out all trash; stay on designated trails; be especially careful not to pollute water; don't disturb plants, wildlife, or archaeological resources; don't pick flowers or collect rocks; and, in general, do your best to have as little impact on the environment as possible. Some hikers go further, carrying a small trash bag to pick up what others may have left. As the Park Service likes to remind us, protecting our national parks is everyone's responsibility. You can learn more about the "Leave No Trace" philosophy at **www.lnt.org.**

YELLOWSTONE

by Eric Peterson

2

Yellowstone has shaped the American public's definition of nature for more than a century, and with good reason: There are more geysers, hot springs, and other thermal features here than on the rest of the planet combined. There's pristine snow-melt cascading into dazzling waterfalls, including one that's twice as high as Niagara Falls. Not to mention a canyon deep and colorful enough to fall into the "grand" category. Best of all, a significant chunk of the park's incredible terrain is reachable by a hiker of just average ability.

Then there's the wildlife: Grizzly bears, bison, gray wolves, and bald eagles are just a few of the species who call the park home.

It's possible to see the highlights of Yellowstone without ever leaving your car—park roads lead past most of the key attractions—but why would you want to? There's so much more to see if you actually get out of your vehicle and venture into the backcountry, something only a small percentage of the park's visitors ever do. You can spend weeks hiking Yellowstone's trails or fishing its streams, and when you do, the crowds and traffic snarls become faint memories.

The beauty of Yellowstone's natural architecture comes from its geology. The area experienced three volcanic periods, beginning 2.1 million years ago, occurring every 600,000 to 800,000 years since. The last big bang happened 640,000 years ago, meaning that the area is ripe for another massive eruption—if Mother Nature's timetable holds to form.

During the biggest eruptions, thousands of square miles of landmass were blown skyward, leaving enormous *calderas* (volcanic depressions). This process has repeated itself several times—some areas hold geologic evidence of 27 layers of lava. Subsequently, glaciers covered the volcanic mountains during the ice ages. The powerful bulldozing caused by the movement of the gigantic blocks of ice shaped the valleys and canyons of the park.

Yellowstone National Park was officially created in 1872, when President Ulysses S. Grant signed legislation making it the first national park in the world. It then suffered from incompetent superintendents and shortages of cash until at last, in 1886, the U.S. Army took possession and helped rein in poaching and establish a sense of order. In 1916, the newly created National Park Service took control of the park. Yellowstone became one of the first parks to come under its stewardship.

FLORA & FAUNA

The park is one of the best places to see wildlife in North America. There are about 300 **grizzly bears,** 100 **gray wolves,** and 3,000 **bison,** as well as notable populations of **black bears, elk, deer, coyotes,** and **bald eagles. Ravens, osprey,** and **white pelicans** are other bird species you might see in Yellowstone.

There are over 3,000 plant species in Greater Yellowstone. The **wildflowers** tend to bloom in May and June, sometimes later in the high country. **Conifer** forests, of which two-thirds burned in the 1988 fires, have recovered nicely, but are still very visibly impacted.

The geysers are home to an invisible population of microbes known as **thermophiles** who not only survive but thrive in the extreme heat of Yellowstone's thermal features.

ESSENTIALS

Getting There & Gateways

To get to Yellowstone from I-90 and **Bozeman,** Montana (91 miles), take U.S. 191 south to the town of **West Yellowstone** and the park's west entrance. **Billings,** Montana, is 129 miles from Yellowstone's northeast entrance over Beartooth Pass (closed in winter). **Cody,** Wyoming, is 52 miles from Yellowstone's east entrance (closed Nov–Apr) on U.S. 14/16/20. To Yellowstone's northeast entrance, it's 67 miles. **Jackson,** Wyoming, is 57 miles south of Yellowstone's south entrance.

THE NEAREST AIRPORTS   You can fly into Bozeman, Montana's airport, **Gallatin Field** (✆ 406/388-8321; www.gallatinfield.com); the **West Yellowstone Airport** (✆ 406/646-7631; www.yellowstoneairport.org); the airport in Billings, Montana, **Logan International** (✆ 406/238-8609; www.flybillings.com); or Cody, Wyoming's **Yellowstone Regional Airport** (✆ 307/587-5096; www.flyyra.com).

Visitor Centers & Information

There are five major visitor centers in the park. **Albright Visitor Center** (✆ 307/344-2263), at Mammoth Hot Springs, is the largest and a good first stop for visitors. It provides visitor information and publications about the park, has exhibits depicting park history from prehistory through the creation of the National Park Service, and also houses displays on wildlife. Another recommended stop, the **Old Faithful Visitor Education Center** (✆ 307/344-2751) has exhibits focusing on the park's thermal features as well as postings of projected geyser-eruption times. There is also the

Canyon Visitor Education Center (✆ 307/344-2550) in Canyon Village, the **Fishing Bridge Visitor Center** (✆ 307/344-2450), near Fishing Bridge on the north shore of Yellowstone Lake, and **Grant Visitor Center** (✆ 307/242-2650) in Grant Village.

To receive maps and information before your arrival, contact **Yellowstone National Park** (✆ 307/344-7381; www.nps.gov/yell). Information regarding lodging, some campgrounds,

Special Regulations & Warnings

It is unlawful to approach within 100 yards of a bear or 25 yards of other wildlife. Feeding any wildlife is illegal. Wildlife calls and artificial attractants are forbidden. Because of wildlife and thermal activity, staying on the trails is especially important.

Yellowstone National Park

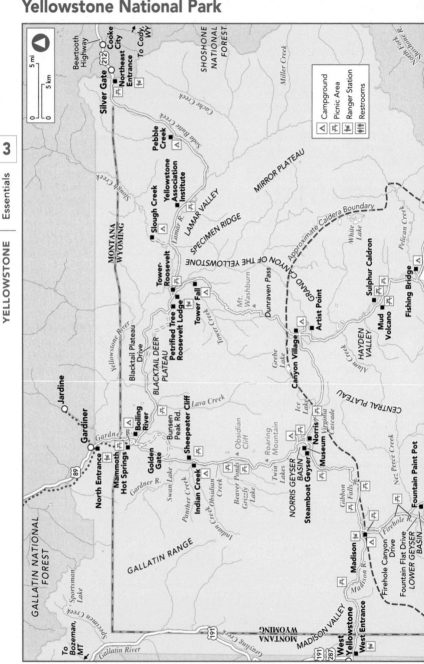

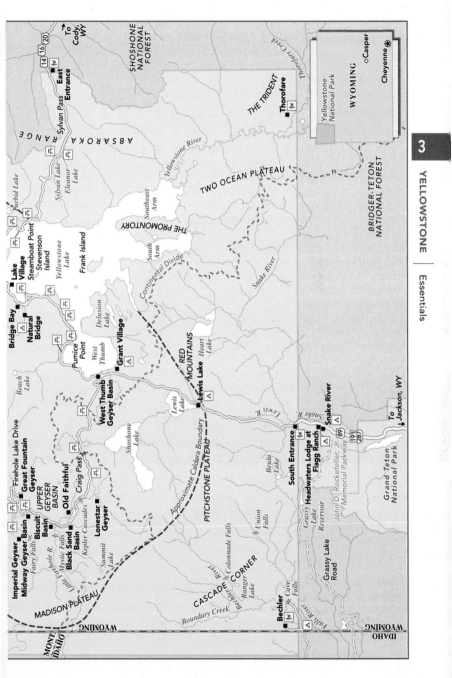

11

tours, boating, and horseback riding in Yellowstone is available from **Xanterra Parks & Resorts** (✆ **866/439-7375** or 307/344-7311; www.yellowstonenationalparklodges. com).

For information regarding educational programs in Yellowstone, contact the **Yellowstone Association** (✆ **406/848-2400;** www.yellowstoneassociation.org), which operates bookstores in park visitor centers, museums, and information stations, and oversees the excellent **Yellowstone Association Institute.** The institute conducts a varied curriculum at the old Lamar Buffalo Ranch in the park's northeast corner and at other locations.

Fees & Permits

A pass to enter Yellowstone costs $25 per vehicle for a 7-day period (no matter the number of occupants) and covers both Yellowstone and Grand Teton national parks. Entering on a snowmobile or motorcycle costs $20 for 7 days, and someone who comes in on bicycle, skis, or foot pays $12. Fees for camping in Yellowstone range from $12 to $20 per night. The RV Campground at Fishing Bridge charges up to $37 per night. You must have a **backcountry permit** for any overnight backpacking trip.

Seasons & Climate

For general information on seasons and climate in the area, see "Seasons & Climate" in chapter 3, which covers nearby Grand Teton National Park. Keep in mind that Grand Teton is a bit lower in elevation than Yellowstone, so snows melt later in Yellowstone and temperatures are slightly lower.

Road Openings

Scheduling a spring driving trip to Yellowstone can be a roll of the dice, because weather can delay openings for weeks, especially at higher altitudes. The same could be said of autumn, as an October snowstorm can compel early closure of the gates. Depending upon weather, most other park roads remain open until the season ends on the first Sunday in November. The only road open year-round is the **Mammoth Hot Springs–Cooke City Road.** Plowing in Yellowstone begins in early March and **roads usually open in April and May for the season.**

EXPLORING THE PARK

Since the roads in Yellowstone are organized into a series of connecting loops that you can reach from any of the park's five entrances, it doesn't really matter where you begin your tour. To simplify things, I discuss attractions going clockwise along each section of the **Grand Loop Road,** beginning at **Madison Junction.** But you can enter the loop and pick up the tour at any point, as long as you travel clockwise.

West Yellowstone to Norris ★

Most of Yellowstone's visitors enter at the **West Yellowstone Entrance,** so I'll use that as a jumping-off point for an extended tour of the park. As you travel the 14 miles from the gate to **Madison Junction,** you will find the **Two Ribbons Trail,** which offers an opportunity to walk through and inspect the effects of the 1988 fire. Madison Junction marks the confluence of the Gibbon and Firehole rivers. The two famous trout streams meet to form the Madison River, one of three that join to form the Missouri. This is also where you'll enter the northern loop toward Norris Junction, along a winding

14-mile section of road that parallels the **Gibbon River.** At **Gibbon Falls,** which is 84 feet tall, you'll see water bursting out of the edge of a thermal vent in a rocky canyon, the walls of which were hidden from view for several hundred years until being exposed by the fire of 1988. Before arriving at Norris Junction, you'll discover the **Artist Paint Pot Trail** in Gibbon Meadows 4.5 miles south of Norris Junction, an interesting yet easy half-mile stroll.

Norris Geyser Basin ★★

Perhaps more than any other area in Yellowstone, this basin is living testimony to the park's unique thermal activity. It changes from year to year as thermal activity and fierce weather create new and different ponds and landscapes. This is the location of one of the park's highest concentrations of thermal features, including the most active geysers. There are two loop trails here, both mostly level with wheelchair access, to the Porcelain Basin and the Back Basin. The **Porcelain Basin Trail** is a .75-mile round-trip that can be completed in 45 minutes; on it are Black Growler Steam Vent, Ledge Geyser, and the descriptively named Whale's Mouth. The 1.5-mile **Back Basin Loop** is easily negotiable in 1 hour and passes by **Steamboat Geyser,** which has been known to produce the world's highest and most memorable eruptions. However, these 400-foot waterspouts occur infrequently, so it will take some luck to see one—it can be years between eruptions.

Norris to Mammoth Hot Springs ★

The 21-mile stretch of road between Norris Junction and Mammoth Hot Springs is another area where you will see dense stands of short trees that have taken root since the 1988 fire. The large **meadow** on the west (left, if you are traveling north) side of the highway that begins 3 miles from Norris is popular with moose, thanks to water from bogs, marshes, and a creek. As you travel alongside **Obsidian Creek,** you'll notice the smell of sulfur in the air, evidence of thermal vents.

Mammoth Hot Springs ★★★

Two of Yellowstone's most fascinating areas are the **Upper** and **Lower terraces.** Strolling through them, you can observe Mother Nature going about the business of mixing and matching heat, water, limestone, and rock fractures to sculpt the area. With the exception of the Grand Canyon of the Yellowstone River, this is the most colorful area of the park; its tapestries of orange, pink, yellow, green, and brown, formed by masses of bacteria and algae, seem to change color before your eyes.

The mineral-rich hot waters that flow to the surface here do so at an unusually constant rate, roughly 750,000 gallons per day, which results in the daily deposit of almost 2 tons of limestone on these ever-changing terraces. Contours are constantly metamorphosing in the hot springs, as formations are shaped by large quantities of flowing water, the slope of the ground, and trees and rocks that determine the direction of the flow. A walk on the **Lower Terrace Interpretive Trail** is one of the best ways to see this area. The hike up the last 150 feet to the **Upper Terrace Loop Drive** is slightly steeper, though there are benches at frequent intervals, and the extra effort is worth the view.

From the 45th parallel parking area on the north entrance road north of Mammoth Hot Springs, a short hike leads to the **Boiling River.** Here you can take a dip during daylight hours, where a hot spring empties into the Gardner River.

AVOIDING the crowds

If a few thousand people on the benches in front of Old Faithful is not your idea of a wilderness park experience, then skip Yellowstone's busy summer season, which is in full swing during July and August. Or if you can't avoid that time of year, head up the trails, away from the roads and car traffic. Fewer than 10% of the park's visitors venture into the backcountry. Although the beautiful seasons between May and mid-June and after Labor Day are no longer the best-kept secret in the Rockies, they attract only a fraction of the midsummer traffic.

Mammoth Hot Springs to Tower Junction ★

Heading east from Mammoth on the Tower Road, an 8-mile drive will bring you to **Blacktail Plateau Drive,** a 7-mile, one-way dirt road that offers wildlife-viewing opportunities and a bit more solitude. You'll emerge on the Mammoth–Tower Road. Turn right and after a mile turn right again onto the half-mile-long road that dead-ends at **Petrified Tree,** a redwood that, while standing, was burned by volcanic ash more than 50 million years ago.

Tower–Roosevelt ★★

Just beyond the Petrified Tree, you'll come to **Tower–Roosevelt,** the most relaxed of the park's villages and a great place to take a break from the more crowded attractions. The center of activity here is **Roosevelt Lodge,** a rustic building that commemorates President Theodore Roosevelt's camping excursion to this area of the park in 1903. At **Specimen Ridge,** 2.5 miles east of Tower Junction, you'll find a ridge that entombs one of the world's most extensive fossil forests. East of Tower, the **Lamar Valley** is the best wildlife-watching area in the park. Beyond it is the northeast entrance and the dinky gateway towns of Cooke City and Silver Gate.

From Tower Junction to Canyon ★★

A few minutes' drive from the Tower area is the **Calcite Springs Overlook,** where a short loop along a boardwalk leads to the overlook at the rim of **The Narrows,** the narrowest part of the canyon. The terrain changes dramatically as the road climbs, as well as along some major hills toward **Mount Washburn.** There are trail heads for the **Mount Washburn Trail,** one of my favorites, on each side of the summit. As you approach **Dunraven Pass** (8,859 ft.), keep your eyes peeled for the shy mountain sheep—this is one of their prime habitats. One mile farther south is the **Washburn Hot Springs Overlook,** which offers sweeping views of the Grand Canyon. On a clear day, you can see 50 to 100 miles south, beyond Yellowstone Lake.

Canyon Village ★★★

You're in for yet another eyeful when you reach the **Grand Canyon of the Yellowstone River.** Compared to the Grand Canyon of Arizona, the Yellowstone canyon is relatively narrow; however, the sheer cliffs are equally impressive, descending hundreds of feet to the bottom of a gorge where the Yellowstone River flows. It's also equally colorful, with displays of oranges, reds, yellows, and golds. You won't find thermal vents in Arizona, but you will find them here, a constant reminder of ongoing underground activity.

An auto tour of the canyon follows **North Rim Drive,** a two-lane, one-way road that begins in Canyon Village, to **Inspiration Point.** A moderately strenuous descent down 57 steps takes you to an overlook with views of the Lower Falls and canyon. Next is the brink of the **Upper Falls,** an overlook where you can hear and feel the power of the waterfall. **South Rim Drive** leads to several overlooks and better views of the Lower Falls. The most impressive vantage point is from the bottom of **Uncle Tom's Trail,** a steep, 500-foot steel staircase that begins at the first South Rim parking lot. South Rim Road continues to a second, lower parking lot and a trail that leads to **Artist Point.** The astounding view here, one of my favorites in the park, is best in the early morning.

Canyon Village to Fishing Bridge ★

The road winds through the **Hayden Valley,** a vast expanse of green meadows accented by brown cuts where the soil is eroded along the banks of the Yellowstone River. You are almost guaranteed to see bison, and it is also prime grizzly bear habitat. Nature is working at her acidic best at the **Sulphur Caldron** and **Mud Volcano** areas, 12 miles south of the Canyon Junction. There's nothing quite like the sound of burping mud pots. The road across the Yellowstone River at **Fishing Bridge** ultimately takes you over Sylvan Pass to Cody, Wyoming. The bridge, built in 1902, spans the Yellowstone River as it exits Yellowstone Lake, and is a prime spawning area for native trout.

Yellowstone Lake Area ★★★

As if the park didn't have enough record-setting attractions: At 7,773 feet, **Yellowstone Lake** is North America's largest high-altitude lake. Home to the largest population of native cutthroat trout in North America, it has great fishing during the summer. **Lake Village,** on the northwest shore of the lake, offers a wide range of amenities, the most prominent of which is the majestic century-old **Lake Yellowstone Hotel.** Just south is the **Bridge Bay Marina,** the center of the park's water activities. **West Thumb Geyser Basin** is notable for a unique series of geysers. Some are right on the shore, and some can be seen beneath the lake surface.

As you depart the West Thumb area, you have two choices: head south toward **Grand Teton National Park,** or head west across the **Continental Divide** at Craig Pass, en route to Old Faithful.

Grant Village to the South Entrance ★

In contrast to the forgettable **Grant Village,** the 22-mile drive to **Grand Teton National Park** (see chapter 3), along high mountain passes and **Lewis Lake,** is beautiful. After the lake loses its winter coat of ice, it is a popular spot for early season anglers who are unable to fish streams clouded by the spring runoff. Beyond the lake, the road follows the Lewis River through an alpine area and along the **Pitchstone Plateau,** a pile of lava more than 2,000 feet high and 20 miles wide that was created some 500,000 years ago.

West Thumb to Old Faithful ★★

The most interesting phenomenon on the Old Faithful route is **Isa Lake** at Craig Pass. The outlet on the east curves west and eventually drains into the Pacific Odean, and the outlet on the west curves east and drains into the Gulf of Mexico. Southeast of Old Faithful 2.5 miles is an overlook at the spectacular **Kepler Cascades,** a 150-foot stairstep waterfall on the Firehole River. Near that parking lot is the trailhead for the second detour, a 5-mile round-trip to the **Lonestar Geyser,** which erupts every 3 hours, sending steaming water 30 to 50 feet from its 12-foot cone.

Old Faithful Geyser Area ★★★

Despite the overwhelming sight of the geysers and steam vents that populate the Old Faithful area, I suggest you resist the temptation to explore until you've stopped at the **Old Faithful Visitor Center** (📞 **307/545-2751**). Check the information board for estimated times of geyser eruptions, and plan accordingly.

The Old Faithful area is divided into four sections: **Upper Geyser Basin,** which includes **Geyser Hill, Black Sand Basin, Biscuit Basin,** and **Midway Geyser Basin.** All of these connect to the Old Faithful area by paved trails and roads. If time allows, hike the entire area; it's fairly level, and distances are relatively short. Between the Old Faithful area and Madison Junction, you'll also find the famous **Lower Geyser Basin,** including **Fountain Paint Pot** and the trails surrounding it. You can see some of these geysers on Firehole Lake Drive.

Though **Old Faithful** is not the largest or most regular geyser in the park, its image has been said to be the West's equivalent of the Statue of Liberty. Like clockwork, the average interval between eruptions is about 90 minutes, though it may vary 30 minutes in either direction. A typical eruption lasts 1½ to 5 minutes, during which 4,000 to 8,000 gallons of water are thrust upward to heights of 180 feet. Plan on arriving early to ensure a first-row view.

An alternative to a spot on the crowded boardwalk is a half-mile stroll from the Old Faithful Geyser up the **Observation Point Trail** to an observation area that provides better views of the entire geyser basin.

Accessible by walkways from Old Faithful Village, the **Upper Geyser Basin Loop** is designated as Geyser Hill on some maps. The 1.3-mile loop trail winds among several thermal attractions. The **Riverside Geyser** is on the bank of the Firehole River, across from a large viewing area. One of the most picturesque geysers in the park, it generates a 75-foot column of water that creates an arch over the river. Just to the south, **Morning Glory Pool** was named for its likeness to its namesake flower in the 1880s, but it has since lost some of its beauty. Vandals have tossed so much debris into its core over the years that it now suffers from poor circulation and reduced temperatures, causing unsightly bacteria to grow on its surface.

Black Sand Basin is a cluster of especially colorful hot springs and geysers located a mile north of Old Faithful. It's interesting primarily because of its black sand, a derivative of obsidian. **Biscuit Basin,** 2 miles up the road, was named for biscuit-like deposits that surrounded colorful **Sapphire Pool** until a 1959 earthquake caused the pool to erupt, devastating the namesake of the area. **Midway Geyser Basin** extends for about a mile along the Firehole River. The major attractions here are **Excelsior Geyser,** the third-largest geyser in the world, and well-known **Grand Prismatic Spring,** the largest hot spring in Yellowstone.

Old Faithful to Madison Junction ★★

Believe it or not, there are more superb geysers and hot springs on **Firehole Lake Drive,** all visible without leaving your vehicle, along a 3-mile, one-way road. The turnoff for Firehole Lake Drive is about 8 miles north of the Old Faithful area. There are three geysers of interest on this road: **Great Fountain Geyser, White Dome Geyser,** and **Pink Cone Geyser.** About a half-mile north of where Firehole Lake Drive rejoins the Grand Loop Road is the **Fountain Paint Pots** area, full of bubbling springs and guttural mud pots.

ORGANIZED TOURS & RANGER PROGRAMS

Within the park, the hotel concessionaire, **Xanterra** (℅ **877/439-7375;** www.yellowstonenationalparklodges.com) offers a variety of general and specialized tours, including bus tours, lake cruises, and horseback rides. Guides are knowledgeable and engaging, and the tours are usually worth the time and the price.

The excellent **Yellowstone Association Institute** (℅ **406/848-2400;** www.yellowstoneassociation.org/institute) offers a slew of guided classes, from daylong hikes to multiday backcountry adventures, often with more of a historical or scientific bent than Xanterra's tours. Participants bunk in cabins at the historic buffalo ranch in Lamar Valley or above Gardiner, Montana, at the new Overlook Field Campus, featuring cabins with shared kitchens and a commanding view.

Ranger-led programs take place throughout the park during the summer, some at campground amphitheaters, some at visitor centers, some on hikes or at key landmarks. It's the best value in the park: free. **Evening campfire programs** run nightly in the summer at campgrounds at Mammoth Hot Springs, Norris, Madison, Grant, Bridge Bay, and Canyon. Many of these activities are accessible to travelers with disabilities. There are more tours and evening programs in the **Old Faithful** area than anywhere else in the park. The talks and walks, which can run as long as 1½ hours, usually focus on the geysers, their fragile plumbing, and their role in the Yellowstone ecosystem. Check the park newspaper when you enter the park for a current listing of ranger programs.

DAY HIKES

West Yellowstone to Madison

Artist Paint Pot Trail ★★　This worthwhile stroll along a relatively level path winds through a lodgepole pine forest in Gibbon Meadows, to a mud pot at the top of a hill. A thermal area, it contains small geysers, hot pools, and steam vents. 1.2 miles RT. Easy. Access: Gibbon Meadow, 4.5 miles south of Norris Junction.

Mammoth Hot Springs Area

Beaver Ponds Loop Trail ★★　Start at Clematis Gulch and make your way to a series of beaver ponds. Your best chance of seeing the big-tailed beasts is early morning or late afternoon, and you might spot a moose, pronghorn, or elk on the way. (I saw a black bear with two cubs here in spring 2009.) There are also some good views, including Mount Everts. 5 miles RT. Moderate. Access: Trail head is located at Mammoth Hot Springs Terrace.

Bunsen Peak Trail ★★　This trail leads to a short but steep 2.1-mile trip to the 8,564-foot summit, with a 1,300-foot gain in elevation. It's favorite for watching the sunrise behind Electric Peak, off to the northwest, which glows with a golden hue. At the top, you'll be 3,000 feet above the valley. 4.2 miles RT. Moderate. Access: Across road from Glen Creek Trailhead, 5 miles south of Mammoth on Mammoth–Norris Rd.

Osprey Falls Trail ★★★　The first 3.3 miles of this hike lead along an old, bike-friendly roadbed at the base of Bunsen Peak. From the Osprey Falls Trail turnoff, it's another 1.5 miles through a series of steep switchbacks in Sheepeater Canyon to a secluded waterfall on the Gardner River. 9.3 miles RT. Moderate. Access: Trailhead is at Bunsen Peak Trailhead, 5 miles south of Mammoth Hot Spring on Mammoth–Norris Rd.

Grand Canyon of the Yellowstone River Area

Mount Washburn Trail ★★★ The Mount Washburn Trail falls into the "If you can only do one hike, do this one" category. The 1,400-foot elevation gain is fairly gradual, and the rises are interspersed with long, fairly level stretches and incredible views to the east of the Absaroka Mountains, south to Canyon and Yellowstone Lake, and west to the Gallatin Mountains. It's a good idea to pack several layers of clothing. There's a warming hut at the summit, as well as viewing telescopes and restrooms. 6 miles RT. Moderate. Access: End of Old Chittenden Rd. and at Dunraven Pass.

North Rim Trail ★★ This trail, which is described more fully in the Canyon Village section above, offers better views and less bustle than you'll find at the paved overlooks. 4 miles RT. Easy. Access: Inspiration Point.

South Rim Trail ★★★ Like the North Rim Trail, this trail gives you more and better views of the canyon and river than you can see from a vehicle, and takes you away from the crowds. There are connecting trails to Clear Lake and Ribbon Lake that allow you to make a loop of it. 6 miles RT. Easy. Access: Parking lot just beyond South Rim Dr. Bridge.

Uncle Tom's Trail ★★★ The short trip is down 328 stairs and paved inclines that lead to an incredible perspective on Lower Falls. The staircase (shackled to the canyon's wall) is rather steep but can be negotiated in an hour, though it will be challenging for inexperienced hikers. 1 mile RT. Moderate. Access: South Rim parking lot.

Yellowstone Lake Area

Elephant Back Loop Trail ★★ The hike is to an overlook that provides photographers with panoramic views of Yellowstone Lake and its islands, the Absaroka Range, and Pelican Valley. 3.6 miles RT. Easy. Access: Just before turnoff for Lake Yellowstone Hotel.

Storm Point Trail ★ The Storm Point Trail follows a level path that terminates at a point jutting into the lake, with panoramic views. In the spring, this is a popular spot with grizzlies, so the trail may be closed. 2.3 miles RT. Easy. Access: Directly across from Pelican Valley Trailhead (on lake side of road), 3.5 miles east of Fishing Bridge.

Old Faithful Area

Fairy Falls Trail ★★ Though considerably longer than the Mystic Falls Trail (see below), the Fairy Falls Trail is equally popular with the park staff because it leads to a taller waterfall. The hike begins at the Imperial Meadows Trailhead, 1 mile south of the Firehole River Bridge on Fountain Flat Drive. It winds through an area populated by elk along Fairy Creek, then past the Imperial Geyser. From here, it joins Fairy Creek Trail and travels east to the base of the falls. The total gain in elevation is only 100 feet. Up to 7 miles RT. Moderate. Access: Imperial Meadows in Biscuit Basin.

Lonestar Geyser Trail ★★★ This trail falls into the "gotta do it" category, and its popularity is its only disadvantage. From the trailhead, you'll wend your way through a forested area along a trail that parallels the Firehole River. The payoff for your effort is the arrival at the geyser, which erupts about every 3 hours, and the eruption lasts about 30 minutes. The trail is popular with cross-country skiers in winter. 4.6 miles RT. Easy. Access: Parking lot opposite Kepler Cascades.

Mystic Falls Trail ★★★ This is a favorite of park rangers. The trail leads to a waterfall on the Little Firehole River that drops more than 100 feet, one of the steepest in the park. The trail starts at Biscuit Basin, crosses the river, and then disappears into the forest. The total distance to the falls is only 1 mile; there's a trail to take you to the top. To make your return more interesting, continue to the Little Firehole Meadows

Trail, which has an overlook that offers a view of Old Faithful in the distance. Best estimates are that the total time for the hike is an easy 2 hours, with an elevation gain of only 460 feet. 2.5 miles RT. Easy. Access: Imperial Meadows in Biscuit Basin.

EXPLORING THE BACKCOUNTRY

The backcountry season in Yellowstone is brief but glorious: For just 2 or 3 months, the snow melts off, the streams drop to fordable levels, and you can go deep into a domain of free-roaming wildlife and pristine natural beauty. Popular routes include the Sportsman Lake Trail on the northwest side of the park, Shoshone Lake and Heart Lake south of Old Faithful, the remote thoroughfare area southeast of Yellowstone Lake, and the waterfall-laden Bechler region in the southwestern corner.

You must have a **backcountry permit** for any overnight trip on foot, on horseback, or by boat, and you can camp only in designated campsites, many of which are equipped with food-storage poles to keep wildlife out of your supplies. You can pick up a permit for hiking or boating the day before a trip, but if you'll be traveling during peak season, make a reservation in advance. It costs $20 to hold a site, and you can start making reservations for the upcoming year beginning April 1. For additional information, contact the **Yellowstone Backcountry Office** (© 307/344-2160; www.nps.gov/yell/planyourvisit/backcountrytripplanner.htm).

OTHER SUMMER ACTIVITIES

BIKING Yellowstone's narrow, twisty roads and lack of bike lanes make life difficult for bikers, and off-road opportunities are limited. The few bike runs we'd recommend include the **Mount Washburn Trail,** leaving from the Old Chittenden Road, which climbs 1,400 feet. **Lonestar Geyser Trail,** accessible at Kepler Cascade near Old Faithful, is an easy 1-hour ride on a user-friendly, partly paved road. Near Mammoth Hot Springs, **Bunsen Peak Road** and **Osprey Falls trails** offer several combination ride-hike.

BOATING The best place to enjoy boating is on **Yellowstone Lake.** The lake is also one of the few areas where powerboats are allowed. Rowboats and outboard motorboats are for rent at **Bridge Bay Marina** (© 866/439-7375). Motorboats, canoes, and kayaks can be used on **Lewis Lake** as well, but there is no marina or rental operation here.

FISHING Seven varieties of game fish live here: native cutthroat, rainbow, brown, brook, and lake trout; grayling; and mountain whitefish. Of the trout, only the cutthroat are native, and they are being pressured in the big lake by the larger lake trout. As a result, you can't keep any pink-meat cutthroat caught anywhere in Yellowstone, and you *must* keep any lake trout. The season typically opens on the Saturday of Memorial Day weekend and ends in early November.

Fishing requires a special permit good only within the park. For anglers 16 and older, it's $15 for a 3-day permit or $20 for 7 days, and $35 for a season permit. Anglers 12 to 15 need a permit, too, but it's free. Children under 12 may fish without a permit when supervised by an adult.

HORSEBACK RIDING People who want to pack their gear on a horse, llama, or mule must get permits to enter the Yellowstone backcountry, or hire an outfitter with a permit. Visitors who want to get in the saddle can put themselves in the hands of the concessionaire, **Xanterra** (© 866/439-7375). Stables are at Canyon Village, Roosevelt Lodge, and Mammoth Hot Springs.

WINTER ACTIVITIES

The average snowfall in a Yellowstone winter is nearly 150 inches (and higher country sees twice that amount), creating a beautiful setting for sightseers and a wonderful resource for outdoor winter recreation. Frozen thermal vapors transform nearby trees into "snow ghosts." Bison become frosted, shaggy beasts, easily spotted as they take advantage of the more accessible vegetation on the thawed ground. Yellowstone Lake's surface freezes to an average thickness of 3 feet, creating a vast ice sheet that sings and moans as the huge plates of ice shift.

Only two of the park's hostelries, **Mammoth Hot Springs** and the **Old Faithful Snow Lodge,** provide accommodations from December through March. The only road that's open for cars is the **Mammoth Hot Springs–Cooke City Road.** Most visitors enter the park in winter from the west or south by snow-coach or snowmobile.

For additional information on all of the following winter activities and accommodations, contact **Xanterra** (✆ **866/439-7375;** www.yellowstonenationalparklodges. com). The **Yellowstone Association Institute** (✆ **406/848-2400;** www.yellowstone association.org/institute) offers winter courses in various areas in the park.

CROSS-COUNTRY SKIING   The Old Faithful area has 40 miles of cross-country trails. Rentals, instruction, ski shuttles, and other services are all available at the **Old Faithful Snow Lodge** and the **Mammoth Hot Springs Hotel.**

SNOW-COACH TOURS   Basically vans with tank treads for tires, snow-coaches provide winter transportation from the north, south, and west entrances to Old Faithful. One-way and wildlife-watching trips range from about $30 to $70, while round-trips cost about $120 to $140. For information, contact **Xanterra Parks & Resorts** (✆ **866/439-7375**).

SNOWMOBILING   A driver's license and guide are required for rental at **Mammoth Hot Springs Hotel** or **Old Faithful Snow Lodge.** Day tours from **Xanterra** (✆ **866/439-7375**) cost about $275 for a single rider or $300 double; custom tours are considerably more costly. A helmet is included with the snowmobile, as is a clothing package for protection against the bitter cold. Snowmobile rentals are also available in Gardiner, Cooke City, and West Yellowstone.

WHERE TO STAY

Inside the Park

If you're coming at the height of summer, you must book ahead! Contact **Xanterra** (✆ **866/439-7375** or 307/344-7311; www.yellowstonenationalparklodges.com) for lodging in the park. Accommodations are open from May to mid-October. Mammoth Hot Springs and Old Faithful Snow Lodge then reopen for the winter season, from mid-December through early March.

MAMMOTH HOT SPRINGS AREA

Mammoth Hot Springs Hotel and Cabins ★   Located just inside the north entrance by the thermal feature of the same name, this historic hostelry offers guest rooms with and without private bathrooms and a cluster of spartan cabins outside. Elk love it here, and there's a number of hikes originating from within walking distance. Inside, the Map Room features an ornate wooden map of the United States and a regular schedule of speakers. I peg this a rung below the Lake Hotel, Old Faithful Snow

CAMPING options

There are 12 campgrounds in Yellowstone, five of them under the efficient management of **Xanterra**, the park concessionaire. The other seven are smaller, less expensive, and often less crowded. The seven campgrounds still run by the **National Park Service** are at **Indian Creek** ★★, **Lewis Lake** ★★, **Mammoth** ★, **Norris** ★★, **Pebble Creek** ★★, **Slough Creek** ★★★, and **Tower Fall** ★. They fill daily on a first-come, first-served basis. My personal favorites are Slough Creek, in the Lamar Valley, and Norris, a shady riverside spot near the Norris Geyser Basin. Both are removed from the large park villages and have a feeling of solitude that is hard to

find at more developed areas like Canyon or Mammoth Hot Springs. Campsite fees are $12 to $20 nightly, except for the RV spaces at Fishing Bridge, which run $37.

Xanterra runs the bigger campgrounds at **Bridge Bay** ★, **Canyon** ★, **Grant Village** ★, **Madison** ★, and **Fishing Bridge** ★. Reservations can be made by calling ☎ **866/439-7375.** The only campground in the park equipped with RV hookups is at **Fishing Bridge RV Park.** It accepts hard-sided vehicles only (no tents or tent trailers) and has full hookups. There are no hookups at other campgrounds, but they all accommodate RVs.

Lodge, and Old Faithful Inn—it is a distinctive historic hotel, but it doesn't quite hit the high notes of the aforementioned trio.

At Mammoth Hot Springs. ☎ **866/439-7375** or 307/344-7311. www.yellowstonenationalpark lodges.com. 212 units, 182 with private bathroom. $87–$130 double; $91–$192 cabin; $229–$241 hot tub cabin; $459–$482 suite. Closed Oct to mid-Dec and early Mar to early May. **Amenities:** 2 restaurants; bar; Wi-Fi (fee).

CANYON VILLAGE AREA

Canyon Lodge and Cabins ★   There are over 600 units here, so the place can be a bit busy—you need to get a little distance if you want solitude. Regardless, the duplex and fourplex cabins here are good options for families and conveniently located at Canyon Village in the heart of the park. There are also more traditional hotel rooms in two lodge buildings. Some of the older cabins are a bit worse for the wear, but that is changing soon—a redevelopment beginning in 2014 will replace a number of cabins with new multistory lodges, the first new construction in the park since the Old Faithful Snow Lodge was rebuilt from the ground up in the 1990s.

In Canyon Village. ☎ **866/439-7375** or 307/344-7311. www.yellowstonenationalparklodges.com. 605 units. $195 double; $105–$199 cabin. Closed late Sept to early June. **Amenities:** 3 restaurants; bar; Wi-Fi (fee).

TOWER–ROOSEVELT AREA

Roosevelt Lodge Cabins ★   Named for Teddy Roosevelt, who camped nearby on a visit to the park, these extremely basic cabins are scattered around a sagebrush-speckled area between the Lamar Valley and Mammoth Hot Springs. They will likely fall a little short of those looking for a traditional hotel—a stay here is more like camping than it is like staying at the Ritz. But families (and aspiring cowboys) tend to like the place, not only for the reasonable rates but for the friendly service and the primo wildlife viewing opportunities nearby. The lodge, fronted by a porch full of rocking chairs and the onsite horse corral, are also key selling points. Guests choose between Frontier cabins which have private bathrooms and a good amount of elbow room and the more primitive Roughrider cabins, which share communal bathhouse and have a woodburning stove for heat.

At Tower Junction. (At junction of Mammoth–Tower Rd. and Tower–Canyon Rd.) (℡ **866/439-7375** or 307/344-7311. www.yellowstonenationalparklodges.com. 80 cabins, 14 with private bathroom. $73–$121 cabin. Closed early Sept to early June. **Amenities:** Restaurant; bar; horseback riding.

LAKE VILLAGE AREA

Lake Lodge Cabins ★★   This is a bit of a hidden gem, with an out-of-the-way setting near the lakeshore and a mix of historic Frontier cabins and Pioneer cabins that date to the 1920s and newer, motel-style units called Western cabins in four- and six-plexes. The namesake and the center of activity, Lake Lodge has a cafeteria and an inviting lobby, but no guestrooms. It's a perfect place to take a load off on one of the rocking chairs that line the front porch. The complex is within easy walking distance of Lake Hotel with its swank restaurant.

In Lake Village. (℡ **866/439-7375** or 307/344-7311. www.yellowstonenationalparklodges.com. 186 cabins. $80 Pioneer cabin; $121 Frontier cabin; $199 Western cabin. Closed mid-Sept to early June. **Amenities:** Restaurant; bar; Wi-Fi (fee).

Lake Yellowstone Hotel and Cabins ★★★   Open since 1891, this iconic yellow hostelry has targeted the well-to-do since the Victorian era. Today it's on the National Register of Historic Places and worth a look even if you're not staying the night. Renovated in 2013–14 with a sense of Art Deco style, the hotel rooms and suites are a cut above other park hotels; they also have such modern perks as a business center and in-room Internet access. That's the hotel; expect the cabins to be much plainer, and we hear that the Wi-Fi rarely reaches them (cell service, too, can be spotty on the property). One of the best features is the dazzling lobby, with ornate, hand-carved water fountains that date to the opening of the hotel and the lounge, full of comfortable seating with great lake views.

In Lake Village. (℡ **866/439-7375** or 307/344-7311. www.yellowstonenationalparklodges.com. 300 units. $158–$399 double; $149 cabin; $549–$629 suite. Closed late Sept to mid-May. **Amenities:** 2 restaurants; bar; Internet access (fee).

GRANT VILLAGE AREA

Grant Village ★   This complex, built in 1984, is one of the newer lodging options in the park, with a pair of six-story wings housing fairly traditional guestrooms. This is the closest lodging on the south entrance and Grand Teton National Park, but its modernity means you trade distinctive character for convenience. I'd recommend it for couples looking for a mid-priced option and some of the perks of civilization, but it doesn't have the definitively Yellowstone character of the older lodges and hotels in the park.

Near West Thumb. (℡ **866/439-7375** or 307/344-7311. www.yellowstonenationalparklodges.com. 300 units. $164 double. Closed early Oct to late May. **Amenities:** 2 restaurants; bar.

OLD FAITHFUL AREA

Old Faithful Inn ★★★   Opened in 1904, this was the prototype for all national park lodges to follow. Considered the biggest log building on the planet, Robert Reamer's design effortlessly blends into the natural surroundings with a palatial, log-cabin look. The lobby, in particular, is quite the sight, a masterwork of exposed beams and knotty pine, with the now off-limits Eagle's Nest in the rafters, the spot for the band when grand Victorian balls took place here a century ago. As for the rooms, they vary wildly. The original rooms are *very* small, and many share bathrooms down the

Where to Stay

YELLOWSTONE

hall. For comfort, many choose rooms in the newer wings as they offer in-room bathrooms and space to open your luggage. *Note:* rooms with geyser views book up a year in advance, so make early reservations.

At Old Faithful. ℂ **866/439-7375** or 307/344-7311. www.yellowstonenationalparklodges.com. 327 units, 254 with private bathroom. $149–$263 double with private bathroom; $109–$199 double with shared bathroom; $433–$539 suite. Closed early Oct to early May. **Amenities:** 2 restaurants; bar.

Old Faithful Lodge Cabins ★ Thin-walled and a bit flimsy, these cabins were hastily constructed in the park's early days. The worst of them have been torn down, so what remain are very simple (some might say austere), but clean, well-maintained and extremely well-located, right in the heart of the park right next to the main attractions in Old Faithful Geyser. A cafeteria and snack bar are located nearby in the central main lodge. The Frontier cabins have private bathrooms while the Budget cabins share a communal facility; all have one double bed, and some have another single or double.

At Old Faithful. ℂ **866/439-7375** or 307/344-7311. www.yellowstonenationalparklodges.com. 96 cabins, 61 with private bathroom. $73–$121 double. Closed late Sept to mid-May. **Amenities:** Restaurant.

Old Faithful Snow Lodge and Cabins ★★★ This new-in-1999 hotel is the snazziest and most modern in the park. Built with plenty of recycled and repurposed materials, a cedar roof, and imposing log columns, the Snow Lodge more than holds its own against its legendary neighbor, the Old Faithful Inn, featuring cozy, stylish rooms, as well as surrounding seasonal cabin units. All in all, the guestrooms are a bit more in tune with modern expectations of size and amenities than some of the historic lodges in the park. *Note:* The summer-only cabins predate the lodge, and are much more basic in terms of both amenities and style, with commensurately lower rates. Lodge rooms are open in both seasons.

At Old Faithful. ℂ **866/439-7375** or 307/344-7311. www.yellowstonenationalparklodges.com. 134 units. $229–$251 double; $99–$165 cabin. Closed late Oct to mid-Dec and early Mar to late Apr. **Amenities:** 2 restaurants; bar; Wi-Fi (fee).

Near the Park
WEST YELLOWSTONE
Moose Creek Inn and Cabins ★★ In a town that's dominated by unremarkable, often poorly maintained motels, these lodgings stand out for the care that has been taken with them. With two facilities—a boutique inn and a cabin complex that once served as employee housing—there are options for all sorts of travelers here, from those looking for kitchenettes, to folks who are just looking for a place to crash. Rooms have a nice sense of subtle Western style, and both locations are very walkable to restaurants and other attractions in West Yellowstone.

119 Electric St. and 220 Firehole Ave. ℂ **406/646-9546.** www.moosecreekinn.com 41 units. $110–$200 double room or cabin. **Amenities:** Free Wi-Fi.

GARDINER
Absaroka Lodge ★ While the décor and furnishings here are what you might find at any given motel along an American roadside, the Absaroka stands out because of its scenic location above the Yellowstone river and the kindly service of the staff here. We also like the fact that some units have small kitchens, and all have plenty of room to spread out after a day in the Park (expect either one or two comfy queen beds in each room).

310 Scott St. at the Yellowstone River Bridge. ℂ **406/848-7414.** www.yellowstonemotel.com. 41 units. Summer $110–$125 double; winter $45–$60 double. **Amenities:** Free Wi-Fi.

COOKE CITY/SILVER GATE

Silver Gate Lodging ★★ This is just the spot for the classic Yellowstone vacation. You've got more peace and quiet than the park villages, a brilliant night sky, and easy access to the Lamar Valley, the best wildlife-watching spot in Yellowstone. All of the historic, real log cabins here have slick, new kitchens, down comforters on comfy new mattresses (as of 2013) and adorable knotty pine furnishings (including rocking chairs on the porch). For a lower rate, there are some basic motel rooms, as well. An onsite general store offers a limited supply of groceries, wine and beer, and souvenirs, and it also rents high-powered scopes ($30/day) to spot wolves and bears.

109 U.S. 212, Silver Gate. ℂ **406/838-2371.** www.pineedgecabins.com. 29 units. $72 double; $125–$195 cabin. **Amenities:** Free Wi-Fi; store.

CODY

The Chamberlin Inn ★★ A lovingly restored historic hotel just off the main drag, the Chamberlin Inn (built in 1900) offers a Victorian alternative to the motels on the outskirts of Cody. The public areas are vibrantly colorful, with period decorations and a real sense of style, and the outdoor courtyard is a shady place to get away from the bustle at the end of a day in Yellowstone. There are several apartments, lofts, and larger suites available, and every room has unique décor. My favorite is the Hemingway King Studio, named for the legendary writer who once bunked here.

1032 12th St. ℂ **888/587-0202** or 307/587-0202. www.chamberlininn.com. 24 units, including 3 apts. $165–$195 double; $250–$750 suite or apt. **Amenities:** Bar; free Wi-Fi.

Pahaska Tepee Resort ★ Established in 1904, Buffalo Bill's old hunting lodge just outside the eastern entrance to Yellowstone—about 25 miles from both Cody and Yellowstone Lake—isn't in Cody proper, but it is perfect for park visitors looking for a wilderness experience. Pahaska was his Lahota name. It means "long hair" and the décor in the main lodge is just as colorful as its moniker. As for the rooms, they range from motel-basic to a few with such nice amenities as hot tubs and kitchens. Some are set in the lodge, while others are scattered in cabins on the grounds.

183 Yellowstone Hwy. ℂ **800/628-7791** or 307/527-7701. www.pahaska.com. 47 units. $100–$180 double or cabin; $575–$625 condo; $995–$1,150 lodge. Closed mid-Oct to Apr. **Amenities:** Restaurant; bar; store; limited free Wi-Fi.

WHERE TO EAT

Inside the Park

At the dining rooms at the Mammoth, Old Faithful, and Lake, reservations are recommended and sometimes required; contact **Xanterra** (ℂ **866/439-7375**). There are fast-food restaurants, snack shops, and cafeterias in the villages as well.

MAMMOTH HOT SPRINGS AREA

Terrace Grille serves fast food at the south end of the building where the dining room is located.

Mammoth Hot Springs Hotel Dining Room ★★ STEAK/SEAFOOD With a view of historic Fort Yellowstone, the fine-dining option at Mammoth is one of the best in the park. Dinner is the most creative menu here, with trout, Montana lamb, and unusual small plates like bison and trout tacos. Earlier in the day, the breakfast buffet is the choice for those with "hiking appetites" and little time, but there are also healthy and hearty menu options. Lunch consists of sandwiches and burgers. The bar has a TV, a rarity in the park.

At Mammoth Hot Springs. (✆ **307/344-7311.** www.yellowstonenationalparklodges.com. Reservations recommended in winter. Breakfast $5–$13; lunch $9–$15; dinner $14–$28. Mid-May to early Oct daily 6:30–10am, 11:30am–2:30pm, and 5–10pm; late Dec to early Mar daily 6:30–10am, 11:30am–2:30pm, and 5:30–9pm.

CANYON VILLAGE AREA

Arrayed around the village parking lot are the **Canyon Glacier Pit Snack Bar,** with the style of a 1950s soda fountain; the **Canyon Lodge Cafeteria,** a fast-food alternative; and the **Canyon Lodge Deli,** with sandwiches and salads.

Canyon Lodge Dining Room ★ STEAK/SEAFOOD More contemporary-looking than the park norm, Canyon's resident sit-down option is known for burgers, Prime rib, and other carnivore's favorites (though it does have some fish and pasta options, as well). It doesn't have the atmosphere of, say, the Lake Yellowstone Hotel's dining room (see below), but the service is friendly, and they won't rush you to finish your meal. Breakfast includes both a buffet and *a la carte* options.

At Canyon Lodge. (✆ **307/344-7311.** www.yellowstonenationalparklodges.com. Reservations not accepted. Breakfast $6–$13; lunch and dinner $9–$22. Early June to late Sept daily 7–10am, 11:30am–2:30pm, and 5–10pm.

TOWER–ROOSEVELT AREA

Roosevelt Lodge Dining Room ★ STEAK/SEAFOOD Roosevelt is as cowboy as Yellowstone gets, and that means barbecued ribs and baked beans for dinner, as well as Old West Dinner Cookouts ($46–$85), complete with horseback or wagon rides to the cookout site. Breakfast is primarily egg dishes and pancakes (no buffet), and lunch is beef and bison burgers and other sandwiches. Beyond ribs, the dinner menu features interesting dishes like bison tamales and barbecue shrimp.

At Tower Junction. (✆ **307/344-7311.** www.yellowstonenationalparklodges.com. Reservations not accepted, except for Old West cookouts. Breakfast $5–$10; lunch $9–$15; dinner $9–$20. Mid-June to early Sept daily 7–10am, 11:30am–9pm.

YELLOWSTONE LAKE AREA

For the eat-on-the-run traveler, a **deli** in the Lake Yellowstone Hotel serves light fare. Down the road, the **Yellowstone Park General Store** has a fast-food option. There is also a **cafeteria** serving three meals a day at Lake Lodge.

Lake Yellowstone Hotel ★★★ CONTINENTAL For the most romantic setting and the best cuisine in Yellowstone, plan ahead—way, way ahead: Many visitors make reservations a year in advance. An upscale atmosphere is matched by the menu of continental fare with regional flair, such as locally raised lamb, Montana trout, and bison bratwurst with cherries and hot peppers, Lunch dishes include entree salads, gourmet sandwiches, and trout. In the morning, there is a breakfast buffet, or you can order off the menu.

On the north side of the lake. (✆ **307/344-7311.** www.yellowstonenationalparklodges.com. Dinner reservations highly recommended. Breakfast $6–$15; lunch $9–$15; dinner $13–$33. Mid-May to early Oct daily 6:30–10:30am, 11:30am–2:30pm, and 5–10pm.

GRANT VILLAGE

The casual choice here is the **Lake House,** specializing in fish, as well as burgers and beer. The **Village Grill** in the Yellowstone General Store also serves three meals daily.

Grant Village Dining Room ★ STEAK/SEAFOOD Trout is the specialty of the house at this fairly standard dining room, lacking historic cachet but making up for it with a menu that spotlights that local fish with a number of preparations. There is also plenty of beef and bison, as well as a breakfast buffet. Dinner reservations are required.

At Grant Village. ☏ **307/344-7311.** www.yellowstonenationalparklodges.com. Breakfast $5–$13; lunch $9–$11; dinner $13–$28. Late May–Sept daily 6–10am, 11:30am–2:30pm, and 5–10pm.

OLD FAITHFUL AREA

For quick and inexpensive, the year-round **Geyser Grill** at the **Old Faithful Snow Lodge** and the cafeterias at the **Old Faithful Lodge Cafeteria and Bake Shop** serve lunch and dinner. There is also an ice-cream stand in the lobby of the **Old Faithful Inn,** and a lunch counter at the **Yellowstone General Store.**

Obsidian Dining Room ★★ STEAK/SEAFOOD The most modern-feeling dining room in the park is adjacent to the slick Firehole Lounge and offers fare that's a bit more creative than some of the other restaurants in Yellowstone. I'm talking bison burgers and antelope sliders to pork osso bucco and seared duck. Lunch is similar but lighter, primarily sandwiches and salads. Obsidian offers breakfast and dinner in summer and three meals a day in winter.

At the Old Faithful Snow Lodge. ☏ **307/344-7311.** www.yellowstonenationalparklodges.com. Breakfast $5–$12; lunch $7–$20; dinner $12–$28. Early May to mid-Oct daily 6:30–10:30am and 5–10:30pm; mid-Dec to mid-Mar daily 6:30–10am, 11:30am–3pm, and 5–9:30pm.

Old Faithful Inn Dining Room ★★ STEAK/SEAFOOD Have a meal here for the experience. This one-of-a-kind structure, said to be the largest log building in the world, features a massive stone fireplace and charm to spare. For those who like lots of eating options, there are buffets—three times a day! Or you can order off the menu; dinner brings inventive and hearty fare like bison pot roast, red trout hash, and a few more exotic options, such as veggie chow main or shrimp creole.

At the Old Faithful Inn. ☏ **307/344-7311.** www.yellowstonenationalparklodges.com. Breakfast and lunch $5–$16; dinner $15–$26. Early May to early Oct daily 6:30–10:30am, 11:30am–2:30pm, and 5–10pm. Closed in winter.

Near the Park

WEST YELLOWSTONE

Beartooth Barbecue ★ BARBECUE They actually do make some pretty good barbecue this far north. This kid-friendly eatery has more-than-respectable ribs, brisket, and pulled pork, and tangy housemade barbecue sauce. The bar serves local microbrew and house wine, but no liquor.

111 Canyon St. ☏ **406/646-0227.** Lunch and dinner $10–$27. Daily noon–10pm. Closed in winter.

GARDINER

The Chico Dining Room ★★★ CONTINENTAL This spot, about 30 miles north of Gardiner, is a favorite of the Hollywood types who frequent the area, serving expertly prepared local meat and seafood with herbs and produce from a greenhouse onsite. Located at the Chico Hot Springs Resort (yes, you can take a soak before the meal), this is the place to head for a splurge on the north side of Yellowstone.

Old Chico Rd., Pray. ☏ **406/333-4933.** www.chicohotsprings.com. Main courses $19–$30. Summer daily 5:30–10pm; winter Sun–Thurs 5:30–9pm, Fri–Sat 5:30–10pm; Sun brunch 8:30–11:30am. Located 30 miles north of Gardiner.

CODY

Cassie's Supper Club ★★ WESTERN   A brothel turned upscale restaurant and bustling country-and-western dance club, Cassie's has a refined dining room and a considerably more casual bar. Fare tends to be carnivorous, with an emphasis on bone-in steaks (though there's also fresh seafood). Featuring some interesting Western murals, the bar has less expensive fare, and the place really gets going after the rodeo ends and the cowboys and cowgirls hit the dance floor.

214 Yellowstone Ave. ℰ **307/527-5500.** www.cassies.com. Lunch $8–$13; dinner $20–$50. Daily 11am–10pm.

Proud Cut Saloon ★ STEAKS   Steaks are the center of the universe at the Proud Cut, and they do a great job with everything from tenderloins to flat iron steaks to Prime rib. There is also some seafood, plus burgers and a thoroughly Wyoming vibe. Expect a wait in the summer if you don't have a reservation.

1227 Sheridan Ave. ℰ **307/527-6905.** Lunch and dinner $10–$30. Mon–Sat 11am–10pm; Sun noon–9pm.

SIDE TRIP: LITTLE BIGHORN BATTLEFIELD NATIONAL MONUMENT

Little Bighorn Battlefield is a relatively easy detour on the way west or east if you are passing through this area, and worth a trip if you are anywhere close by.

This is where Lt. Col. George Armstrong Custer and the 647 men of the 7th Cavalry were wiped out on June 25, 1876, after Custer and his troops attacked an American Indian village along the banks of the Little Bighorn River. Custer had divided his troops into three companies—he led one, while Maj. Marcus Reno and Capt. Frederick Benteen commanded the others. Custer expected little resistance, but he was surprised by what some have estimated at several thousand Lakota Sioux, Cheyenne, and Arapaho warriors, who surrounded and killed the soldiers.

In late 2001, Congress approved $2.3 million for construction of a memorial at the national monument to the American Indian warriors who fought at Little Big Horn. The striking memorial, dedicated in 2003, includes bronze tracings of three warriors—a Sioux, a Cheyenne, and an Arapaho—and what is described as a "spirit gate."

Essentials

WHEN TO GO

The national monument is popular, and visitation is highest between Memorial Day and Labor Day. The best advice if you wish to avoid crowds is to avoid these months, or to arrive early in the morning or late in the day. This is also good advice because summers in eastern Montana can get very hot, and there is no shade on the battlefield.

GETTING THERE

For driving directions from the monument to Yellowstone, see "Getting There & Gateways," earlier in this chapter. If you are coming from the west, from Billings, Montana, take **I-90** east 61 miles to the Little Bighorn Battlefield off-ramp at **U.S. 212** (exit 510). If you are coming from the south, from Sheridan, Wyoming, take I-90 north (approx. 70 miles) to the same off-ramp at U.S. 212. If you are coming from the east, from the

Black Hills of South Dakota, you will already be on U.S. 212. The battlefield is 42 miles west of Lame Deer, Montana.

INFORMATION & VISITOR CENTER

At the **visitor center** just inside the park entrance, you'll see actual uniforms worn by Custer, read about his life, and view an eerie reenactment of the battles on a small-scale replica of the battlefield. Contact **Little Bighorn Battlefield National Monument** (𝒞 **406/638-3214** or 406/638-3217; www.nps.gov/libi) for more.

PARK HOURS & FEES

The park is open daily 8am to 9pm from Memorial Day through July, and 8am to 8pm August to Labor Day; spring and fall hours are 8am to 6pm; winter hours are 8am to 4:30pm. The visitor center is open the same hours. The park is closed on January 1, Thanksgiving, and December 25. The admission fee is $10 per vehicle, $5 per person on foot or bike.

Exploring the Monument

It's possible to view the site in less than a half-hour, but you should plan to spend enough time to explore the visitor center, listen to interpretive talks presented by rangers (see below) and then tour the site. You'll leave with a greater appreciation for the monument and understanding of the history that led up to the battle.

After stopping at the **visitor center,** drive 4.5 miles south to the **Reno-Benteen Monument Entrenchment Trail,** at the end of the monument road, and double back. Interpretive signs at the top of this bluff show the route followed by the companies under Custer, Benteen, and Reno as they approached the area from the south, and the positions from which they defended themselves from their American Indian attackers.

As you proceed north along the ridge, you'll pass **Custer's Lookout,** the spot from which the general first viewed the Indian village. This was the spot at which Custer sent for reinforcements, though he continued marching north.

Capt. Thomas Weir led his troops to **Weir Point** in hopes of assisting Custer, but was immediately discovered by the Indian warriors and forced to retreat to the spot held by Reno.

The **Medicine Trail Ford,** on the ridge, overlooks a spot well below the bluffs in the Medicine Trail Coulee on the Little Bighorn River, where hundreds of warriors who had been sent from the Reno battle pushed across the river in pursuit of Custer and his army.

Farther north, the Cheyenne warrior Lame White Man led an attack up **Calhoun Ridge** against a company of the 7th Cavalry that had charged downhill into the coulee. When the opponents' resistance overwhelmed the army, troops retreated back up the hill, where they were killed.

As you proceed to the north, you will find detailed descriptions of the events that occurred on the northernmost edges of the ridge, as well as white markers that indicate the places where army troops fell in battle. The bodies of Custer, his brothers Tom and Boston, and nephew Autie Reed all were found on Custer Hill.

Indian casualties during the rout are estimated at 60 to 100 warriors. Following the battle, which some say began early in the morning and ended within 2 hours, the Indians broke camp in haste and scattered to the north and south. Within a few short years, they were all confined to reservations.

The survivors of the Reno-Benteen armies buried the bodies of Custer and his slain army where they fell. In 1881, the graves that could be located were opened, and the bones reinterred at the base of a memorial shaft found overlooking the battlefield. Custer's remains were eventually reburied at the U.S. Military Academy at West Point.

There are three **walking trails** within the monument for visitors wishing to explore the battle in greater depth.

The adjacent **National Cemetery,** established in 1879, incorporates a self-guided tour to the graves of some of the more significant figures buried there. The **Indian Memorial** is also in this area.

RANGER PROGRAMS & GUIDED TOURS Regular **interpretive talks** help visitors understand the battle and its participants. Subjects vary during the day and include discussion of the culture and life of the Northern Plains tribes that engaged in the battle, army life in the 1870s, weapons and tactics, and the significance of the battle. There is a free cellphone-based audio tour available; call the park for information.

For a unique perspective, take a guided tour with **Apsaalooke Tours** (© **406/638-3114**); American Indian guides lead 1-hour bus tours by reservation. The cost is $150 (cash only) for a group of any size.

GRAND TETON

by Eric Peterson

E very time you focus your camera in Grand Teton, the frame will likely center on one of its many stately peaks. As a whole, the towering mountains of the Teton Range define this park, unlike neighboring Yellowstone, which is distinguished by its thermal features and subtle beauty. You'll still see wildlife—eagles and osprey along the Snake River; moose and, if you're lucky, a black bear in the vicinity of the Jackson Lake; and pronghorn on the valley floor—but it is the landscape that makes Grand Teton.

Consider that the tops of the Tetons, which sit on a 40-mile-long fault, were displaced by geological upheaval that caused 30,000 feet of movement of the earth's crust over the last 13 million years—the valley floor dropped by 24,000 feet as the mountains shot up 6,000 feet. Ice-age glaciers, which also gouged out hundreds of lakes in the park, carved the canyons that punctuate the mountains.

The first homesteaders arrived in the area in the 1880s. By 1907, cattle ranchers discovered that wealthy Eastern hunters were attracted to the area as a vacation site, and the dude-ranching industry secured its first foothold in Jackson Hole, the great valley that runs the length of the Tetons to the east. But when cattle interests learned of a movement to convert the valley floor into a national park, a tug-of-war began. Congress had designated the area south of Yellowstone the Teton Forest Reserve in 1897 and attempted to create a larger sanctuary in 1918, but local opposition stymied the move. In 1923, Congress set aside 96,000 acres as a national park in 1929.

Next, John D. Rockefeller, Jr., anonymously accumulated more than 35,000 acres of land between 1927 and 1943. His goal was to donate the property for an enlarged park, but opponents in Congress prevented the government from accepting his gift. Finally, in 1950, the Feds and the locals reached a compromise: The government agreed to reimburse Teton County for revenue that would have been generated by property taxes and to honor existing leaseholds, and present-day Grand Teton National Park was born.

FLORA & FAUNA

Grand Teton is home to grizzly and black bears, wolves, elk, and deer, but its most notable wild population is probably moose. Willow Flats is the best place to spot moose in the park, as well as along the Moose–Wilson Road en route to Jackson. There are thousands of plant species, ranging from wildflowers to evergreen, and the valley floors have plenty of sagebrush.

AVOIDING the crowds

Most of the travelers who visit Grand Teton are visiting Yellowstone on the same trip, and this means that when winter closes in on Yellowstone, the crowds abandon both parks. Grand Teton usually holds out against winter a bit longer than the higher plateau to the north, so you may enjoy a wonderful, traffic-free visit in early June and late October. But I emphasize the word *may*: Snow can fall as early as September and as late as June. In spring, higher trails are still blocked by snow or mud. This soggy season can last well into June. Fall nights can be cold and icy winds sometimes blow.

If crowds make you claustrophobic, the key months to avoid are July and August. But most of the people who come through the gates in midsummer go only to the developed campgrounds and lodges. If you have the energy to hike up into Cascade Canyon and beyond, you'll see an entirely different landscape, with wildflowers blooming well into July and wildlife always in evidence.

ESSENTIALS

Getting There & Gateways

The park is essentially the east slope of the Tetons and the valley below; if you drive to it, you enter from the south, east, or north. From the north, you can enter Grand Teton from Yellowstone National Park via the **John D. Rockefeller, Jr., Memorial Parkway** (U.S. 89/191/287). From December to March, Yellowstone's south entrance is open only to snowmobiles and snow coaches. You can also approach the park from the east, on **U.S. 26/287.** This route comes from Dubois, 55 miles east on the other side of the Absaroka and Wind River mountains, and crosses Togwotee Pass, where you'll get your first and one of the best views of the Tetons from above the valley. Coming from Jackson, you drive 12 miles north on **U.S. 26/89/191** to the park's south entrance.

THE NEAREST AIRPORT Jackson Hole Airport (© 307/733-7682; www.jackson holeairport.com) is just inside the southern boundary of Grand Teton National Park.

Visitor Centers & Information

Grand Teton National Park has three visitor centers. The most extensive is the **Craig Thomas Discovery and Visitor Center** (© 307/739-3399), a half-mile west of Moose Junction at the southern end of the park. The **Jenny Lake Visitor Center** (© 307/739-3343), at South Jenny Lake, has maps, publications, and a geology exhibit. The **Colter Bay Visitor Center** (© 307/739-3594), the northernmost center, is also the home of the **Indian Arts Museum.** On the Moose–Wilson Road, you'll find the **Laurence S. Rockefeller Preserve Center** (© 307/739-3654).

To receive park maps and information before your arrival, contact **Grand Teton National Park** (© 307/739-3300; www.nps.gov/grte). The **Grand Teton Association** (© 307/739-3403;

Special Regulations & Warnings

It is unlawful to approach within 100 yards of a bear or within 25 yards of other wildlife. Feeding any wildlife is illegal.

Grand Teton National Park

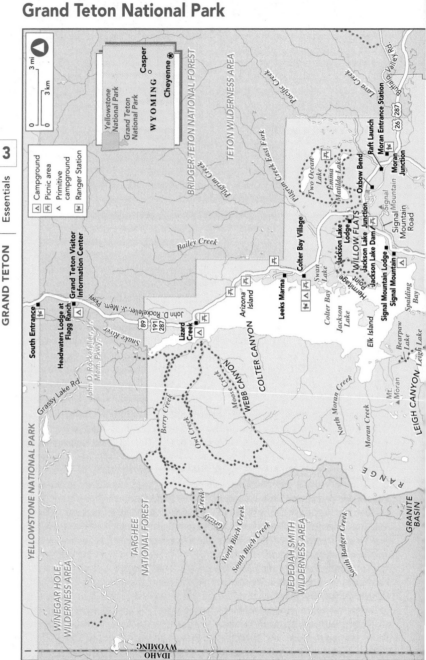

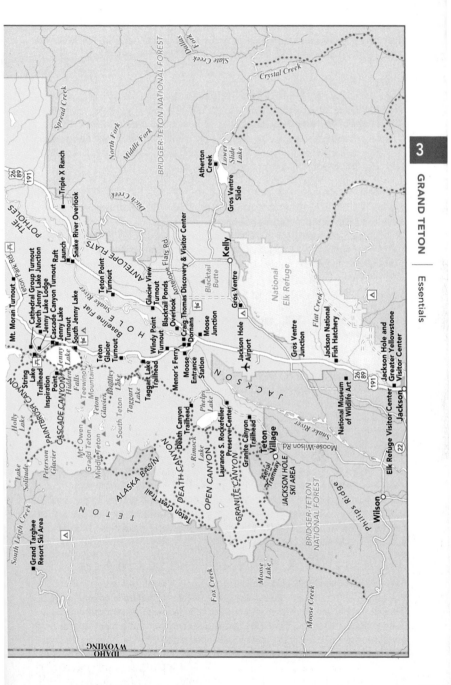

www.grandtetonpark.org) also provides information about the park and books of interest to visitors at the visitor centers.

The **Jackson Hole Chamber of Commerce** (© **307/733-3316;** www.jacksonhole chamber.com) provides information about the area. In town, stop at the **Jackson Hole and Greater Yellowstone Visitor Center,** 532 N. Cache St.

Fees & Permits

There are no park gates on U.S. 26/89/191, so the views are free as you pass through the park on that route, but if you want to get off the highway and explore, you'll pay $25 per automobile for a 7-day pass (good for both Yellowstone and Grand Teton).

Fees for **camping** in Grand Teton are $21 per night ($8 for hike- and bike-in sites). You must have a **permit** to sleep in the backcountry. See "Exploring the Backcountry," later this chapter, for information.

Seasons & Climate

Spring is likely to be chilly and spitting snow or rain here. Snow and mud still clog trails. Cold and snow may linger into May, though temperatures are generally warming. A jacket, rain gear, and water-resistant walking shoes are advised. **Summer** is finally under way in mid-June; wildflowers start to bloom in May in the lower valleys and plains, and in July in the higher elevations. Temperatures are typically pleasant in the lower elevations and are especially comfortable because of the lack of humidity. Nights, however, will be cool, even during the warmest months, with temperatures dropping into the low 40s (single digits Celsius), so you'll want to pack a light jacket. Thunderstorms are common. As **fall** approaches and temperatures begin to cool, you'll want an additional layer of clothing. The first snows typically fall by November 1 and continue through May. **Winter** is a glorious season, though it's not for everyone—it can get *very* cold. But the air is crystalline, the snow is powdery, and the skiing is fantastic. You'll need appropriate gear for the often inhospitable climate. If you drive in the park in the winter, carry sleeping bags, extra food, flashlights, and other safety gear.

If you're planning on visiting Yellowstone as well as Grand Teton, and are considering making your trip to the parks before the middle of June, think about beginning your exploration in Grand Teton before working north to Yellowstone—elevations here are slightly lower and snow melts earlier.

EXPLORING THE PARK

We begin at the northern end of the park. But you could also start exploring from the southern end, near Jackson. From Jackson, it's 13 miles to the Moose Entrance Station, another 7 miles to the Jenny Lake Visitor Center, another 12 miles to the Jackson Lake Junction, and 5 miles to Colter Bay.

Jackson Lake & the North End of the Park

Many people enter Grand Teton National Park from the north end, emerging from Yellowstone's south entrance with a 7-day park pass that is good for admission to Grand Teton as well. Yellowstone connects to Grand Teton by a wilderness corridor called the **John D. Rockefeller, Jr., Memorial Parkway,** through which the highway runs for 8 miles, over the Snake River, past meadows sometimes dotted with elk, along the shores of Jackson Lake, and through forests.

Giant **Jackson Lake,** a huge expanse of water that fills a deep gouge left 10,000 years ago by retreating glaciers, dominates the north end of the park. Stream flow from the dam is regulated both for potato farmers downstream in Idaho and for rafters in the canyon, so, for better or ill, we have an irrigation dam in a national park. Elsewhere on the lake, things look quite natural, except when water gets low in the fall.

As the road follows the east shore of the lake from the north, the first development that travelers encounter is **Leeks Marina.** Just south of Leeks is **Colter Bay,** a busy outpost of park services—a visitor center, a general store, laundry, restaurants, cabins, and a campground.

From Colter Bay, the road swerves east and then south again past Jackson Lake Lodge. Numerous trails emanate from here, both to the lakeshore and east to **Emma Matilda Lake.** The road then comes to **Jackson Lake Junction,** where you can either continue west along the lakeshore or go east to the park's Moran Entrance Station.

If you're here to enjoy the park, you should turn right (west) on **Teton Park Road** at Jackson Lake Junction. After 5 miles, you will arrive at **Signal Mountain,** with the full array of visitor services. If you turn east instead of west off Teton Park Road at Signal Mountain, you can drive up to the **top of the mountain,** 700 feet above the valley, where you'll have a fine view of the ring of mountains—Absarokas, Gros Ventres, Tetons, and Yellowstone Plateau—that create the Jackson "Hole."

Jenny Lake & the South End of the Park

Continuing south along Teton Park Road, you move into the park's southern half, where the tallest peaks rise abruptly above a string of smaller lakes strung together in the foothills—**Leigh Lake, String Lake,** and **Jenny Lake.** At North Jenny Lake Junction, you can take a turnoff west to Jenny Lake Lodge. The road continues as a one-way loop along the lakeshore before rejoining Teton Park Road 4 miles later.

Jenny Lake gets a lot of traffic throughout the summer, both from hikers who circumnavigate the lake on a 6-mile trail and others who pay for a boat ride across the lake. The parking lot at **South Jenny Lake** is often jammed, and there can be a long wait for the boat ride, so get there early. Or you can save your money by taking the 2-mile hike around the lake—it's level and easy. The trip costs $12 round-trip for adults, $7 for children 5 to 12, and free for children under 5. Contact **Jenny Lake Boating Company** (© **307/734-9227;** www.jennylakeboating.com); reservations are recommended.

South of the lake, Teton Park Road crosses open sagebrush plains with views of the mountains. You'll pass the Climbers' Ranch and some trail heads for **hikes to Taggart Lake** and elsewhere. The **Teton Glacier Turnout** presents a view of a glacier that grew for several hundred years until, pressured by hotter summer temperatures in the past century, it reversed direction and began retreating.

The road arrives at the park's south entrance and the **Craig Thomas Discovery and Visitor Center** in Moose, also home to park headquarters and a village with shops, restaurants, and lodgings. Behind the visitor center is **Menor's Ferry.** Bill Menor had a store and operated a ferry across the Snake River at Moose in the late 1800s. The ferry and store have been reconstructed. **Dornan's** is a small village area just south of the visitor center with a grocery store, rental cabins, restaurants, and a wine shop.

Four miles south on the Moose–Wilson Road is the **LSR Preserve** around Phelps Lake. Until 2007, this was the Rockefellers' former private

> ### Road Openings
>
> **Teton Park Road** opens for the summer season around May 1. The **Moose–Wilson Road** opens to vehicles at about the same time. Roads close to vehicles on November 1 and open for snowmobiles in mid-December.

retreat, since donated to the National Park Service. Buildings came down and a 8-mile trail system went in, along with a staffed visitor center with exhibits geared towards getting visitors to reflect on their own relationship with nature.

The East Side of the Park

At Moose Junction, just east of the visitor center, drivers can rejoin the highway and turn south to Jackson and the Gros Ventre turn, or cruise north up U.S. 89/26/191 to Moran Junction. This 18-mile trip is the fastest route through the park and, because of its distance from the mountains, offers views of a broader mountain tableau.

The junction of U.S. 89 with **Antelope Flats Road** is 1.25 miles north of the Moose Junction. The 20-mile route beginning here is a good biking route. It's all on level terrain, passing by the town of Kelly and the Gros Ventre campground before looping back to U.S. 26/89/191 at the Gros Ventre Junction to the south.

Less than a mile farther along U.S. 26/89/191, on the left, **Blacktail Ponds Overlook** offers an opportunity to see how beavers build dams and how they affect the flow of the streams. The area is marshy early in summer, but it's worth the quarter-mile hike down to the streams, where you can view the beaver activity more closely.

Traveling 2 miles farther along U.S. 89 brings you to the **Glacier View Turnout,** which offers views of an area that 150,000 years ago was filled with a 4,000-foot-thick glacier. The view of the gulch between the peaks offers testimony to the power of the glaciers that carved this landscape. The **Snake River Overlook,** 4 miles down the road, is the most famous view of the Snake River, immortalized by Ansel Adams. A half-mile north of the overlook is the road to **Deadman's Bar.** Many float trips launch here, and there is also some fishing access.

If you head down the highway in the other direction (south) from Moose Junction on U.S. 26/89/191, you can turn east on the **Gros Ventre River Road** 5 miles before you reach Jackson and follow the river east into its steep canyon. A few miles past the little town of **Kelly,** you leave the park and enter **Bridger-Teton National Forest.**

In 1925, a huge slab of mountain broke off the north end of the Gros Ventre Range on the east side of Jackson Hole, a reminder of nature's violent and unpredictable side. The slide left a gaping open gash in the side of Sheep Mountain, sloughing off nearly 50 million cubic yards of rock and forming a natural dam across the Gros Ventre River half a mile wide. Two years later, the dam broke, and a cascade of water rushed down the canyon and through the little town of Kelly, taking several lives. The town of **Kelly** is a quaint, eccentric community with a large number of yurts. Up in the canyon formed by the Gros Ventre River is a roadside display with photographs of the slide area and a nature walk from the road down to the residue of the slide and **Lower Slide Lake.** Signs identify the trees and plants that survived or grew in the slide's aftermath.

ORGANIZED TOURS & RANGER PROGRAMS

The **Grand Teton Lodge Company** (*C* 307/543-2811; www.gtlc.com) runs half-day bus tours of Grand Teton ($50 adults, $20 children 3–11) and full-day tours of Yellowstone ($80 adults, $45 children 3–11) from late May to early October, weather permitting.

The **Teton Science Schools** (*C* 307/733-1313; www.tetonscience.org) has an excellent curriculum for students of all ages. Classes take place at campuses in Jackson and Kelly, and other locations in Jackson Hole. The school's **Wildlife Expeditions**

(📞 **877/404-6626**) offers tours that bring visitors closer to the park's wildlife. These trips range from a half-day to a week.

Within the park, ranger programs include a ranger-led 3-mile hike from the Colter Bay Visitor Center to Swan Lake, as well as a relaxed evening chatting with a ranger on the deck of the Jackson Lake Lodge while you watch for moose and birds through a spotting scope. Check the schedules in the park's newspaper, *The Teewinot,* available at any visitor center.

Youngsters 8 to 12 can join the **Junior Ranger program** at Colter Bay or Jenny Lake and learn about the natural world for 2 hours while hiking with a ranger. Signups are at the visitor centers (the fee is a mere $1), and the kids will need basic hiking gear.

DAY HIKES

Colter Bay Area

Hermitage Point Trails ★   There are several loop options on trails that lead past Swan Lake and Cygnet Pond to the end of the peninsula at Hermitage Point. When choosing your route, keep in mind that the three trails have virtually identical foliage and terrain. The numerous options can be confusing, so carry a map. Up to 9.4 miles RT. Easy. Access: Colter Bay Visitor Center parking lot.

Lakeshore Trail ★   Originating in the Colter Bay area, this short jaunt starts at the marina and leads out to pebble beaches on the west side of Jackson Lake. The trail is wide and shady, and views of the entire Teton Range leap out at you from across the lake when you arrive at the end of the trail. 2 miles RT. Easy. Access: Marina entrance.

Jackson Lake Lodge Area

Christian Pond Trail ★★   This trail begins with a half-mile walk through a grassy, wet area to a pond with nesting trumpeter swans and other waterfowl. You can circle the pond, adding another 3 miles to the trip. In May and June, this is a great wildflower walk, but it's also prime habitat for bears (and mosquitos), so check with rangers first. The south end of the pond is covered with little grassy knolls upon which the birds build their nests and roost; beavers have constructed a lodge here, too. 1 mile RT. Easy. Access: 200 yards south of Jackson Lake Lodge entrance (it's unmarked, so look carefully).

Signal Mountain Summit Trail ★★   This trail gives you a few hours of solitude, en route to the final grand panorama of a glacially carved valley. After negotiating a steep initial climb, you'll come to a broad plateau with lodgepole pines, grassy areas, and seasonal wildflowers. Cross a paved road to a lily-clad pond, and just beyond you'll choose one of two trails—take the right one up (ponds, wildlife, maybe moose) or the left one down (ridges with views). 8 miles RT. Moderate. Access: Near Signal Mountain Lodge entrance, or 1 mile (by car) up Signal Mountain Rd. to a pond on the right.

Two Ocean & Emma Matilda Lake Trails

Emma Matilda Lake Trail ★★   Circumnavigating this lake is a pleasant, up-and-down journey with great views of the mountains and a good chance of seeing wildlife. The hike winds uphill for a half-mile from the parking area to a large meadow favored by mule deer. The trail follows the north side of the lake through a pine forest 400 feet above the lake, then descends to an overlook where you'll have panoramic views of the Tetons, Christian Pond, and Jackson Lake. 12 miles RT. Easy to moderate. Access: Emma Matilda Lake trail head on Pacific Creek Rd., or trail head off Two Ocean Lake Rd. north of Jackson Lake–Moran Rd.

Two Ocean Lake Trail ★★ Take your time and take a picnic on this delightful, underused trail around Two Ocean Lake. You can start at either end, the walk around the lake is fairly level, and ducks, swans, grebes, and loons are common. As usual, awesome views of the Tetons abound; for the best perspective, take the 1.3-mile trip up 600 feet to Grand View Point. It's possible to branch off onto the Emma Matilda Lake Trail at the east end of Two Ocean Lake. 5.8 miles RT. Easy to moderate. Access: Two Ocean Lake trail head on Two Ocean Lake Rd., or Grand View Point trailhead.

Jenny Lake Area

Amphitheater Lake Trail ★★★ Here's a trail that can get you up into the high mountains and out in a day, if you're in good shape and acclimated to the altitude (you'll climb 3,000 ft.). You'll cross glacial moraines, meadows quilted with flowers, and forests of fir, lodgepole, and whitebark pine. (Bear food—be alert!) Finally, you clear the trees and come into a massive rock amphitheater topped by Disappointment Peak, with the Grand and Teewinot in view. Surprise Lake and Amphitheater Lake sit in this dramatic setting, with a few gnarled trees struggling to survive on the slopes. 9.6 miles RT. Strenuous. Access: Lupine Meadows trail head between Moose and Jenny Lake.

Cascade Canyon Trail ★★★ For those who have time to go a little farther, Cascade Canyon Trail is the most popular in the park. You can begin the hike from South Jenny Lake, but you can shave 2 miles off each way by riding the boat across the lake and beginning your hike at the dock. After the steep 1-mile hike from Inspiration Point, which is as far as many visitors go, you make a brief climb to the glacially rounded canyon, where the trail levels out in a wonderland of wildflowers, waterfowl, and busy pikas. 9.1 miles RT. Moderate to strenuous. Access: Inspiration Point.

Hidden Falls & Inspiration Point Trail ★★ Many people cross Jenny Lake, either by boat or on foot around the south end, and then make the short, forest-shaded uphill slog to Hidden Falls (less than 1 mile of hiking if you take the boat, 5 miles round-trip if you walk around), which tumbles down a broad cascade. Some think that's enough and don't go another steep half-mile to Inspiration Point. Up there you get a great view of Jenny Lake below, and you can see the glacial moraine that formed it. 1.8–5.8 miles RT. Moderate. Access: East or west shore boat dock.

Jenny Lake Loop Trail ★★★ Another lake to circumnavigate, following the shore. You can cut the trip in half by taking the Jenny Lake boat shuttle from the east shore boat dock to the west shore boat dock. The lake occupies a pastoral setting at the foot of the mountain range, providing excellent views throughout the summer. The trails to Hidden Falls, Inspiration Point, and Moose Ponds on the southwest shore of the lake. 6.5 miles RT. Easy to moderate. Access: Trail head at east shore boat dock.

EXPLORING THE BACKCOUNTRY

Grand Teton is a favorite of backpackers, with more than 250 miles of backcountry trails. You must have a **permit** from the Park Service to sleep in the backcountry—the permits are free, but reservations are not. The permit is valid only on the dates for which it is issued. There are two methods of securing permits: They may be picked up at park visitor centers the day before you start your trip, or you can make a reservation for a permit in advance of your arrival, for a $25 fee. Reservations are accepted from January 1 to May 15; it's wise to reserve a camp area if you're going in July or August.

Reservations may be made by writing the **Permits Office,** Grand Teton National Park, P.O. Drawer 170, Moose, WY 83012, or online at **www.nps.gov/grte.**

Remember that this region has a short summer and practically no spring. Although the lower-elevation areas of the park are open in May, some of the high-country trails may not be clear of snow or high water before late June or early July.

Perhaps the most popular backcountry trail in Grand Teton is the 19-mile **Cascade Canyon Loop,** which starts on the west side of Jenny Lake, winds northwest 7.2 miles on the **Cascade Canyon Trail** to Lake Solitude and the Paintbrush Divide, then returns on the 10-mile-long **Paintbrush Trail** past Holly Lake.

This kind of backcountry trip is really an expedition, and it requires skill and experience. Go over your plans with park rangers, who can help you evaluate your ability to take on the challenge.

OTHER SUMMER SPORTS & ACTIVITIES

BIKING Road bikers should try **Antelope Flats,** beginning at a trail head 1 mile north of Moose Junction and going east. Sometimes called **Mormon Row,** this paved route crosses the flats below the Gros Ventre Mountains, past old ranch homesteads and the small town of Kelly. It connects to the unpaved **Shadow Mountain Road,** which actually goes outside the park into national forest, climbing through the trees to the summit. Total distance is 7 miles, and the elevation gain is 1,370 feet; you'll be looking at Mount Moran and the Tetons across the valley. Banned on park trails, mountain bikers gravitate to the **River Road,** a 15-mile dirt path along the Snake River's western bank. (Bison use it, too, and you'd be smart to yield.)

Mountain bikers have a few more options: Try **Two Ocean Lake Road** (reached from the Pacific Creek Rd. just north of Moran Junction) or the **River Road,** a 15-mile dirt path along the Snake River's western bank. (Bison use it, too, and you'd be smart to yield.) Ambitious mountain bikers may want to load their overnight gear and take the **Grassy Lake Road,** once used by American Indians, west from Flagg Ranch on a 50-mile journey to Ashton, Idaho.

BOATING If you bring your own boat, you must register it: For human-powered craft, it's $10 for 7 days, or $20 for a 1-year permit; motorized skippers pay $20 for 7 days and $40 for an annual permit, which you can buy at the Colter Bay and Moose visitor centers. Boat and canoe rentals, tackle, and fishing licenses are available at **Colter Bay** and **Signal Mountain** (rental fees of $30–$60 per hour for motorboats include permits; kayaks, canoes, and deck cruisers are also available). Sailboat tours are also available at Signal Mountain. The **Jenny Lake Boating Company** (© 307/733-9227) runs shuttles to the west side of Jenny Lake and offers scenic cruises for $15 adults, $7 kids. **Scenic cruises** of Jackson Lake are conducted daily by the **Grand Teton Lodge Company** (© 307/543-2811; www.gtlc.com). You can rent kayaks and canoes at **Adventure Sports** at Dornan's in the town of Moose (© 307/733-3307; www.dornans.com/adventures), which is within the boundaries of Grand Teton National Park.

CLIMBING Two top-notch operations offer classes and guided climbs of Grand Teton: **Jackson Hole Mountain Guides** in Jackson (© 800/239-7642 or 307/733-4979; www.jhmg.com) and **Exum Mountain Guides** in Moose (© 307/733-2297; www.exumguides.com). Expect to pay around $700 to $1,000 for a guided 2-day climb of Grand Teton, or $150 to $200 for a class. The **Jenny Lake Ranger Station** (© **307/739-3392;** open only in summer) is the center for climbing information; climbers are encouraged to stop in and obtain information on routes, conditions, and regulations.

FISHING The lakes and streams of Grand Teton are popular fishing destinations. Jackson, Jenny, and Phelps lakes are loaded with lively cutthroat trout, whitefish, and mackinaw (lake) trout. Jackson has produced monsters weighing as much as 50 pounds, but you're more likely to catch fish under 20 inches, fishing deep with trolling gear from a boat during hot summer months. You need a Wyoming state **fishing license** and must check creel limits, which vary from year to year and place to place.

FLOAT TRIPS The park's 27-mile stretch of the Snake River is wonderful for viewing wildlife, with moose, eagles, and other animals coming, like you, to the water's edge. Most of the commercial float operators in the park operate from mid-May to mid-September (depending on weather and river flow conditions). Try **Grand Teton Lodge Company** (© **307/543-2811;** www.gtlc.com) or **Signal Mountain Lodge** (© **307/543-2831;** www.signalmtnlodge.com). Scenic float trips cost about $50 to $60 for adults, with discounts for children under 12.

HORSEBACK RIDING The **Grand Teton Lodge Company** (see below) offers tours from stables next to popular visitor centers at Colter Bay and Jackson Lake Lodge. Choices are 1- and 2-hour guided trail rides daily aboard well-broken, tame animals for $40 to $75 per rider.

WINTER SPORTS & ACTIVITIES

Park facilities pretty much shut down during the winter, except for a skeleton staff at the Moose Visitor Center.

SKIING You can ski flat or you can ski steep in Grand Teton. The two things to watch out for are hypothermia and avalanches. Check with local rangers and guides for trails that match your ability. Among your flat options is the relatively easy **Jenny Lake Trail,** starting at the Taggart Lake Parking Area, about 8 miles round-trip of flat and scenic trail that follows Cottonwood Creek. Skiers who come to Jackson Hole are usually after the steep stuff at the **Jackson Hole Mountain Resort,** but the area is also a mecca for backcountry skiers.

SNOWMOBILING Snowmobiling is a popular winter option. Snowmobiling is allowed on the frozen surface of Jackson Lake and in the nearby **Bridger-Teton National Forest,** the area to the immediate east of Grand Teton National Park. There are numerous outfitters in Jackson that rent snowmobiles and offer guided tours, including **Jackson Hole Snowmobile** (© **306/733-3692;** www.jacksonholesnowmobile.com).

WHERE TO STAY

Inside the Park

You can get information about or make reservations for Jackson Lake Lodge, Jenny Lake Lodge, and Colter Bay Village through the **Grand Teton Lodge Company** (© **800/628-9988** or 307/543-2811; www.gtlc.com). For Signal Mountain Lodge, contact **Signal Mountain Lodge** (© **307/543-2831;** www.signalmountainlodge.com). In Moose, **Dornan's Spur Ranch Cabins** (© **307/733-2522;** www.dornans.com)

sleep four to six for $185 to $265 in the summer. Nearby, **Moulton Ranch Cabins** (© **307/733-3749;** www.moultonranchcabins.com) charges $95 to $249 for a cabin.

COLTER BAY VILLAGE AREA

Colter Bay Village ★ Think "summer camp for grown-ups" and you'll be fine with the digs at this extremely rustic complex. It features both genuine log cabins (they look like something out of a Laura Ingalls Wilder book and are as bare of amenities—like air conditioning, rugs on the cold floors or coffeemakers—as a, well, early pioneer home would have been); and even more spartan permanent tents with bunk beds (guests bring their own bedding for those). Families tend to choose the place more than couples do perhaps because the beds are all doubles and twins. Or it could be they're drawn here by the fair prices, the abundance of on-site activities (hiking trails, rental canoes, a friendly guest lounge with Wi-Fi) and the presence of other families. *Note:* Many of the cabins and all the tents make use of shared bathroom facilities, so inquire about what you're renting if that's a deal-breaker.

At Colter Bay on Jackson Lake. © **800/628-9988** or 307/543-2811. www.gtlc.com. 166 units. $77 log cabin with shared bathroom; $141–$239 log cabin with private bathroom; $59 tent cabin. Closed late Sept to late May. **Amenities:** 2 restaurants; free Wi-Fi.

Jackson Lake Lodge ★★ A midcentury gem, it was built in 1955, by Gilbert Stanley Underwood, a prolific National Parks architect (he's the man behind the Awahnee Lodge in Yosemite and the Old Faithful Lodge in Yellowstone). Here he concentrated on the site's strengths: the views, which he framed with 60-foot picture windows. Look through them and you get a spectacular panorama of the Cathedral Group, the most-photographed mountains in the Teton Range. Not surprisingly, the best rooms are those with views, so avoid the dated and viewless "classic cabins" and pick one of the slickly designed lodge rooms instead. The Grand Teton Lodge Company has put a lot of money into the rooms over the years, probably to compete with the upscale norm in nearby Jackson and Teton Village, and it shows. Amenities are a cut above the national park norm, including coffeemakers and hair dryers and subtle "New West" decor.

At Jackson Lake. © **800/628-9988** or 307/543-2811. www.gtlc.com. 385 units. $249–$355 double; $705–$845 suite. Closed mid-Oct to mid-May. **Amenities:** 2 restaurants; outdoor heated pool; free Wi-Fi.

Signal Mountain Lodge ★★ Operated by Forever Resorts, this has a more laid-back, less corporate vibe than the Grand Teton Lodge Company properties, and therefore a loyal cadre of repeat guests. It is easy to see why: a picture-perfect location between Jackson Lake and Signal Mountain, a full slate of recreational activities (including sailboating), and a wide range of lodge rooms, bungalows, and cabins (a number with usable kitchens and fold-out sofas, making them a good choice for families and larger groups). Some units are contemporary, others are rustic, but they all share a nice sense of style.

At Jackson Lake. © **307/543-2831.** www.signalmountainlodge.com. 80 units. $162–$334 double. Pets accepted ($20 per night). Closed late Oct to early May. **Amenities:** 2 restaurants; bar; boat rentals.

JENNY LAKE AREA

Jenny Lake Lodge ★★★ This is as swank—and pricey—as national-park lodging comes. Tucked away from the main road near a trail that takes you to Jenny Lake, the location feels more isolated than it really is, and the rockers on each porch is just the place to watch the sun set over the Tetons. The lodging is exclusively cabins, and each is individually decorated with quilts and Western art, a rustic-meets-chic style.

The breakfast and dinner are included, and—along with the recreational opportunities—make the lodge worth the splurge.

At Jenny Lake. © **800/628-9988** or 307/543-2811. www.gtlc.com. 37 units. $655 double; $830–$915 suite. Extra person $155 a night. Rates include breakfast and dinner, horseback riding, and use of bicycles. Closed mid-Oct to May. **Amenities:** Restaurant; bar; horseback riding.

Near the Park

FLAGG RANCH AREA

Flagg Ranch offers travelers cabins, a campground, an above-average restaurant at Headwaters Lodge, and a gas station. However, there's not much to do here except watch the Snake River.

Headwaters Lodge ★ Acquired by the Grand Teton Lodge Company in 2012, this longstanding complex (formerly Flagg Ranch Resort) has both plusses and minuses to it. And some can be both. Take the location, which is 20-plus miles from a town in either direction, and sits between the Yellowstone and Grand Teton national parks (but is a fairly substantial drive from either). Some enjoy the remoteness, others find it a hassle (there's no cellphone coverage, so the lodge throws in free long-distance calls on in-room phones). Nearby, however, is excellent fishing, and the lodge can set up float trips, horseback rides, and more. Lodgings are divided into three categories, each slightly plusher than the next. First is the campground (which is pricier than those in the parks); a step up from that are the Camper Cabins, opened in 2012. They come without bathrooms, electricity, or bedding (they have beds, but you need a sleeping bag or sheets and blanket to stay warm) but are a good options for park-goers on a budget. Finally, are the recently renovated, spacious duplex and fourplex cabins set in the woods, each with a nice patio and rocking chair. They're not swank, but most find them comfortably appointed.

At Flagg Ranch. © **800/443-2311** or 307/543-2861. www.gtlc.com. 92 cabins, 171 campsites. $180–$257 cabin double; $70 Camper Cabin; $64 RV site; $35 tent site. **Amenities:** Restaurant; bar.

IN JACKSON & TETON VILLAGE

Clustered together near the junction west of downtown where Wyo. 22 leaves U.S. Hwy. 26/89 and heads north to Teton Village are numerous chain franchises, and there are numerous older motels closer to Town Square. Below is what we recommend.

A Teton Tree House ★★ For more than 40 years, innkeeper Denny Becker has been building and tweaking and rebuilding his B&B, literally located in the treetops in Wilson, about 10 minutes from Jackson at the foot of Teton Pass. From the road, it is almost 100 steps up to the front door, and the curious design is a perfect fit for the surroundings, and an ideal spot for bird watching—no, it is not an actual treehouse, but an architectural marvel that melds the best of a treehouse with a real home. Most rooms have decks and views of Jackson Hole; some can accommodate up to 4 guests. Heart-healthy breakfasts with no eggs or meat include breakfast banana splits with yogurt, and Denny is an awesome resource for exploring Grand Teton National Park.

6175 Heck of a Hill Rd., Wilson. © **307/733-3233.** www.atetontreehouse-jacksonhole.com. 6 units. $215–$285 double; 3-night minimum. Rates include complimentary full breakfast. 8 miles west of Jackson. Closed mid-Oct to mid-May. Located 8 miles west of Jackson. **Amenities:** Free Wi-Fi.

The Hostel ★ Formerly known as Hostel X, this classic budget ski lodge was destined for a date with a wrecking ball, but the economic winds shifted and it survived. A 2011 renovation gave the place a nice update, and there are plenty of

CAMPING options

Jenny Lake Campground ★★★, with 51 tent-only sites, is in a quiet, wooded area near the lake. It's worth it to arrive first thing in the morning to get a site. This is one of the loveliest places imaginable to see the sun set or rise. The largest campground, **Gros Ventre ★**, is the last to fill, if it fills up at all—probably because it's on the east side of the park, a few miles from Kelly on the Gros Ventre River Road. It lacks the scenery of Jenny Lake, and is more of a last resort because of its location on the sagebrush plain. **Signal Mountain Campground ★★**, with views of the lake and access to the beach, is another recommended spot that fills first thing in the morning. **Colter Bay Campground and Trailer Village ★** has 350 sites, some with RV hookups, showers, and a launderette. Thanks to its size, there almost always seems to be someone coming or going, so steer clear if you are after peace and quiet. **Lizard Creek Campground ★★** is at the north end of Grand Teton National Park near Jackson Lake in a nicely wooded area that is more private than Colter Bay but not as pretty as Jenny Lake. At all campgrounds, sites run $21 nightly, or $8 for hike-in sites. For recorded information on campgrounds, call ℂ **307/739-3603.**

communal perks: kitchen facilities, ping-pong, and TVs. Rooms are more than worth the rate, an unbeatable value in ski season—or any other time of year. If you are on a budget and do not want to camp, look no further.

3315 W. Village Dr., Teton Village. ℂ **307/733-3415.** www.thehostel.us. 55 rooms, 20 dormitory-style bunks. $89–$99 double; $18–$34 bunk. **Amenities:** Game room; Wi-Fi (fee).

Wyoming Inn ★★ Renovated to the nines in 2013, the Wyoming Inn is a cut above most of its mid-priced competitors in Jackson proper and our mid-priced pick in a relatively expensive market. The subtle "New West" design in both the rooms and public areas pleases the eye, and there are nice perks like free laundry machines and in-room fireplaces in premium units. The hotel is a walkable mile to Town Square.

930 W. Broadway, Jackson. ℂ **800/844-0035** or 307/734-0035. www.wyominginn.com. 68 units. $199–$249 double; $259–$309 suite. **Amenities:** Restaurant; free Wi-Fi.

WHERE TO EAT

Inside the Park

COLTER BAY

Colter Bay Village ★ AMERICAN   The Colter Bay Complex features a grocery store, snack shop, and a pair of more substantial restaurants in **John Colter Café Court** and the **Ranch House.** The former offers fast-food-style fare and meals to go, while the latter offers a woodsy atmosphere and hearty steaks, burgers, and local rainbow trout.

At Colter Bay Village on Jackson Lake. ℂ **307/543-2811.** www.gtlc.com. Breakfast and lunch $5–$15; dinner $7–$21. John Colter Café Court: Daily 11am–10pm. Ranch House: Daily 6:30–10:30am, 11:30am–1:30pm, and 5:30–9pm. Closed early Sept to May.

JACKSON LAKE JUNCTION

The casual dining choice at the Jackson Lake Lodge is the **Pioneer Grill.** The **Blue Heron** lounge at Jackson Lake Lodge is a nice spot for a cocktail.

The Mural Room ★★★ STEAKS/GAME   Even with so much to look at—the stunning panorama of the Tetons outside and the namesake Western murals by Carl Roters inside—the food manages to shine as some of the best in any national park. From quinoa scrambles and a hearty breakfast buffet to cobb salads and curried tofu at lunch, there are plenty of creative spins coming from the kitchen. Dinners are excellent, from the requisite beef and game dishes, to a number of vegetarian entrees.

At Jackson Lake Lodge. ✆ **307/543-3100.** www.gtlc.com. Reservations recommended. Breakfast $6–$16; lunch $12–$19; dinner $18–$38. Summer daily 7–9:30am, 11:30am–1:30pm, and 5:30–9pm.

Signal Mountain Lodge ★★ AMERICAN/MEXICAN   There are three dining options at the resort: Most expensive is the upscale **Peaks,** with steaks and seafood on one of the best menus in the park, and the best views this side of the Mural Room. Less expensive and formal is the casual **Trapper Grill,** serving burgers, chili, and burritos. Budget travelers love the **Deadman's Bar,** known for its blackberry margaritas and a mountain of a nacho plate that is nearly impossible to finish and perhaps the best value in all of Jackson Hole at $16.

At Signal Mountain Resort. ✆ **307/543-2831.** www.signalmountainlodge.com. Breakfast and lunch $7–$17; dinner $9–$32. Summer daily 7–10am and 11:30am–10pm.

JENNY LAKE AREA

Jenny Lake Lodge Dining Room ★★★ CONTINENTAL   This eatery has set the standard for national-park dining for decades. The breakfast and five-course dinner is included in the rate for overnight guests, but are prix-fixe for others. Lunch is perhaps the best meal for outsiders, because the prices are lower and you will get a peek at the beautiful lodge when it is not dominated by the overnight guests, That said, dinners—with a nice selection of local and regional fare—are some of the best in the Rockies, featuring game delicacies like huckleberry-port elk chops and juniper-scented venison. Jackets are recommended.

At Jenny Lake Lodge. ✆ **307/733-4647.** www.gtlc.com. Reservations required. Prix-fixe breakfast $24; lunch $11–$14; prix-fixe dinner $78, not including alcoholic beverages. Summer daily 7:30–9am, noon–1:30pm, and 6–8:45pm.

Near the Park

Nora's Fish Creek Inn ★★ AMERICAN   Topped by a massive rainbow trout, hit this landmark diner in Wilson, 6 miles northwest of Jackson, for breakfast: The huevos rancheros are world-famous, and rightfully so, topped with spicy green chile, and the pancakes are truly enormous. Lunch brings top-notch sandwiches and burgers, and the standout dinner is trout.

5600 W. Wyo. 22, Wilson. ✆ **307/733-8288.** www.norasfishcreekinn.com. Reservations accepted for dinner. Breakfast and lunch $6–$15; dinner $12–$39. Mon–Fri 6:30am–2pm; Sat–Sun 6:30am–1:30pm; Thurs–Sun 5–9pm. Call for winter hours.

Rendezvous Bistro ★★ NEW AMERICAN   This locally beloved eatery hits all of the right notes, from its casual vibe to its raw bar to its creative menu, inspired equally by regional and international cuisines. It changes regularly, but salmon, steak, and shellfish are almost always featured, as well as game, poultry, and pork. You might have such selections as organic chicken, vegetarian gnocchi, and steak frites. There are also less expensive sandwiches, daily specials, and an excellent wine list.

380 S. Broadway. ✆ **307/739-1100.** www.rendezvousbistro.net. Reservations recommended. Main courses $12–$27. Tues–Sat 5:30–10pm.

In winter, the U.S. Fish & Wildlife Service feed the elk alfalfa at the **National Elk Refuge,** just north of Jackson on U.S. Hwy. 26/89 (© **307/733-9212;** www.fws.gov/refuge/national_elk_refuge), keeping them out of the haystacks at area ranches. Thousands of elk, some with huge antlers, dot the snow for miles. Horse-drawn sleigh rides are available in winter, embarking at the **Jackson Hole and Greater Yellowstone Visitor Center,** 532 N. Cache St., from 10am to 4pm. Tickets are $19 for adults, and $15 for kids 5 to 12.

Snake River Brewing Co. ★ MICROBREWERY   One of the best brewpubs in the West, the Snake River Brewing Co. is equally well-known for its award-winning beers (Zonker Stout is a favorite), its top-notch pub grub, and its status as "Jackson's living room." The menu includes ribs, pizza, burgers, and creative spins on pub standards. On a budget? Drop in for the $7 lunch special.

265 S. Millward St. © **307/739-2337.** www.snakeriverbrewing.com. Most dishes $8–$15. Daily 11:30am–11pm. Bar open later.

Snake River Grill ★★★ NEW AMERICAN   This grill tops many "best of" lists for the state of Wyoming. From starters like prosciutto-fig pizza to the housemade eskimo bars for dessert, the menu is a regularly changing revelation. Main courses might include lamb chop "lollipops" and pumpkin ravioli. If the prices are too rich, have an appetizer and a cocktail at the bar for the atmosphere, then head to a less spendy place for your main course.

84 E. Broadway, on the Town Square. © **307/733-0557.** www.snakerivergrill.com. Reservations recommended. Main courses $19–$52. Daily 5:30–10pm (opens 6pm in winter). Closed Nov and Apr.

3

GRAND TETON — Where to Eat

GLACIER

by Eric Peterson

M ajestic and wild, this vast preserve beckons visitors with stunning mountain peaks (many covered year-round with glaciers), verdant mountain trails, and a huge diversity of plant and animal life. Every spring, Glacier is a postcard come to life: Wildflowers carpet its meadows; bears emerge from months of hibernation; and moose, elk, and deer play out the drama of birth, life, and death. The unofficial mascot in these parts is the grizzly, a refugee from the high plains.

Here you'll see nature at work: The glaciers are receding (the result of global warming, many say), and avalanches have periodically ravaged Going-to-the-Sun Road, the curving, scenic 50-mile road across the park. For the time being, the park is intact and very much alive, a treasure in a vault that opens to visitors.

Named in honor of the slow-moving glaciers that carved awe-inspiring valleys throughout this expanse of more than 1 million acres, Glacier National Park exists because of the efforts of George Bird Grinnell, a 19th-century magazine publisher and cofounder of the Audubon Society. Following a pattern established with Yellowstone and Grand Teton, Grinnell lobbied for a national park to be set aside in the St. Mary region of Montana, and in May 1910 his efforts were rewarded. Just over 20 years later, it became, with its northern neighbor Waterton Lakes National Park in Canada, **Glacier-Waterton International Peace Park**—a gesture of goodwill and friendship between the governments of two countries.

If your time is limited, motor along Going-to-the-Sun Road, viewing the dramatic mountain scenery. Visitors with more time will find diversions for both families and hard-core adventurers; while some hiking trails are suitable for tykes, many more will challenge those determined to conquer and scale the park's tallest peaks. The park's lakes, streams, ponds, and waterfalls are equally engaging. Travelers board cruise boats to explore the history of the area; recreational types can fish, row, and kayak.

To truly experience the park requires more effort, interest, and spunk than a simple drive through—abandon the pavement for even a short, easy hiking trail, and you'll discover a window into Glacier's soul.

FLORA & FAUNA

The park has notable populations of **grizzly bears, mountain goats, gray wolves, elk,** and **moose,** not to mention a small population of rare **bog lemmings.** Over 270 species of birds call the park home for at least part of the year, including harlequin ducks and golden eagles. There are more than 1,000 plant species that take root in the park, including abundant

AVOIDING the crowds

The simplest way to leave the crowds behind is to avoid visiting the park in its peak season, from mid-June to Labor Day. July is the busiest month. Late September and October, when fall colors light up the park, are excellent months to visit. A highlight is the display the larch trees put on throughout the western portions of the park. Entire hillsides turn bright yellow, fading to a dull orange glow as October wanes.

If visiting in the off season isn't possible, consider the following: Find a trail head that is equidistant from two major points, and head for the woods. Because most people congregate in proximity to the major hotels, this strategy should gain you a measure of solitude. If you must drive, to make the trip more enjoyable (and traffic-free), journey across the Going-to-the-Sun Road before 8:30am; you'll be astounded at the masterful job Mother Nature does of painting her mountains. You can always see more wildlife in the early morning (or just before dark) than at other times.

coniferous and **deciduous forests** as well as spring **wildflowers** in the wake of the spring thaw.

ESSENTIALS
Getting There & Gateways

Glacier National Park is in the northwest corner of Montana, on the Canadian border. The closest cities with airline service are **Kalispell,** 29 miles southwest of the park; **Great Falls,** 200 miles southeast; and **Missoula,** 150 miles south. If you're driving, the easiest ways to reach the park are from **U.S. 2** and **U.S. 89.**

Among the park's entrances are those at West Glacier, Camas Road, St. Mary, Many Glacier, Two Medicine, and Polebridge. Access is primarily at either end of Going-to-the-Sun Road: at West Glacier on the southwest side and St. Mary on the east. From the park's western boundary, you may enter at Polebridge to reach Bowman and Kintla lakes or take Camas Road to Going-to-the-Sun Road. The following east-side entrances are primarily hiking trails designed to access specific places and do not necessarily take you into the heart of the park: Essex, East Glacier, Two Medicine, Cut Bank, and Many Glacier. Entrance is restricted during the winter, when most of Going-to-the-Sun Road is closed.

THE NEAREST AIRPORTS **Glacier Park International Airport** is north of Kalispell at 4170 U.S. 2 (✆ **406/257-5994;** www.glacierairport.com).

BY RAIL Amtrak's *Empire Builder* (✆ **800/872-7245;** www.amtrak.com), a Chicago-Seattle round-trip train, stops from May to October at East Glacier and year-round at West Glacier and Essex.

Visitor Centers & Information

For up-to-date information on park activities, contact the superintendent, **Glacier National Park** (✆ **406/888-7800;** TDD 406/888-7806; www.nps.gov/glac). A vast array of publications is available from the **Glacier Association** (✆ **406/888-5756;** www.glacierassociation.org). Once you get to the park, check in at visitor centers at

BIKING   Bikes are restricted to established roads, bike routes, and parking areas, and are not allowed on trails. Restrictions apply to the most hazardous portions of Going-to-the-Sun Road during peak travel times, from around mid-June to Labor Day; call ahead or check the website to find out when the road will be closed to bikers. During low-visibility periods of fog or darkness, a white front light and a red back reflector are required.

BOATING   Although boating is permitted on some of Glacier's lakes, motor size is restricted to 10 horsepower on Bowman and Two Medicine lakes. A detailed list of other regulations is available at park headquarters and staffed ranger stations. Park rangers may inspect or board any boat to determine regulation compliance.

FISHING   A fishing license is not required within the park's boundaries; however, there are guidelines, so check with rangers at visitor centers or ranger stations for regulations. Fishing outside the park in Montana waters requires a state license; check in at a local fishing shop to make certain you're within the law.

VEHICLES   RVs and vehicles longer than 21 feet or wider than 8 feet are prohibited on the 24-mile stretch of Going-to-the-Sun Road between Avalanche Campground and Sun Point; vehicles over 10 feet are discouraged. Snowmobiling is prohibited.

Apgar, Logan Pass, and **St. Mary;** Travel Alberta staffs a center at **West Glacier.** St. Mary is open from mid-June through mid-October; Logan Pass, from mid-June through late September; and Apgar, from May through October (and weekends during the winter). Park information is also available from the **Two Medicine, Polebridge,** and **Many Glacier** ranger stations or from park headquarters.

Fees & Permits

A vehicle pass good for 7 days costs $25; an individual pass for walk-ins, bicycle riders, and motorcyclists, also good for 7 days, is $12. In winter, the fees drop to $15 and free, respectively. An annual park pass costs $35. Visitors to Waterton Lakes National Park (which is located in Canada) pay a separate entrance fee.

Camping fees are $10 to $23 per night at the park's drive-in campgrounds. Shared hiker-biker sites run $5 to $8 per person. If you plan to backpack overnight, you'll need a backcountry permit before your trip (see "Exploring the Backcountry," later in this chapter).

Seasons & Climate

Glacier is magnificent at any time of the year, but some roads are closed and park access is limited in the winter. By far the most popular time to visit is during the summer, when Going-to-the-Sun Road is fully open; in summer, sunrise is around 5am and sunset is nearly 10pm, so you have plenty of time for exploring. Spring and fall are equally magnificent, with budding wildflowers and variegated leaves and trees, but these sights can be viewed only from the park's outer boundaries and a limited stretch of the scenic highway. In winter, Glacier shuts itself off from much of the motorized world. Going-to-the-Sun Road, which is generally fully open only from mid-June to mid-September, is usually plowed from West Glacier to the head of Lake McDonald.

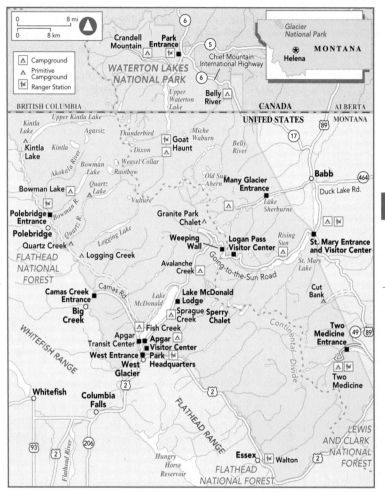

0 8 mi
0 8 km

△ Campground
△ Primitive Campground
🛉 Ranger Station

Crandell Mountain
Park Entrance
Chief Mountain International Highway

WATERTON LAKES NATIONAL PARK

Glacier National Park
Helena ⊛ MONTANA

BRITISH COLUMBIA

Upper Waterton Lake
Belly River
CANADA
ALBERTA

Kintla Lake
Upper Kintla Lake
UNITED STATES
MONTANA

Agassiz
Thunderbird
Miche Wabun
Goat Haunt
Belly River

Kintla Lake
Kintla
Dixon

Akokala River
Bowman Lake
Weasel Collar
Rainbow

Old Sun
Ahern
Many Glacier Entrance
Babb
Duck Lake Rd.

Bowman Lake
Quartz Lake
Vulture
Lake Sherburne

Polebridge Entrance
Granite Park Chalet

Polebridge
Quartz Creek
Logging Lake
Weeping Wall
Logan Pass Visitor Center
Rising Sun
St. Mary Entrance and Visitor Center

FLATHEAD NATIONAL FOREST
Logging Creek
Avalanche Creek
Going-to-the-Sun Road
St. Mary Lake

Camas Creek Entrance
Camas Rd.
Lake McDonald
Lake McDonald Lodge

Big Creek
Sprague Creek
Sperry Chalet

WHITEFISH RANGE
Fish Creek
Apgar Transit Center
Apgar Visitor Center
Continental Divide

West Entrance
Park
West Glacier
Headquarters
Two Medicine Entrance

Whitefish
Columbia Falls
FLATHEAD RANGE
Two Medicine

Hungry Horse Reservoir
Essex
Walton
FLATHEAD NATIONAL FOREST
LEWIS AND CLARK NATIONAL FOREST

4

GLACIER | Exploring the Park by Car

U.S. 89 provides access to the St. Mary area. The North Fork Road from Columbia Falls is open for winter travel to North Fork and the Polebridge Ranger Station. Temperatures sometimes drop to –30°F (–34°C), so appropriate dress is essential.

EXPLORING THE PARK BY CAR

Because of the massive mountains that surround Glacier National Park, visitors inevitably compare it to Grand Teton. Perhaps the most significant difference is that here one drives among the mountain peaks; at Teton, you view the mountains from a distance, unless you're willing to head for the hiking trails.

Going-to-the-Sun Road is by far the most driver-friendly avenue on which to enjoy the park and see some of the more spectacular views.

You can easily circumnavigate the lower half of the park in 1 long day, without traveling at warp speed. Along the way, you'll get a bird's-eye view of Big Sky country. After a leisurely breakfast in West Glacier, you'll be in East Glacier in plenty of time for lunch at the Glacier Park Lodge (see "Where to Stay," later in this chapter) and at St. Mary or Many Glacier for dinner. (*Note:* Going-to-the-Sun Road's multiyear rehabilitation will cause 30-min.- to 4-hr. delays for several years.)

U.S. 2 between West Glacier and East Glacier, which is approximately 57 miles, is a well-paved, two-lane affair that winds circuitously around the western and southern edges of the park and follows the Middle Fork of the Flathead River. In the summertime, you'll see inner tubes and white-water rafts galore. As you descend to the valley floor, you'll drive through beautiful Montana ranchland and farmland. Shortly after entering the valley, look to the north and admire the park's massive peaks—spires as beautiful as any on the planet. The Goat Lick parking lot, on U.S. 2 just east of Essex, gets you off the beaten path and provides a view into a canyon carved by the Flathead River; if you have time, take the short hike down to the stream and look on the hillside for mountain goats.

Beyond East Glacier, as you head northwest on Mont. 49 and west toward Two Medicine, you'll notice that the earth appears to fall off. The contrast is inescapable—mountains tower in the west, but to the east the Hi-Line begins, with a horizon that extends far and flat. But round a corner on the Two Medicine Road, and suddenly you'll find yourself faced with three red-hued mountains: Appistocki Peak, Mt. Henry, and Bison Mountain. Ten miles later, continuing the route north on U.S. 89, you'll come across a wide panorama of mountain peaks, valleys, ridges, and forested mountains that truly characterize Glacier's personality. Conclude the bottom half of your long loop by winding downward from these high elevations to the village of St. Mary.

There are two ways to see the park's western boundary and to reach the Polebridge area, in the north; one is slow and uncomfortable, the other slightly faster and less uncomfortable. The **North Fork Road** (Mont. 486) from Columbia Falls takes about an hour to negotiate. It's a sometimes-paved (often gravel- and pothole-filled) stretch that follows the North Fork of the Flathead River; spectacular views ameliorate the condition of the drive. Not much is there besides water and scenery, but the area around Polebridge is a popular spot for the outdoor crowd—an excellent location to experience Montana's natural beauty.

The **Inside North Fork Road,** just north of Apgar, also runs to Polebridge. However, it's totally unpaved, takes an hour longer, and is much rougher—take the faster route and spend that extra hour relaxing on a riverbank.

ORGANIZED TOURS & RANGER PROGRAMS

Ranger-guided activities and evening campfire and slide-show programs run daily throughout the park. The park's *Glacier Visitor Guide* publication—free upon entering the park and also available at visitor centers—is a thorough source for days, times, and locations of various educational programs. Local tribal members provide programs highlighting **American Indian culture and history.** Most programs are free; there may be a minimal charge for some of the American Indian programs and those including boat trips.

For kids, there is a **Junior Ranger** program with an activity book; backpacks with kid-oriented naturalist activities can also be checked out at the Logan Pass, St. Mary, and Apgar visitor centers.

The park offers a **free shuttle bus service.** Visitors simply park their cars at the Apgar Transit Center on the west side or the St. Mary Visitor Center and take the shuttle to about 20 stops throughout the park, most of them on Going-to-the-Sun Road. The shuttles connecting the two lots run from about 7am to 7pm. For detailed information on the schedule and routes, visit the park's website or check the insert in the *Glacier Visitor Guide.*

Glacier Park Boat Co. (© **406/257-2426;** www.glacierparkboats.com) offers narrated boat tours from Lake McDonald, St. Mary, Two Medicine, and Many Glacier from mid-June to mid-September. These "scenicruises" combine the comfort of an hour-long lake cruise with a short hike or picnic. Spectacular views of Lake McDonald sunsets, the awe-inspiring Grinnell Glacier, and the panoramic rugged cliffs ringing St. Mary Lake are just a few of the possible photo opportunities you may have while aboard. The boats typically depart every hour, usually seven times each day (although schedules are subject to change in late season or if the weather is inclement). Ticket prices top out at $23. Check ahead for a complete listing of prices and departure times. The concessionaire also offers charter service for larger groups and guided hikes in the park.

"Jammer" coach tours run along Going-to-the-Sun Road and north to Waterton. Thirty-three classic bright-red coaches from the 1930s, long identified with Glacier, are in service after a restoration project that began in 1999. Drivers provide insightful commentary about the park and its history, and you don't have to worry about how close you may be to the edge of the often-precipitous road! For schedules, contact **Xanterra** (© **303/6004300;** www.xanterra.com).

Historical-cultural 25-passenger **motor coach tours** of Going-to-the-Sun Road conducted by guides from the Blackfeet Nation. Contact **Suntours** (© **800/786-9220;** www.glaciersuntours.com). The guides focus on Glacier as point of the Blackfeet spirituality, making for a much different, but equally insightful, experience from the "Jammer" tour.

The **Glacier Institute** (© **406/755-1211;** www.glacierinstitute.org) conducts summer field classes that examine the park's cultural and natural resources. These 1- to 4-day courses include transportation, park fees, and even college credit. Highly skilled instructors bring an intimate knowledge of the region and subject matter to each course. The classroom is Glacier National Park and other areas in northwest Montana; courses cover wildflowers, grizzlies, weather systems, and nature photography. Prices range from $65 to $500 per course. (The pricier classes include lodging.) Contact the institute or visit the website for a listing of the current catalog.

Finally, **Glacier Guides** (© **800/521-7238** or 406/387-5555; www.glacierguides. com) organizes backpacking trips into the Glacier National Park backcountry. The company has been the exclusive backpacking guide service in the park since 1983. See "Exploring the Backcountry," below.

DAY HIKES

With more than 700 miles of maintained trails, the park is best explored by hiking. Many of the longer trails described there can be done fully (or at least partially) in a day, and are likely to take you farther off the beaten path than the shorter routes, and away from the crowds.

Trail maps are available at outdoor stores in Whitefish and Kalispell, as well as at visitor centers and the major ranger stations at each entry point. The park's new free shuttle can take you to numerous trail heads; there is a comprehensive guide in the *Glacier Visitor Guide* newspaper.

Before setting off, check with the nearest visitor center or ranger station to determine the accessibility of your destination, trail conditions, and recent bear sightings. It can be a bummer when, 10 miles into a trip, a ranger turns you back.

The Park Service asks you to stay on trails to keep from eroding the park's fragile components. Also, do not traverse snowbanks, especially the steeper ones. Before approaching any trail head, you should have proper footwear and rain gear, enough food, and, most important, enough water. A can of **pepper spray** can also come in handy when you're in grizzly habitat.

Lake McDonald Area

Trout Lake ★★ This is a good workout. The hike is straight up and straight down, 2,100 feet each way. The trail takes you from the north end of Lake McDonald to the foot of Trout Lake and back. 8.4 miles RT. Moderate. Access: North end of Lake McDonald, 1.5 miles west on Lake McDonald Rd.

Logan Pass Area

Hidden Lake Overlook Nature Trail ★★ This trail climbs 460 feet and requires more spunk than others in the area, yet it's not too hard. It's a popular trail, but if you go past the overlook up to the lake, you'll get past most of the crowds. This is an interpretive nature trail, with signs along the way that point out what you are seeing. 3 miles RT. Easy to moderate. Access: Logan Pass Visitor Center.

The Loop ★★★ Not considered easy mainly because of its altitude gain of 2,200 feet, The Loop is a popular hiking trail that winds up to Granite Park Chalet and back. Many people use it as a continuation of the Highline Trail, but this is the section to do if you're short on time. The Highline Trail is 7.6 miles one-way to the chalets, but not nearly as steep as the Loop; see the descriptions of the chalets on page 59. If you want to spend the night in a chalet, contact **Granite Park Chalet** for reservations (© **888/345-2649;** www.graniteparkchalet.com). 8 miles RT. Moderate. Access: Along Going-to-the-Sun Rd., about halfway btw. Avalanche Campground and Logan Pass Visitor Center.

Sunrift Gorge Trail ★★★ Most hikers approach Siyeh Pass from the Piegan Pass trail head, but I prefer ascending to this gorgeous glacial valley from Sunrift Gorge. The creekside trail climbs through a forest and switches back to reveal a hanging glacier and several waterfalls, before ascending the pass up a wall that is prime bighorn habitat. 11 miles RT. Difficult. Access: Sunrift Gorge parking area, 10 miles west of St. Mary.

Many Glacier Area

Iceberg Lake ★★★ This beautiful hike traverses flower-filled meadows to a high lake backed against a mountain wall. Even in summer, there may be snow on the ground and ice floating in the lake. Look for mountain goats or bighorn sheep on the cliffs above, and keep an eye out for the grizzlies. 9.6 miles RT. Moderate. Access: Trail head in a cabin area east of the Swiftcurrent Coffee Shop and Campstore.

Swiftcurrent Nature Trail ★★ This is a fun hike along the shore, through the woods, and near a marsh. You may see deer and birds—watch for blue grouse. If you have time, continue on the trail as it circles Lake Josephine, another easy hike that adds 2.8 miles to the trip. Dramatic Mount Gould towers above the far end of the lake. Midsummer wildflowers can be spectacular. Access to a longer, 10-mile round-trip trail to Grinnell Glacier, the park's largest, is also from this area. 2.5 miles RT. Easy. Access: Picnic area .5 mile west of the hotel turnoff.

Two Medicine Area

Appistoki Falls ★★   This trail, with an elevation gain of only 260 feet, climbs through a forest of fir and spruce, then runs along Appistoki Creek before ending at an overlook that provides views of a 65-foot waterfall. 1.2 miles RT. Easy. Access: .25 mile east of Two Medicine Ranger Station.

Twin Falls Trail ★★   The most popular hiking path in this area is the one to Twin Falls, which originates at the campground. Hikers may walk the entire distance to Twin Falls on a clearly identified trail, or boat across Two Medicine Lake to the foot of the trail head and hike the last mile. 7.6 miles RT. Easy. Access: Two Medicine Campground.

Polebridge Area

Bowman Lake ★★★   This trail (14 miles to Brown Pass) is similar to the Kintla Lake hike in difficulty and, like the Kintla Lake Trail, passes the lake on the north. After a hike through rolling hills sheathed in foliage, the trail climbs out of reach for anyone not in top shape, ascending 2,000 feet in less than 3 miles to join the Kintla Lake Trail at Brown Pass. A left turn takes you back to Kintla Lake (23 miles), and a right takes you to Goat Haunt at the foot of Waterton Lake (9 miles). 7.1 miles one-way. Moderate. Access: Bowman Lake Campground; follow Glacier Rte. 7 to Bowman Lake Rd., just north of Polebridge, then follow signs to Bowman Lake Campground.

Quartz Lake ★★   The loop runs up and over an 1,800-foot ridge and down to the south end of Lower Quartz Lake. From there it's a level 3-mile hike to the west end of Quartz Lake, then 6 miles back over the ridge before dropping back to Bowman Lake. 12 miles RT. Moderate. Access: Bowman Lake Picnic Area.

EXPLORING THE BACKCOUNTRY

Depending upon your point of view, negotiating the backcountry may translate to a leisurely stroll or a strenuous experience in the high country. Choices range from 4-mile day hikes to multiday treks, so consider your experience and fitness level before heading out. Study a park map that illustrates trails and campsites in the area you want to explore.

Backcountry campgrounds have maps at the entrance to show you the location of each campground, the pit toilet, food-preparation areas, and, perhaps most important, food-storage areas. In addition, you can obtain a free loan of bear-resistant food containers at most backcountry permit-issuing stations. If you fish while camping, it's recommended you exercise catch-and-release to avoid attracting wildlife in search of food. If you eat the catch, be certain to puncture the air bladder and throw the entrails into deep water at least 200 feet from the nearest campsite or trail. When backpacking in Glacier, especially in the high country, it's important to remember to pack as lightly as possible and make sure you're aware of the trail's degree of ascent. And remember the cardinal rule: Pack it in, pack it out. No exceptions.

Wherever you decide to go, remember that you must secure a **backcountry permit** before your overnight trip. Advance reservations can be made June 15 to October 31 for $30; a fee of $5 per night per camper is also charged. Call ☎ **406/888-7857** for additional information.

A GUIDED BACKCOUNTRY TRIP   Many folks like to let someone else make the arrangements, leaving themselves free to concentrate on the hiking experience. The exclusive backpacking guide service in Glacier National Park is **Glacier Guides** (☎ **800/521-7238** or 406/387-5555; www.glacierguides.com). For a price, the company will put together any kind of trip; it has several regularly scheduled throughout the season, from the end of June through the beginning of September. These include a 3-day "taste" of the park for $465 per person, and an entire week in the wilderness for about $900 per person. Custom trips run $180 a day per person, with a four-person minimum. Glacier Guides will even organize a trip that lets you spend the day hiking and the night cuddled in a comfy inn inside the park or in the Granite Park Chalet (see page 59). Gear rentals are also available.

OTHER SUMMER SPORTS & ACTIVITIES

BOATING   At Apgar and Lake McDonald, you will find kayaks, canoes, rowboats, and motorboats for rent; gas-powered outboard motors of 10 horsepower or less are permitted at Two Medicine Lake and Bowman Lake. You can also rent kayaks, canoes, rowboats, and electric motorboats at Two Medicine. At Many Glacier, you can rent kayaks, canoes, and rowboats. For details, contact **Glacier Park Boat Co.** (☎ **406/257-2426**; www.glacierparkboats.com).

FISHING   The crystal-clear mountain streams and lakes of Glacier are home to many native species of trout. Anglers looking to hook a big one should try the North Fork of the Flathead for cutthroat, and any of the three larger lakes in the park (Bowman Lake, St. Mary Lake, and Lake McDonald) for lake trout and cutthroat. For equipment or sage advice, or to schedule a guided foray ($350 for one or two people for a half-day), contact **Glacier Anglers** (☎ **800/235-6781**; www.glacierraftco.com) at the Glacier Outdoor Center in West Glacier.

HORSEBACK RIDING   If you want to saddle up Old Paint and take an Old West approach to transportation, **Swan Mountain Outfitters** (☎ **406/387-4405**; www.swanmountainoutfitters.com) offers horseback riding at Lake McDonald, Apgar Village, and Many Glacier. The company offers hourly ($40) to full-day rides ($170) into the nearby wilderness.

MOUNTAIN CLIMBING   The peaks of Glacier Park rarely exceed elevations of 10,000 feet, but these are incredibly difficult climbs; you must inquire at a visitor center or ranger station regarding climbing conditions and closures. In general, the peaks are unsuitable except for experienced climbers or those traveling with experienced guides. The park administration does not recommend climbing because of the unstable nature of the rock.

RAFTING & FLOAT TRIPS   Though the waters in the park don't lend themselves to white-water rafting, the boundary forks of the Flathead River are some of the best in the northwest corner of the state. For just taking it easy and floating along in the summer sun, the North Fork of the Flathead River stretching from Polebridge to Columbia Falls and into Flathead Lake is ideal. The same may be said for the Middle Fork of the Flathead, which forms the southern border of the park.

For white-water voyagers, the North Fork of the Flathead River (classes II and III) and the Middle Fork (class III) are the best bets. Flow rates change dramatically as snow melts or storms move through the area; inquire at any ranger station for details and conditions. The names of certain stretches of the Middle Fork are instructive (the Narrows, Jaws, Bonecrusher), but you can book a trip with several outfitters that offer expert, sanctioned guides.

Established in 1975, **Glacier Raft Company** (© **800/235-6781;** www.glacierraftco. com), is Montana's oldest raft company. Offerings include half-day trips ($52 adult, $42 child under 13) and full-day excursions ($89 adult, $65 child) as well as multiday trips. Prices include all equipment and food. The company also offers scenic trips, inflatable-kayak rentals, and other services.

WINTER SPORTS & ACTIVITIES

All unplowed roads become trails for snowshoers and cross-country skiers, who rave about the vast powdered wonderland here. Guided trips into the backcountry are a great way to experience the park in winter, or you can strap on a pair of snowshoes and explore on your own. *Note:* Snowmobiles are prohibited.

SNOWSHOEING & CROSS-COUNTRY SKIING Glacier has many cross-country trails, the most popular of which is the **Upper Lake McDonald Trail** to the Avalanche picnic area. This 8-mile trail offers a relatively flat route up Going-to-the-Sun Road with views of McDonald Creek and the mountains looming above the McDonald Valley. For the advanced skier, the same area presents a more intense trip that heads northwest in a roundabout fashion to the Apgar Lookout.

The most popular trail on the east side is the **Autumn Creek Trail** near Marias Pass. Avalanche paths cross this area, so inquire about weather conditions before setting out. Yet another popular spot is in Essex along the southern boundary of the park at the **Izaak Walton Inn.**

WHERE TO STAY
Inside the Park

The hostelries in Glacier National Park fall into two categories. Lake McDonald Lodge, Glacier Park Lodge, and Many Glacier Hotel are first-tier properties that have been popular destinations since early in the 20th century. Swiftcurrent Motor Inn is typical of the casual motel-style properties at the other end of the spectrum that provide more-than-acceptable accommodations for far less money.

Although the lodges have a certain stately charm, don't expect in-room hot tubs or even air-conditioning. The structures may have been constructed to withstand natural disasters, but little thought was given to interior soundproofing. If you're an eavesdropper, you'll be in heaven; if you're a light sleeper, bring earplugs. Although all the lodges are comfortable, their greatest attribute, aside from the architecture, may be their stunning setting.

Reserve well in advance; July and August dates may fill before the spring thaw. For more information on the Xanterra-operated properties (and all but one are) and to make reservations, contact **Xanterra** (© **303/600-3400;** www.xanterra.com). For St. Mary Lodge and Glacier Park Lodge, contact **Glacier Park, Inc.** (© **406/892-2525;** www.glacierparkinc.com).

Apgar Village Lodge ★ A basic budget alternative to the park's Xanterra-managed properties, the complex features both motel rooms and log cabins. The motel units are small and can accommodate up to three people; the cabins can sleep as many as six, and most have kitchens but few other amenities. The Apgar Village Lodge is in Apgar Village on the south side of Lake McDonald.

In Apgar Village. ✆ **406/888-5484.** www.westglacier.com. 28 cabins, 20 motel rooms. $95–$135 double; $120–$309 cabin. Some units have a 2-night minimum. Closed Oct to mid-May. **Amenities:** Restaurant; boat rentals.

Lake McDonald Lodge, Cabins & Motor Inn ★★ One of the classic railroad hotels built to entice passengers to hop onboard and visit some of the most scenic areas of the U.S., the Lodge opened in 1914 and except for a flash flood in the 1960s it hasn't changed all that much since. Lanterns still dangle in the soaring lobby, antlered deer heads stare down at you, and the balconies on each of the three floors are carved with words in the Kootenai tongue for "Welcome" and other hospitable phrases. You'll feel the same welcome in the dignified main lodge rooms, though they are tiny (remember, people were smaller when this place was built). To make up for their size, there's a longer list of amenities here than in most National Park Lodges. We prefer the lodge rooms to the viewless attached motel rooms and even the larger cabin units (which are plain to a fault). The sublime lakeside location, nestled in a lush forest, is a highlight.

On Lake McDonald. ✆ **303/600-4300.** www.xanterra.com. 62 lodge and motel units, 38 cottage units. $182–$191 lodge room; $315–$331 lodge suite; $135–$142 motel unit; $130–$191 cottage. Closed late Sept to late May. **Amenities:** 2 restaurants; bar; free Wi-Fi.

Many Glacier Hotel ★★★ Another railway hotel (this one in 1915 by the Great Northern Railway), this palatial hostelry is a Montana icon. It is also my favorite place to hang my hat while "roughing it" in Glacier by day. What makes it so good? The secluded location on Swiftcurrent Lake, for one, and the remarkable sunset views from the veranda. It's also the most steeped in Glacier lore, reflected by the performances by David Walburn, who captures the park in song on Tuesday through Saturday evenings. The best rooms have a view of the lake from a private balcony, but all of the units have a woodsy, homey appeal. There are also family rooms with more space. Guests can also board a historic wooden boat for a tour that offers an up-close look at nearby glaciers.

On Swiftcurrent Lake. ✆ **303/600-4300.** www.xanterra.com. 215 units. $155–$255 double; $320–$336 suite. Closed mid-Sept to early June. **Amenities:** 3 restaurants; bar; free Wi-Fi.

Rising Sun Motor Inn & Cabins ★ Rising Sun is a good value, but the complex lacks the character of some of the statelier lodges in the vicinity. The view of St. Mary Lake is its most remarkable feature, and, to be fair, the lodge offers many conveniences, with a store, gas station, and restaurant on the premises. Rooms and cabins date to the 1940s though they have been well maintained. This is a good choice for travelers who plan on spending more time outdoors than anywhere else.

About 6 miles west of St. Mary. ✆ **303/600-4300.** www.xanterra.com. 63 units. $128–$142 double; $130–$137 cabin. Closed mid-Sept to mid-June. **Amenities:** Restaurant; free Wi-Fi.

Swiftcurrent Motor Inn & Cabins ★ Like Rising Sun Motor Inn, this property is a fairly typical motel-and-cabin complex, with relatively low rates by Glacier National Park standards. The motel units are spartan but a good fit for visitors who aren't planning on spending a lot of time in their room. (And why would you want to do that here?) The cabins, built 20 years before the motel units in the 1930s and nestled

in a nicely wooded area, have a bit more historic personality (though they're just as rustic and some share a communal bathroom). This is a good pick for families, with plenty of room for the kids to roam.

Near Swiftcurrent Lake. ℂ **303/600-4300.** www.xanterra.com. 88 units and cabins, some cabins without private bathroom. $128–$142 double in motor inn; $76–$101 double in cabin. Closed mid-Sept to mid-June. **Amenities:** Restaurant.

Village Inn at Apgar ★★ A favorite among hikers—trails radiate from the property into the Glacier wilderness—this is also the smallest property Xanterra operates in Glacier, so it feels like you're really staying in a national park rather than a Disneyland hotel (as can be the case at some of the larger lodges in other parks). Units include a number of kitchenettes and some larger rooms that sleep up to six guests, and are pleasant but unremarkable, with a warm and woodsy feel. Though there's no onsite restaurant, guests have many dining options at nearby Lake McDonald Lodge and the Apgar Village Lodge.

In Apgar Village. ℂ **303/600-4300.** www.xanterra.com. 36 units. $139–$261 double. Closed mid-Sept to early June. **Amenities:** None.

Near the Park

If the convenience of staying on Glacier's back porch is important to you, these are the towns to stay in. For greater variety in lodging, dining, and nightlife, head for Whitefish.

IN EAST GLACIER

Glacier Park Lodge ★★ Built in 1912–13 by the Great Northern Railway in East Glacier, this grand lodge has all sorts of unexpected amenities for a park lodge—including a nine-hole golf course, a pool, and a spa—probably because it is not in the park, but rather, just outside of it. It is a good pick for travelers with a penchant for historic hotels, and an architectural marvel that's supported by 60 massive timbers. The lobby is dominated by a number of these immense logs, and perhaps the second grandest lobby in a national-park lodge after the Old Faithful Inn in Yellowstone. Rooms are pleasant but fairly typical, with hardwood floors; some have private balconies.

1 Midvale Creek Rd., East Glacier. ℂ **406/892-2525.** www.glacierparkinc.com. 161 units. $152–$244 double; $377–$480 suite. Closed Oct to late May. **Amenities:** 2 restaurants; bar; outdoor pool; golf course; spa; free Wi-Fi.

IN ESSEX

Izaak Walton Inn ★★ Originally temporary housing for railroad workers in the 1930s, the Izaak Walton Inn—named for the British author of *The Compleat Angler*—highlights its legacy in the form of cabooses and other railcars that have been converted into posh guestrooms. The lodge rooms and cabins are likewise comfortable and aesthetically pleasing, with rail-themed touches in the décor to boot. Not surprisingly, Essex remains an Amtrak stop to this day. The inn also a great spot to stay in winter for cross-country skiers, with trails emanating from the property on the southern boundary of Glacier National Park.

290 Izaak Walton Inn Rd., Essex. ℂ **406/888-5700.** www.izaakwaltoninn.com. 33 units, 4 caboose cottages, 1 locomotive lodging. $119–$179 double; $239–$279 suite; $189–$300 cabins, caboose, and railcar cabins. 2-night minimum stay in cabins, cabooses, and locomotive. **Amenities:** Restaurant; bar; free Wi-Fi.

CAMPING & chalets

You can spend your evenings at the park in the hotel lounge looking over your cocktail at the folks in the campground, or vice versa. For those who prefer the latter—and it's a wonderful way to get closer to nature (as well as save money)—Glacier offers 13 campgrounds, 8 of which are accessible by paved road. Fees range from $10 to $23 a night during summer.

Most campgrounds are available on a first-come, first-served basis and offer restrooms with flush toilets and cold running water. Fish Creek and St. Mary campgrounds may be reserved through the **National Park Service Reservation System** (✆ **877/444-6777;** www.recreation.gov). Despite its proximity to the center of the hotel and motel activity, the **Many Glacier Campground ★★** is a well-forested, almost secluded campground that provides as much privacy in a public area as you'll see anywhere. The campground has adequate space for recreational vehicles and truck-camper combinations, but space for vehicles pulling trailers is limited. It is a veritable mecca for tent campers.

Apgar Campground ★★ is at the bottom of Lake McDonald, near the West Glacier entrance and the Apgar Visitor Center. Besides the beautiful lakeside location and bathrooms with running water, it has an extensive calendar of ranger programs at the amphitheater and, as a result, is an excellent pick for families with curious minds. The **Avalanche Campground ★★★** may be the nicest of all, because it is 4 miles north of Lake McDonald on Going-to-the-Sun Road in a heavily treed area adjacent to the creek. But I also like **Bowman Lake Campground ★★★** at the end of a primitive dirt road in the northwest section of the park (accessible through the Polebridge entrance). Water is only available from spigots here and there are pit toilets, but the trade-off for primitive facilities is the feeling that you've really and truly gotten away from it all. The bad news about the **Cut Bank Campground ★★** road is that it's not paved. The good news is that it's only 5 miles from the pavement of U.S. 89 to the ranger station and campground, which are in the southeast portion of the park between St. Mary and Two Medicine. And the unpaved road deters many from heading into the outback to this primitive campground, which sits in the shadow of Bad Marriage and Medicine Wolf mountains.

Fish Creek Campground ★★ is 2 miles from Apgar, on the western shore of Lake McDonald. It's a good pick for its lakeside location and proximity to hiking trails, but I prefer Sprague Creek and Avalanche because they have fewer sites. **Kintla Lake Campground** is in the northwest section of the park, reached by primitive dirt roads through the Polebridge entrance station. Like Bowman Lake, it is relatively primitive (read: hand pumps and pit toilets) but its remoteness and small size (13 sites) makes it a very good option for those looking for a break from modern civilization. **Logging Creek ★★** and **Quartz Creek ★★** are two more primitive campgrounds that are accessible by dirt roads through the Polebridge entrance. Both are quiet and remote, but lack the scenic lakeside views of Kintla and Bowman campgrounds. **Sprague Creek Campground ★★** is on the eastern shore of Lake McDonald. It is quite small

(25 sites) and immediately on the lakeside. No towed trailers or vehicles longer than 21 feet are allowed. **St. Mary Campground** ★, outside the village of St. Mary, is a last resort as it lacks shade and while the views are plenty dramatic, it not as well located for touring as some of the campgrounds in the interior. **Rising Sun Campground** ★, 6 miles west of St. Mary, is near the public showers at Rising Sun Motor Inn, so it is good for those looking for good hygiene, but the trade-off is a campground that feels less removed from it all. The **Two Medicine Campground** ★★ is in the shadows of major mountains near three lakes and a stream. It is a forested area that has beautiful sites, plenty of shade, and opportunities to wet a fishing line or dangle your feet in cool mountain water.

BACKCOUNTRY CAMPING

Glacier has 65 backcountry campgrounds. Fortunately, many are at lower elevation, so inexperienced backpackers have an opportunity to experience them. For an accurate estimation of your itinerary's difficulty and advice on what you may need, check with rangers in the area you contemplate visiting. One of the main dangers of staying in these campgrounds is running into a bear.

Visitors planning to camp overnight in Glacier's backcountry must stop at a visitor center, ranger station, or the Apgar Backcountry Permit Office and obtain a **backcountry use permit.** Backcountry permits may be reserved in advance (see "Exploring the Backcountry," p. 53). Permits are good only for the prearranged dates and locations, with no more than 3 nights allowed at each campground. Certain campgrounds have a 1-night

limit. There are separate fees for advance reservations ($30 per permit) and backcountry camping ($5 per person per night or $2.50 for kids under 16).

You can obtain backcountry camping permits in person from the backcountry office at Apgar, Waterton Townsite, and St. Mary, or the ranger stations at Many Glacier, Two Medicine, and Polebridge. During summer months, permits may be obtained no earlier than 24 hours before your trip.

CHALETS

Two of the park's most popular destinations, Granite Park and Sperry Chalets, are National Historic Landmarks built by the Great Northern Railway between 1912 and 1914. Granite Park is a basic hikers' shelter, and Sperry is a full-service chalet.

Granite Park Chalet has 12 rooms (all with single bunk beds) and sleeps two to six per room. The chalet runs $98 for the first person, and $79 for each additional person in the same room, plus tax, with an optional linen/bedding service at $20 per person (and an optional preorder menu). Onsite kitchen facilities are shared.

Sperry Chalet, a rustic backcountry chalet, is accessible by trail only. It operates from mid-July through mid-September. Services include overnight accommodations and full meal service for $202 for the first person, and $142 for each additional person in the room. Reservations are required. For information and reservations for either chalet, contact **Belton Chalets** (© **888/345-2649;** www.graniteparkchalet.com or www.sperrychalet.com).

IN POLEBRIDGE

North Fork Hostel and Square Peg Ranch ★ Located just across the North Fork of the Flathead River from the park, this is one of my favorite value-priced lodgings in Montana. That may have to do with the hospitality as much as the digs: Proprietor Oliver Meister is a Glacier ranger and a great source of advice and information. And at this picturesque spot, there is something for everyone, from shared hostel rooms to small, bare-bones cabins to fully equipped, solar-powered log homes. There is also a pair of tipis and a campground, as well as a shared kitchen in the main house.

80 Beaver Dr., Polebridge. ✆ **406/888-5241** or 406/253-4321. www.nfhostel.com. 7 bunks, 2 private rooms, 2 cabins, 2 log homes. $20 bunk; $45–$50 tipi; $50 cabin; $80 log home. 3-night minimum stay in log home. Reservations required in winter. **Amenities:** Bike and boat rentals; free Wi-Fi.

IN ST. MARY

St. Mary Lodge, Cabins & Motel ★★ At the St. Mary end of Going-to-the-Sun Road, this longstanding lodge is owned and managed by Glacier Park, Inc., and a good bet for visitors coming to the park from the east. The lodge is at the center of a tidy little village with a store, gas station, and other facilities. There's a wide variety of options here, from basic rooms in a pair of 1950s-era motels to more upscale lodge rooms to the luxury Sun Cabin, complete with a large deck and a loft-style bedroom.

U.S. 89 and Going-to-the-Sun Rd., St. Mary. ✆ **406/892-2525.** www.glacierparkinc.com. 115 units. $98–$345 double; $240–$440 cabin. **Amenities:** 2 restaurants; bar; free Wi-Fi.

IN WEST GLACIER

Belton Chalets and Lodge ★★ This has been the slickest place to hang your hat in West Glacier since it opened in 1910. Restored in 2000, the lodge happily feels more off the beaten path than it is. Guestrooms and cottages are clad in antiques and subtle earth tones, with comfy beds and chairs and some have private balconies. The legendary taproom is just the place to unwind at the end of the day, with plenty of local beer on tap.

12575 U.S. 2, West Glacier. ✆ **888/235-8665** or 406/888-5000. www.beltonchalet.com. 25 rooms, 2 cottages. $155–$325 double or cottage. **Amenities:** Restaurant; bar; Wi-Fi (fee).

IN WHITEFISH

Garden Wall Inn ★★★ The Garden Wall Inn is the best B&B in the Glacier National Park area, bar none. Just a short walk south of downtown Whitefish and a 30-mile drive to the park, it strikes the perfect balance between comfort and style, featuring Art Deco touches, ornate woodwork, and memorable breakfasts made largely with local ingredients. Rooms are furnished with antiques and the bathrooms are masterfully outfitted with black and white tile, rainshower showerheads, and premium soaps. Innkeepers Chris Schustrom and Rhonda Fitzgerald are not just great hosts, but knowledgeable outdoorspeople with great tips for exploring the park.

504 Spokane Ave., Whitefish. ✆ **888/530-1700** or 406/862-3440. www.gardenwallinn.com. 4 units. $155–$215 double; $275–$315 suite. Rates include full breakfast and afternoon refreshments. **Amenities:** Free Wi-Fi.

Hidden Moose Lodge ★★ Tucked in the woods north of Whitefish, Hidden Moose Lodge has the best of both worlds—it manages to balance the privacy and style of a boutique hotel with the perks of a B&B. The former is evidenced by the comfortable guestrooms located in the main house and an adjacent newer structure. The latter comes in the form of scrumptious breakfasts served in the great room, where a fire often crackles in the handsome stone fireplace.

1735 E. Lakeshore Dr., Whitefish. ☏ **888/733-6667** or 406/862-6516. www.hiddenmooselodge. com. 13 units, including 2 suites. $99–$159 double; $149–$249 suite. Rates include full breakfast. **Amenities:** Outdoor hot tub; free Wi-Fi.

WHERE TO EAT

Inside the Park

Food options inside the park are primarily dining rooms operated by park concession-aire Xanterra. Breakfasts range from about $5 to $10, lunch entrees $6 to $15, and most dinner entrees cost $10 to $30.

You'll find above-average food served at above-average prices in the dining rooms at the major properties (see below) along with fast-food options at all the lodges. Alternatives to the latter include second-tier restaurants in proximity to the hotels, most of which are comparable to chain restaurants in both quality and price. The **Two Dog Flats Grill** at the Rising Sun Motor Inn serves "hearty American fare." The **Swift-current Motor Inn Restaurant** offers lunch and dinner combinations of salads, sandwiches, pasta dishes, and create-your-own pizzas. At Apgar you'll find a deli and a family dining eatery.

Russell's Fireside Dining Room ★ AMERICAN   Russell's has a hunting-lodge atmosphere with rough-hewn beams and hunting trophies. The menu changes from season to season, but expect such American classics as steaks, seafood, and pasta for dinner, as well as meatless main dishes like wild mushroom and onion tarts. In the morning, there's a full buffet breakfast. The lunch menu includes salads, sandwiches, wraps, burgers, and the like.

At Lake McDonald Lodge. ☏ **406/888-5431** or 303/600-4300. www.xanterra.com. Main courses $7–$17 breakfast and lunch; $15–$30 dinner. Summer daily breakfast, lunch, and dinner.

Swiss Room ★ AMERICAN   Feel like fondue? That's one of the specialties at this, yes, Swiss restaurant, which looks like it belongs up in the Alps. It's menu includes more American dishes, such as Montana meatloaf made with buffalo instead of beef, and Rocky Mountain trout. Lunch is lighter, with a variety of wraps, salads, and healthy fare, and breakfast is a hot and hearty buffet.

At Many Glacier Hotel. ☏ **406/732-4411** or 303/600-4300. www.xanterra.com. Main courses $7–$17 breakfast and lunch; $15–$30 dinner. Summer daily breakfast, lunch, and dinner.

Near the Park

IN EAST GLACIER & VICINITY

Glacier Park Lodge has two eating options: the Western-themed **Great Northern Dining Room** (beef, barbecued ribs, fish, and chicken, plus a full breakfast buffet); and the **Empire Bar & Grill,** which offers a hearty bar menu.

Two Sisters Cafe ★★ AMERICAN   "Aliens Welcome" is written in large letters on the roof and license plates from all 50 states on the walls—yes, this roadside eatery has personality to spare. The food is similarly out of this world from rainbow trout with huckleberry aioli to bison sirloin, as well as plump sandwiches and juicy burgers. At the full bar, I recommend the huckleberry margaritas.

4 miles north of St. Mary on U.S. 89, Babb. ☏ **406/732-5535.** www.twosistersofmontana.com. Most main courses $10–$20. Daily 11am–10pm. Closed Oct to May.

4

GLACIER | Where to Eat

IN WHITEFISH

Tupelo Grille ★★ CAJUN/NEW AMERICAN   For an address so far north of New Orleans, the Tupelo Grille does Cajun surprisingly well. The kitchen plates up spicy Southern comfort foods like catfish, jambalaya, and shrimp and grits, as well as a nice selection of steaks, pasta, and seafood. All things considered, this is the most reliable eatery in Whitefish.

17 Central Ave. (✆ **406/862-6136.** www.tupelogrille.com. Main courses $14–$32. Summer daily 5:30–10pm; winter Mon–Sat 5:30–9:30pm.

SIDE TRIP: WATERTON LAKES NATIONAL PARK

Located in Alberta, Canada, Waterton is the place where the Canadian mountains meet the rolling prairie, which means it has an incredible variety of flowers and animals. As you travel along the high ridge, you'll see meadows and boggy areas that are ideal habitat for moose; later you'll find lakes all around and the Canadian Rockies filling the horizon.

The park's **Visitor Reception Centre** (✆ 403/859-5133; www.parkscanada.gc.ca/waterton) is just inside the park. Park entrance costs about C$8 (about US$8) per person, with a maximum of about C$20 (US$19) per vehicle.

The 11-mile **Crypt Lake Trail** has long been rated as one of Canada's best hikes—except for those prone to seasickness: To reach the trail head, hikers take a 2-mile boat ride across Upper Waterton Lake. Contact the **Waterton Shoreline Cruise Company** (✆ 403/859-2362; www.watertoncruise.com) for details about the boat shuttle. After that, the trail leads past Hellroaring Falls, Twin Falls, and Burnt Rock Falls before reaching Crypt Falls and a passage through a 60-foot rock tunnel. The elevation gain is 2,300 feet.

At the west end of the village is **Townsite Campground,** a Parks Canada–operated facility with 235 sites. There are also a number of designated **wilderness campgrounds** with dry toilets and surface water, some of which have shelters. If you want a roof over your head, the **Prince of Wales Hotel** (✆ 403/236-3400 or 406/892-2525; www.glacierparkinc.com) compares with the finest park hostelries in Glacier.

ROCKY MOUNTAIN

by Eric Peterson

Snow-covered peaks stand watch over lush valleys and alpine lakes, creating the perfect image of America's most dramatic and beautiful landscape: the majestic Rocky Mountains. Here the pine- and fir-scented forests are deep, the air is crisp and pure, and the mountain peaks reach up to grasp the deep-blue sky.

What makes Rocky Mountain National Park unique is not only its breathtaking scenery, but also its variety. In relatively low areas, up to 9,000 feet, ponderosa pine and juniper cloak the sunny southern slopes, with Douglas fir on the cooler northern slopes. The thirstier blue spruce cling to the banks of streams, along with occasional groves of aspen. Elk and mule deer thrive. Lodgepole pine are often here, too, a population that's been devastated by Rocky Mountain pine beetles in recent years. On higher slopes, forests of Engelmann spruce and subalpine fir dominate, interspersed with wide meadows vibrant with wildflowers in spring and summer. This is also home to bighorn sheep, which have become a symbol of the park. Above 11,500 feet, the trees become increasingly gnarled and stunted, until they disappear altogether and alpine tundra takes over. Fully one-third of the park is in this bleak, rocky world, where many of the plants are identical to those found in the Arctic.

Within the park's 415 square miles are 17 mountains above 13,000 feet. Longs Peak, at 14,259 feet, is the highest.

Trail Ridge Road, which cuts west through the middle of the park from Estes Park, then south down its western boundary to Grand Lake, is one of America's most scenic highways. Climbing to 12,183 feet, it's the highest continuously paved highway in the United States. The road is usually open from Memorial Day into October, depending on snowfall. The 48-mile drive from Estes Park to Grand Lake takes about 3 hours, allowing for stops at numerous view points. Exhibits at the Alpine Visitor Center at Fall River Pass, 11,796 feet above sea level, explain life on the alpine tundra.

Fall River Road, the original park road, leads from Estes Park to Fall River Pass via Horseshoe Park. As you negotiate its graveled switchbacks, you get a clear idea of what early auto travel was like in the West. This road, too, is closed in winter. Among the few paved roads in the Rockies that lead into a high mountain basin is Bear Lake Road, which stays open year-round, with occasional half-day closings to clear snow.

5

FLORA & FAUNA

Rocky Mountain National Park is home to notable populations of **elk, deer, bighorn sheep,** and **black bears,** as well as **marmots** and **pikas** in the higher country. Most of the trees are **coniferous,** and the spring and summer brings an impressive **wildflower** bloom. The **Rocky Mountain pine beetle** has devastated many of the forests here, particularly on the west side of the park.

ESSENTIALS

Getting There & Gateways

Entry to the park is from either the east (through the town of **Estes Park**) or the west (through the town of **Grand Lake**). Connecting the east and west sides of the park is **Trail Ridge Road,** open during summer and early fall, but closed to all motor vehicle traffic by snow the rest of the year. Most visitors enter the park from the Estes Park side. The Beaver Meadows Entrance, west of Estes Park on U.S. 36, leads to the Beaver Meadows Visitor Center and park headquarters; it is the most direct route to Trail Ridge Road. U.S. 34 west from Estes Park takes you to the Fall River Visitor Center, just outside the park, and into the park through the Fall River Entrance, which is north of the Beaver Meadows Entrance. From there you have access to Old Fall River Road or Trail Ridge Road.

Estes Park is about 71 miles northwest of Denver, 44 miles northwest of Boulder, and 42 miles southwest of Fort Collins.

The most direct route from Denver is **U.S. 36** through Boulder. At Estes Park, that highway joins **U.S. 34,** which runs up the Big Thompson Canyon from I-25 and Loveland, and continues through Rocky Mountain National Park to Grand Lake. An alternative scenic route to Estes Park is **Colo. 7,** the "Peak-to-Peak Scenic Byway" that transits Central City (Colo. 119), Nederland (Colo. 72), and Allenspark (Colo. 7). *Note:* Floods seriously damaged all three of these roads in fall 2013, but all were slated to reopen by the beginning of 2014.

Heading south from Estes Park on Colo. 7, you can reach two trail heads in the southeast corner of the national park, but there are no connecting roads to the main part of the park from those points. These are **Longs Peak Trailhead** (the turnoff is 9 miles south of Estes Park and the trail head about another mile) and **Wild Basin Trailhead** (another 3.5 miles south to the turnoff and then 2.25 miles to the trail head).

Every day from late spring to early fall, free national park **shuttle buses** take hikers to some of the more popular spots and trail heads on the park's east side. There is a

Rocky Mountain National Park

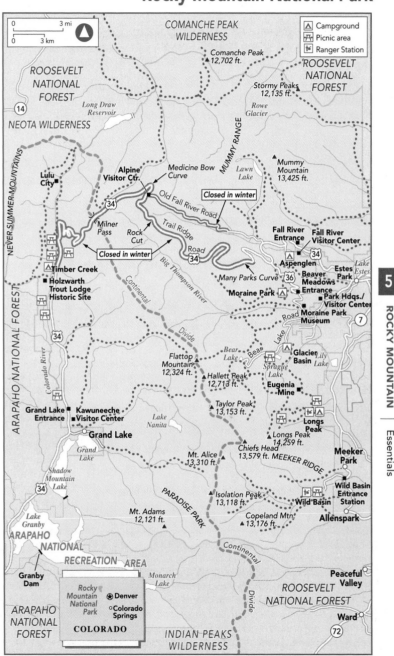

Rocky Mountain National Park's high elevation and extremes of climate and terrain are among its most appealing features, but also its greatest hazards. Hikers should try to give themselves several days to acclimate to the altitude before hitting the trails that climb above timberline, and hikers with respiratory or heart problems would do well to discuss their plans with their physicians before leaving home. Hikers need to be prepared for rapidly changing conditions, including sudden afternoon thunderstorms in July and August. If lightning threatens, stay clear of ridges and other high points.

Park and Ride parking area west of Glacier Basin Campground; one route goes to Bear Lake, and the other goes to Moraine Park and several nearby trail heads. Contact park offices or visit the website for the current schedule.

From late June to Labor Day, the town of Estes Park also operates a free summer **shuttle service** that connects the Estes Park Visitor Center with downtown, the surrounding campgrounds, and the Rocky Mountain National Park's hiker shuttles.

Those who want to enter the national park from the west can take **U.S. 40** north from I-70 through Winter Park and Tabernash to Granby, and then follow U.S. 34 north to the village of Grand Lake and on into the park.

THE NEAREST AIRPORT Visitors usually fly into **Denver International Airport** (© 303/342-2000; www.flydenver.com), 90 miles southeast of the park's east entrances. It's served by most major airlines and car-rental companies. From the airport, travelers can also get to Estes Park on **Estes Park Shuttle** (© 970/586-5151; www.estesparkshuttle.com). The 2-hour trip costs $45 per person one-way or $85 per person round-trip.

Visitor Centers & Information

When entering the park, it's wise to make your first stop one of the visitor centers. All can be contacted through the main park phone number (© 970/586-1206). Visitor center hours vary seasonally and are based on available staff. Full information can be had at **Rocky Mountain National Park** (© 970/586-1206; www.nps.gov/romo). The **Rocky Mountain Nature Association** (© 800/816-7662 or 970/586-0108; www.rmna.org) also offers a variety of trip-planning tools.

The **Beaver Meadows Visitor Center,** on U.S. 36 on the east side of the park, has a good interpretive exhibit that includes a relief model of the park, a free film, and a bookstore. It's open daily year-round. Just outside the park on U.S. 34, just east of the Fall River entrance on the east side of the national park, is the **Fall River Visitor Center.** It is open daily from late spring through early fall, and weekends only the rest of the year. The **Kawuneeche Visitor Center,** at the Grand Lake end of Trail Ridge Road, is open daily year-round. *Kawuneeche* (Kah-wuh-*nee*-chee) is an Arapaho word that translates as "Valley of the Coyote."

At 11,796 feet above sea level, the **Alpine Visitor Center,** at Fall River Pass, has exhibits that explain life on the alpine tundra. The center is usually open late May through early October, weather permitting, and closed the rest of the year. The **Moraine Park Visitor Center and Museum** is a great spot for families. It is on Bear Lake Road, about 1.5 miles from the Beaver Meadows entrance station, in a log building that dates from 1923. The museum is open daily from late spring to early fall.

Fees & Permits

Park admission costs $20 per vehicle for up to 1 week and $10 for solo bicyclists, motorcyclists, and pedestrians. Camping in developed campgrounds costs $20 per night during the summer and $14 in the off season when the water is turned off, usually from late September to May. Required **overnight backcountry permits** cost $20 from May through October and are free the rest of the year (see "Exploring the Backcountry," p. 70).

Seasons & Climate

Even though the park is open year-round, **Trail Ridge Road,** the main east-west thoroughfare, is always closed in winter. Assume that you will not be able to drive clear across the park from mid-October until Memorial Day—even into June and again in September, snow can close the road for hours or even a day or more.

In summer, temperatures typically climb into the 70s (20s Celsius) during the day and drop into the 40s (single digits Celsius) at night, but because of the park's high elevation and range of elevations, temperatures vary greatly. The higher into the mountains you go, the cooler it gets. Rangers say that for every 1,000 feet in elevation gain, the climate changes the equivalent of traveling 600 miles north. The tree line in the park—the elevation at which trees can no longer grow—varies but is at about 11,500 feet.

Winters usually see high temperatures in the 20s and 30s (below 0 Celsius) and lows from –10°F (–23°C) to 20°F (–7°C). Spring and fall temperatures can vary greatly, from pleasantly warm to bitterly cold and snowy. For this reason, spring and fall are when you need to be flexible and ready to adjust your itinerary to suit current conditions. Particularly at higher elevations, wind-chill factors can be extreme. Hypothermia can be a problem at any time, even in summer, when afternoon thunderstorms sometimes cause temperatures to drop dramatically and suddenly.

EXPLORING THE PARK BY CAR

Although Rocky Mountain National Park is generally considered the domain of hikers and climbers, it's easy to enjoy this park without working up a sweat. For that we can thank **Trail Ridge Road,** built in 1932 and undoubtedly one of America's most scenic highways. This remarkable 48-mile road rises to over 12,000 feet in elevation and crosses the Continental Divide. Along the way it offers spectacular vistas of snow-capped peaks, deep forests, and meadows of wildflowers full of browsing bighorn sheep, elk, and deer. Allow at least 3 hours for the drive, and consider a short walk or hike from one of the many vista points.

To get a close-up look at the tundra, pull off Trail Ridge Road into the **Rock Cut Parking Area** (elev. 12,110 ft.), about halfway along the scenic drive. You'll have splendid views of glacially carved peaks along the Continental Divide, and on the .5-mile **Tundra Nature Trail** you'll find signs identifying and discussing the hardy plants and animals that inhabit this region.

Trail Ridge Road is left unplowed and closed by winter snows. In recent years, it has usually been clear by late May and closed sometime in October, depending how fast winter comes. But even well into June and again in September and through early October, the road can be closed due to snow.

There are two other roads within the park. **Old Fall River Road,** 9 miles long and unpaved, is one-way uphill only (you'll return on Trail Ridge Rd.). It's usually open from July 4 through mid-October. **Bear Lake Road,** the access road to Bear Lake, is open year-round.

ORGANIZED TOURS & RANGER PROGRAMS

Campfire talks and other programs occur between June and September. Activities vary from talks on the park's wildlife and geology to photo walks, fly-fishing, and orienteering programs. At night, rangers lead night-sky programs using the park's computerized telescopes. They also give nightly talks during the elk rutting season. Winter visitors will find a variety of activities, including moonlight hikes and snowshoe and cross-country ski trips. Check at visitor centers for current schedules. The **Rocky Mountain Nature Association** (*©* **970/586-0108;** www.rmna.org) offers a wide variety of seminars and workshops, lasting from a half-day to 1 full day, to several days. Subjects vary but might include songbirds, painting, wildlife photography, animal tracking, and edible mushrooms. Rates are $35 to $100 for half- and full-day programs and $140 and up for multiday programs.

DAY HIKES

The park contains over 350 miles of hiking trails, ranging from short, easy walks to extremely strenuous hikes that require climbing skills. Trail difficulty can also vary by time of year—the higher elevations usually have snow until at least mid-July. Many of the park's trails, such as Longs Peak, can be either day hikes or overnight backpacking trips. Hikers are strongly advised to discuss their plans with park rangers before setting out. The following are some favorites; there are many more.

Shorter Trails

Alberta Falls Trail ★★   With an elevation change of only 210 feet, this is an easy, scenic walk along Glacier Creek to Alberta Falls. Along the sunny trail, you'll see beaver dams and an abundance of golden-mantled ground squirrels. 1.2 miles RT. Easy. Access: Glacier Gorge parking area.

Bierstadt Lake Trail ★★   This trail climbs 566 feet through an open forest of aspen to Bierstadt Lake. From the northwest side of the lake, you'll have good views of Longs Peak. This trail connects with several other trails, including one that leads to Bear Lake. 2.8 miles RT. Moderate. Access: North side of Bear Lake Rd., 6.5 miles from Beaver Meadows.

Emerald Lake Trail ★★★   Spectacular scenery on its route past Nymph and Dream lakes to its destination, Emerald Lake is the appeal of this trail. The .5-mile hike to Nymph Lake is easy, climbing 225 feet. The trail is then rated moderate to Dream Lake (another .6 mile) and Emerald Lake (another .7 mile), which is 605 feet higher than the starting point at Bear Lake. In addition to the mountain lakes, you'll see the surrounding mountains, which are especially pretty reflected in the surface of Nymph Lake or towering over Dream Lake. In summer, an abundance of wildflowers borders the path between Nymph and Dream lakes. 3.6 miles RT. Easy to moderate. Access: Bear Lake.

Eugenia Mine Trail ★★   This walk to an abandoned mine follows the Longs Peak Trail for about .5 mile and then forks off to the right, heading through groves of aspens and then evergreens before arriving at the site of the mine. There you'll see hillside tailings, the remnants of a cabin, and abandoned mine equipment. The trail has an elevation gain of 508 feet. 3.3 miles RT. Moderate. Access: Longs Peak Ranger Station.

Gem Lake Trail ★★   A relatively low-elevation trail, starting at only 7,740 feet, this route has an elevation change of 1,090 feet. It offers good views of Estes Park and Longs Peak; the destination is a pretty lake. 4 miles RT. Moderate. Access: Lumpy Ridge trail head on Devil's Gulch Rd., north of Estes Park.

Mills Lake Trail ★★★   Hike to a mountain lake nestled in a valley among towering mountain peaks. Among the best spots in the park for photographing Longs Peak (the best lighting is usually in late afternoon or early evening), this is also the perfect place for a picnic. The trail has an elevation change of about 750 feet. 5 miles RT. Moderate. Access: Glacier Gorge Junction.

Ouzel Falls Trail ★★★   This trek climbs about 950 feet and crosses Cony Creek on two bridges before delivering you to a picture-perfect waterfall, among the park's prettiest. The trail passes through areas that were burned in 1978—good spots to see wildlife—and also offers fine views of Longs Peak and Mount Meeker. *Note:* The bridge at Ouzel falls was destroyed by the 2013 floods. 5.4 miles RT. Moderate. Access: Wild Basin Ranger Station.

Longer Trails

East Inlet Trail ★★   This trail is an easy walk for the first .3 mile, to scenic Adams Falls. It then wanders along some marshy areas, crosses several streams, and, becoming more strenuous, climbs sharply in elevation to Lone Pine Lake, about 5.5 miles from the trail head. It is another 1.5 miles, partly through a subalpine forest, to Lake Verna. The trail continues, unmaintained, after the lake. Total elevation gain to Lake Verna is 1,809 feet. 14 miles RT. Moderate to strenuous. Access: West portal of Adam's Tunnel, southeast of the town of Grand Lake.

East Longs Peak Trail ★★★   Recommended only for experienced mountain hikers and climbers in top physical condition, this trail climbs 4,855 feet along steep ledges and through a narrows to the top of 14,259-foot Longs Peak, the highest point in the park. The trek takes most hikers about 15 hours to complete and can be done in 1 or 2 days. Those planning a 1-day hike should consider starting extremely early, so they will be well off the peak before the summer afternoon thunderstorms arrive. For a 2-day hike, go 5 or 6 miles the first day, stay at a designated backcountry campsite (a permit is required), and complete the trip the following day. Those making the hike in early summer (usually until mid-July) should be prepared for icy conditions. 16 miles RT. Strenuous. Access: Longs Peak Ranger Station.

Lulu City Trail ★★   This trail gains just 300 feet in elevation as it winds along the river floodplain, through lush vegetation, past an 1880s mine and several mining cabins, and then along an old stage route into a subalpine forest before arriving at Lulu City. Founded in 1879 by prospectors hoping to strike gold and silver, it was abandoned within 10 years. Little remains except the ruins of a few cabins. An interpretative brochure is available. 7.4 miles RT. Moderate. Access: Colorado River trail head, near the western park boundary.

Ute Trail ★★   An excellent way to see the tundra, this moderate hike can become fairly easy if you can get a ride to the top and walk down the 3,300-foot descent to Beaver Meadows. The hike down the side of a canyon provides great views. 6 miles one-way. Moderate. Access: Ute Trail turnout on Trail Ridge Rd.

EXPLORING THE BACKCOUNTRY

The park allows numerous opportunities for backpacking and technical climbing, and hikers and climbers will generally find that the farther they go into the backcountry, the fewer humans they see. Some of the day hikes discussed above can also be done as overnight hikes; for example, the East Longs Peak Trail, which takes most people about 15 hours round-trip, is often completed over 2 days. Hikers can also combine various shorter trails to produce loops that can keep them in the park's backcountry for up to a week.

The park has well over 100 small **backcountry campsites,** which may be reserved. Backpackers should carry portable stoves, because wood fires are permitted at only a few sites with metal fire rings. In addition to the designated backcountry campsites, there are two-dozen cross-country zones, in some of the least accessible sections of the park, which are recommended only for those with good map and compass skills.

The park's **Backcountry Office** should be the first stop for those planning backpacking trips. Rangers there know the trails and camping areas well and are happy to advise hikers on the best choices for their abilities and expectations. **Backcountry permits** are required for all overnight hikes. Technical climbers who expect to be out overnight usually set up a bivouac—a temporary open-air encampment that is normally at or near the base of a route or on the face of a climb. Designated bivouac zones have been established; **permits** are required.

Backcountry and bivouac permits are available at park headquarters and ranger stations. They cost $20 from May through October and are free from November through April. For information, call ✆ **970/586-1242.**

OTHER SPORTS & ACTIVITIES

BIKING As in most national parks, bikes are not permitted on the trails, only established roads. Bicyclists here will, in most cases, share space with motor vehicles along narrow roads with 5% to 7% grades. However, bikers still enjoy the challenge and scenery. A free park brochure provides information on safety, regulations, and suggested routes. One popular 16-mile ride, with plenty of beautiful mountain views, is the **Horseshoe Park/Estes Park Loop.** It goes from Estes Park west on U.S. 34 past Aspenglen Campground and the park's Fall River Entrance, and then back east at the Deer Ridge Junction, following U.S. 36 through the Beaver Meadows Entrance. Rentals are available from **Estes Park Mountain Shop,** 2050 Big Thompson Ave., Estes Park (✆ **303/586-6548**), for about $40 to $60 a day.

CLIMBING & MOUNTAINEERING The **Colorado Mountain School** (✆ **800/836-4008;** www.coloradomountainschool.com), is the sole concessionaire for technical climbing and instruction in Rocky Mountain National Park. The school offers a wide range of programs, including half-day classes for $190 and a guided hike up Longs Peak for $425. The school also offers lodging in a hostel-type setting ($25 per bed per night).

CROSS-COUNTRY SKIING & SNOWSHOEING A growing number of people have discovered the joys of exploring the park on cross-country skis and snowshoes, which are conveniently available for rent at area stores outside the park.

If you're headed into the backcountry for cross-country skiing or snowshoeing, stop by park headquarters for maps, information on where the snow is best, and a free backcountry permit if you plan to stay out overnight. Keep in mind that trails are not groomed. On winter weekends starting in February, rangers often lead guided snowshoe walks on the east side of the park and guided cross-country ski trips on the west side. Participants must supply their own equipment.

Popular winter recreation areas include Bear Lake, south of the Beaver Meadows Entrance. A lesser-known part of the park is Wild Basin, which is south of the park's east entrances, off Colo. 7 about a mile north of the community of Allenspark. A 2-mile road, closed to motor vehicles for the last mile in winter, winds through a subalpine forest to the Wild Basin trail head, which follows a creek to a waterfall, a rustic bridge, and eventually another waterfall. Total distance to the second falls is 2.7 miles.

Among shops that rent winter gear is **Estes Park Mountain Shop,** 2050 Big Thompson Ave. (© **970/586-6548;** www.estesparkmountainshop.com), which charges $12 per day for a cross-country ski package and $5 per day for snowshoes.

FISHING   Four species of **trout** are fished in the park: brown, rainbow, brook, and cutthroat. Anglers must get a state fishing license and are permitted to use only artificial lures or flies. About a half-dozen lakes and streams, including Bear Lake, are closed to fishing; a free park brochure lists open and closed waters, and gives regulations and other information.

HORSEBACK RIDING   Many of the national park's trails are open to horseback riders. Several outfitters provide guided rides inside and outside the park, including a 1-hour ride ($35) and the very popular 2-hour rides ($50). There are also all-day rides ($120, including lunch), plus breakfast and dinner rides and multiday pack trips. Recommended companies include **SK Horses** (www.skhorses.com), which operates **National Park Gateway Stables,** at the Fall River entrance of the national park on U.S. 34 (© **970/586-5269**), and the **Cowpoke Corner Corral,** at Glacier Lodge, 3 miles west of town, 2166 Colo. 66 (© **970/586-5890**). **Hi Country Stables** (www. sombrero.com) operates two stables inside the park: **Glacier Creek Stables** (© **970/ 586-3244**) and **Moraine Park Stables** (© **970/586-2327**).

SNOWMOBILING   On the park's west side, a 2-mile section of the North Supply Access Trail is open to snowmobiles. It leads from the park into the adjacent **Arapaho National Forest.** This trail leaves U.S. 34 just north of the Kawuneeche Visitor Center and follows County Roads 491 and 492 west into the forest. Contact park visitor centers for current information.

WHERE TO STAY

With the exception of campgrounds (see p. 73) there's no lodging in the park.

Estes Park Area (East Side of the National Park)

In addition to the properties that follow, the best value in town is the **Alpine Trail Ridge Inn,** 927 Moraine Ave. (© **800/233-5023** or 970/586-4585; www.alpinetrail ridgeinn.com) with summer rates $85 to $155 double, or $145 to $250 for a suite or family unit. Just outside the Fall River Entrance to Rocky Mountain National Park, **McGregor Mountain Lodge,** 815 Fall River Rd. (© **800/835-8439** or 970/586-3457; www.mcgregormountainlodge.com), is another good mid-priced option, with rates of $126 to $139 double and $156 to $319 for a cottage or a suite in summer.

Allenspark Lodge Bed & Breakfast ★★   This three-story lodge was built in 1933 and is my pick for those looking to focus on the Wild Basin unit of Rocky Mountain National Park. Woodsy to the nines, the property captures the national-park vibe better than its peers in Estes Park proper. The Great Room is one for the ages, and the upstairs guest rooms, though small, have period charm, with quilts on the bed, and original, handmade pine furnishings. There's a sizeable family room with a queen bed and twin bunks, as well as a full kitchen. The complimentary breakfast is first rate, as are the complimentary cookies set out each evening.

184 Main St., Colo. 7 Business Loop (PO Box 247), Allenspark. ✆ **303/747-2552.** www.allenspark lodge.com. 13 units, 7 with bathroom. $105–$150 double. Rates include full breakfast. Children 13 and under not accepted. **Amenities:** Bar; indoor Jacuzzi; free Wi-Fi.

Baldpate Inn ★★   Pure Colorado and full of quirks, the Baldpate Inn has stood since its 1917 opening under the watchful gaze of the Twin Sisters, aptly named peaks summited by trails right out of the front door. Named after the 1913 mystery novel, "The Seven Keys to Baldpate," the "key room" here has 20,000 keys hanging from the ceiling and walls, donated by guests over the years. Rooms are a bit creaky and small, as you might expect for a historic hotel, with quilts on the beds, solid wood furnishings and shared or private bathrooms; there are also a quartet of larger cabins here that can accommodate up to six guests. Rooms aside, the location and personality are the biggest draws, and the restaurant is known for its tasty soup-and-salad buffets.

4900 S. Colo. 7, Estes Park. Located 7 miles south of Estes Park. ✆ **866/577-5397** or 970/586-6151. www.baldpateinn.com. 12 units (2 with private bathroom), 4 cabins. $130 double with shared bathroom; $150 double with private bathroom; $230 cabin per double ($15 per additional person). Rates include full breakfast. Closed Nov–Apr. **Amenities:** Restaurant; free Wi-Fi.

Estes Park Center/YMCA of the Rockies ★★   The family-friendliest lodging in family-friendly Estes Park, this huge complex backs right up to the boundary of Rocky Mountain National Park. Perfect for weekend getaways as well as family reunions, the overnight options range from lodge rooms to yurts to sizable cabins (the largest sleep 10 people)—more than 700 units in all—and four pay-as-you-go restaurants. The list of activities is mind-boggling: Guests can a ride horse, tackle a challenge course, make crafts, hike, bike, play a round of mini-golf and—after dark—roast marshmallows on a campfire.

2515 Tunnel Rd., Estes Park. ✆ **970/586-3341** or 303/448-1616. www.ymcarockies.org. 510 lodge rooms, 205 cabins. Summer $114–$169 double, $129–$409 cabin; winter $79–$99 double, $99–$284 cabin. YMCA memberships get $15 discount. Pets accepted in the cabins but not the lodge rooms. **Amenities:** 4 restaurants; bike rentals; children's program; indoor heated pool; tennis courts (3 outdoor); free Wi-Fi.

Romantic RiverSong Inn ★★   Located at the dead end of a dirt road, it is hard to find a much more secluded place to hang your hat in the Rocky Mountain National Park vicinity than the Romantic RiverSong Inn. Comprised of rooms in a historic Craftsman-style home and adjacent cottages, the B&B is one of the best in the Rockies, and the standout room is Meadow Bright, with a picture-perfect rock fireplace and log-canopy bed. Hearty breakfasts are cooked with hikers in mind, including potato pancakes and French toast.

1765 Lower Broadview Rd., Estes Park. ✆ **970/586-4666.** www.romanticriversong.com. 10 units. $165–$350 double. Rates include full breakfast. Not suitable for small children. **Amenities:** Free Wi-Fi.

CAMPING options

The park has five campgrounds with a total of almost 600 sites. Nearly half of the sites are at **Moraine Park ★**, which has good access to Estes Park in a ponderosa pine forest, but is notably busy. **Aspenglen ★**, close to the Fall River Entrance, is less crowded but not exactly off the beaten path. **Glacier Basin ★** was closed in 2013 due to road construction; its reopening date was uncertain at press time, and it may not reopen at all due to budget cuts. All three accept reservations from Memorial Day through early September, and they are strongly recommended, especially on holiday weekends (☎ **877/444-6777;** www.recreation.gov). In summer, arrive early if you hope to snare one of the first-come, first-served campsites (my favorites in the park) at **Longs Peak ★★**, notable for its views of and access to the trails up the iconic mountain of the same name, and **Timber Creek ★★**, a nicely treed campground (and the only one of the west side of the park). Campsites cost $20 per night during the summer or $14 in the off season, when water is turned off. No showers or RV hookups are available. Camping is limited to 7 nights per summer.

Stanley Hotel ★★   F.O. Stanley of Stanley Steamer fame opened this iconic hotel above Estes Park in 1909, but another event in 1974 changed its reputation forever: horror writer Stephen King checking in to room 217 in 1974. King's experience served as the formation for "The Shining," and this, in tandem with already-existing ghost stories galore, makes a stay an absolute must for any aficionado of paranormal lodgings. (The $15 **ghost tours** are popular with guests and non-guests alike.) While Stanley Kubrick did not film his 1980 adaptation here, you can just imagine Jack Nicholson bellying up to the ethereal-looking Whiskey Bar, a relatively new addition, with the largest selection of whiskeys in Colorado. Standard rooms are small but stylish, king rooms and suites are larger (as are the one- to three-bedroom condos located on hotel grounds), and you will pay a serious premium for the privilege of sleeping in 217 or another allegedly haunted room. Next door is the recently renovated **Lodge at the Stanley,** a smaller replica of the hotel built in 1911 and now offering a luxurious, B&B-like atmosphere.

333 Wonderview Ave., Estes Park. ☎ **800/976-1377** or 970/577-4000. www.stanleyhotel.com. 140 units. $149–$399 double; $300–$700 suite or presidential cottage. Lodge at Stanley rates include continental breakfast. **Amenities:** Restaurant; lounge; exercise room; outdoor heated pool (seasonal); spa; tennis court (outdoor); free Wi-Fi.

Grand Lake Area (West Side of the National Park)

Grand Lake Lodge ★★   This 1920 gem reopened in 2011 after a 5-year shutdown, with new ownership immediately bringing it back up to speed. Perched above Grand Lake, the remodeled and modernized cabins are mostly duplexes, offering several bed combinations in one room with a small bathroom; there are also a couple of larger units that sleep more than 10 people. The lodge, fronted by the swings of "Colorado's Favorite Front Porch," is a classic, with a good restaurant, taxidermy galore, and plenty of places to sit and play antique pin-games or just while away the time around the colossal fireplace.

Off U.S. 34, Grand Lake. ☎ **855/585-0004** or 970/627-3967. www.grandlakelodge.com. 70 units, including 2-, 3-, and 8-bedroom cabins. $130–$150 double; $215–$875 2-bedroom cabin or larger. Pets accepted ($10/night). Closed Oct–May. **Amenities:** Restaurant; lounge; free Wi-Fi.

WHERE TO EAT

There are no dining facilities inside the park.

Estes Park Area (East Side of the National Park)

Dunraven Inn ★★ ITALIAN   The place to go for an upscale Italian dinner for a generation, the Dunraven Inn is tucked away in the trees on Colo. 66, halfway before it dead-ends. Countless renditions of the Mona Lisa hang on the walls and more than $16,000 worth of dollar bills wallpaper the bar. The Italian dishes are uniformly good, from lobster ziti to chicken parmesan, and there are also steaks and seafood specialties. I'm a fan of the gorgonzola-stuffed filet mignon and the namesake dish, the Lord Dunraven, a center-cut charbroiled sirloin steak.

2470 Colo. 66. ℭ **970/480-0396.** www.dunraveninn.com. Main courses $13–$34. Daily 4–9pm.

Rock Inn ★★ AMERICAN   Built in 1937 as a big-band dance hall, this is my favorite spot in Estes Park. It is not just the woodsy atmosphere, which has the best national-park-lodge feel in the area, from the stuffed animal heads to the log beams. It's also that the patio has great views, the beer is cold, and the food is first-rate, from roasted beets for starters to the steaks, pastas, burgers, and pizzas for the main event. Expect live music and a bit of a wait in peak season.

1675 Colo. 66, south of the intersection with U.S. 36. ℭ **970/586-4116.** www.rockinnestes.com. Main courses $9–$33. Summer daily Sun–Wed 4–9pm, Thurs–Sat 4–10pm; shorter hours in winter. Bar open later.

Grand Lake Area (West Side of the National Park)

Grand Lake Lodge (see p. 73) also has an excellent restaurant with the best view on this side of the park. Open for three meals a day in peak season, the menu offers sandwiches and entrees like buffalo burgers, rainbow trout, and honey pepper salmon ($10–$24). In town at the Daven Haven Lodge, the **Backstreet Steakhouse** (ℭ **970-627-8144;** www.backstreetsteak.com) serves dinner nightly in summer and around Christmas and Thursday through Sunday in other seasons. The house specialty, Jack Daniel's pork chops (breaded, baked, and served with a creamy Jack Daniel's mushroom sauce), has been featured in *Bon Appétit* magazine. Also on the menu (main courses are $9–$31) are steaks, burgers, pasta, chicken, and fish dishes, plus slow-roasted prime rib and children's items.

Sagebrush BBQ & Grill ★ AMERICAN   I love the atmosphere at this old-fashioned place that always draws a crowd. The appeal is understandable. The barbecue is excellent (especially the pulled pork and sausage with mustard barbecue sauce), you can throw your nutshells on the floor, and the full bar pours draft microbrew. There are also burgers, steaks and game, and seafood, plus pasta, pizza, and burritos for good measure, as well as hearty breakfasts such as huevos rancheros and biscuits and gravy.

1101 Grand Ave. ℭ **970/627-1404.** www.sagebrushbbq.com. Main courses $6–$13 breakfast; $7–$26 lunch and dinner. Sun–Thurs 7am–9pm; Fri–Sat 7am–10pm.

BADLANDS

by Eric Peterson

It's a strange and seemingly complicated place. From the ragged ridges and saw-toothed spires to the wind-ravaged desolation of Badlands Wilderness Area, Badlands National Park is an awe-inspiring sight and an unsettling experience. Few leave here unaffected by the vastness of this geologic anomaly, which spreads across 381 square miles of moonscape.

The Lakota Indians who once traversed this incredible land named it *mako sica,* or "land bad." Early French-Canadian trappers labeled it *les mauvaises terres à traverser,* or "bad lands to travel across."

Steep canyons, towering spires, and flat-topped tables all appear among Badlands buttes. Despite their apparent complexity, the unusual formations of the Badlands are essentially the result of two basic geologic processes: deposition and erosion.

The layered look of the Badlands comes from sedimentary rocks composed of fine grains that have been cemented into a solid form. Layers with similar characteristics are grouped into units called **formations.** The bottom formation is the **Pierre Shale,** deposited 68 to 77 million years ago during the Cretaceous period, when a shallow, inland sea stretched across the Great Plains. The mud of the sea floor hardened into shale, leaving fossil clamshells and ammonites that confirm a sea environment. The sea eventually drained away, and the upper layers of shale were weathered into soil, now seen as Yellow Mounds.

The **Chadron Formation,** deposited 34 million to 37 million years ago during the Eocene epoch, sits above the Pierre Shale. By this time, a flood plain had replaced the sea, and each time the rivers flooded, they deposited a new layer of sediment on the plain. Alligator fossils indicate that a lush, subtropical forest covered the region. However, mammal fossils dominate. The Chadron is best known for large, elephant-size mammals called *titanotheres.*

Some of the sediment carried by rivers and wind was volcanic ash, the product of eruptions associated with the creation of the Rocky Mountains. This ash mixed with river and stream sediments to form clay stone, the main material from which Badlands buttes are constructed. After the Eocene epoch, the climate began to dry and cool, and tropical forests gave way to open savanna. Rivers deposited the **Brule** and **Sharps formations** during the Oligocene epoch from 28 to 34 million years ago, and today these formations contain the most rugged peaks and canyons of the Badlands.

Actually, the impressive serrated ridges and deep canyons of the Badlands did not exist until about 500,000 years ago, when water began to cut through the layers of rock, carving fantastic shapes into what had been a flat flood plain. Once again, the ancient fossil soils, buried for millions of years, became exposed. That erosion continues: Every time rain falls, or snow melts in spring, more sediment is washed from the buttes in this ongoing work of sculpting the earth. On average, the buttes erode an inch a year; scientists believe that the buttes will be gone in another 500,000 years.

In addition to its scenic wonders, the Badlands are one of the richest Oligocene fossil beds known to exist. Remains of three-toed horses, dog-size camels, saber-toothed cats, giant pigs, and other species have been found here; all date from 28 million to 37 million years ago.

FLORA & FAUNA

Largely a mixed-grass prairie, the park contains 56 types of **grasses,** most of which are native species, including green needlegrass and buffalo grass. **Wildflowers,** including curlycup gumweed and pale purple coneflower, add color, with the best wildflower displays in June and July. You won't find many trees.

Wildlife to watch for include **bison, Rocky Mountain bighorn sheep, pronghorns,** and **mule deer.** Darting in and out of the grass are **cottontail rabbits. Prairie dogs** thrive here; a prairie dog town is just 5 miles down Sage Creek Rim Road. You might also see a **prairie rattlesnake** slithering through the grass, plus several **nonpoisonous snake species.**

ESSENTIALS
Getting There & Gateways

Located in extreme southwestern South Dakota, Badlands National Park is easily accessible by car either on **S. Dak. 44** east of Rapid City, or off **I-90** at Wall or Cactus Flat. Westbound I-90 travelers take exit 131 south (Cactus Flat) onto S. Dak. 240, which leads to the park boundary and the **Ben Reifel Visitor Center** at Cedar Pass. This road becomes **Badlands Loop Road,** the park's primary scenic drive. After passing through the park, S. Dak. 240 rejoins I-90 at exit 110 at Wall. Eastbound travelers will start in Wall and rejoining I-90 at exit 131.

THE NEAREST AIRPORT   Rapid City Regional Airport (*(C)* **605/393-9924;** www.rcgov.org/Airport) 10 miles southeast of Rapid City on S. Dak. 44, provides easy access to the Badlands, Black Hills, and Mount Rushmore.

Visitor Centers & Information

For Badlands National Park information, contact **Badlands National Park** (*(C)* **605/433-5361;** www.nps.gov/badl). From the home page, click on "Badlands Visitor Guide" and you'll get excellent and thorough information.

For information about the area, contact **South Dakota Tourism** (✆ **800/S-DAKOTA** [732-5682]; www.travelsd.com), or the **Black Hills Visitor Information Center,** north side of I-90 at exit 61 (✆ **605/355-3600;** www.blackhillsbadlands.com).

The Badlands Visitor Guide, published by the nonprofit **Badlands Natural History Association,** (✆ **605/433-5489;** www.badlandsnha.org), provides up-to-date information on visitor center hours, park programs, camping, and hiking trails.

Visitor centers are at Cedar Pass and White River. The **Ben Reifel Visitor Center** at Cedar Pass is open year-round and features exhibits on the park's natural and cultural history. The **White River Visitor Center,** on the Pine Ridge Indian Reservation, is open June through late August only. It includes exhibits about Oglala Sioux history. The National Park Service distributes a wide variety of brochures on topics including geology, prairie grasses, backpacking, biking, wildlife, plants, and the use of horses in the park. You can pickup the brochures at these centers or download them from the park's website.

Fees

Park entry fees are $15 per passenger vehicle (up to 7 days), motorcycles $10, and each person on foot or bike pays $7. Camping costs $16 per site per night at the Cedar Pass Campground; sites with electrical hookups are $28 per night. Camping at Sage Creek Primitive Campground is free.

Seasons & Climate

Badlands weather is often unpredictable. Heavy rain, hail, and high, often damaging winds are possible, particularly during spring and summer. Lightning strikes are common. Summer temperatures often exceed 100°F (38°C), so sunscreen, a broad-brimmed hat, and plenty of drinking water are essential to avoid severe sunburn, dehydration, and heat stroke. Winter travelers should be aware of approaching storms and be prepared for sleet, ice, heavy snow, and blizzard conditions.

ORGANIZED TOURS & RANGER PROGRAMS

A limited schedule of **naturalist-led walks** and programs generally begins in mid-June; offerings become more frequent as visitation increases. Check the activities board at the Ben Reifel Visitor Center or campground bulletin boards for times, locations, and other details. Activities vary each year but often include guided walks on the prairie, talks covering fossils and the geological history of the park, and stargazing and other evening programs at the amphitheater at the Cedar Pass Campground.

Special Regulations & Warnings

Water in the Badlands is too full of silt for humans to drink and will quickly clog a water filter. When hiking or traveling in the park, always carry an adequate supply of water. Drinking water is available only at the Cedar Pass area, the White River Visitor Center, and the Pinnacles Ranger Station. No campfires are allowed. Climbing Badlands buttes and rock formations is allowed, but it can be extremely dangerous due to loose, crumbly rock. Unpaved roads in the park can be dangerous in winter and during thunderstorms, when surfaces may become extremely slippery.

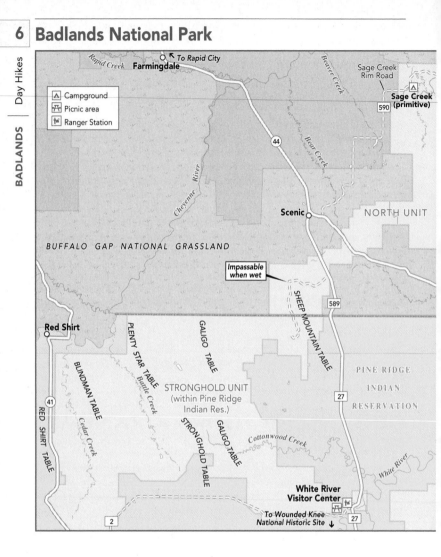

DAY HIKES

Numerous hiking trails provide a closer look at the Badlands for those adventurous enough to leave the confines of their vehicles. All developed trails start from parking areas within 5 miles of the Ben Reifel Visitor Center at Cedar Pass.

Castle Trail ★★　Winding some 5 miles (10 miles round-trip) through the mixed-grass prairie and badlands, this is the longest developed trail in the park and runs parallel to some interesting formations. The fairly level trail connects the Fossil Exhibit Trail and the Door and Window parking area. Just walking this trail a short distance from the parking area brings the hiker close to outstanding formations. Walk the Castle Trail from the Door parking area in the early morning for wonderful views of the

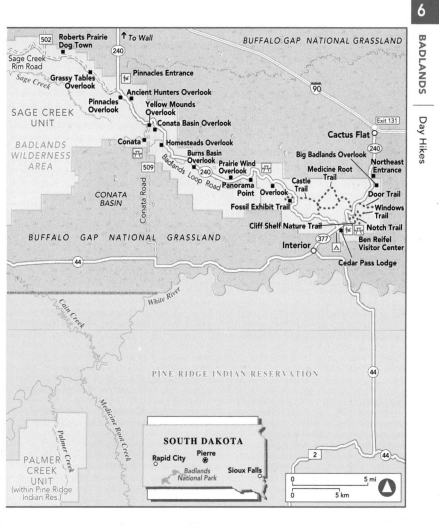

formations. Walk a bit farther in the late day for beautiful color and patterns. To make this a loop, follow the signs and turn off onto the well-marked Medicine Root Trail. The trail is not heavily used, making it an ideal spot to escape the crowds, but it can be treacherously slick during and just after a heavy rain and, with no tree cover, can be hot on some summer days. 10 miles RT. Moderate. Access: Trail heads at Fossil Exhibit Trail and at Door Trail parking area.

Cliff Shelf Nature Trail ★ This popular trail takes you through a "slump" area where a good supply of water supports an oasis of green, which stands out in contrast to the stark badlands formations. You can pick up a brochure for a self-guided excursion at the Visitor Center desk. The trail includes some steep sections and boardwalk stairs. .5 mile RT. Moderate. Access: .5 mile north of Ben Reifel Visitor Center.

Door Trail ★★ This trail winds through some of the "baddest" of the Badlands. The first 100 yards, to a beautiful view at "The Door," are mostly downhill and accessible, with assistance, to those in wheelchairs. The more rugged section takes off to the right of the viewing area; striped posts mark the way, indicating the safest route. .6 mile RT. Moderate. Access: 2 miles northeast of Ben Reifel Visitor Center.

Fossil Exhibit Trail ★ This easy boardwalk loop will give you an idea of what animal life was like 30 million years ago. Wheelchair accessible. .25 mile RT. Easy. Access: 5 miles northwest of Ben Reifel Visitor Center.

Notch Trail ★ This trail takes you up a wash between the buttes, up a 45-degree angle wood-and-rope ladder, a climb that may rattle those afraid of heights. Follow the wash to the "Notch"; you'll find a striking view over the Cliff Shelf area and the White River Valley. 1.5 miles RT. Moderate. Access: North end of Door Trail parking area.

Saddle Pass Trail ★★ In less than .25 mile, this trail rises steeply 200 feet from the bottom of the Badlands Wall to the top, connecting with the Castle and Medicine Root trails. It's impassable after rains, so ask about trail conditions at the visitor center before you set out. .5 mile RT. Moderate to strenuous. Access: Branches off Castle Trail just west of intersection with Medicine Root Trail and leads to Badlands Loop Rd.

Window Trail ★★ A 100-yard boardwalk trail leads to a spectacular view through a "window," or opening, in the Badlands Wall. Wheelchair accessible. .25 mile RT. Easy to moderate. Access: Trail head at center of Door Trail parking area.

EXPLORING THE BACKCOUNTRY

The park encompasses the largest prairie wilderness in the United States, where expansive grasslands make cross-country travel unique. Vast ranges of classic badlands provide rugged, challenging terrain for even skilled hikers. Wildlife is close and abundant. Best of all, it's never crowded; hikers often have hundreds of acres to themselves.

The Badlands has no formal system of backcountry permits or reservations. Let friends and relatives know when you depart and when you expect to return. Rangers at the Ben Reifel Visitor Center can assist in planning a safe, enjoyable excursion by offering directions, safety tips, maps, and information sheets.

When planning your backcountry hike, examine past, present, and forecasted weather carefully. With even a small amount of precipitation, some trails can become slick and impassable. Carry water if you think you could be out for as little as a half-hour. Cross-country hikers are encouraged to carry a map, compass, and water, and to wear or carry appropriate clothing. No campfires are allowed. All overnight backcountry hikers should discuss their route with a park ranger before departure.

Spring and fall may be the best times to experience the Badlands backcountry. Days are often pleasant, and nights are cool. In summer, temperatures often exceed 100°F (38°C) and pose health hazards. Avoid heat sickness by drinking plenty of water and avoiding the midday sun. Only the hardiest hikers attempt winter backpacking trips.

OTHER SPORTS & ACTIVITIES

AERIAL TOURS Those looking for a hot-air-balloon adventure can contact **Black Hills Balloons** (© **605/673-2520;** www.blackhillsballoons.com), which offers flights over the Badlands and Black Hills year-round. Rates are about $250 to $300 per passenger for a 1-hour flight.

CAMPING options

Camping is available inside Badlands National Park at the Cedar Pass Campground and the Sage Creek Primitive Campground, on a first-come, first-served basis. Both are suitable for tents and small RVs, and offer scenic views but little shade. Campfires are not permitted. **Cedar Pass Campground ★**, with 96 sites, is just off the Loop Road and has an amphitheater and the Night Sky Interpretive Area. Nightly fees are $16, or $28 for RV sites. **Sage Creek Campground ★** is at the end of Sage Creek Rim Road, a gravel road that begins at the point where the park's Loop Road turns toward the Pinnacles Entrance. It is free but has little in the way of facilities aside from pit toilets and picnic tables. Impassable roads may limit access in winter. Backcountry camping is also permitted; it is free and permits are not required.

BIKING Off-road biking is not allowed in the park, but the Loop Road is accessible to bikes. There are bike racks at the Ben Reifel Visitor Center. The 22-mile route from Pinnacles Overlook to the Ben Reifel Visitor Center is mostly downhill (though there are several steep passes to climb). Many bikers ride along Sage Creek Rim Road, past the prairie dog town, to spectacular views of the Badlands wilderness. During summer, though, car traffic is heavy and the temperatures hot. There are no bike rentals available in the park.

HORSEBACK RIDING Several companies offer guided trail rides through the backcountry of the Badlands (and the Black Hills). They include family-run **Dakota Badland Outfitters** (✆ **605/574-3412;** www.ridesouthdakota.com). Ninety-minute rides are typically $30 to $40 per rider.

WHERE TO STAY

Cedar Pass Lodge ★ Located near the Ben Reifel Visitor Center in the park's North Unit, this is the only lodging in park boundaries, but it is a pretty good one despite its lack of competition. All of the cabins were replaced with new environmentally friendly, LEED-certified units for the 2013 season, incorporating beetlekill pine woodwork, on-demand hot water, and low-flow plumbing, and attractive Western furnishings. Most are freestanding, but there is also one older duplex cottage with a kitchen that was not replaced in 2013. Cabins come with either a queen bed and two doubles, one king, or two queens.

In Badlands National Park. ✆ **877/386-4383.** www.cedarpasslodge.com. 25 cabins. $130–$140 double. Closed mid-Oct to mid-Apr. **Amenities:** Restaurant; free Wi-Fi.

WHERE TO EAT
Inside the Park

Cedar Pass Lodge Restaurant ★ AMERICAN This is the only place to sit down for a meal in Badlands National Park. The options range from traditional American fare (steaks and seafood at dinner, and burgers, wraps, and the like for lunch) but

WALL DRUG or bust

You'll see the signs offering FREE ICE WATER at **Wall Drug,** 510 Main St., Wall, about 8 miles north of Badlands National Park on S. Dak. 240 and I-90. And you'll see them almost everywhere you go throughout the Black Hills region, all telling you how many miles it is to the small town of Wall and its eponymous drugstore. In fact, there are now more than 3,000 of these signs, all over the world. The advertising gimmick saved a small-town drugstore in an isolated community from bankruptcy during the Great Depression. Dorothy and Ted Hustead's marketing also turned their little establishment into a block-long Old West emporium that draws crowds from all over the United States and the world. You can buy pancakes or dough-nuts (some of the best in the state, in fact), American Indian crafts, books, jew-elry, and Western apparel, and watch the animatronic "cowboy band" perform every 15 minutes. Do you want a "genu-ine" jackalope? Yes, they've got those, too. Oh, and the ice water is still free. There's free entry to this 76,000-square-foot icon. Want to know more? Go to **www.walldrug.com.**

those in the know order a Sioux Indian Taco, a regional delicacy of spiced buffalo on fry bread. The views of the park's trademark spires are excellent.

Cedar Pass Lodge. ⓒ **605/433-5460.** www.cedarpasslodge.com. Breakfast and lunch $5–$10; din-ner $8–$20. Summer 7am–9pm; shorter hours early and late in season. Closed mid-Oct to mid-Apr.

Near the Park

The towns around Badlands National Park, Interior, and Wall (see the sidebar "Wall Drug or Bust," above) offer several dining choices.

SIDE TRIP: MOUNT RUSHMORE & THE BLACK HILLS

Chiseled in granite high on a pine-clad cliff in South Dakota's fabled Black Hills are the portraits of four of America's greatest leaders. Since 1941, George Washington, Thomas Jefferson, Abraham Lincoln, and Theodore Roosevelt have gazed quietly across the Great Plains and a land they did so much to mold.

Widely regarded as one of the man-made wonders of the world, Mount Rushmore is as much a work of art as it is an engineering marvel. Its creator, sculptor Gutzon Borglum, wanted to symbolize in stone the very spirit of a nation and, through four of its most revered leaders—George Washington, Thomas Jefferson, Abraham Lincoln, and Theodore Roosevelt—the country's birth, growth, preservation, and development. A half-century after its completion, Mount Rushmore remains one of America's most enduring icons.

In 1924, Borglum visited the Black Hills, looking for a place to carve a lasting legacy for himself and the nation. He hoped to locate a mountain with a suitable mass of stone, as well as a southeasterly exposure that would take advantage of the sun's rays for the greatest portion of the day. He decided on a rock outcropping named Mount Rushmore.

Inclement weather and lack of funds often stalled progress on the memorial. All told, the monument was completed at a cost of about $1 million during 6½ years of work over a 14-year period.

Most of the 2.7 million people who visit each year spend an hour or so at the memorial, maybe eating a sandwich, then moving on to Yellowstone National Park or some other "major" destination. But those with the time and inclination will discover much to enjoy at Mount Rushmore and the other attractions of the Black Hills. Within an hour's drive, you will find not only **Wind Cave National Park** and **Jewel Cave National Monument,** but also **Custer State Park** and the **Crazy Horse Memorial** (see sidebar on page 84)—a work in progress that will be far larger than Mount Rushmore. And if you are willing to get off the beaten path—something that relatively few visitors do—you will find a backcountry dotted with trails through the region's pine forests, a nearly untrammeled wilderness where you can escape the crowds for days, or perhaps just an hour. As a bonus, you are almost certain to view a variety of wildlife matched in few places in the United States.

Geologists predict the presidents will continue their earthly vigil at **Mount Rushmore National Memorial** for many centuries, as they erode less than 1 inch every 10,000 years.

As the "crown jewel" of South Dakota's state park system, **Custer State Park** offers 71,000 acres of prime Black Hills real estate, the largest and most diverse population of wildlife, the best accommodations and facilities, including four historic lodges, and the most memorable natural resources of any park in the state.

Located east of the town of Custer, the park is home to four lodges, four fishing lakes, wildlife loops, campgrounds, scenic drives, and granite spires so impressive that they make you want to get out of the car and walk the forest floor. With rolling meadows and foothills, pine forests, and the giant fingerlike granite spires of the Needles, Custer State Park is a must on any Black Hills itinerary.

Even after more than 100 years since the establishment of the park, there is still something to discover in the darkened depths of **Wind Cave National Park.** Although the cave formations here are generally not as ornate as those in some of the West's other caves, such as Carlsbad Cavern, Wind Cave has its share of fairyland-style decorations, including popcorn, shimmering needle-shaped crystals, and an abundance of formations called **"boxwork,"** which sometimes looks like fine lace. With more than 132 miles of mapped passageway, Wind Cave is one of the longest caves in the world. And with each succeeding expedition, the interconnecting network of known passages continues to grow, sometimes by a few paces, other times by several hundred feet. Barometric wind studies estimate that only 5% of the total cave has been discovered.

But there's a great deal more to Wind Cave than just its geological wonders. Aboveground, 28,295 acres of rolling prairie and ponderosa pine forests are ablaze

---

Guided Tours of the Black Hills

A number of charter bus park tours and guide services are available. **Gray Line of the Black Hills** (($ 800/456-4461 or 605/342-4461; www.blackhillsgrayline. com) offers daily bus tours of the area in season. **Golden Circle Tours Inc.**

(($ **605/673-4349;** www.goldencircle tours.com) gives guided van tours of the area. Gray Line has slightly less expensive rates (about $50 vs. $100), but Golden Circle offers more easily customized trips for small groups and families.

6 CRAZY HORSE MEMORIAL: the "fifth face"

Known by locals as the "Fifth Face" in the Black Hills, the sculpture of the legendary Lakota Sioux Chief Crazy Horse began with the dedication of the work on June 3, 1948. More than a half-century later, work continues on what is expected to be the world's largest sculpture. The chief's nine-story-high face has been completed, and work has begun on carving the 22-story-high horse's head.

Begun by the late sculptor Korczak Ziolkowski (pronounced Jewel-cuff-ski), and carried on by his widow, sons, and daughters, the mountain sculpture memorial is dedicated to all American Indians.

"My fellow chiefs and I would like the white man to know the red man has great heroes, too," Sioux Chief Henry Standing Bear wrote Ziolkowski in 1939, inviting him to create the mountain memorial. Seven years later, the sculptor agreed and began carving the colossal work.

When the sculpture is completed, Crazy Horse will sit astride his mount, pointing over his stallion's head to the sacred Black Hills. So large is the sculpture (563 ft. high) that all four presidents on Mount Rushmore would fit in Crazy Horse's head.

Visitors driving by the site on U.S. 16/385, 5 miles north of the town of Custer, might hear dynamite blasts, a sure-fire signal that work on the mountain carving is progressing. When night blasts are detonated, they tend to be among the most impressive events in the Black Hills.

In addition to viewing the carving in progress and watching an audiovisual display about the work, visitors may stop at the **Indian Museum of North America** at Crazy Horse, which is home to one of the most extensive collections of American Indian art and artifacts in the country. The museum's gift shop features authentic American Indian crafts.

For more information, go to www.crazy horsememorial.org or © **605/673-4681.**

with wildflowers and teeming with wildlife. Bison and pronghorn antelope graze on the park's lush grasslands, while prairie dogs watch from the relative safety of their "towns." In the fall, elk can be heard "bugling" throughout the confines of the park, and overhead, hawks, eagles, and vultures float on the thermal currents that rise from the rocky ridges of the Black Hills.

In the limestone labyrinth that rests below the Black Hills, **Jewel Cave National Monument** offers a mysterious, mazelike network of caverns and passageways. It is filled with delicate speleothems (cave formations) and beautiful crystal-like paths that have yet to be fully explored.

Essentials

GETTING THERE & GATEWAYS

Rapid City is the most popular gateway to the Black Hills and its bountiful selection of national and state parks, monuments, and memorials.

The most direct route to the Black Hills by car is I-90. To reach **Mount Rushmore,** take exit 57 to U.S. 16 (Mt. Rushmore Rd.) and continue approximately 23 miles southwest of Rapid City to the memorial entrance.

Custer State Park, between Mount Rushmore and Wind Cave National Park, is accessible via S. Dak. 79 and S. Dak. 36 from the east, U.S. 16A from the north and west, and S. Dak. 87 from the north and south.

Wind Cave National Park is best accessed via U.S. 385 north of Hot Springs, South Dakota, or S. Dak. 87 from Custer State Park, which shares its southern boundary with Wind Cave's northern perimeter. It's about an hour's drive south from Mount Rushmore.

Jewel Cave National Monument is just off U.S. 16, 13 miles west of Custer.

The Crazy Horse Memorial is 5 miles north of Custer on U.S. 16/385.

INFORMATION & FEES

For information on Mount Rushmore, contact Mount Rushmore National Memorial (© 605/574-2523; www.nps.gov/moru). For information about Custer State Park, contact the park (© 605/255-4515; www.custerstatepark.com). To get information about Wind Cave, contact Wind Cave National Park (© 605/745-4600; www.nps.gov/wica). For details on Jewel Cave, contact Jewel Cave National Monument (© 605/673-8300; www.nps.gov/jeca).

Mount Rushmore has no entrance fee, but parking runs $11 per vehicle. Custer State Park charges $15 for 7 days per vehicle ($10 for motorcycles). Wind Cave is free to enter above ground, but most cave tours run $7 to $9 for adults (half price for kids 6–16 and seniors, those 5 and under are free). Likewise, the surface is free at Jewel Cave, and most cave tours run $4 to $8.

MESA VERDE

by Don & Barbara Laine

With about 5,000 archaeological sites, Mesa Verde National Park is the largest archaeological preserve in the United States. Among the sites are some of the largest cliff dwellings in the world, as well as mesa-top pueblos, pit houses, and kivas (subterranean rooms used for meetings and religious ceremonies)—all of which were built by the ancestral Puebloans. The sites here tell the story of a 700-year period (A.D. 600–1300) during which these people shifted from a seminomadic hunter-gatherer lifestyle to a largely agrarian way of life centered on large communities.

Mesa Verde must have looked inviting to the ancestral Puebloans, whose descendants are such modern Pueblo tribes as the Hopi, Zuni, and Acoma. On the mesa's north side, 2,000-foot-high cliffs form a natural barrier to invaders. The mesa slopes gently to the south, and erosion has carved numerous canyons, most of which receive abundant sunlight and have natural overhangs for shelter.

The mesa tops were covered with *loess,* a red, windblown soil good for farming. They grew beans, corn, and squash; raised turkeys; foraged in the pinyon-juniper woodland; and hunted rabbits and deer. They wove sandals and clothing from yucca fibers, and traded for precious stones and shells, which they used to make jewelry.

To us today, their most impressive accomplishments are the multistory cliff dwellings, which were largely unknown until two local ranchers chanced upon them in 1888. Looting of artifacts followed their discovery until a Denver newspaper's stories aroused national interest in protecting them. In 1906, the 52,000-acre site was declared a national park.

Cliff Palace, the park's largest and best-known site, is a must-see. This four-story apartment complex is accessible by guided tour only and is approached by a quarter-mile downhill path. Its towers, walls, and kivas sit back beneath the rim of a cliff. Another ranger-led tour takes visitors up a 32-foot ladder to explore the interior of **Balcony House.** Each of these tours runs only in summer and early fall (see park website for information).

Two other important sites—**Step House** and **Long House,** both on Wetherill Mesa—are open to visitors in summer only. Rangers lead tours to **Spruce Tree House,** a major cliff-dwelling complex, only in winter, when other park facilities are closed; during the summer, you can see Spruce Tree House on your own.

AVOIDING the crowds

With over a half million visitors annually, Mesa Verde can seem packed at times. But park officials point out that the numbers are much lower just before and after the summer rush, from mid-June to mid-August 15, so go in early June or late August. Another way to beat the crowds is to drive to the lesser-visited **Wetherill Mesa,** where a free tram takes you to various archeological sites (see "Getting Around," below).

ESSENTIALS

Getting There & Gateways

Mesa Verde National Park is in southwestern Colorado, just under 400 miles southwest of Denver and 252 miles northwest of Albuquerque. The park entrance is on U.S. 160, 10 miles east of the town of Cortez and 6 miles west of Mancos.

From Cortez, **U.S. 491** runs north to Monticello, Utah, and south to Gallup, New Mexico and I-40. **U.S. 160** runs east through Durango to Walsenburg and I-25, and west through the Four Corners area into Arizona.

THE NEAREST AIRPORT Cortez Municipal Airport (© 970/565-7458; www.cityofcortez.com), about 3 miles southwest of town off U.S. 491 and U.S. 160, is served by **Great Lakes Airlines,** which offers daily service between Cortez and Denver and has rental cars from **Hertz** and **Budget.**

Visitor Centers & Information

The **Visitor Center,** 14 miles southwest of the park entrance, has an information desk, a display of American Indian art, and a small bookstore. It's open year-round, from 7:30am to 7pm daily in summer, with shorter hours at other times.

The staff at the small **Morefield Ranger Station** in Morefield Village also provides park information. It's open daily on summer mornings only.

The **Chapin Mesa Archaeological Museum,** open daily year-round (8am–6:30pm from early Apr to mid-Oct, closing earlier at other times), has interpretive displays on Pueblo culture, an information desk, and a bookstore.

If you'd like more information before you arrive, contact **Mesa Verde National Park,** P.O. Box 8, Mesa Verde N.P., CO 81330 (© 970/529-4465; www.nps.gov/meve).

For area information, stop at the **Colorado Welcome Center at Cortez** and **Cortez Area Chamber of Commerce,** 928 E. Main St. (© 970/565-3414; www.cortezchamber.com); or contact the **Mesa Verde Country Visitor Information Bureau** (© 970/565-8227; www.mesaverdecountry.com).

Special Regulations & Warnings

To protect the park's many archaeological sites, the Park Service has outlawed backcountry camping and off-trail hiking. It's also illegal to enter cliff dwellings without a ranger present. The road to Wetherill Mesa cannot accommodate vehicles over 25 feet or over 8,000 pounds gross vehicle weight. Cyclists must have lights to pedal through the tunnel on the park entrance road.

Fees

Admission to the park for up to 1 week for private vehicles is $15 from Memorial Day weekend through Labor Day weekend and $10 the rest of the year; rates for those on motorcycles, bikes, and on foot are $8 and $5 per person, respectively.

Getting Around

Mostly you will be driving your personal motor vehicle at Mesa Verde, though not if you want to see the archaeological sites on Wetherill Mesa. The Park Service operates **trams**—52-passenger biodiesel busses—in the Wetherill Mesa area during the summer. They run from a ranger kiosk to the main archaeological sites and are real time-savers, because your only other choice is to hike; cars aren't permitted beyond the Kiosk. Check at the visitor center for the current schedule.

Seasons & Climate

With elevations up to 8,572 feet, summer temperatures are cool, and even in July, the hottest month, highs average a bearable 87°F (30°C), and nighttime lows dip into the mid-50s (lower teens Celsius). Daytime highs average in the upper 30s and low 40s (single digits Celsius) in winter. Spring tends to come late, with winter weather common through March, but warm autumns are not uncommon.

EXPLORING THE PARK BY CAR

The main scenic drive in the park is the **Mesa Top Loop Road.** Each of the 12 stops along this 6-mile loop either overlooks cliff dwellings or is a short walk from mesa-top dwellings. Highlights include the **Square Tower House Viewpoint,** where binoculars are handy for spotting the myriad cliff dwellings in the canyon; **Sun Point Pueblo,** where a tunnel links a *kiva*—a subterranean room used for ceremonies—to a lookout tower; and the mysterious **Sun Temple,** a D-shaped structure that may have been a shrine or community gathering area. On your way back to the Visitor Center, stop at the **Far View Sites Complex,** 1 mile south of the visitor center. Six sites are within walking distance, including what seem to be the remains of an ancient reservoir. *Note:* If you want to see the archeological sites on **Wetherill Mesa,** you'll be parking at the ranger kiosk and hopping on the tram. See "Getting Around," above.

ORGANIZED TOURS & RANGER PROGRAMS

Three of the park's spectacular cliff dwellings—Cliff Palace, Balcony House, and Long House—can be visited only during ranger-guided tours. Tickets ($3 per person, regardless of age) can be purchased at the Visitor Center, Morefield Ranger Station, and the Colorado Welcome Center in Cortez. Visitors may tour Long House and either Cliff Palace or Balcony House on the same day, but not tour both Cliff Palace and Balcony House in a day.

The 1-hour **Cliff Palace tour** ★★★ involves a 100-vertical-foot descent to the dwelling and a climb to the same height to exit. In between, you'll have to scale four 10-foot-high ladders. The effort is well worth it. With 151 rooms and 23 kivas, Cliff Palace is the largest cliff dwelling in the Southwest and one of the largest in the world. Especially striking is the original red-and-white wall painting inside a four-story tower.

what's in a NAME?

The prehistoric inhabitants of the ancient villages of the Four Corners region have long been known as the **Anasazi.** That word is being phased out, however, in favor of the terms **"ancestral Puebloans"** or **"ancestral Pueblo people,"** because modern American Indians who trace their roots to the ancestral Puebloans consider the word *Anasazi* demeaning. *Anasazi* is a Navajo word that means "enemy of my people" (the Navajos considered the ancestral Puebloans their enemies).

Merely reaching the 45-room **Balcony House ★**, the most fortresslike of the Mesa Verde dwellings, will make you appreciate the agility of the ancestral Puebloans, who used hand- and footholds and log ladders to scale the cliffs. During the 1-hour tour, you'll descend 90 vertical feet of stairs, climb 32- and 20-foot-long ladders, and slip through a narrow 12-foot-long crawl space.

Some people remember the **Long House tour ★★** for its .75-mile walk, the flight of 52 stairs, and the two 15-foot-high ladders they climb. Others recall the dwelling itself, with its 21 kivas and 150 rooms stretching across a long alcove. At its center is a large plaza where the community gathered and danced. Granaries are tucked like mud dauber nests into two smaller alcoves (one above the other) to the rear of the large one. The 90-minute tours meet at the Wetherill Mesa Kiosk.

Cliff Palace tours run from early April to early November, a few weeks longer than the season for Balcony House. Wetherill Mesa, site of Long House, is open only from Memorial Day weekend through Labor Day. During the off season, there are free ranger-guided tours of Spruce Tree House, a self-guided area in summer.

In summer, rangers also lead 90-minute **twilight tours ★★** of Cliff Palace. The 7pm tours are limited to 20 people and cost $10 per person. Tickets are available only at the Visitor Center. Rangers also lead several **guided hikes,** ranging from 2 hours to 8 hours, with charges of $18 to $40 per person for all ages. Tickets can be purchased online at www.recreation.gov or by calling ℰ **877/444-6777.** There are also **free ranger-led walks** daily (sometimes including birding hikes), and **evening programs** at Morefield Campground and Far View lodge (bring a flashlight). Schedules are available at the Visitor Center.

From late spring through early fall, park concessionaire Aramark offers a **bus tour** that includes a few short hikes to archaeological sites on Chapin Mesa. The 4-hour **700 Years Tour ★★** costs $48 for adults, $37 for children 5 to 11, and free for children under 5. Tour tickets are available at Far View Lodge, Far View Terrace, Morefield Campground Store, and online at www.visitmesaverde.com.

DAY HIKES

Check at the visitor center for hours these trails are open. Although none of the trails are strenuous, the 7,000-foot elevation can be tiring for those not used to the altitude.

Shorter Trails on Chapin Mesa

Far View Sites Trail ★★   This gravel trail takes hikers to Far View House and four other small mesa-top villages, plus a dry reservoir, in what was one of the most densely populated areas of the mesa between A.D. 900 and 1300. .75 mile one-way. Easy. Access: 4 miles north of Chapin Mesa Archaeological Museum.

Spruce Tree House Trail ★★★ This paved walk takes you to Spruce Tree House, a dwelling with 130 rooms and 8 kivas. Because Spruce Tree House sits in an 89-foot-deep alcove, this is the best-preserved dwelling at Mesa Verde. Rangers are here to answer questions during high season. Off season, guided tours are offered here. The trail is accessible to those with wheelchairs, although they may require assistance on some of its grades. .25 mile one-way. Easy. Access: Chapin Mesa Archaeological Museum.

Longer Trails on Chapin Mesa

Several backcountry trails on Chapin Mesa are open to day hikers. Before hiking either of these two trails, register at the trail head or museum where you can buy a booklet for the self-guided tour on the Petroglyph Point Loop.

Petroglyph Point Loop Trail ★★★ This trail travels just below the rim of a side canyon of Spruce Canyon. It eventually reaches Petroglyph Point, one of the park's most impressive panels of rock art. Just past the petroglyphs, the trail climbs to the rim. It stays on the relatively flat rimrock for its return to the Chapin Mesa Archaeological Museum. 2.4 miles RT. Moderate. Access: Short paved trail to Spruce Tree House site, just below Chapin Mesa Archaeological Museum and Chief Ranger Station.

Spruce Canyon Trail ★★ This loop descends 500 feet into a tributary of Spruce Canyon. Turning to the north, it travels up the bed of Spruce Canyon before climbing in steep switchbacks to the rim. It reaches the rim near the park's picnic area, a short walk from the Chapin Mesa Archaeological Museum. The vegetation along the bottom of the canyon includes Douglas firs and ponderosa pines, which flourish in the moist canyon bottom soil. 2.4 miles RT. Moderate. Access: Short paved trail to Spruce Tree House site, just below Chapin Mesa Archaeological Museum and Chief Ranger Station.

Trails on Wetherill Mesa

Badger House Community Trail ★★ This trail visits mesa-top sites on Wetherill Mesa. Usually uncrowded, the gravel and paved trail is accessible from one of three tram stops or by making a longer walk from the parking area. The 12-stop self-guided tour details 600 years of history. 2.4 mile RT. Easy. Access: Wetherill Mesa Kiosk.

Nordenskiold Site No. 16 Trail ★★ Begin this quiet hike by taking the tram to its trailhead or walking from the parking area. Mostly flat, the dirt trail descends over rocks for the last few yards before it reaches an overlook of Site No. 16, a 50-room cliff dwelling. 2 miles RT. Easy. Access: Wetherill Mesa Kiosk.

Trails Near Morefield Campground

Knife Edge Trail ★★ This trail follows the old Knife Edge Road, the only automobile route into the park until a tunnel was blasted in 1957. Now, during wet years, wildflowers brighten the old roadbed, which hugs the side of Prater Ridge on one side and drops off all the way to the Montezuma Valley on the other. A self-guided tour identifies many of the plants along the way. From the trail's end you can watch the sun set behind Sleeping Ute Mountain. 2 miles RT. Easy. Access: Near Morefield Village.

Point Lookout Trail ★ This trail rises in tight switchbacks from the northeast corner of the campground to the top of Point Lookout, a monument conspicuous from near the park's entrance. It then traverses the top of this butte to a stunning overlook of the Montezuma Valley. Sheer drops in several places make the trail unsuitable for small children. 2.2 miles RT. Moderate. Access: Near Morefield Village.

CAMPING options

The Morefield Campground ★★, operated by park concessionaire Aramark (www.visitmesaverde.com; *ℂ* **800/449-2288**), has 267 sites, including 15 with full RV hookups. It's fully open from early May to mid-October, and open for primitive camping for a few weeks at the beginning and end of the season. The campground sits on rolling hills in a grassy area with scrub oak and brush, and at dusk on most nights mule deer browse in the bushes.

Showers are available just outside the campground entrance at Morefield Village, which also has a coin-operated laundry (not within easy walking distance of most campsites). The campground has toilets, drinking water, and an RV dump station. Campsites cost $25, $35 with hookups. Reservations are available for sites without hookups and strongly recommended for the sites with hookups.

WHERE TO STAY

If you don't stay in the park you'll likely be bedding down in Cortez. Contact the chamber of commerce there for information. See "Visitors Centers & Information," above.

Inside the Park

Far View Lodge ★★   This is the best place to stay while exploring Mesa Verde because it's in the park where everything is happening. The standard rooms are just that—standard motel rooms—although the colorful bedspreads and light-colored furnishings make them appealing. Most standard rooms have one queen-sized bed or two doubles, and private balconies, but do not have air conditioning. The nicer "Kiva" rooms have air-conditioning plus more upscale furnishings, private balconies, and one king-sized or two double beds. Neither type has TVs, and smoking is not permitted.

Mesa Verde National Park. Aramark, P.O. Box 277, Mancos. *ℂ* **800/449-2288.** www.visitmesaverde.com. 150 units. $125–$158 double; about $25 less at the beginning of the season. Closed late Oct to mid-Apr. Pets accepted in standard rooms with deposit and $10 fee per pet per night. **Amenities:** 2 restaurants; free Wi-Fi.

WHERE TO EAT

Inside the Park

In addition to the three below, the campground serves an all-you-can-eat pancake breakfast in summer.

Far View Terrace Café ★ AMERICAN/REGIONAL   This looks like a shopping mall food court, but the food is better, in part because visitors get to play a hand in its preparation. We especially like the build-your-own breakfast burrito and omelet bar in the morning and the create-your-own sandwich bar for lunch. There's a pasta and salad buffet at dinner, plus a variety of regional specialties such as the Navajo taco.

Picnic & Camping Supplies

A **general store** in Morefield Village sells camping supplies and groceries from late April through late October.

Across from the Visitor Center, near Far View Lodge. Buffets $10–$15. Daily 7–10am, 11am–3pm, 5–8pm. Closed mid-Oct to early May.

Metate Room Restaurant ★★ SOUTHWESTERN Big windows provide splendid views, and the kitchen serves up the best food in the park at this casually elegant restaurant. It specializes in ancestral Puebloan–inspired dishes, using wild game, corn, squash, and beans; as well as variations on contemporary favorites. Specialties include our top choice, the mixed grill, which might include elk or wild turkey in a red chile cilantro demi glace; the elk shepherd's pie with roasted corn and black beans; or the pan seared blue corn and pine nut dusted trout. There are also vegetarian items. Reservations aren't accepted, so get there early during high season.

Far View Lodge, across from the Visitor Center, 17 miles down the park entrance road. Main courses $16–$34. Daily 5–9:30pm. Closed late Oct to mid-Apr.

Spruce Tree Terrace Café ★ AMERICAN At this busy cafeteria you'll pick up your food and either find a table in the dining room or head outside to the patio for grand views of the park. The most popular item here is the Navajo taco, but you can also choose from fast-food staples such as hamburgers, hot dogs, and salads.

Across from Chapin Mesa Archaeological Museum. Most items $6–$11. Late May to mid-Aug daily 9am–6:30pm; shorter hours the rest of the year.

NEARBY ATTRACTIONS

The **Four Corners** area—where the states of Colorado, New Mexico, Arizona, and Utah meet—is the most important archaeological area of the United States, and has dozens of archeological sites outside Mesa Verde National Park.

Among sites you may want to check out is **Hovenweep National Monument,** which preserves some of the most striking and isolated archaeological sites in this area. *Hovenweep* is the Ute word for "deserted valley," appropriate because its inhabitants apparently left around A.D. 1300. The monument contains six separate sites and is noted for mysterious, 20-foot-high sandstone towers, some square, others oval, circular, or D-shaped. A ranger station, with exhibits, restrooms, and drinking water, is at the **Square Tower Group,** in the Utah section of the monument, the most impressive and best preserved of the sites. Also there is a campground, open year-round. For information, contact **Hovenweep National Monument,** (✆ 970/562-4282, ext. 10; www.nps.gov/hove).

Set aside by the Ute Mountain tribe to preserve its heritage, **Ute Mountain Tribal Park** includes wall paintings, ancient petroglyphs, and hundreds of surface sites and cliff dwellings that are similar in size to those in Mesa Verde. Access to the park is limited to guided tours, which start at the **Ute Mountain Visitor Center & Museum** (✆ 970/749-1452) at the junction of U.S. 491 and U.S. 160, 20 miles south of Cortez. Contact **Ute Mountain Tribal Park** (✆ 800/847-5485; www.utemountainute.com/tribalpark.htm) for details.

A stunning setting and well-preserved ruins make the long drive to **Chaco Culture National Historical Park** in northwestern New Mexico worthwhile. The stark desert seems strange as a center of culture, but the ancient ancestral Puebloan people (the group here are also called Chacoans) successfully farmed and built elaborate structures. From about A.D. 850 to 1250, Chaco was the religious and economic center of the area, with 2,000 to 5,000 residents. The stone walls of their buildings rose more than four stories high, and some are still in place today. The key ruin is **Pueblo Bonito,** one of the largest prehistoric dwellings excavated in the American Southwest with 800 rooms covering more than 3 acres. The primary entrance is off **U.S. 550** and San Juan County roads 7900 and 7950, but check the park's website for recommended routes. For information, contact **Chaco Culture National Historical Park** (✆ 505/786-7014; www.nps.gov/chcu).

YOSEMITE

by Eric Peterson

Yosemite's sky-scraping geologic formations, lush meadows, swollen rivers, and spectacular waterfalls make it a destination for travelers from around the world. It's home to three of the world's 10 highest waterfalls and the largest single piece of exposed granite anywhere, not to mention one of the world's largest trees and the most recognized rock formation.

The greatest thing about all this is that you don't have to be a mountaineer to enjoy the beauty. Yosemite's most popular attractions are accessible to everyone. No matter where you go, you'll see a view worth remembering. In the span of a mile, you can behold the quiet beauty of a forest, walk through a pristine meadow, observe a sunset from a towering granite cliff, hike to a half-mile-high waterfall, enjoy a moonlit night as bright as day, climb a rock, and eat a gourmet meal.

Yosemite Valley, the destination of 95% of park visitors (more than three million people a year), is just a small sliver of the park—around 1% of its land area—but it holds the bulk of the region's jaw-dropping features. This is the place of record-setting statistics: the highest waterfall in North America and three of the tallest in the world (Upper Yosemite, Sentinel, and Ribbon falls), the biggest and tallest piece of exposed granite (El Capitan), and stands of giant sequoia.

The flip side is that 94% of the park is designated wilderness, and only a tiny fraction of visitors dive into it. While Yosemite is in some ways being loved to death, there are plenty of hiking destinations that will take you away from the roar of traffic and the crush of the crowds to places you can have, if just for one perfect moment, all to yourself.

FLORA & FAUNA

Yosemite is not Yellowstone—it is better known for geology than biology—but it has **black bears, deer, numerous bird species,** and a few stands of **giant sequoia trees.** Tuolumne Meadows is rife with **wildflowers** in spring, especially following a wet winter.

ESSENTIALS

Getting There & Gateways

Yosemite is a 3½-hour drive from San Francisco and a 6-hour drive from Los Angeles. From the west, the Big Oak Flat Entrance is 88 miles from Manteca on **Calif. 120** and passes through the towns of Groveland, Buck Meadows, and Big Oak Flat. The Arch Rock Entrance is 75 miles northeast of Merced on **Calif. 140** and passes through Mariposa and El Portal. The

Yosemite National Park

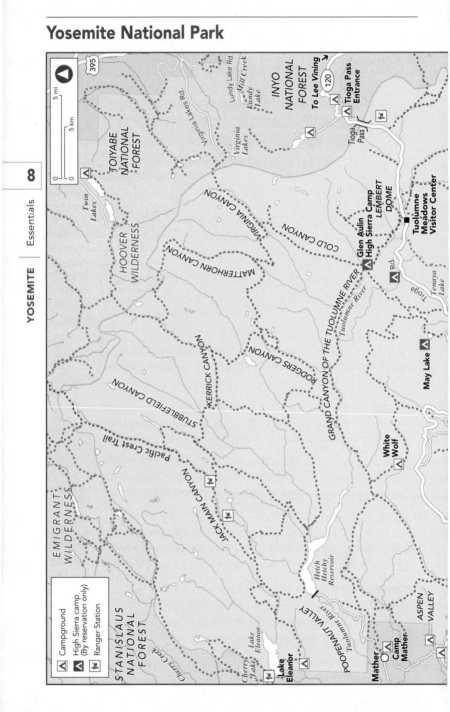

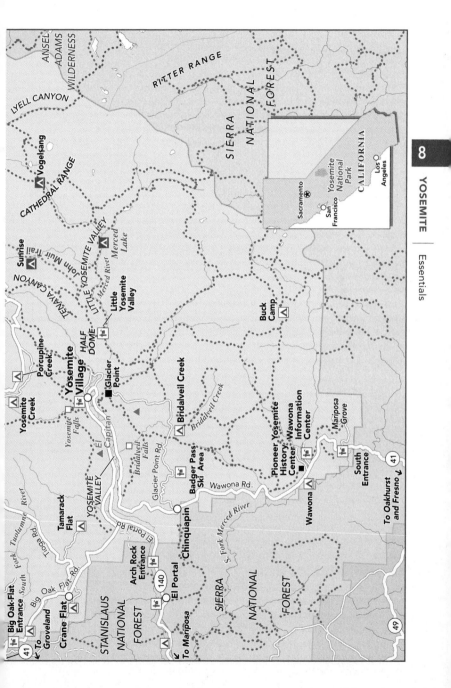

AVOIDING the crowds

Yosemite has its highest number of visitors during summer, especially during school vacations, so the best advice for avoiding crowds is to go when schools are in session. The campgrounds and lodgings are often full from June through August, and you can expect some crowds in late spring and early fall as well. Because of Yosemite's proximity to California's population centers, you'll also want to try to avoid weekends, especially holiday weekends. Winter is a great time to visit Yosemite—not only is the park almost empty, but it offers a number of activities, from skiing at Badger Pass to sledding, ice-skating, and snowshoeing. Keep in mind that the high country along Tioga Pass Road is inaccessible to vehicles from mid-fall to early June, depending on snow levels.

Other ways to avoid humanity at any time of the year are to explore the less-visited sections of the park—which generally means anywhere outside Yosemite Valley—and to walk away from the crowds by getting out on the trails. The farther you go from the trail heads, the fewer people you'll encounter. Time of day is also important. Most people tour the park between 10am and 4pm, meaning that early morning, late afternoon, and early evening are the best times to see the park.

South Entrance is 64 miles north of Fresno and passes through Oakhurst, Bass Lake, and Fish Camp. From the east, the Tioga Pass Entrance is the only option. It is 10 miles west of Lee Vining on Calif. 120; the route is usually open only in the summer.

Daily bus transportation into the park from Merced, Mariposa, and nearby communities is provided by **YARTS,** the **Yosemite Area Regional Transportation System** (© 877/989-2787; www.yarts.com). Buses are not subject to park entrance delays during peak season.

THE NEAREST AIRPORTS **Fresno–Yosemite International Airport** (© 559/621-4500; www.flyfresno.com), 90 miles from the South Entrance at Wawona, is the nearest major airport.

Visitor Centers & Information

In the park, the best and biggest visitor center is the **Valley Visitor Center** in Yosemite Village (© 209/372-0200). The year-round center offers tour information, daily ranger programs, lodging, and restaurants. The rangers here are helpful, insightful, and knowledgeable. Inside, information boards update road conditions and campsite availability, and serve as message boards. Maps, books, and videos are for sale; the free park newspaper, the *Yosemite Guide,* is a vital source of information. There are several exhibits on the park, its geologic history, and the history of the valley. Nearby is **Yosemite Valley Wilderness Center,** a small room with high-country maps, information on necessary equipment, and trail information. A ranger at the desk answers questions and issues permits. Elsewhere, the **Wawona Information Station** and **Big Oak Flat Information Center** dispense general park information. In the high country, stop at the **Tuolumne Meadows Visitor Center** for information and advice.

For advance-of-your-trip advice, contact **Yosemite National Park** (© 209/372-0200; www.nps.gov/yose). The **Yosemite Conservancy** (© 209/379-2317; www.yosemiteconservancy.org) sells relevant books and supports the park.

Fees & Permits

It costs $20 per vehicle per week to enter the park, or $10 per person per week if arriving on bike or on foot. Camping costs $5 to $20 a night. Camping in the backcountry and fishing both require permits.

Seasons & Climate

For general information on the climate of Yosemite, see the "Seasons & Climate" section of chapter 9, which covers nearby Sequoia and Kings Canyon parks. The climate there is similar to Yosemite's. The high country in Yosemite receives up to 20 feet of snow annually, and visitors who plan a winter trip should be well experienced in winter travel.

EXPLORING THE PARK

It's relatively easy to find your way around Yosemite. You'll soon realize that everything leads to a one-way road that hugs the valley's perimeter. To get from one side to the other, you can either drive the entire loop or travel one of the few bridges over the Merced River. It's easy to find yourself heading in the wrong direction on the one-way road, so be alert whenever you merge.

In addition to the year-round shuttle bus in Yosemite Valley, Wawona, and Tuolumne Meadows offer a similar service during summer months. Driving in any of these places during peak season—or even off-season in the valley—is a surefire way to miss important sights and spend too much time stuck in traffic.

Yosemite Valley

Many people come to Yosemite National Park solely to see Yosemite Valley, which can be simply described as a giant study in shadow and light. In spring, after winter snow begins melting in the high country, waterfalls encircle the valley, shimmering like a diamond necklace. There are wide, beautiful meadows, towering trees, and the ever-present sound of rushing water in the background.

Yosemite Valley consists of three developed areas. Just about all the hotels, restaurants, and shops are in **Yosemite Village, Yosemite Lodge,** and **Curry Village.** Curry Village (also called Camp Curry) and Yosemite Lodge offer the bulk of the park's overnight accommodations. Yosemite Lodge is at stop no. 8.

Yosemite Village is the most-developed region in the valley. It is home to the park's largest visitor center. The village has a host of stores and shops, including a grocery, restaurants, the valley's only medical clinic, a dentist, a post office, a salon, and an ATM.

Also check out the **Yosemite Pioneer Cemetery,** a peaceful graveyard in the shade of tall sequoias with headstones dating from the 1800s. There are about 36 marked graves, identifiable by horizontal slabs of rock, some etched with crude or faded writing. Buried here are some notables in Yosemite history, such as James Lamon, an early settler known for his apple trees—they still bear fruit—who died in 1875.

Next door, you'll find the **Yosemite Museum** and **Indian Cultural Exhibit.** Both are free and provide a historic picture of the park, before and after it was settled and secured as a national treasure. The museum entrance is marked by a crowd-pleaser—the cross-section of a 1,000-year-old sequoia with memorable dates identified on the tree's rings. Highlights include the signing of the Magna Carta in 1215, the landing of Columbus in the New World, and the Civil War. The ring was cut in 1919 from a tree that fell in the Mariposa Grove south of the valley in Wawona. The Indian Cultural

Special Regulations & Warnings

In addition to the usual regulations about not damaging the natural resources, staying on established trails, and the like, special regulations at Yosemite are aimed at protecting the park's **bear** population, which has become much too familiar with the habits of humans. Under no circumstances should food be left in tents, cabins, or cars. There are storage lockers and bear-proof containers throughout the park—use them. Never feed a bear, or any animal, for that matter.

Exhibit strives to explain the life of the American Indians who once lived here, and members of regional tribes regularly speak or give demonstrations of traditional arts.

The village of the **Ahwahneechee** is behind the museum and Indian Cultural Exhibit; a free self-guided walking tour is accessible from the back door of the visitor center. This exhibit guides visitors through the transformation of the Ahwahneechee, the tribe that inhabited Yosemite Valley until the mid-1850s.

The **Ansel Adams Gallery** (© **888/361-7622** or 209/372-4413; www.anseladams. com) sells prints and cards of images made by the famed photographer. The shop also serves as a small gallery for current artisans, some with works for sale.

One mile east of Yosemite Village on a narrow, dead-end road is the majestic old **Ahwahnee** hotel (see p. 106), a must for fans of design.

The **LeConte Memorial Lodge** is an educational center and library. Built in 1903 in honor of University of California geologist Joseph LeConte, the Tudor-style granite building schedules educational programs. Talks are listed in the *Yosemite Guide.*

At the valley's far eastern end, beyond Curry Village, is the **Happy Isles Nature Center.** In summer, the nature center offers exhibits and books on the animal and plant life of Yosemite and is a super place for children to explore. This is also where the park's Little Cub and Junior Ranger programs are held. Happy Isles is named for three nearby inlets labeled by Yosemite's guardian in 1880.

North of the Valley

Hetch Hetchy and **Tuolumne Meadows** are remarkably different regions on opposite sides of the park. Hetch Hetchy is on the western border; take the turnoff just outside the park's Big Oak Flat Entrance. Tuolumne Meadows is on the eastern border, just inside Tioga Pass, and is inaccessible by motor vehicle during the winter.

Hetch Hetchy is home to the park's reviled reservoir, fought over for years by conservationist John Muir. In the end, Muir lost and the dam was built, ensuring water for the city of San Francisco. Many believe the loss exhausted Muir and hastened his death in 1914, a year after a bill was signed to fund the dam project. Construction began on the dam in 1919, and it was completed in 1923.

South of Hetch Hetchy, inside the park, are two large stands of giant sequoias. The Merced and Tuolumne groves offer a quiet alternative to the Mariposa Grove of Big Trees in Wawona. Both groves are accessible only on foot. The **Merced Grove** is a 4-mile round-trip walk that begins on Big Oak Flat Road inside the Big Oak Flat Entrance. Although the trees don't mirror the majesty of the Mariposa Grove, the solitude makes this area a real treat for hikers.

To get into Yosemite's **high country,** go about 1½ hours east along Tioga Road, which is closed in winter between Big Oak Flat and Tioga Pass. This subalpine region is low on amenities, which makes it a frequent haunt of those who enjoy roughing it, but even cushy-soft couch potatoes can enjoy the beauty up here. Glistening granite domes tower above lush green meadows, which are cut by silver swaths of streams and lakes. Many of Yosemite's longer hikes begin or pass through here.

Olmsted Point, midway between White Wolf and Tuolumne Meadows, offers one of the most spectacular vistas anywhere in the park. Here the enormous walls of the Tenaya Canyon are exposed, and an endless view stretches all the way to Yosemite Valley. In the distance are Cloud's Rest and the rear of Half Dome. To the east, easily accessible Tenaya Lake, one of the park's larger lakes, glistens like a sapphire.

About 8 miles east of Tenaya Lake is **Tuolumne Meadows,** a huge subalpine area surrounded by domes and steep granite formations that offer exhilarating climbs. The meadow is a beautiful place to hike and fish, or just to admire the scenery while escaping the crowds of Yosemite Valley. North of the meadow is Lembert Dome at about 2 o'clock, and then, working clockwise, Johnson Peak at 7 o'clock, Unicorn Peak at 8 o'clock, Fairview Dome at about 10 o'clock, and Pothole Dome at 11 o'clock. Up the road is the central region of Tuolumne, where you'll find a visitor center, campground, canvas tent-cabins, and a store. Continue east to reach Tioga Lake and Tioga Pass.

South of the Valley

This region, which includes Wawona and the Mariposa Grove of Big Trees, is densely forested. It has a handful of granite rock formations, none as spectacular as those found elsewhere in the park. En route to Wawona you'll come across several wonderful views of Yosemite Valley. **Tunnel View,** a turnout just before the tunnel to Wawona, provides one of the park's most recognizable vistas, memorialized by Ansel Adams. To the right is Bridalveil Fall, opposite El Capitan. Half Dome lies straight ahead.

Halfway between Yosemite Valley and Wawona is Glacier Point Road (closed in winter past the turnoff to Badger Pass Ski Area), which runs 16 miles to spectacular **Glacier Point.** From the parking area, it's a short hike to an amazing overlook that provides a view of the glacier-carved granite rock formations all along the valley and beyond. You will be at eye level with **Half Dome,** which looks close enough to reach out and touch. Far below, Yosemite Valley resembles a green-carpeted ant farm.

Continue south on Wawona Road to reach **Wawona,** a historic small town 30 miles from the valley. It was settled in 1856 by homesteader Galen Clark, who built a rustic waystation for travelers en route from Mariposa to Yosemite. The property's next owners, the Washburn brothers, built much of what is today the Wawona Hotel, including the large white building to the right of the main hotel, which was constructed in 1876. As Yosemite grew in popularity, so did Wawona. When Wawona was added to the park in 1932, it was allowed to remain under private ownership.

Nearby, the **Mariposa Grove** is a stand of giant sequoias, some of which have been around for 3,000 years. They stretch almost 300 feet tall, are 50 feet in circumference, and weigh an average of 2 million pounds. The 500 trees here are divided into the Upper Grove and the Lower Grove. The easiest way to see the trees is from the open-air tram (© **209/372-4386**) that runs during summer. Cost is $26.50 for adults, $25 for seniors, and $19 for children; kids under 5 ride free. Trams leave from the Mariposa Grove parking area; call for current hours. A guide provides commentary during the trip, which lasts about an hour. It makes regular stops at the Grizzly Giant, Wawona Tunnel Tree, and Mariposa Grove Museum. It's worth hopping out and walking around as often as possible. Just take the next tram back. All of the area is also accessible on foot. It is an uphill walk to the upper grove, 2.5 miles each way.

The Grizzly Giant is the largest tree in the grove. At "just" 200 feet, it is shorter than some of its neighbors, but its trunk measures more than 30 feet in diameter at the base. A huge limb halfway up measures 6 feet in diameter and is bigger than many of the "young" trees in the grove.

ORGANIZED TOURS & RANGER PROGRAMS

The park offers a number of **ranger-guided walks, hikes, and other programs.** Check at one of the visitor centers or the park newspaper for current topics, start times, and locations. Walks may vary from week to week, but you can always count on nature hikes, evening discussions, and photo workshops aimed at replicating some of Ansel Adams's works.

Southern Yosemite Mountain Guides (✆ 800/231-4575; www.symg.com) runs hiking, backpacking, fishing, and rock-climbing trips. A day hiking trip usually runs $350 to $400 for up to six people. DNC's **Yosemite Mountaineering** (✆ 209/372-8344; www.yosemitemountaineering.com) offers a variety of guided group hikes covering 2 to 8 miles for $20 to $80 per person.

Guided bus tours are also available. You can buy tickets at tour desks at Yosemite Lodge, the Ahwahnee, Curry Village, or beside the Village Store in Yosemite Village. Advance reservations are suggested for all tours; space can be reserved in person or by phone (✆ 209/372-4386; www.yosemitepark.com). Adult prices range from $25 for a 2-hour tour to $95 for a full-day trip with lunch. Children's rates are usually half that, and discounts are also offered for seniors.

Spring through fall, the **Yosemite Theater** offers inexpensive theatrical and musical programs. Favorites include a conversation with noted John Muir impersonator Lee Stetson, films on Yosemite, and musical performances.

The nonprofit **Yosemite Conservancy** (✆ 209/379-2317; www.yosemiteconservancy.org) offers dozens of **Outdoor Adventures,** covering subjects from backpacking to natural history to photography. Most of the programs are multiday, with charges of about $100 per person per day (not including lodging and meals), and often include hikes or backpacking trips.

DAY HIKES

A nature-lover's paradise, Yosemite has some of the most beautiful scenery anywhere, and the best way to experience the park is to get out onto the trails.

In & Near the Valley

Columbia Rock ★★   This hike mirrors the initial ascent of the waterfall trail but stops at Columbia Rock, 1,000 feet above the valley. You won't have a valley view, but the sights here are still impressive. The trail is also less likely to get an accumulation of snow, because it's on the sunny side of the valley. 2 miles RT. Moderate. Access: Trail head for Upper Yosemite Fall.

Four-Mile Trail to Glacier Point ★★   This trail climbs 3,200 feet, but your efforts will be rewarded with terrific views of Yosemite Valley's north rim. Check on current trail conditions before setting out; it's usually closed in winter. The trail ends at Glacier Point. If you'd like to extend the hike, you can connect there to the

Panorama Trail. You can also catch a shuttle ($25) back. The combined round-trip distance is 14 miles. 9.6 miles RT. Strenuous. Access: Trail head 1.25 miles from Yosemite Village, at Four Mile parking area.

Half Dome ★★★ About 1,000 hikers do this long, steep trail *each summer day*, despite the fact that it climbs 4,900 feet. From Happy Isles, take the Mist Trail or the John Muir Trail past Vernal and Nevada falls, and up into Little Yosemite Valley. Leave the John Muir Trail for the Half Dome Trail. Hiking the final 600 feet up the back of Half Dome requires the use of cables—and a strong heart is helpful, too. Half Dome has a small level spot on top, at an elevation of 8,800 feet. It's possible to cut the length of the trip by camping in Little Yosemite Valley (you'll need a wilderness permit). 17 miles RT. Very strenuous. Access: Happy Isles (shuttle bus stop no. 16).

Mist Trail to Vernal Fall ★★ This hike begins on the famous 211-mile John Muir Trail to Mount Whitney in Sequoia National Park. From the Happy Isles Bridge, the trail climbs 400 feet to the Vernal Fall Bridge, which offers a good view of what lies ahead, as well as water and restrooms. From this point, you can either take switchbacks along the side of the mountain and come out above the fall, or ascend the Mist Trail (my preference), which is a steep climb with 500 steps—it's wet, picturesque, and refreshing (the spray from the fall drenches anyone who tackles this route, especially in spring). You can continue up 1.2 miles to Nevada Fall and leave the crowds behind for a round-trip of 5.4 miles. 3 miles RT. Moderate to strenuous. Access: From Happy Isles (shuttle bus stop no. 16), walk to Happy Isles Bridge. Cross bridge and follow signs to the trail.

Upper Yosemite Fall ★★★ Climb 2,700 feet on this trail and you'll be rewarded with spectacular views from the ledge above the fall. This hike is not for the faint of heart. Take it slow, and rest often. One mile up, you'll reach Columbia Rock, which offers a good view. The rest of the trail dips and climbs, and you'll get a bit of mist from the fall above. The last quarter mile is rocky and steep, with a series of tortuous, seemingly endless switchbacks that ascend through underbrush before opening at a clearing near the top of the fall, but beware—the view here can induce vertigo. After completing the trail, it's a worthwhile walk upstream to see the creek before it takes its half-mile tumble to the valley floor below. Hikers with the proper permits and equipment can stay here overnight. 7.2 miles RT. Strenuous. Access: Shuttle bus stop no. 7; trail head next to Camp 4 Walk-in Campground, behind Yosemite Lodge.

South of the Valley

Chilnualna Falls from Wawona ★★ This trek offers a satisfying glimpse of a stunning waterfall. One of the tallest outside Yosemite Valley, the fall cascades down two chutes. The one at the bottom is narrower and packs a real punch after a wet winter. A series of switchbacks leads to the top fall. 8.2 miles RT. Moderate. Access: From Wawona, take Chilnualna Rd., just north of the Merced River's south fork, until it dead-ends at "The Redwoods," a little more than 1.25 miles. This is the trail head.

Grizzly Giant ★★ The walking alternative to the Mariposa Grove tram tour (p. 99), it's a nice stroll to see an impressive tree, and the hike climbs only 400 feet. 1.6 miles RT. Easy. Access: Sign near map dispenser at east end of Mariposa Grove parking lot.

Mariposa Grove ★★ The hike sounds long, but a one-way option in the summer uses the Wawona shuttle bus service for the return trip, cutting the distance almost in half. The trail climbs through a forest, then ascends the Wawona Dome and Wawona Basin, both of which provide excellent views. 12 miles RT. Moderate to strenuous. Access: Park at Wawona Store parking area and walk east .25 mile to Forest Dr. Trail head is on the right.

Sentinel Dome ★★★   Take this one for broad views of Yosemite Valley. At the starting point, you'll be able to see Sentinel Dome on your left. The trail descends slightly and, at the first fork, bears right. It winds through manzanita and pine before beginning its ascent. It's a steep scramble to the top of Sentinel Dome, and you have to leave the trail on the north side to scramble up. The view from the top offers a 180-degree panorama of Yosemite Valley that includes a host of impressive and recognizable geologic landmarks. 2.2 miles RT. Moderate. Access: Glacier Point Rd. to Sentinel Dome parking lot, about 3 miles from Glacier Point.

North of the Valley

Cathedral Lakes ★★   These lakes are set in granite bowls cut by glaciers, and the views of the peaks and domes around both Lower and Upper Cathedral lakes are worth the hike alone. Lower Cathedral Lake is next to Cathedral Peak and is a good place to stop for a snack before heading up the hill to enjoy the upper lake. 8 miles RT. Moderate. Access: Trail head off Tioga Rd., at west end of Tuolumne Meadows, west of Budd Creek.

Cloud's Rest ★★★   This hike descends through a wooded area, heading toward Sunrise Lake. Ascend out of Tenaya Canyon and bear right at the junction (watch for the signposts); the vistas will appear almost at once. The last stretch to the top is a little spooky, with sheer drops on each side, but your perseverance will be amply rewarded with spectacular views of the park's granite domes. Overnight stays (with a permit) offer the added incentive of beautiful sunrises. 14 miles RT. Strenuous. Access: Tioga Rd. to Tenaya Lake. Trail leaves from parking area on east side of road near southwest end of lake.

Glen Aulin ★★★   This hike takes you to an impressive waterfall with grand views along the way. Start by heading across a flat meadow toward Soda Springs and Glen Aulin. The hike offers a view of the landmarks of Tuolumne Meadows. Behind you, Lembert Dome rises almost 900 feet above the meadow. About .4 mile from the trail head, the road forks; head right up a grassy slope. In less than 500 feet is a trail that leaves the road on the right and a steel sign that says GLEN AULIN IS 4.7 MILES AHEAD. Along the way you'll pass Fairview Dome, Cathedral Peak, and Unicorn Peak. The crashing noise you'll hear in early to midsummer is Tuolumne Falls, a cascade of water that drops first 12 feet, then 40 feet down a series of ledges. There's a hikers' camp nearby if you want to spend the night. 11 miles RT. Strenuous. Access: Tioga Rd. toward Tuolumne Meadows, about 1 mile east of Tuolumne Meadows Visitor Center and just a few yards east of the bridge over Tuolumne River. Follow marked turnoff and take the paved road on your left. The trail head begins about .3 mile ahead, at a road that turns right and heads up a hill toward the stables.

Lembert Dome ★★   This hike offers a bird's-eye view of Tuolumne Meadows—and it's a great vista. A well-marked trail leads you to the top, and from there you'll see the peaks that encircle the valley and get good views of this lovely meadow. It's a great place to watch sunrises and sunsets. 2.8 miles RT. Moderate. Access: Trail head at parking lot north of Tioga Rd. in Tuolumne Meadows, at road marker T-32. Follow nature trail that starts here and take off at marker no. 2.

Lyell Canyon ★★   This section of the John Muir Trail follows the Lyell Fork of the Tuolumne River up an idyllic green canyon to the rocky Donohue Pass, nearly 12 miles from the trail head and over 2,000 feet above it. While this is a good starting point for a backcountry expedition, a shorter hike up Lyell Canyon—say, 3 miles each way—is perfect for a picnic-centered day hike for most any group of hikers. Backpackers can continue into the Ansel Adams Wilderness Area; day hikers loop back through the Vogelsang area. Up to 12 miles one-way. Easy to strenuous. The trail head is at the Dog Lake parking lot near Tuolumne Meadows Lodge.

Mono Pass ★ You'll pass some historical cabin sites, then hike down to Walker Lake, and return by the same route. The hike loops into the Inyo National Forest and the Ansel Adams Wilderness, and it climbs to an elevation of 10,600 feet. Hikers enjoy a stupendous view of Mono Lake from the top of the trail. 8 miles RT. Moderate to strenuous. Access: Trail head on south side of Tioga Rd. as you enter the park from Lee Vining. Drive about 1.5 miles from park entrance to Dana Meadows, where trail begins on an abandoned road and up alongside Parker Creek Pass.

Mount Dana ★★ This climb is an in-your-face reminder that Mount Dana is Yosemite's second-highest peak. The mountain rises 13,053 feet, and the trail gains a whopping 3,100 feet in 3 miles. The views at the top are wonderful, and once you catch your breath, you can again stand upright. You can see Mono Lake from the summit. In summer, the wildflowers add to this hike's beauty. 7 miles RT. Very strenuous. Access: Trail head on southeast side of Tioga Rd./Calif. 120 at Tioga Pass.

North Dome ★★ Amazing views of Yosemite Valley are the lure with this hike. Walk south down the abandoned road toward the Porcupine Creek Campground. A mile past the campground, the trail hits a junction with the Tenaya Creek and Tuolumne Meadows Trail. Pass a junction toward Yosemite Falls and head uphill toward North Dome. The ascent is treacherous because of loose gravel, but from the top you can catch an all-encompassing view of Yosemite Valley, second only to the view from Half Dome. 10 miles RT. Moderate. Access: Tioga Rd. east to Porcupine Flat Campground, past White Wolf. About 1 mile past campground is a sign for Porcupine Creek, at a closed road. Park in designated area.

Polly Dome Lake ★★ Easily the road least traveled, this hike to Polly Dome Lake is a breeze, and you'll find nary another traveler in sight. Several lakes beneath Polly Dome can accommodate camping. The trail fades in and out, so watch for markers. It crosses a rocky area en route, then skirts southeast at a pond just after the rocky section. Polly Dome Lake is at the base of—you guessed it—Polly Dome, a visual aid to help hikers stay the course. 13 miles RT. Easy to moderate. Access: Tioga Rd. past White Wolf to Tenaya Lake. Drive about .5 mile to picnic area midway along lake. Trail head is across road from picnic area.

Tioga Lake to Dana Lake ★★ This is a less crowded alternative to the hike to Mount Dana; it doesn't top the mountain, although that option is available for experienced hikers on the Mount Dana Trail. The trail is not maintained, although it is fairly visible. This area is easily damaged, so be sure to tread lightly. Mount Dana looms large from the lake's shore. 4.6 miles RT. Moderate to strenuous. Access: Calif. 120 to Tioga Lake. Trail head is on west side of lake, about 1 mile east of the pass.

Vogelsang ★★★ The reward at the end of this hike is a high meadow offering spectacular views. The trail goes south through the woods to a footbridge over the Dana Fork. Cross the bridge and follow the John Muir Trail upstream. Head right at the next fork. The trail crosses the Lyell Fork on a footbridge. Take the left fork a couple hundred feet ahead. Continue onward, and just before you cross the bridge at Rafferty Creek, you'll reach another junction. Veer right and prepare for switchbacks up a rocky slope. The trail climbs steeply for about .25 mile, then levels off as it darts toward and away from Rafferty Creek for the next 4 miles. The trail ascends to Tuolumne Pass, crossing many small creeks and tributaries en route. Two small tarns mark the pass. One drains south and the other north. Just south of the tarns, the trail splits. Veer left. (The right fork offers a 2-mile round-trip jaunt to Boothe Lake.) You'll climb to a meadow with fab views, at 10,180 feet. 14 miles RT. Moderate to strenuous. Access: Tioga Rd. to Tuolumne Meadows; watch for signposted trail head for John Muir Trail and Lyell Fork.

Near Hetch Hetchy

Carlon Falls ★★   This trail off the road to Hetch Hetchy takes visitors through a nicely treed canyon to a year-round waterfall and a swimming hole. It's a bit of a local secret and an escape from the crowds. 4.5 miles. Easy. Access: From the turnoff to Hetch Hetchy, park immediately after the 1st bridge and take the trail west of the river.

Wapama Falls ★★   You'll circumnavigate the shores of Hetch Hetchy from O'Shaughnessy Dam to the powerful Wapama Falls. It is very misty here—be prepared to get drenched. If you continue another 4.2 miles, you make it to another waterfall, popular backpacking destination Rancheria Falls. 5 miles. Moderate. Access: The trail begins at O'Shaughnessy Dam at the end of Hetch Hetchy Rd.

OVERNIGHT HIKES

Of the more than four million people who visit Yosemite each year, 95% never leave the valley, but the brave 5% who do are well rewarded. A wild, lonelier Yosemite awaits just a few miles from the crowds. You'll find some of the most grandiose landscapes in the Sierra, as well as excellent opportunities for backpacking.

All overnight backpacking stays require a **wilderness permit,** available by phone, by mail, by fax, or in the park. Permits can be reserved 2 days to 4 months in advance and cost $5 plus $5 each individual on the permit. You can download a reservation form at www.nps. gov/yose/planyourvisit/wpres.htm to fax it to 209/372-0739, or call ℭ **209/372-0740.**

If planning isn't your style, first-come, first-served permits are available up to 24 hours before your trip. Permit stations are at the Yosemite Valley Visitor Center and Wawona Information Station year-round, and at Big Oak Flat Information Station in Tuolumne Meadows in summer.

OTHER SPORTS & ACTIVITIES

About the only thing you can't do in Yosemite is surf. In addition to sightseeing, the park is a great place to bike, ski, rock-climb, fish, and even golf.

BICYCLING   Twelve miles of designated bike trails cross the eastern end of Yosemite Valley, which is the best place to ride because roads and shuttle bus routes are usually crowded and dangerous for bicyclists. Children under 18 are required by law to wear helmets. Single-speed bikes are for rent by the hour ($12) or the day ($32) at Curry Village in summer only, and at Yosemite Lodge year-round. Bike rentals include helmets. Call ℭ **209/372-4386** for more information.

CROSS-COUNTRY SKIING   The park has more than 350 miles of skiable trails and roads, including 25 miles of machine-groomed track and 90 miles of marked trails in the Badger Pass area. Equipment rentals, lessons, and day and overnight ski tours are available from **Badger Pass Cross-Country Center and Ski School** (ℭ **209/372-8444;** www.yosemitepark.com).

FISHING   Several species of trout can be found in Yosemite's streams. California fishing licenses are required for those 16 and older; information is available from the **California State Department of Fish and Game** (ℭ **831/649-2801;** www.dfg. ca.gov). **Village Sport Shop** in Yosemite Valley has fishing gear and sells licenses.

GOLF   The park has one golf course, at **Wawona** (ℭ **209/375-6572**), a 9-hole, par-35 course that alternates between meadows and fairways. Greens fees are $21 to $26 for 9 holes, and carts are about $20.

HORSEBACK RIDING   Several companies offer guided horseback rides in and just outside the national park, with rates starting at about $64 for 2 hours. **Yosemite Stables** (© **209/372-8348**) offers rides from Yosemite Valley, Tuolumne Meadows, and Wawona; it leads multiday pack trips into the backcountry (call for details). **Yosemite Trails Pack Station** (© **559/683-7611;** www.yosemitetrails.com) offers rides just south of Wawona.

ICE SKATING   The outdoor ice rink at Curry Village, with great views of Half Dome and Glacier Point, is open from early November to March, weather permitting. Admission is $10 for adults, $9 for children; skate rental costs $4.

RAFTING   A raft-rental shop is located at Curry Village (© **209/372-4386**). Daily fees are $30 for a raft, paddles, mandatory life preservers, and transportation from Sentinel Beach to Curry Village. Swift currents and cold water can be deadly. Talk with rangers and shop people before venturing out to be sure you're planning a trip that's within your capabilities.

ROCK CLIMBING   Yosemite is considered one of the world's rock climbing areas. The **Yosemite Mountaineering School** (© **209/372-8344;** www.yosemitemountaineering.com) provides instruction for beginning, intermediate, and advanced climbers in the valley and Tuolumne Meadows from April through October. Classes last anywhere from a day to a week, and private lessons are available. Rates vary according to the class or program. All equipment is provided.

SKIING   Yosemite's **Badger Pass Ski Area** (© **209/372-8430;** www.yosemitepark.com) is usually open from mid-December to early April, weather permitting. This small resort, located 22 miles from Yosemite Valley, was established in 1935, making it the oldest downhill operation in California. There are 10 runs, rated 35% beginner, 50% intermediate, and 15% advanced, plus a terrain park and tubing area, with a vertical drop of 800 feet from the highest point of 8,000 feet. There are five lifts—one triple chair, three double chairs, and a cable tow. Full-day lift tickets cost $40 to $47 for adults, $22 to $40 for kids 7 to 17 (kids under 7 are free). Seniors 65 and over ski free Monday through Thursday. There are ski shuttles from Yosemite Valley and Oakhurst, as well as some great ski-and-stay packages.

Facilities at the ski area include several casual restaurants; a ski shop; ski repairs; a day lodge; lockers; and an excellent ski school, thanks to the late "Ski Ambassador" Nic Fiore, a Yosemite ski legend who arrived in the park in 1947 to ski for a season and never left. Fiore became director of the ski school in 1956, and park officials credit him with making Badger Pass what it is today—a family-oriented ski area where generations have learned the art of skiing.

WHERE TO STAY

Choices abound in and near Yosemite National Park. Yosemite Valley is the hub for lodging, dining, and other services in the park. It is usually quite crowded in summer, but it offers the best location, close to Yosemite's main attractions and with easy access to the park's shuttle bus system. A narrower scope of choices is available outside the valley, but still in the park, during the summer. In addition, there are some delightful (and generally less expensive) accommodations outside the park in the gateway communities of El Portal, Mariposa, Oakhurst, and Groveland.

CAMPING options

Important note: When camping in this area, proper food storage is *required* for the sake of the black bears in the parks, as well as for your safety.

INSIDE THE PARK

For the 13 developed campgrounds, reservations are a really good idea. Reservations are accepted in 1-month blocks beginning on the 15th of each month and can be made up to 5 months in advance (𝒞 877/444-6777; www.recreation.gov). Make your reservations as soon as you can, especially for sites in the valley. Nightly fees range from $5 to $20 per site.

The busiest campgrounds in the park are in Yosemite Valley. All four of the following have flush toilets and access to the showers nearby at Curry Village. **Upper Pines ★** is pretty and shady, but you won't find peace and quiet here in the summer. **Lower Pines Campground ★** is wide open, with lots of shade but limited privacy. Still, it's a nice place with clean bathrooms, and sits just south of a picturesque meadow. **North Pines ★★**, which I particularly like, is beautifully situated beneath a grove of pine trees that offer little privacy but a lot of shade. It's near the river, roughly a mile from Mirror Lake. **Camp 4 ★** (also called Sunnyside Walk-In) has tent sites only. It's a small campground that's become a magnet for hikers and climbers taking off or just returning from trips. It's behind Yosemite Lodge and the trail head for Yosemite Fall, and near rocks frequently used by novice rock climbers. Pets are not permitted.

Elsewhere in the park, **Bridalveil Creek Campground ★** at Glacier Point has flush toilets. Near beautiful Glacier Point, this campground is set off from the valley crowds but a moderate drive from the valley sights. It's along Bridalveil Creek, which flows to Bridalveil Fall, a beauty of a waterfall, especially after a snowy winter or wet spring. The campground can accommodate some pack animals; call park offices for information. Take Wawona Road (from either direction) to Glacier Point Road. The campground is about 8 miles down the road.

Several campgrounds are near Big Oak Flat Entrance, roughly 20 to 25 miles from Yosemite Valley. About 1 mile inside the entrance is **Hodgdon Meadow ★**, which has flush toilets and RV and tent sites,

Inside the Park

Most lodging in the park is under the management of **DNC Parks & Resorts at Yosemite** (𝒞 **801/559-4884;** www.yosemitepark.com). In addition, more than 130 private homes in the park can be rented through the **Redwoods in Yosemite** in Wawona (𝒞 **877/753-8566;** www.redwoodsinyosemite.com). Offerings range from cabins to vacation homes, all furnished and equipped with linens, cookware, and dishes. Summer rates range from about $200 a night for a one-bedroom cabin to $800 or more for a six-bedroom spread; there are usually 3-night minimum stays in summer, 2-night minimums the rest of the year. You'll find a similar operation at **Yosemite West Lodging** (𝒞 **559/642-2211;** www.yosemite westreservations.com), which rents private homes, cottages, and condo units in a forested area in the park about 10 miles from Yosemite Valley and 8 miles from Badger Pass. Nightly rates range from $175 to $325 in summer.

The Ahwahnee ★★★   Steve Jobs, Queen Elizabeth II, Dwight D. Eisenhower, John F. Kennedy, Ronald Reagan, and the Shah of Iran all stayed at the Ahwahnee over the years, and we're guessing they felt it was one of the most magnificent places they'd ever bunked. A masterpiece of "parkitechture," opened in 1927, the Ahwahnee melds including some walk-in sites. It's open all year and requires reservations from May through September. This campground is along North Crane Creek, near the Tuolumne River's south fork. About 8 miles farther, not far from the Tioga Road turnoff, is **Crane Flat ★**, a large but pleasant campground with flush toilets. It's near the Big Trees and away from valley crowds. **Tamarack Flat Campground ★** is a bit off the beaten path and therefore more secluded and less busy than most.

Campgrounds in the White Wolf area include **Porcupine Flat ★**, which has shade, shrubs, and trees, although facilities are pretty much limited to pit toilets. It's near Yosemite Creek; you may find a spot here if you're in a pinch. The **White Wolf Campground ★★**, secluded in a forest, is a delightful campground where you might want to spend several days. It has flush toilets and offers easy access to nearby hiking, with trails that lead to several lakes, including Grant Lake and Lukens Lake. On the down side, mosquitoes make their presence felt here in summer.

Among Yosemite's other campgrounds are **Tuolumne Meadows ★**, the biggest campground in the park and, amazingly, often the least crowded. Its location in the high country makes this a good spot from which to head off with a backpack. It's also near the Tuolumne River, making it a good choice for anglers. In addition to its standard RV and tent sites, the campground has 25 walk-in spaces for backpackers and 8 group sites that can accommodate up to 30 people each. There are flush toilets and showers nearby at Tuolumne Lodge (for a fee).

Wawona Campground ★, which requires reservations from May through September and is first come, first served the rest of the year, has flush toilets and can accommodate pack animals; call park offices for information. There's not much seclusion here, but the location, shaded beneath towering trees, is beautiful. The campground is near the Mariposa Grove of Big Trees and close to the Merced River, which offers some of the better fishing in the park. It's about 1 mile north of Wawona. The **Yosemite Creek Campground ★**, along Yosemite Creek, has pit toilets and little else, but it may have sites available when the park's other campgrounds are full.

Native American, Arts and Crafts, and Art Deco influences into a majestic design, which features hand-stenciled beams, fabulous murals, and in the dining room, 34-foor high windows framed by stained glass. (Not all is as handmade as it seems, though: the exterior only looks wooden—it's actually concrete poured into molds to resemble redwood timbers.) Rooms have a Native American motif with fine wood furnishings, and spectacular views (99 are in the lodge and another 24 are in surrounding cottages). The Ahwahnee plays host to a full calendar of special events, including the Renaissance-inspired Bracebridge Dinner in December and vintner's and chef's holidays throughout the year.

Yosemite Valley. (© **801/559-4884.** www.yosemitepark.com. 123 units. $497–$599 double; $616–$1,226 suite. **Amenities:** Restaurant; bar; outdoor pool; free Wi-Fi.

Curry Village ★   Since 1899, this has been the budget option in Yosemite Valley. The majority of the 500 units are bare-bones canvas tent-cabins that share a communal bathhouse, but there are wooden cabins (with and without private bathrooms) and a few motel-style units. Curry Village is convenient, with everything from groceries to a pool to restaurants, but is a little thin when it comes to modern conveniences. It's also a busy spot, so not exactly the spot to get away from it all, but it can be good pick for families who want a camping-like experience without all of the gear, dirt, and other camping rigmarole.

Yosemite Valley. ℂ **801/559-4884.** www.yosemitepark.com. 500 units. $124–$129 double tent-cabin; $131–$139 double cabin without bathroom; $180–$301 double cabin with bathroom; $199 double motel room. Lower winter rates. **Amenities:** 4 restaurants; outdoor pool; bike rentals; free Wi-Fi.

Housekeeping Camp ★ A smaller version of Curry Village, and here all of the units are canvas tent-cabins with shared bathrooms and no electricity. Onsite is a basic camp store and laundry machines. The prices are right, but if you're hooked on modern conveniences, you may want to look elsewhere.

Yosemite Valley. ℂ **801/559-4884.** www.yosemitepark.com. 266 canvas tent-cabins, all with shared bathrooms and shower facilities. $80–$99 for up to 4 people. Closed Nov–Mar. **Amenities:** Free Wi-Fi.

Tuolumne Meadows Lodge ★ Not unlike Housekeeping Camp or White Wolf Lodge, this is a collection of seasonal canvas tent-cabins that can accommodate up to four guests. You don't get private bathrooms or electricity, but this does offer a much more secluded atmosphere compared to Curry Village in Yosemite Valley. Which makes sense as here you're at 8,775 feet above sea level, so be prepared for cold nights and chilly morning, and a relative dearth of oxygen. That being said, there are some signs of civilization, most notably a camp store and restaurant.

Tioga Rd., Tuolumne Meadows. ℂ **801/559-4884.** www.yosemitepark.com. 69 canvas tent-cabins, all with shared bathrooms and shower house. $124 double. **Amenities:** Restaurant.

Wawona Hotel ★★ The Wawona Hotel was built in 1879 before the area was part of the national park, and its as gracious and inviting as it ever was. Today a National Historic Landmark, it showcases the Yosemite history better than any of its in-park peers, thanks to its décor of authentic and reproduction period pieces (we love the fact that each room opens onto the verandah). That being said, the rooms without bathrooms are small; the larger units feature tub-shower combos. The Wawona also has as many facilities as any lodging in Yosemite Valley, with a restaurant, store, a number of trailheads, tennis court, swimming tank, nearby stables and even a 9-hole golf course.

In Wawona Village. ℂ **801/559-4884.** www.yosemitepark.com. 104 units (54 with shared bathroom). $159 double with shared bathroom; $235 double with private bathroom. Lower winter rates. **Amenities:** Restaurant; outdoor pool; golf course; tennis court; swimming tank; free Wi-Fi.

White Wolf Lodge ★ This is as off the beaten path as lodging in Yosemite gets, and my favorite of all the tent-cabin complexes in the park. The cabins have woodburning stoves and the area is rich on the atmosphere as the lodge is set in a subalpine meadow (prime wildflower territory) bordered by lodgepole pines. There are also four more substantial wooden cabins onsite with private bathrooms, electricity, and propane heating.

Off Tioga Rd., White Wolf. ℂ **801/559-4884.** www.yosemitepark.com. 24 canvas tent-cabins, 4 wood cabins. All canvas cabins share restrooms and shower facilities. $124–$140 double. Closed mid-Sept to mid-June. **Amenities:** Restaurant.

Yosemite Lodge at the Falls ★★ This is the most modern lodging in Yosemite, and it also has the best views of Yosemite Falls, which splashes down to the valley floor right across the road. Guestrooms have a contemporary mountain feel with sturdy wooden furnishings and a good amount of light; a handful of larger family units contain multiple beds and pull-out sofas, perfect for large groups. It feels more removed than it is, as you are a little ways from the hustle and bustle in the middle of Yosemite Village.

In Yosemite Valley. ℂ **801/559-4884.** www.yosemitepark.com. 249 units. $200–$220 double. Lower rates in winter. **Amenities:** Restaurant; outdoor pool; bike rentals; free Wi-Fi.

HIGH SIERRA CAMPS

The park has five **High Sierra Camps ★★** that provide food and shelter, allowing hikers to shun heavy backpacking gear with the knowledge that someone a few miles ahead has everything under control. All camps fill quickly via a lottery system, and advance reservations are necessary. The camps—**May Lake, Glen Aulin, Vogelsang, Sunrise,** and **Merced Lake**—are situated about a day's walk apart, and each is a sort of rustic resort. Tent-cabins are furnished with woodstoves, and a folding table and chairs, and beds with blankets or comforters—but guests must bring your own sheets and towels. Soap and candles are also provided. Most tents sleep four, but some accommodate only two people. This means you'll often be sharing your tent with strangers, but the camps tend to attract people who rank high on the camaraderie scale, so that's not usually a problem. Breakfast and dinner are served family style in a dining tent. The food is excellent and portions are generous. One dinner meal included pasta, filet mignon, soup and salad, eggplant Parmesan, and cookies. Breakfast is substantial as well. Box lunches are available for an additional charge. All you need to bring is day-hike gear (including plenty of water or a purifier), plus a flashlight, personal toiletries, something to sleep in, a change of clothes, and bed linen. In spring, trekking poles are also handy for crossing streams.

Camps are open from mid-June to around Labor Day, conditions permitting. Each camp accommodates 30 to 60 guests; demand exceeds supply, so accommodations are assigned by lottery. Applications are accepted from September 1 to November 1. The lottery drawing is held in December, and guests are notified by mid-January. Cancellations are frequent, however, so it's worth a last-minute call to see if space is available. Overnights at the camps cost $161 per adult and $102 per child for lodging and meals (breakfast and dinner; sack lunches are available for an extra fee); there are also packages for multiday saddle trips and guided hikes. A meals-only option is available (about $55 per adult, reservations required) if you want to bring your own tent and eat at the camp. Sack lunches run about $16. For information or to request an application for High Sierra Camp accommodations, call ✆ **559/253-5672** or visit **www.yosemitepark.com.**

Outside the Park

If you choose to stay outside the park, you'll find a plethora of choices, many of which are less expensive than the lodging in the park. Keep in mind that many of the gateways are an hour's drive to Yosemite Valley.

ALONG CALIF. 120 (WEST OF THE PARK)

Evergreen Lodge ★★ This complex dates back to the 1930s, and was completely reinvented in 2004 as an upscale, family-oriented resort well off of the beaten path on the road to Hetch Hetchy Reservoir. Today it is one of the best places to stay in the Yosemite area, with a great slate of recreational activities and some of the slickest cabins in the Sierra Nevada (colorful décor, vaulted ceilings, interesting art on the walls). You can choose from a few different sizes of cabins, a 2,500-square-foot house, or a "Custom Camping" site (tents, sleeping bags, and lantern included). Come nighttime, the restaurant is excellent, and the tavern has character to spare.

33160 Evergreen Rd., Groveland. ✆ **209/379-2606.** www.evergreenlodge.com. 88 units, plus 1 private house and 15 Custom Camping sites. $180–$400 double; $875–$1,150 private house; $85–$120 campsite. 2-night minimum stay. Lower winter rates (camping not available in winter). **Amenities:** Restaurant; bar; outdoor pool; free Wi-Fi.

Sunset Inn ★★ Just the place for sunsets and stargazing, the aptly named inn, comprised of a trio of lovingly restored cabins, is just 2 miles outside the Yosemite entrance, nestled on a quiet property that was spared when the 2013 fires devastated nearby forests. Surrounded by chicken coops, a frog pond, and plenty of open space, the cabins have small kitchens and beautiful woodwork, with rockers on the porches. The property has a faraway feel that is a world away from busy park lodgings.

33569 Harden Flat Rd., Groveland. ✆ **888/962-4360** or 209/962-4360. www.sunsetinn-yosemite cabins.com. 3 cabins. $180–$285 cabin. 4-night minimum stay required at peak times. Lower winter rates. **Amenities:** Kitchens; free Wi-Fi.

ALONG CALIF. 140 (SOUTHWEST OF THE PARK)

Yosemite Bug Rustic Mountain Resort ★★★   This funky mountain resort is my favorite lodging in the Yosemite area, with a big personality that captures the soul of the Sierra Nevada. Douglas Shaw and Caroline McGrath started the Bug as a hostel in 1997, and the property has snowballed into a true destination in the years since. Today the complex encompasses shared dorm-style lodging as well as cabins, motel-style units painted in the colors of wildflowers, a terrific restaurant, and a spa, not to mention the swimming hole down the hill. It is also a bus stop for the YARTS buses, making it a snap to get into the park.

6979 Calif. 140, Midpines. ✆ **866/826-7108** or 209/966-6666. www.yosemitebug.com. 64 hostel beds, 16 private rooms with private bathroom, 8 private rooms with shared bathroom, 16 tent-cabins, 1 studio, 1 private house. Hostel beds $23–$26 per person; $75–$155 double; $65–$100 double with shared bathroom; $45–$75 tent-cabin; $155–$285 studio/private house. Minimum stay may apply. Lower winter rates. **Amenities:** Restaurant; spa; free Wi-Fi.

ALONG CALIF. 41 (SOUTH OF THE PARK)

Tenaya Lodge at Yosemite ★★   This large resort is managed by DNC, the prime concessionaire in Yosemite National Park, and features handsomely outfitted rooms (down bedding, solid furniture, high quality linens), plenty of recreation, and great access to the park, but not as much personality as some of the independent properties in the area. Rooms are hotel-style units with all of the modern technology, and on the whole more spacious and sophisticated than their counterparts in the park. The hotel has an impressive lobby, centered on a massive river-rock fireplace, and facilities running the gamut from restaurants to outdoor and indoor pools and top-notch spa and fitness center.

1122 Calif. 41, Fish Camp. ✆ **888/514-2167** or 559/683-6555. www.tenayalodge.com. 244 units, 53 cottages. $189–$379 double; $309–$719 suite. Pets accepted ($75 one-time fee). **Amenities:** 4 restaurants; bar; concierge; outdoor pool; spa; free Wi-Fi.

ALONG U.S. 395 (EAST OF THE PARK)

El Mono Motel ★   Off-beat and fun, this renovated 1920s motel hits all of the right notes for budget travelers, from the warm and colorful guestrooms (love the 60s vibe comforters) to the resident coffeehouse, Latte Da, which serves excellent java and a raft of organic baked items. The place has a very social vibe, is a favorite of foreign visitors to Yosemite, and has great access to Mono Lake and its fascinating formations. Rooms are basic (no TV, no fridge), and the cheaper ones have shared bathrooms, but they are well-kept and are a good match for the needs of park-goers. Plus there's few happier places to hang than on the porch swing in the gardens here.

51 U.S. 395, Lee Vining. ✆ **760/647-6310.** www.elmonomotel.com. 11 units (6 with shared bathroom). $69–$99 double. Closed Nov to late Apr. **Amenities:** Restaurant; free Wi-Fi.

Lake View Lodge ★   This is a good mom-and-pop motel on the south side of Lee Vining with large, lush lawns that are perfect for kids with excess energy. Rooms are functional and nicely maintained, and there are larger family units and some nice standalone cottages. True budgeters take the camping cabins with shared bathrooms.

51285 U.S. 395, Lee Vining. © **800/990-6614** or 760/647-6543. www.lakeviewlodgeyosemite.com. 46 units, 7 cottages. $119–$159 double; $119–$255 cottage; $59 camping cabin. Lower winter rates. **Amenities:** Free Wi-Fi.

WHERE TO EAT

In the Valley

You'll find numerous fast-food options and cafeteria-style restaurants in Yosemite Valley, including a buffet, coffee shop, pizzeria, and taqueria at **Curry Village;** a food court at **Yosemite Lodge at the Falls;** a cafe and other fast-food fare at **Degnan's;** and the **Village Grill,** a fast-food place in Yosemite Village.

The Ahwahnee Dining Room ★★★ AMERICAN/CONTINENTAL This majestic room, sporting 350-foot ceilings, granite pillars, and space for 350, is without a doubt the finest restaurant in Yosemite. The regularly changing dinner menu is a study in continental cuisine, with steaks, duck, and seafood, as well as creative dishes like Moroccan braised lamb with kale and lemon yogurt. Breakfast is hearty American fare and lunch salads and sandwiches, but fast for a spell before coming for the "Grand Brunch" on Sunday—it has everything from oysters and catfish to blintzes and omelets. The dinner dress code requires men to wear a collared shirt and long pants and women to wear a dress, skirt, or pants with a blouse; breakfast and lunch are casual. Reservations are required for dinner.

The Ahwahnee, Yosemite Valley. © **209/372-1489.** www.yosemitepark.com. Breakfast $7–$21; lunch $13–$17; dinner $25–$50; Sun brunch $43 adults, $12 children. Mon–Sat 7–10am, 11:30am–2pm, and 5:30–8:30pm (until 9pm Fri–Sat); Sun 7am–2pm and 5:30–8:30pm.

Mountain Room Restaurant ★★ AMERICAN It is hard to look away from the view of Yosemite Falls, even when your meal arrives. Not that the food is not up to snuff—some prefer this restaurant to the Ahwahnee—but the 2,424-foot waterfall, framed within floor-to-ceiling windows is bound to take your breath away. The menu's focus is on local ingredients and sustainable seafood, and that includes gluten-free options. Selections shift with the season—you might find have the choice of halibut, rainbow trout, and quinoa falafel—but there's always a selection of expertly grilled steaks.

Yosemite Lodge at the Falls, Yosemite Valley. © **209/372-1403.** www.yosemitepark.com. Main courses $14–$35. Sun–Thurs 5–8pm; Fri–Sat 5–8:30pm.

Elsewhere in the Park

Tuolumne Meadows Lodge ★★ AMERICAN There are not many options in the high country of Yosemite, but despite the lack of competition, the fare here is top-notch. Hearty breakfasts like eggs, pancakes, and granola make good fuel for hikers, then at the end of the day dinner options include prime rib, mountain trout and vegetarian dishes. Reservations are required for dinner.

Tuolumne Meadows, Calif. 120. © **209/372-8413.** Breakfast $7–$14; dinner main courses $8–$30. Daily 7–9am and 5:45–8pm.

Wawona Dining Room ★★ AMERICAN To jibe with the Victorian ambiance here, the menu consists of tried and true—and deliciously prepared—American classics like pot roast, meatloaf, and flat iron steak for dinner (as well as several vegetarian entrees). Breakfast features hearty dishes like the "Grizzly Giant" (pancakes, one egg, and a choice of breakfast meat) and lunch brings salmon burgers and veggie paninis as well as big salads and barbecue chicken and cheeseburgers. In summer, you can sit in the adjacent veranda. There are also Saturday barbecue cookouts at the hotel on summer nights.

Wawona Hotel, Wawona Rd. ℂ **209/375-1425.** www.yosemitepark.com. Breakfast and lunch $10–$15; dinner main courses $20–$30. Daily 7:30–10am and 11:30am–1:30pm; Sun–Thurs 5:30–8:30pm; Fri–Sat 5:30–9pm.

White Wolf Lodge ★★ AMERICAN   This is the only option outside of Tuolumne Meadows Lodge at the higher elevations in Yosemite, and it is likewise reliably good. Breakfasts are eggs, granola, and dinner is served family-style. Selections vary throughout the season, but you can expect beef, seafood, and vegetarian options (also a box lunch for the trail). Dinner reservations are required.

White Wolf, Tioga Rd. ℂ **209/372-8416.** Breakfast $6–$12; dinner main courses $8–$30. Daily 7:30–9:30am and 6–8pm.

Near the Park

Cafe at the Bug ★★ AMERICAN   After a day of hiking the trails in Yosemite, there are few places I'd rather hoist a pint of beer and eat dinner than the deck at the Yosemite Bug. The service is well-oiled, the vibe is friendly and social, and the healthy food is first-rate. That being said, the operation is casual—you order at the counter and get your salad, roll, and drink, then take a seat and your meal gets delivered a few minutes later. Breakfasts include pancakes and egg and tofu scrambles, lunch ranges from black bean quesadillas to Vietnamese salads, and dinners change often—expect fresh and local ingredients in savory dishes like an African pea-and-plantain stew.

At the Yosemite Bug Rustic Mountain Resort and Spa, 6979 Calif. 140, Midpines. ℂ **209/966-6666.** www.yosemitebug.com. Breakfast and lunch $7–$11; dinner main courses $9–$20. Daily 7am–9pm.

Iron Door Saloon and Grill ★ AMERICAN   Said to be the oldest bar in California, the Iron Door has been open for business since 1852. It is named for its fireproof iron doors, imported from England a century and a half ago, and remains a must-see stop in Groveland en route to Yosemite. Black-and-white photos detail the life and times of local legends Black Bart and John Muir, long-dead animal heads gaze at your from the walls and there's local color to spare. The fare is typical American: eggs and bacon for breakfast, hamburgers for lunch and dinner.

18761 Calif. 120, Groveland. ℂ **209/962-6244.** www.iron-door-saloon.com. Breakfast, lunch, and dinner main courses $6–$10. Sun–Thurs 7am–9pm; Fri–Sat 7am–10pm. Shorter winter hours. Bar open later.

Savoury's ★★ NEW AMERICAN   This is my pick for a nice dinner in Mariposa. The contemporary space features plenty of open space and colorful art, with a menu that offers top-quality beef, poultry, and seafood, as well as several vegetarian dishes. I'm a sucker for the spicy shrimp diablo, but the food is uniformly excellent. Do not pass on dessert—the strawberry panna cotta is a memorable finish to any meal.

5034 Charles St. (Calif. 140), Mariposa. ℂ **209/966-7677.** www.savouryrestaurant.com. Main courses $16–$26. Summer Thurs–Tues 5–9:30pm; winter Thurs–Tues 5–8:30pm.

Whoa Nellie Deli ★★ DELI/NEW AMERICAN   This restaurant is in a gas station, but dismiss any preconceived notions of gas-station grub now—this is the best restaurant in the Lee Vining area. The far-flung menu includes ahi sashimi, fish tacos, chicken pizza, and buffalo meatloaf, served with massive salads and fresh fruit. The servings are designed for big appetites. Breakfast is much more basic, and the gas station has a store with a good selection of necessities and souvenirs.

Calif. 120, just west of U.S. 395, Lee Vining. ℂ **760/647-1088.** www.whoanelliedeli.com. Breakfast and lunch $6–$12; dinner main courses $10–$20. Daily 6:30am–9:30pm. Closed Nov–Apr.

8

SEQUOIA & KINGS CANYON

by Eric Peterson

In the heart of the Sierra Nevada, just south of Yosemite, are Sequoia and Kings Canyon national parks, home to the largest giant sequoia trees in the world, vast wilderness areas, and a deep, beautiful canyon. Sequoia and Kings Canyon are separate adjacent parks that are managed jointly. Their peaks stretch across 1,350 square miles and include 14,505-foot Mount Whitney, the tallest point in the continental United States. The parks are also home to the Kaweah Range, a string of dark, beautiful mountains nestled amid the Sierra, and three powerful rivers: the Kings, Kern, and Kaweah. Despite their size and scenic beauty, these two parks attract less than half the number of Yosemite's annual visitors, making them a welcome alternative for those looking to avoid huge crowds.

The parks owe their existence to a small band of determined 19th-century conservationists. Alarmed by the wholesale destruction of the region's sequoia forests, these farsighted people pushed to make the area a protected park. Sequoia National Park was created in 1890, along with the tiny General Grant National Park, which was established to protect Grant Grove. In 1926, the park was expanded eastward to include the Kern Canyon and Mount Whitney, and in the 1960s Kings Canyon was finally protected. In 1978, Mineral King was added to Sequoia's half of the park.

FLORA & FAUNA

There are populations of **deer, black bear, lizards, newts,** and more than 200 **bird species,** but you probably came here for the trees, namely the **giant sequoia trees.** General Sherman is widely considered the largest living thing on earth—52,000 cubic feet, give or take.

ESSENTIALS

Getting There & Gateways

There are two main entrances to the parks. **Calif. 198** through Visalia and the town of Three Rivers leads to the **Ash Mountain Entrance** in Sequoia National Park. **Calif. 180** from Fresno leads straight to the **Big Stump Entrance** near Grant Grove in Kings Canyon National Park. Three dead-end entrance roads are open only in the summer: the Kings Canyon Highway (a continuation of Calif. 180) to **Cedar Grove** in Kings Canyon

Sequoia & Kings Canyon National Parks

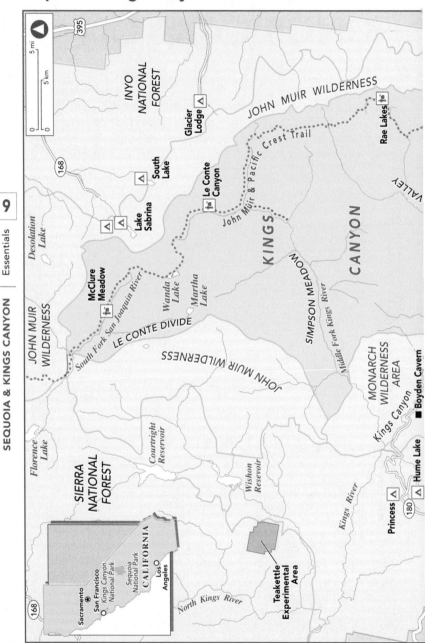

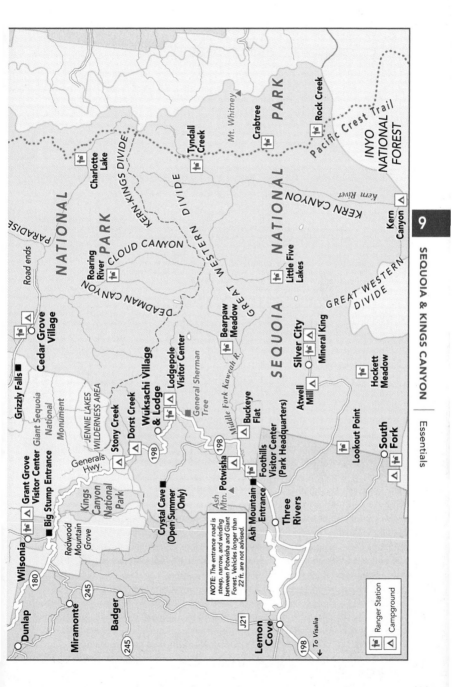

AVOIDING the crowds

Though Sequoia and Kings Canyon receive far fewer visitors than nearby Yosemite, they still get crowded, especially in summer. Luckily, it's relatively easy to find solitude. To get the most from the parks while avoiding traffic, try to visit before Memorial Day or after Labor Day, keeping in mind that snow can limit access in the high elevations. Fall provides some scenic color.

You can also try taking a dead-end road into the parks. Mineral King, South Fork, and, to a lesser extent, Cedar Grove all lack the through traffic prevalent on the larger highways.

National Park, and two smaller roads to **Mineral King** and to **South Fork** in the southern part of Sequoia National Park.

The parks are roughly equidistant (5 hr. by car) from San Francisco and Los Angeles. The Ash Mountain Entrance is 36 miles, or about an hour, from Visalia. The Big Stump Entrance is 53 miles from Fresno, also about an hour's drive.

The National Park Service and the City of Visalia have put together a transportation system that makes it possible to explore Sequoia National Park without a car. From Visalia (or Three Rivers), the **Sequoia Shuttle** (✆ **877/404-6473;** www.sequoia shuttle.com) will take you to the Giant Forest Museum for just $15 round-trip. From here, riders can connect with the **free park shuttle** to get to Wuksachi Lodge or one of the numerous trail heads en route.

THE NEAREST AIRPORTS The closest major airport is **Fresno-Yosemite International Airport** (✆ **559/621-4500;** www.flyfresno.com), 53 miles from the Big Stump Entrance in Kings Canyon.

Visitor Centers & Information

The largest visitor center in Sequoia National Park is at **Lodgepole** (✆ 559/565-4436), 4.5 miles north of Giant Forest Village. The **Foothills Visitor Center** (✆ **559/565-3135**), just inside the Ash Mountain Entrance to Sequoia National Park on Calif. 198, includes exhibits on the chaparral region's ecosystem. The visitor center in **Grant Grove** in Kings Canyon National Park (✆ 559/565-4307) shows exhibits on logging and forest fires, and the **Giant Forest Museum** (✆ 559/565-4480) has exhibits on giant sequoias. The small visitor center at **Cedar Grove** and ranger station at **Mineral King** are open only during the summer.

For further information before your trip, contact **Sequoia & Kings Canyon National Parks** (✆ **559/565-3341;** www.nps.gov/seki). Information about other attractions and facilities in the monument are discussed elsewhere in this chapter. For additional information, contact **Giant Sequoia National Monument** ✆ **559/338-2251;** www.fs.usda.gov/sequoia).

Fees & Permits

It costs $20 per motor vehicle ($10 for individuals on foot, bike, or motorcycle) to enter the parks for up to a week. Park campgrounds charge $12 to $20 a night.

All overnight backpacking trips require a $15 **wilderness permit** per party (free in winter), available by mail, by fax, or in person at the ranger station closest to the hike you want to take.

Seasons & Climate

Sequoia and Kings Canyon, for the most part, share a climate that varies considerably depending on the region of the park. A good rule of thumb is that the higher you go, the cooler it gets. During the summer, temperatures at lower elevations can climb into the 90s (30s Celsius) or higher, and drop into the 50s (10s Celsius) at night. Afternoon temperatures average in the 60s and 70s (upper teens and 20s Celsius) in spring and fall, and evenings are usually cool. Afternoon showers are fairly common year-round. Winter days average in the 40s and 50s (single digits and 10s Celsius) and seldom drop below zero, although much of the land is beneath several feet of snow. A particularly wet winter often leads to stunning wildflowers and spectacular waterfalls (and dangerous rivers and creeks) in spring and early summer.

EXPLORING THE PARKS

Sequoia National Park

The best-known stand of sequoias in the world is in **Giant Forest,** part of Sequoia National Park. Named in 1875 by explorer and environmentalist John Muir, this park consists mostly of huge meadows and a large grove of giant trees. At the northern edge of the grove, you can't miss the **General Sherman Tree,** considered the largest living tree on the planet (although it is neither the tallest nor the widest). It is believed to be about 2,100 years old, and it's still growing. Every year it adds enough new wood to make another 60-foot-tall tree. The tree is part of the 2-mile **Congress Trail,** a foot trail that includes groups of trees with names such as the Senate and the House.

Another interesting stop in Giant Forest is **Tharp's Log,** a cabin named after the first non–American Indian settler in the area, Hale Tharp, who grazed cattle among the giant sequoias and built a summer cabin in the 1860s from a fallen sequoia hollowed by fire. It is the oldest cabin remaining in the park. You'll also encounter **Tunnel Log,** a toppled tree that you can drive under.

Also in the area is **Moro Rock,** a large granite dome that offers one of the most spectacular views in the Sierra. From atop the rock, the high-elevation, barren mountains in the Kaweah Range appear dark and ominous. The walk to the top takes visitors up hundreds of stairs and requires about a half-hour to complete.

South of the Giant Forest is the turn-off for **Crystal Cave,** one of more than 200 caves in the park and one of just two in the area that offer guided tours. (Boyden Cavern in the neighboring Giant Sequoia National Monument is the other.) The cave consists of limestone that has turned to marble, and it contains a wonderful array of formations, many still growing, that range from sharply pointed stalactites and towering stalagmites to beautiful flowing draperies. To reach the entrance, drive 7 miles down the narrow, winding road (RVs, trailers, and buses are prohibited); the cave is an additional

> ### Special Regulations & Warnings
>
> The roads are steep and winding, and those in RVs will find it easiest to travel on Calif. 180 from Fresno. All groundwater should be boiled, filtered, or otherwise purified before drinking. Rattlesnakes are common; look where you step and touch. In the foothills, check your clothes for ticks. Beware also of black bears. When camping, store all food in lockers and put all garbage in bear-proof containers.

half-mile walk down a steep path (which you'll have to hike up after your cave tour). The Sequoia Natural History Association conducts 45-minute tours daily mid-June to Labor Day, daily every half-hour from 10:30am to 4:30pm; from mid-May to mid-June and after Labor Day to late October, daily every hour from 11am to 3pm (with slightly longer weekend hours). The cost is $15 for adults, $13 for seniors 62 and older, and $8 for children 5 to 12 (free for children under 5). A special discovery tour is offered in summer only, Monday through Friday at 4:15pm. It is less structured and limited to 16 people, has a minimum age requirement of 13, and costs $16 per person. Information is available at visitor centers, online at www.sequoiahistory.org, or by calling ⓒ **559/565-3759.** It gets cold underground, so take a sweater or jacket.

Lodgepole, the most developed area in both parks, lies just northeast of the Giant Forest on the Generals Highway. Here you'll find the largest visitor center, a large market, several places to eat, a laundry, and a post office. Nearby is Wuksachi Village, with a restaurant, lodge, and gift shop.

About 16 miles south of Giant Forest is the region of the park known as the **Foothills.** Located near the Ash Mountain Entrance, the Foothills has a visitor center, several campgrounds, and **Hospital Rock,** a boulder with ancient pictographs believed to have been painted by the Monache Indians, who once lived here. Nearby are about 50 grinding spots once used to smash acorns into flour. A short trail leads down to a beautiful spot along the Kaweah River where the water gushes over rapids into deep pools.

Mineral King is a relatively undeveloped region in the southern part of the park. This high-mountain valley was carved by glaciers and is bordered by the tall peaks of the Great Western Divide. To reach this area, patient drivers must follow the marked highway sign 3 miles outside Sequoia National Park's Ash Mountain Entrance. From the turnoff to Mineral King, it's a 28-mile trip that makes many tight turns and usually takes over an hour. Trailers, RVs, and buses are not allowed, and the road is closed in winter.

The rocky landscape in Mineral King is as colorful as a rainbow—red and orange shales mix with white marble and black metamorphic shale and granite. In winter, this area is prone to avalanches. The most prominent point in the area is **Sawtooth Peak,** which reaches 12,343 feet. The trails in Mineral King begin at 7,500 feet and climb from there.

Kings Canyon National Park

With its rugged canyon, huge river, and desolate backcountry, Kings Canyon is a hiker's dream. It consists of Grant Grove and Cedar Grove, as well as portions of the Monarch Wilderness and Jennie Lakes Wilderness. Between Grant Grove and Cedar Grove is a stretch of land that lies not in the park, but in Giant Sequoia National Monument.

Grant Grove is the most crowded region in either park. Not only is it just a few miles from a main entrance, but the area is also a thoroughfare for travelers heading from Giant Forest to the south or Cedar Grove to the east. The grove was designated General Grant National Park in 1890 and was incorporated into Kings Canyon National Park when it was created in 1940.

Here you'll find the towering **General Grant Tree** amid a grove of spectacular giant sequoias. The tree was discovered by Joseph Hardin Tomas in 1862 and named 5 years later to honor Ulysses S. Grant. It measures 267 feet tall and 108 feet around, is among the world's largest living trees, and is possibly 2,000 years old. This tree has been officially declared "The Nation's Christmas Tree" and is the cornerstone of the park's annual Christmas tree ceremony.

To the southwest, at **Panoramic Point** visitors can stand atop a 7,520-foot ledge and see across a large stretch of the Sierra and across Kings Canyon. **Grant Grove Village** also has a restaurant, shops, a post office, and visitor center.

The **Cedar Grove** section of the park is known for its lush landscape, tumbling waterfalls, and miles upon miles of solitude. Getting to it is half the fun. You drive through **Kings Canyon,** with sheer granite canyon walls towering above you and the wild South Fork of the Kings River racing by. One mile east of the Cedar Grove Village turnoff is **Canyon View,** where visitors can see the glacially carved U shape of Kings Canyon. Easily accessible nature trails in Cedar Grove include Zumwalt Meadow, Roaring River Falls, and Knapp's Cabin. **Zumwalt Meadow** is dotted with ponderosa pine and has good views of two rock formations, the **Grand Sentinel** and **North Dome.** The top of Grand Sentinel is 8,504 feet above sea level; North Dome, which some say resembles Half Dome in Yosemite, towers over the area at 8,717 feet.

Roaring River Falls is a 5-minute walk from a parking area 3 miles east of the turnoff to the village. Even during summer and dry years, water crashes through a narrow granite chute into a cold green pool below. During a wet spring, these falls are powerful enough to drench visitors who venture too close.

Ten miles west of Cedar Grove, in the national monument and back toward Grant Grove, is the entrance to **Boyden Cavern.** Although it's not as impressive as Sequoia's Crystal Cave, Boyden is a scenic cave, known for a wide variety of formations including rare shields. For information, contact **Boyden Cavern (© 888/965-8243;** www. boydencavern.com).

In Cedar Grove is a small summer-only village with a store and gift shop, restaurant, laundry, showers, lodge, and campgrounds.

The **Monarch Wilderness** is a 45,000-acre region protected under the 1984 California Wilderness Act that adjoins wilderness in Kings Canyon National Park. The **Jennie Lakes Wilderness,** at 10,500 acres, includes the 10,365-foot Mitchell Peak and wide lowland meadows. This region lies between the Generals Highway and Calif. 180, east of Grant Grove.

ORGANIZED TOURS & RANGER PROGRAMS

The **Sequoia Field Institute (© 559/565-4251;** www.sequoiahistory.org) offers a wide variety of "Ed Ventures" spanning backpacking expeditions (about $60 a day) to writing and pottery workshops (usually about $200), as well as a "Hire A Guide" service starting at $200 for one of the institute's naturalists for 4 hours.

Ranger programs include free walks and talks at Giant Forest, Lodgepole, Grant Grove, Mineral King, and Foothills. Some of the highlights include weekend wildflower walks at Foothills, talks at General Sherman, and evening campfire programs at Lodgepole. Call the park (© **559/565-3341**) or check bulletin boards and visitor centers for the current schedule.

DAY HIKES

Near Giant Forest

Big Trees Trail ★★   A scenic loop walk among the sequoias, Big Trees Trail skirts the edge of a pretty meadow and has trailside exhibits that explain why this area is such a good habitat for sequoias. There are usually abundant wildflowers in Round Meadow in early summer. The trail, which has a 60-foot elevation change, is mostly paved, with some wooden boardwalk sections, and is wheelchair accessible. .7 mile RT. Easy. Access: Giant Forest Museum.

Congress Trail ★★★   This walk circles some of Sequoia National Park's best-known and best-loved giants. The trail is a paved loop with a 200-foot elevation gain. Here you'll find the General Sherman Tree, considered the largest living tree on the planet. 2 miles RT. Easy. Access: General Sherman Tree, just off the Generals Hwy., 2 miles northeast of Giant Forest Museum.

Crescent Meadow Loop ★★   The meadow is a large, picturesque clearing dotted with high grass and wildflowers, encircled by a forest of firs and sequoias. The park's oldest cabin (Tharp's Log) is along this paved route. 1.8 miles RT. Easy. Access: Crescent Meadow parking area.

High Sierra Trail ★★★   This is one gateway to the backcountry, but the first few miles also make a great day hike. Along the way are spectacular views of the Kaweah River's middle fork and the Great Western Divide. The trail runs along a south-facing slope and is warm in spring and fall. Get an early start in summer. From the trail head, cross two wooden bridges over Crescent Creek until you reach a junction. Tharp's Log is to the left, the High Sierra Trail to the right. Hike uphill and a bit farther on through the damage done by the Buckeye Fire of 1988, a blaze ignited by a discarded cigarette 3,000 feet below, near the Kaweah River. After .75 mile you'll reach Eagle View, which offers a picturesque vision of the Great Western Divide. To the south are the craggy Castle Rocks. At 3.25 miles is Panther Rock. Follow a few more creeks to reach the last fork of Panther Creek, down a steep, eroded ravine. 9 miles RT. Moderate. Access: Near Crescent Meadow parking area restrooms.

Huckleberry Trail ★★   This is a great hike with a lot of beauty and not a lot of people. The first mile takes you along the Hazelwood Nature Trail. Head south at each junction until you see a big sign with blue lettering, which marks the start of the Huckleberry Trail. You pass a small creek and meadow before reaching a second sign for Huckleberry Meadow. The next mile is steep and runs beneath sequoias, dogwoods, and white firs. At the 1.5-mile point is a Squatter's Cabin, built in the 1880s. East of the cabin is a trail junction. Head north (left) up a short hill. At the next junction, veer left along the edges of Circle Meadow for about a quarter-mile before you reach a third junction. The right is a short detour to Bear's Bathtub, a pair of sequoias hollowed by fire and filled with water. Legend has it that an old mountain guide once surprised a bear taking a bath here. Continue on the trail heading northeast to the Washington Tree, almost as big as the General Sherman Tree, then on to Alta Trail, then turn west (left) to Little Deer Creek. At the next junction, head north (right) on the last leg of the Huckleberry Trail to the parking area. 4 miles RT. Moderate. Access: Hazelwood Nature Trail parking area.

Moro Rock and Soldiers Loop Trail ★★   This hike cuts cross-country from the Giant Forest to Moro Rock. An early section is parallel to a main road, but the trail quickly departs from the traffic and heads through a forest dotted with giant sequoias. A carpet of ferns occasionally hides the trail. It pops out at Moro Rock, and then it's just a quick heart-thumper to the top for a superlative view. 4.6 miles RT. Moderate. Access: 30 yards west of cafeteria at Giant Forest Museum.

Near Grant Grove

Azalea Trail ★   From the visitor center, walk past the amphitheater to Sunset Campground and cross Calif. 180. The first mile joins the South Boundary Trail as it meanders through Wilsonia and criss-crosses Sequoia Creek in a gentle climb. After 1.5 miles is the third crossing of Sequoia Creek. It may be dry in late summer, but the banks are lush with ferns and brightly colored azaleas. Return the way you came. 3 miles RT. Easy. Access: Kings Canyon Visitor Center.

Boole Tree Loop ★★   This trail loops through the once-proud forest in the ravaged Converse Basin to the 269-foot Boole Tree, one of the last reminders of the giants that were logged here. The world's eighth-largest sequoia (it was once thought to be the largest), the Boole Tree, is the highlight of the loop, and there are terrific views of Kings Canyon. 2.5 mile RT. Moderate. Access: The end of the Converse Basin Rd. north of Grant Grove in Giant Sequoia National Monument.

Hitchcock Meadow Trail ★   This trail takes you to pretty Viola Falls. After passing through the stumps and logging debris on the Big Stump Trail, hike another quarter-mile to Hitchcock Meadow, a large clearing in Sequoia National Forest that is surrounded by sequoia stumps. Notice the small sequoias in this area—these are the descendants of the giant sequoias logged in the last century. From here the trail climbs slightly to a ridge, where it reenters Kings Canyon National Park before descending a short series of steep switchbacks to Sequoia Creek. Cross the creek and look for a sign directing you to Viola Falls, a series of short steps that join into one fall when the water level is high. It is very dangerous to venture down the canyon, but above it are several flat places that make great picnic spots. 3.5 miles RT. Easy. Access: Big Stump Picnic Area near the entrance to Grant Grove from Kings Canyon.

Sunset Trail ★★   The hike climbs 1,400 feet past two waterfalls and a lake. After crossing the highway, the trail heads left around a campground. After 1.25 miles, follow the South Boundary Trail toward Viola Falls. You'll reach a paved road where you can head to the right to see the park's original entrance. Return the way you came, or follow the road to the General Grant Tree parking area and walk to the visitor center. 6 miles RT. Moderate to strenuous. Access: Across the road from Kings Canyon Visitor Center.

Near Cedar Grove

Bubbs Creek Trail ★★★   The trail begins by crossing and re-crossing Copper Creek. This site was once an American Indian village, and shards of obsidian can still be found on the ground (please leave them in place). After the first mile, you'll enter a swampy area that offers a good place to watch for wildlife. The trail here closes in on the river, where deer and bear drink. At 2 miles, you'll come to a junction. The trail to Paradise Valley heads north (left); the hike to Bubbs Creek veers right and crosses Bailey Bridge, over the South Fork of the Kings River.

Continue hiking east over four small wooden bridges that cross Bubbs Creek. The creek was named after John Bubbs, a prospector and rancher who arrived here in 1864. The trail climbs on the creek's north side, following a few steep switchbacks, which provide alternating views of the canyon of Paradise Valley and Cedar Grove. At 3 miles is a large, emerald pool with waterfalls, and far above is a rock formation that John Muir named "the Sphinx." At 4 miles you reach Sphinx Creek, a good area to spend the day or night (with a wilderness permit). There are several campsites nearby. Hike back the way you came or along the Sentinel Trail. 8 miles RT. Moderate to strenuous. Access: East end of parking area at Road's End.

Mist Falls ★★   This is one of the more popular trails leading to the backcountry, but it's also a nice day hike. The first 2 miles, before you reach Bubbs Creek Bridge, are dry. Take the fork to the left and head uphill. The first waterfall is not your destination, although it is a pretty spot to take a break. From here, the trail meanders along the river, through forest and swamp areas, before it comes out at the base of Mist Falls, a wide fall that flows generously in spring. There are dozens of great picnic spots along the way. Return along the same route, or cross over at Bubbs Creek Bridge and head back on the Sentinel Trail. 8 miles RT. Moderate to strenuous. Access: Short-term parking area at Road's End; pass Cedar Grove Village and follow signs.

Sentinel Trail ★★★   Essentially, this hike encircles a small length of the South Fork of the Kings River. After following the river's north side for 2 miles, the trail splits and heads north to Mist Falls and Paradise Valley or east across Bailey Bridge toward Bubbs Creek. Follow the eastern trail, but instead of hiking to Bubbs Creek, follow a sign that reads ROAD'S END—2.6 MILES. This will take you through dense groves of pine and cedars, with occasional views of Grand Sentinel. You'll cross Avalanche Creek before emerging in a huge meadow and returning near the riverbank. At 2 miles, you can see Muir's Rock, the huge, flat boulder that Sierra Club founder John Muir used as a pulpit for some of his most famous speeches At 2.25 miles, you'll find a footbridge that points back to the parking area. 4.6 miles RT. Easy. Access: Short-term parking area at Road's End; pass Cedar Grove Village and follow signs.

Zumwalt Meadow ★★   Cross the bridge and walk left for 100 yards to a fork. Take the trail that leads right for a bird's-eye view of the meadow before descending 50 feet to the ground below. The trail leads along the meadow's edge, where the fragrance of ponderosa pine, sugar pine, and incense cedar fills the air. The loop returns along the banks of the South Fork of the Kings River. Grand Sentinel and North Dome rise in the background. 1.5 miles RT. Easy. Access: Zumwalt Meadows parking area, 1 mile west of Road's End, on Calif. 180 past Cedar Grove Village.

Other Hikes

Cold Springs Nature Trail ★★   This easy loop illustrates the natural history and beauty of the region. It passes near private cabins that predate the area's addition to Sequoia National Park in 1978. The walk offers views of the Mineral King Valley and surrounding peaks. It can get hot and dry in summer, so carry additional water. 2 miles RT. Easy. Access: Mineral King's Cold Springs Campground, across from ranger station.

Marble Fork Trail ★★   This is one of the most scenic hikes in the Foothills area. The walk leads to a deep gorge where the roaring Marble Falls spill in a cascade over multicolored boulders. From the parking area, begin hiking north up the Southern California Edison flume. After crossing the flume on a wooden bridge, watch for a sign to the trail and head east (uphill). The trail will begin to flatten out and settle into a slight slope for the rest of the hike up to the waterfalls. Look for large yuccas and California bay along the way. After 2 miles, you can see the waterfalls as the hike cuts through white and gray marble, a belt of the rock that is responsible for seven caves in the park, including Crystal Cave near Giant Forest. Once you reach the falls, it's almost impossible to hike any farther; only very experienced hikers should attempt a walk downstream. The marble slabs break very easily, and the boulders in the area can get very slick. Be extra careful when water is high. This is a good hike, but it can be very hot during summer afternoons. 6 miles RT. Strenuous. Access: Dirt road at upper end of Potwisha Campground, 3.5 miles east of the Ash Mountain Entrance. A parking area is past campsite no. 16.

EXPLORING THE BACKCOUNTRY

All overnight backpacking trips require a $15 **wilderness permit** per party (free in winter), available by mail, by fax, or in person at the ranger station closest to the hike you want to take. First-come, first-served permits can be issued the morning of your trip or after 1pm on the previous afternoon. **Reservations** can be made at least 14 days in advance, March 1 to September 10. To reserve a permit, you must provide a name, address, and telephone number; the number of people in your party; the method of travel (snowshoe, horse, foot); number of stock, if applicable; start and end dates; start and end trail heads; a principal destination; and a rough itinerary. Download the application from the park's website and mail it to **Wilderness Permit Reservations,** Sequoia and Kings Canyon National Parks, 47050 Generals Hwy. #60, Three Rivers, CA 93271, or fax it to ✆ **559/565-4239.** Reserved permits must be picked up by 9am. If your hike crosses agency boundaries, get the permit from the agency on whose land the hike begins. Only one permit is required.

Note: Eight ranger stations lie along the John Muir and Pacific Crest trails, and six are in the southern part of the park in the Sequoia backcountry. Most are not staffed from fall to spring. To find the ranger station closest to your trail head, consult the park map.

Some warnings: Be aware of **bears,** and in the summer take insect repellent for protection against mosquitoes. Stay off high peaks during thunderstorms, and don't attempt any climb if it looks as if a storm is rolling in; exposed peaks are often struck by lightning. In winter, snow buries many of these routes.

OTHER SPORTS & ACTIVITIES

CROSS-COUNTRY SKIING   There are 35 miles of marked backcountry trails in the parks. Call park concessionaires for information (✆ 559/335-5500 in Grant Grove; ✆ 559/565-4070 in the Wuksachi Lodge area). The **Pear Lake Ski Hut** is open to the public all winter for backcountry accommodations in Sequoia for $30 to $40 per person per night. Reservations are by a November lottery, but there are often openings during the season. Call ✆ 559/565-4222 for more information or check out **to register for the lottery** online.

FISHING   A section of the south fork of the **Kings River,** the **Kaweah** drainage, and the parks' lakes are open all year for trout fishing—rainbow, brook, German brown, and golden. California **fishing licenses** are required for anglers 16 and older, and you should also get a copy of the National Park Service's fishing regulations, available at visitor centers.

HORSEBACK RIDING   In Kings Canyon, **Cedar Grove Pack Station** (✆ 559/565-3464) is about 1 mile east of Cedar Grove Village, and **Grant Grove Stables** (✆ 559/335-9292) is near Grant Grove Village.

SNOWSHOEING   Free ranger-led snowshoe tours take place in both parks on Saturdays and holidays when conditions permit. Call ✆ 559/565-4480 (Wuksachi) or ✆ 559/565-4307 (Grant Grove). There are also several snowshoe trails near **Wuksachi Lodge** (✆ 559/565-070); rentals are available at the lodge.

WHITE-WATER RAFTING   The Kaweah and Upper Kings rivers in the parks are not open to boating, but several companies run trips just outside the parks. The thrilling roller-coaster ride through the rapids is a great way to not only see, but also to experience these scenic rivers. Offering trips on the Kaweah, Kings, Merced, and other rivers is **Whitewater Voyages** (✆ 800/400-7238; www.whitewatervoyages.com), with rates that range from $109 to $229 for half- and full-day trips, and multiday trips are also available.

WHERE TO STAY
Inside the Parks

Lodging in the parks ranges from rustic cabins to well-equipped, motel-style accommodations, usually with a mountain-lodge atmosphere and great views. Besides the options that follow, there is the **Bearpaw High Sierra Camp** (✆ 866/807-3598; www.visitsequoia.com), an 11-mile hike from Crescent Meadow in Sequoia National Park

CAMPING options

There are numerous camping opportunities both within and surrounding Sequoia and Kings Canyon national parks. It's important to remember that proper food storage is required for the sake of the black bears in the parks, as well as for your safety. See local bulletin boards for instructions.

INSIDE SEQUOIA NATIONAL PARK

The only national park campgrounds that accept reservations are Dorst Creek and Lodgepole (www.recreation.gov; © 877/444-6777); the other campgrounds are first come, first served. Reservations for Dorst and Lodgepole can be made up to 6 months in advance.

The two biggest campgrounds in the park are in the Lodgepole area. The **Lodgepole Campground** ★ has flush toilets and is often crowded, but it's pretty and near big trees and enough backcountry trails to offer some solitude. In summer, you'll find a grocery store nearby, a restaurant, visitor center, and other facilities. From Giant Forest, drive 5 miles northeast on the Generals Highway. **Dorst Creek Campground** ★★, 14 miles northwest of Giant Forest on the Generals Highway, is a high-elevation campground that offers easy access to Muir Grove and pleasant backcountry trails. It has flush toilets and evening ranger programs.

Group campsites are available by reservation.

In the Foothills area, **Potwisha Campground** ★ is small, with well-spaced sites tucked beneath oak trees along the Marble Fork of the Kaweah River. However, it does get hot in summer. The **Buckeye Flat Campground** ★, which is open to tents only, sits in a pretty spot among oaks along the Middle Fork of the Kaweah River, but also gets hot in summer. **South Fork Campground** ★ just inside Sequoia's southwestern boundary, is the smallest and most remote campground in the park. It is along the South Fork of the Kaweah River and has pit toilets only. From the town of Three Rivers, go east on South Fork Road 23 miles to the campground.

The two campgrounds in the Mineral King area are open to tents only—no RVs or trailers. Pretty, small **Atwell Mill Campground** ★★ is near the East Fork of the Kaweah River, at Atwell Creek. **Cold Springs Campground** ★★, which also has pit toilets, is a beautiful place but not very accessible. Once you get there, you'll be rewarded with lovely scenery. From Three Rivers, take Mineral King Road east for about 20 miles to get to these campgrounds.

For additional information, call the general **information line** (© **559/565-3341**).

---

proper. It features six tent cabins (each can sleep three people) and a central bathroom that has toilets and hot showers. Bedding, breakfast, and dinner are included in the price ($250 per double nightly).

Cedar Grove Lodge ★   This property in itself is nothing special, but the location is unbelievable. The 1920s-era motel, with fairly standard rooms, is right alongside the Kings River, and the only place to sleep with a roof over your head in the general vicinity. I like the patio rooms, with queen beds, more than the standards, with doubles, because they are not only roomier, but the private patio are perfect places to kick back after a day on the nearby trails. The lodge's small size makes for a less busy area than some of the other villages in the park, but it has all of the necessary facilities.

At Cedar Grove. © **877/436-9615** or 559/565-0100. www.visitsequoia.com. 18 units. $120–$140 double. Closed Nov–Apr. **Amenities:** Restaurant.

IN KINGS CANYON NATIONAL PARK

All of the campgrounds in Kings Canyon are first come, first served only; reservations are not available. All have flush toilets.

In the Grant Grove area are three nice campgrounds near the big trees—**Azalea ★★**, **Crystal Springs ★★**, and **Sunset ★★**. There are four campgrounds in the Cedar Grove Village area, all accessible from Calif. 180 and close to the facilities in Cedar Grove Village. **Sentinel ★★**, the first to open for the season, tends to fill quickly; **Moraine ★★** is the farthest from the crowds. **Sheep Creek ★** and **Canyon View ★** are open when there is high demand.

For additional information, call the general Sequoia/Kings Canyon **information line** (✆ **559/565-3341**).

IN GIANT SEQUOIA NATIONAL MONUMENT

The U.S. Forest Service operates a number of campgrounds in **Giant Sequoia National Monument.** They provide a delightful forest camping experience and are usually less crowded than national park campgrounds. There is also primitive camping available—no fee, no facilities.

In the Hume Lake area, all the Forest Service campgrounds have pit toilets except the beautiful **Hume Lake Campground ★★**, which is on the banks of the lake and has flush toilets. The largest campground in this area is **Princess ★★**, on Calif. 180; two smaller campgrounds, both beyond Hume Lake on Ten Mile Road, are **Landslide ★** and **Upper Ten Mile ★**. In the Stony Creek/Big Meadows area, you'll find vault toilets at all U.S. Forest Service campgrounds except **Stony Creek Campground ★**, off Generals Highway in Stony Creek Village, which has flush toilets. Among the larger campgrounds in this area is **Big Meadows ★**, which sits along Big Meadows Creek. Nearby trails lead to the Jennie Lakes Wilderness.

For additional information, contact **Giant Sequoia National Monument** (✆ **559/338-2251;** www.fs.usda.gov/sequoia). You can make reservations at Hume Lake, Princess, or Stony Creek during the summer by calling ✆ **877/444-6777** or visiting **www.recreation.gov.**

OUTSIDE THE PARKS

You'll pass many of these establishments as you travel to different sections of the parks. Accessible only by trail, **Sequoia High Sierra Camp** (✆ **866/654-2877;** www.sequoiahighsierracamp.com) in Giant Sequoia National Monument bring luxury to the backcountry. For $250 per person, you get 330-square-foot bungalows with plush furnishings and three gourmet meals a day.

Grant Grove Cabins ★   Whether you have just a few shekels or buckets full of them, you should be able to find welcome shelter from the elements here. All the accommodations are cabins, but they range in comfort from permanent canvas tents to handsome "honeymoon cabins" with indoor plumbing, a queen size bed, private patio and lots of charm. Those high-end cabin are some of the few cabin that have running water (most share a central bathhouse). I like the "Rustic Cabins" with an outdoor woodburning stove and room for a family because they have the most character, and because they really feel like they belong in this spectacular setting, but they share the central bathhouse with other guests. Kings Canyon visitors looking for a more hotel-like experience should probably look elsewhere.

At Grant Grove Village. ✆ **877/436-9615** or 559/335-5000. www.visitsequoia.com. 53 units, 9 with private bathroom. $70–$95 cabin with shared bathroom; $130–$145 cabin with private bathroom. **Amenities:** Restaurant; free Wi-Fi.

John Muir Lodge ★★   Built in the 1990s, this is a relatively modern lodging, tucked away from the hustle and bustle of the cabins. Named for the legendary conservationist, the lodge is neck and neck with Wuksachi in Sequoia as the most upscale in either park. The warm and sunny rooms are attractively decorated with handcrafted wooden furniture and one king bed or two queens, and have phones, iPod docks, and other conveniences you would expect in a modern hotel with a more urban setting.

At Grant Grove Village. ℂ **877/436-9615** or 559/335-5000. www.visitsequoia.com. 30 units. $180–$195 double. Register at Grant Grove Village Registration Center, btw. the restaurant and gift shop. **Amenities:** Free Wi-Fi .

Silver City Mountain Resort ★★   The Mineral King unit of Sequoia tends to attract backpackers and campers, but for those looking for a roof over their head, this is a top pick (for both couples and families). The variety of cabins here is notably wide: Some are less than 10 years old and others date back to the 1930s; they range from about 200 to 1,500 square feet; and some share bathrooms, while others approach luxury in their own folksy sort of way. Built at the site of a mining town that once had 3,000 residents, the resort has more personality than the lodgings in more well-trod parts of the parks, and all have access to the miraculous pies baked at the Silver City restaurant.

In Mineral King. ℂ **559/561-3223.** www.silvercityresort.com. 13 cabins, 7 with shared central bathhouse. $100–$395 cabin. 2- to 3-night minimum. Discounts approx. June 1–15 and after Sept 18. Closed late Oct to Memorial Day. **Amenities:** Restaurant; free Wi-Fi.

Wuksachi Lodge ★★   This downright swank mountain lodge dates to 1999, making it one of the newest in any national park. It offers not just eye-pleasing style, but a terrific location in the forest at about 7,200 feet above sea level, surrounded by hiking trails that are great skiing routes in wintertime. For those who like modern conveniences as much as they love national parks, this is the best fit in Sequoia. The onsite restaurant (see p. 128) is also quite good.

Near Lodgepole and Calif. 180 and 198. ℂ **866/807-3598** or 801/559-4930. www.visitsequoia. com. 102 rooms. $140–$275 double. **Amenities:** Restaurant; free Wi-Fi .

In Giant Sequoia National Monument

Montecito Sequoia Lodge ★   This classic family mountain resort has one of the best recreation programs in the Sierra Nevada, running the gamut from archery and arts and crafts to swimming and tennis. It is best known for its 6-night "Family Camps" that include all recreation and meals for about $1,000 per person for the week. There are also 4-night "Adventure Camps." Attractive guestrooms outfitted with quilts and rustic Western decor are in cabin-style units around a central lake, and there are 37 lodge rooms open year-round. In winter, the lodge turns into a mecca for cross-country skiers, as trails originate at the property.

63410 Generals Hwy., Giant Sequoia National Monument. ℂ **800/227-9900,** 800/843-8667, or 559/565-3388. www.mslodge.com. 36 units, 13 cabins. $99–$299 double; $209–$499 suite; $1,495–$5,995 room or suite for 6-night Family Camp. 4- or 6-night minimum most summer weeks except Sat. **Amenities:** Restaurant.

Stony Creek Lodge ★   This lodge offers fairly standard motel rooms and a pleasant lobby highlighted by a big river-rock fireplace. We recommend it for its convenient location in between Grant Grove and Lodgepole, though it is far from the most distinctive property in the area. That being said, the rooms are well-maintained and functional, and we like the laid-back vibe of Stony Creek Lodge.

On Generals Hwy., Giant Sequoia National Monument. ☏ **866/522-6966** or 559/335-5500. www.
sequoia-kingscanyon.com. 11 units. $159–$189 double; $240–$320 suite or cabin Closed Sept–
May. **Amenities:** Restaurant.

In the Nearby Gateway Towns

Buckeye Tree Lodge ★★   Immediately outside Sequoia National Park, the
Buckeye has a vintage motel feel and a spectacular riverside location. To better appreciate that locale, all of the rooms have a patio or balcony looking out to the main fork
of the Kaweah River. The sister property across the street, the **Sequoia Village Inn**
(www.sequoiavillageinn.com) offers nice cabin-style rooms big enough for families.
Frankly, because of their careful upkeep and superb location, I like both properties
much more than the motels in the heart of Three Rivers.

46000 Sierra Dr., Three Rivers. ☏ **559/561-5900.** www.buckeyetree.com. 12 units. $134–$160
double; lower rates in winter. Rates include continental breakfast. Pets accepted by prior arrangement ($10/night). **Amenities:** Free Wi-Fi.

Lake Elowin Resort ★   They don't make them like Lake Elowin Resort anymore.
This funky, eccentric, thoroughly Californian kind of place, centered on the small lake
of its name, is a worthy base camp for adventures in Sequoia National Park. It features
picturesque wooden bridges and a number of outdoor sculptures, a vintage lighted sign
by the road, and a lush setting that feels more off the beaten path than it is. The cabins
are fairly basic (though the "Master Cabin" boasts a Jacuzzi, fireplace, and deck), and
include kitchens with cookware and utensils, the use of a canoe, and an outdoor barbecue (but no phones, TV, or Wi-Fi). The property has a lot of shady nooks and cran-
nies, and much more personality than the motels in Three Rivers.

43840 Dineley Dr., Three Rivers. ☏ **559/561-3460.** www.lake-elowin.com. 10 cabins. $120–$300
double or cabin. **Amenities:** Boat rentals.

Visalia Marriott ★★   This is one of the few, large full-service hotels in the general vicinity of Sequoia National Park, though its walking distance to numerous restaurants in vibrant downtown Visalia. If you need a dose of civilization head here. The
hotel has the types of amenities and décor you'd expect at, well, a big-city Marriott
along with convention facilities.

300 S. Court St., Visalia. ☏ **559/636-1111.** www.visaliamarriotthotel.com. 195 units. $59–$119 double; $189–$299 suite. **Amenities:** Restaurant; outdoor heated pool; outdoor hot tub; free Wi-Fi.

WHERE TO EAT

Inside the Parks

For a quick bite, there are many fast-food restaurants at the Lodgepole Market in
Sequoia and Cedar Grove in Kings Canyon. There's also a seasonal pizzeria at Stony
Creek Lodge, on Generals Highway between Grant Grove and Wuksachi.

Grant Grove Restaurant ★ AMERICAN   This is the center of activity in Grant
Grove in summer, with a menu focused on American standards for three meals a day.
It is a family-friendly eatery and fairly reliable, but not as memorable as the restaurants
at Wuksachi and Silver City.

Grant Grove Village, Kings Canyon National Park. ☏ **559/335-5000.** www.visitsequoia.com.
Breakfast and lunch $7–$15; dinner main courses $10–$30. Late May to early Sept daily 7–9pm;
shorter hours early and late in season. Closed Oct–Apr.

The Peaks ★★ NEW AMERICAN   Located in Wuksachi Lodge, this is easily the nicest dining room in either park. With contemporary mountain style and great views of the surrounding forest and mountains, the upscale eatery is a good bet for breakfasts—the buffet is hearty and good for hiking diets—as well as lunch, with sandwiches and burgers. Dinner brings creative preparations of wild game, beef, and other meat dishes, as well as a vegan burger for the herbivorous. Reservations are required for dinner.

Wuksachi Lodge, Sequoia National Park. ✆ **559/565-4070,** ext. 0. www.visit.sequoia.com. Breakfast and lunch $6–$15; dinner main courses $12–$30. Daily 7–10am, 11:30am–2:30pm, and 5–10pm.

Silver City Mountain Resort ★★ AMERICAN   If you want a home-cooked meal in Mineral King, this is your only option, but it's a pretty good one despite the lack of competition. It serves three hearty American meals a day Thursday through Monday and only pie and coffee on Tuesday and Wednesday—but don't skip it any day of the week. The house-baked pie is a revelation—they ship to restaurants down the valley in Three Rivers and beyond.

Mineral King, Sequoia National Park. ✆ **559/561-3223.** Menu items $7–$14. Thurs–Mon 8am–8pm; Tues–Wed 8am–5pm (pie and coffee only). Closed Oct to Memorial Day.

Outside the Parks

Anne Lang's Emporium ★ DELI   This is a fun little shop is a one-stop-shop for coffee, sandwiches, ice cream, and souvenirs. It is an old-fashioned type of place, with a nice deck on the Kaweah River. If you plan on hiking in Sequoia, get your picnic lunch to go here in the morning.

41651 Sierra Dr. (Calif. 198), Three Rivers. ✆ **559/561-4937.** Most items $3–$7. Mon–Fri 10am–4pm; Sat–Sun 11am–4pm. Store/ice-cream parlor Mon–Fri 9am–5pm; Sat–Sun 9am–5:30pm.

Brewbakers Brewing Company ★★ BREWPUB   A swell micro-brewery—you'll see the huge vats from the brass rail of the bar; try the excellent flagship Sequoia Red—Brewbakers has a classic pub ambiance. That means brick walls, stained glass windows, lots of friendly regulars and a pub menu to match of affordably priced steaks, burgers, massive salads, and pizza. Kids love the place as it also "brews up" homemade sodas. Live music some nights.

219 E. Main St., Visalia. ✆ **559/627-2739.** www.brewbakersbrewingco.com. Main courses $7–$24. Daily 11:30am–10pm. Bar open later.

Vintage Press ★★★ NEW AMERICAN/CONTINENTAL   Owned and operated by the Vartanian family since 1966, this is the best restaurant in the Sequoia region and a true fine-dining experience, with white tablecloths, plush red leather banquettes and excellent service. The menu encompasses a wide range of influences, meaning you could order the excellent lamb kebobs while your companion feasts on chile relleno. Classic American dishes are also quite well done, especially the restaurant's famed filet mignon. The wine list is similarly superlative. Reservations are recommended for dinner.

216 N. Willis St., Visalia. ✆ **559/733-3033.** www.thevintagepress.com. Main courses $12–$27 lunch, $20–$40 dinner. Mon–Sat 11:30am–2pm and 5:30–10pm; Sun 10am–2pm and 5–9pm.

DEATH VALLEY

by Eric Peterson

Americans looking for gold in California's mountains in the winter of 1849–50 got lost in the parched desert here while trying to avoid snowstorms in the nearby Sierra Nevada. One person perished along the way, and the land became known as Death Valley.

Little about the valley's essence has changed since. Its mountains stand naked, unadorned. The bitter waters of saline lakes evaporate into odd, thorn-like crystal formations. Jagged canyons jab deep into the earth. The ovenlike heat, frigid cold, and dry air combine to make this one of the world's most inhospitable locations. Death Valley is raw, bare earth, the way things must've looked before life began. Here, Earth's forces are exposed with dramatic clarity; just looking out on the landscape, you'll find it impossible to know what year, or century it is. It is no coincidence that many of Death Valley's topographical features are associated with hellish images: Funeral Mountains, Furnace Creek, Dante's View, Coffin Peak, and Devil's Golf Course. However, the valley can be a place of serenity as well.

Death Valley was designated a national monument in February 1933, protecting a vast and wondrous land and transforming one of the earth's least habitable spots into a tourist destination. In 1994, Death Valley National Park became the largest national park outside Alaska, with more than 3.3 million acres. Though remote, it attracts upwards of a million visitors a year.

FLORA & FAUNA

Little sign of life is found at the lowest elevations; any groundwater is highly saline and supports predominantly algae and bacteria. One notable exception is the unique **desert pupfish,** an ancient species that has slowly adapted to Death Valley's increasingly harsh conditions. In the spring, you can see the tiny fish in the marshes of Salt Creek, halfway between Furnace Creek and Stovepipe Wells, where a boardwalk lined with interpretive plaques allows an up-close look.

Hardy desert shrubs such as **mesquite, creosote,** and **arrowweed** flourish wherever there's groundwater below or snowmelt trickling from above. There are a surprising number of small animals that live at the lower elevations, including **rabbits, bats, snakes, roadrunners,** and **coyotes.** At the higher elevations, where **pinyon** and **juniper** blankets the slopes, animals are more plentiful and can include **bobcats, mule deer,** and **bighorn sheep.** Above 10,000 feet, look for **bristlecone pine;** some specimens on Telescope Peak are more than 3,000 years old.

AVOIDING the crowds

Visitors tend to avoid the summer and crowd Death Valley on weekends and holidays the rest of the year, especially in the spring.

ESSENTIALS

Getting There & Gateways

All the routes into the park involve crossing one of the steep mountain ranges that isolate Death Valley. The most common access route from Los Angeles and points south is **Calif. 127** from I-15 at the town of Baker. From Las Vegas, **Nev. 160** leads to Pahrump, 2 miles past which the route heads west to Death Valley Junction on Belle Vista Road. Perhaps the most scenic entry is on **Calif. 190** from the west, reached from Calif. 14 and U.S. 395 by taking Calif. 178 from Ridgecrest. You can also approach the park from Nevada by taking **Nev. 374** from Beatty, via U.S. 95.

THE NEAREST AIRPORT The nearest major airport is Las Vegas's **McCarran International Airport** (℘ 702/261-5211; www.mccarran.com).

Visitor Centers & Information

The **Furnace Creek Visitor Center** (℘ 760/786-3200) is open daily year-round in Furnace Creek, 15 miles inside the eastern park boundary on Calif. 190. There's also an information center at **Scotty's Castle** (℘ 760/786-2392). It's open daily year-round. The ranger stations are at **Stovepipe Wells** and **Grapevine.**

For information about the park, call ℘ 760/786-3200, visit www.nps.gov/deva, or contact the **Death Valley Natural History Association** (℘ 800/478-8564; www.dvnha.org), which operates park bookstores.

Fees

Entry to the park for up to 7 days costs $20 per car (or $10 per person on foot, motorcycle, or bike). There are nine campgrounds within park boundaries. Four are free; overnight fees elsewhere range from $12 to $18.

Seasons & Climate

Although Death Valley is one of the world's driest deserts, altitudes in the park range from 282 feet below sea level to over 11,000 feet above—so "desert" doesn't always equal "hot." From June to September, temperatures in the valley can soar above 120°F (49°C), making the mountain sections of the park a relief, with temperatures in the 70s and 80s (20s Celsius). From November to February, when valley temperatures are comfortable, many higher areas are frigid and snowy.

EXPLORING THE PARK BY CAR

A network of roads, ranging from washboard remnants of old mining days to well-maintained highways built during the 1930s, crisscross Death Valley National Park. You'll find that most of the popular destinations, as well as the five major entry routes, have superior-quality roads suitable for passenger vehicles, as well as trailers and RVs.

Death Valley National Park

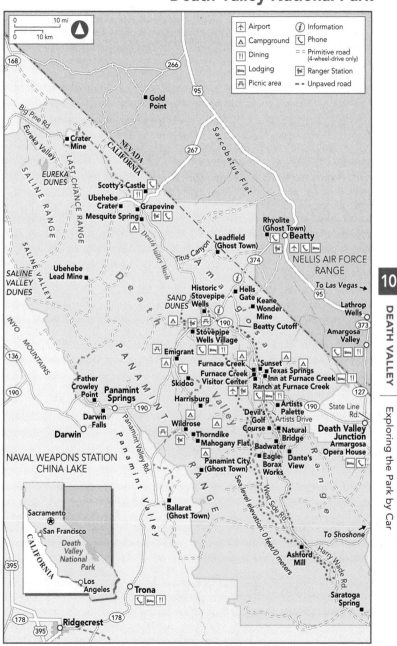

Dehydration is your most urgent concern, particularly in summer. Recommended minimum amounts are 1 gallon of water per person per day, twice that if you're hiking. Also bring sunscreen and protective clothing, including a wide-brimmed hat and sunglasses. Watch your temperature gauge, especially if you have an older vehicle. Turn off the air-conditioning on uphill grades if your car overheats.

Some of the most beautiful sites have handy access roads, vista turnouts, or loop drives to facilitate viewing. These include **Artists Palette,** where the 9-mile (one-way) Artists Drive takes you through a colorful display hidden from the main road. Over millions of years, mineral deposits have created brilliant swaths of color across the rocky hills. There's a scenic overlook at the beginning of the drive, as well as a parking area farther along, in case you want to stop and scramble amid the pink, blue, red, orange, and green patches. (Sci-fi buffs, take note: This area served as a location in the original *Star Wars.*)

About 10 miles south of Artists Drive is **Badwater,** whose name indicates the lowest, hottest, and (curiously) wettest spots on the valley floor. The basin bottoms out at the continental superlative of 282 feet below sea level. The water in the spring-fed pools here at first seemed like relief to early travelers—until they tasted the chloride, sodium, and sulfate. It isn't poisonous, and it is home to beetles, soldier fly larvae, and a snail that slowly adapted to these harsh conditions.

A similar site is 25 miles north on Calif. 190: **Salt Creek,** home to the **Salt Creek pupfish,** found nowhere else on Earth. In the spring, you can glimpse this little fish, which has made some amazing adaptations to survive in this arid land, from a wooden boardwalk nature trail. In spring, a million pupfish might be wriggling in the creek; they're not visible at any other time of year.

Your car will also take you all the way to two of the best lookout points around, both along Calif. 190 southeast of Furnace Creek. Before sunrise, photographers set up their tripods at **Zabriskie Point,** 5 miles southeast of Furnace Creek off Calif. 190, and aim their cameras down at the pale mudstone hills of Golden Canyon and the great valley beyond. The panoramic view is magnificent.

Another grand park vista is at **Dante's View,** 25 miles south of Furnace Creek by way of Calif. 190 and Dante's View Road. This 5,475-foot point looks out over the shimmering Death Valley floor backed by the high Panamint Mountains.

Nearly everyone takes the scenic drive up Scotty's Castle Road to visit the park's major man-made attraction, **Scotty's Castle** (see below). While you're there, it's worth taking the 15-minute drive to **Ubehebe Crater,** 9 miles west of the castle. The otherworldly pockmark resulted from a volcanic explosion that occurred as recently as 300 years ago. You'll know that you're close when the landscape begins to darken from layers of cinders that were spewed from the half-mile crater. A convenient loop road takes you up to the most scenic lip. An explanatory sign graces the parking area, and there's a hiking path (for those willing to brave the often-gusting winds) to an even more dramatic overlook and a field of smaller craters.

10

Exploring the Park by Car

DEATH VALLEY

ORGANIZED TOURS & RANGER PROGRAMS

In addition to providing hourly **Scotty's Castle** "Living History" tours (see below), Death Valley rangers offer lectures and film presentations on varied topics, and guided hikes are available on a seasonal basis. Contact park headquarters for a seasonal schedule of day and evening events; nearly all programs (except for year-round Scotty's Castle tours) cease in summer.

PARK ATTRACTIONS

Scotty's Castle ★★★, the Mediterranean-style hacienda in the northern part of the park wows visitors with Spanish tiles, well-crafted furnishings, and ahead-of-its-time solar water heating. Even more compelling is the colorful history of this villa in remote Grapevine Canyon, brought to life by rangers dressed in 1930s uniforms. Chicago millionaire Albert Johnson built the "castle" as a winter retreat in the 1920s. The insurance tycoon's unlikely friendship with prospector/cowboy/spinner-of-tall-tales Walter Scott (a.k.a. Scotty) put the $2.3-million structure on the map and captured the public's imagination. Scotty would tell visitors the castle was his place, and Johnson would always oblige his fibs because he was so fond of his larger-than-life tall tales.

Guided tours depart about every 20 minutes from 9am to 5pm in the winter and 9:30am to 4pm in the summer; they fill up quickly, so arrive early for the first available spots. The 50-minute tour costs $11 for adults, $9 seniors, $6 children 6 to 15, and is free for kids under 6. During busy periods, you may have to wait an hour or more, perusing the gift shop, relaxing in the snack bar, or hiking to Scotty's grave on the hill behind the castle. Or, you can order tickets (at least 24 hr. in advance) at www.recreation.gov or ✆ **877/444-6777.** There's also a self-guided walking tour (excluding the interiors) from stable to pool, from bunkhouse to powerhouse.

For yet another side of the human experience here, visit the **Harmony Borax Works,** 1 mile north of Furnace Creek off Calif. 190. Death Valley prospectors called borax "white gold," and though it wasn't a glamorous substance, it was a profitable one. From 1883 to 1888, more than 20 million pounds of it were transported from the Harmony Borax Works; some borax mining continues in Death Valley to this day. A short trail with interpretive signs leads past the ruins of the old borax refinery.

Transport of borax was the stuff of legends, too. The famous 20-mule teams hauled the huge loaded wagons 165 miles to the rail station at Mojave. To learn more about this colorful era, visit the **Borax Museum** at the Ranch at Furnace Creek (see p. 137).

DAY HIKES

Wherever you hike, never forget to carry enough water; even in seemingly mild weather conditions, hikers can become dehydrated quickly.

Shorter Trails

Eureka Dunes ★★★ These magnificent dunes are the tallest in California, and surprisingly full of plant and animal life. The view from atop the highest dune (about 700 ft.) takes in the contrast of creamy sand against the layer-cake band of nearby rock, and small avalanches of sand create the trademark "singing" peculiar to such dunes. 5 miles RT. Moderate. Access: Eureka Valley, at the end of South Eureka Rd.

MOJAVE NATIONAL PRESERVE: a desert wonderland

To most Americans, the eastern Mojave is a bleak, interminable stretch of desert to be crossed as quickly as possible. But many consider the national preserve, just southeast of Death Valley National Park along California's I-15 and I-40, the crown jewel of the California desert.

This is a hard land to get to know—it has no accommodations or restaurants, few campgrounds, and only a handful of roads suitable for the average passenger vehicle. But hidden within this natural fortress are some true gems—its 1.6 million acres include the world's largest Joshua tree forest; abundant wildlife; spectacular canyons, caverns, sand dunes, and volcanic formations; tabletop mesas; and a dozen mountain ranges.

There's much more life in the Mojave Desert than the human eye can immediately discern. Many animals are well camouflaged or nocturnal (or both), but if you tread lightly and keep your eyes open, the experience is rewarding. Wildlife includes the hopping kangaroo rat, ground squirrels, cottontails and jackrabbits, bobcats, coyotes, lizards, snakes, and the threatened desert tortoise. Consider yourself lucky to spot elusive bighorn sheep or shy mule deer. Migrating birds that stop off in the Mojave are met by permanent residents such as quail, pinyon jays, sparrows, noisy cactus wrens, and the distinctive roadrunner.

You'll see familiar desert plants such as the fragrant creosote bush, several varieties of cacti (including the deceptively fluffy-looking cholla, or "teddy bear"), and several strains of yucca. On and around Cima Dome grows the world's largest and densest **Joshua tree forest.** Botanists say that Cima's Joshuas are more symmetrical than their cousins elsewhere in the Mojave. The dramatic colors of the sky at sunset provide a breathtaking backdrop for Cima's Joshua trees, some more than 25 feet tall and over 100 years old.

Other desert flora include Mormon tea, cliff rose, desert sage, desert primrose, and cat's-claw; these flowering plants are among many that make the spring wildflower season a popular time to visit. Junipers, nut-bearing pinyon pines, and scrub oaks are found in the preserve's higher elevations.

Kelbaker Road provides an excellent opportunity to sample the preserve with a minimal expenditure of time or trouble. The well-paved two-lane road, crossing the preserve roughly from north to south between I-15 and I-40, takes about 1 hour one-way without stops.

You'll drive through the eerie blackened landscape of **lava beds** and **cinder cones,** visit the restored **Kelso Depot,** home to an interesting museum, and see the towering golden mounds of **Kelso Dunes.** This 45-square-mile formation of sculpted sand dunes is famous for its "booming," a low rumble emitted when small avalanches or blowing sands pass over the underlying layer. Geologists speculate that the extreme dryness of the East Mojave Desert, combined with the wind-polished, rounded nature of the sand grains, has something to do with the musicality. **Hole-in-the-Wall** is an interesting geological phenomenon with all sorts of pockmarked volcanic formations that have been slowly shaped by the ravages of the desert climate, featuring a trail that includes rungs bored into the rock for hikers to descend.

Entry to the preserve is free. Campsites at two developed campgrounds cost $12, but dispersed camping is free. There are hiking opportunities. For more information, **Mojave National Preserve** (𝐶 **760/252-6100;** www.nps.gov/moja).

Golden Canyon Interpretive Trail ★★   A good choice for a quick hike in just about any weather, Golden Canyon is convenient to Furnace Creek accommodations and offers an opportunity to get up close with an interesting rock formation. The fairly level trail twists and turns a mile up Golden Canyon, to the foot of the aptly named Red Cathedral. 2 miles RT. Easy. Access: 2 miles south of Calif. 190 on Badwater Rd.

Little Hebe Crater Trail ★★★   Black cinders and volcanic fragments cover the countryside surrounding the apocalyptic-looking Ubehebe Crater, which erupted as recently as 300 years ago. Fierce winds can hamper your progress, but you'll get an exhilarating feeling, as though you're visiting another planet. High-top boots or shoes are recommended for the pebbly path. Adventurous types can also descend a short, steep trail to the crater floor, about 500 feet below the rim. 1.5 miles RT. Moderate. Access: Trail head leads up from parking area for Ubehebe Crater, 7 miles northwest of the Grapevine Ranger Station.

Mosaic Canyon ★★   This short stroll requires a bit of rock scrambling into a canyon where water has polished the marble into white, gray, and black mosaics. The first mile is easy, suitable for every skill level; children will love running their hands over the water-smoothed rock walls. More adventurous climbers can continue up a series of chutes and dry waterfalls in the latter half of the hike. .5 to 4 miles RT. Moderate. Access: End of a short, graded dirt road just east of Stovepipe Wells on Calif. 190.

Natural Bridge Canyon ★   This short walk takes you into a colorful narrow canyon. The loose gravel underfoot makes for a tiring walk, but it's less than .5 mile to the distinctive formation that gives the canyon its name: a rock bridge overhead, formed when rushing waters cut through softer lower layers. If you wish to hike past the bridge, it's another .5 mile to the end of the canyon, making for a 2-mile hike. 1 mile RT. Moderate. Access: Take Badwater Rd. 15 miles south of Furnace Creek and continue 2 miles on unpaved spur road suitable for passenger vehicles.

Salt Creek Nature Trail ★★   A leisurely hike on a wooden boardwalk leads you along the unique salt marshes, passing a few plants (including the unusual pickleweed) along the way. In the spring, watch for the amazingly adaptive Salt Creek pupfish flashing about in the shallow water. .5 mile RT. Easy. Access: Take Calif. 190 14 miles north of Furnace Creek or 13 miles east of Stovepipe Wells, then follow 1-mile graded dirt spur road.

Titus Canyon Narrows ★★   The canyon's rock walls are an amateur geologist's dream—layers of orange, black, and blue-gray volcanic sediment streaked with threads of gleaming white calcite. Though you can augment this easy hike by continuing through the canyon, there's a broad pullout from the road at 1.5 miles; it's a good place to enjoy the view, and perhaps a picnic, before returning the way you came. More adventurous types can hike 5 miles more to walls bedecked with petroglyphs near Klare Springs. *Note:* As you hike, watch for vehicle traffic coming one-way from the other direction. 3 miles RT. Easy. Access: Up a signed dirt road off Scotty's Castle Rd. (about 15 miles north of Calif. 190) that leads to the mouth of Titus Canyon, where it meets a one-way road for four-wheel-drive vehicles from Nev. 374; trail begins where the road becomes one-way coming toward you (from Nevada).

A Word on Biking

Cycling is allowed on the 1,000 miles of dirt and paved roads used by motor vehicles in the park, but not on hiking trails or anywhere else. Weather conditions between May and October make bicycling at the lower elevations dangerous at times other than early morning.

Longer Trails

Gower Gulch Loop ★★★   Start by hiking along the once-paved route that allowed cars to drive into the canyon but which was destroyed by flash flooding. Soon you'll be scrambling around the badlands, hills of mud and silt deposited by ancient lakes. Those with more stamina can continue past Manly Beacon (a sandstone formation), across gullies and washes, and then up to Zabriskie Point for panoramic views of the forbidding badlands. *Note:* If you hike beyond Manly Beacon, bring a map—it is easy to lose your bearings in this area. 4 miles RT. Easy to moderate. Access: Golden Canyon parking lot along Calif. 178, about 2 miles south of the Inn at Furnace Creek.

Jayhawker Canyon ★★   This out-of-the-way route follows the path of a desperate group of pioneers who attempted to find a way out of Death Valley in 1849–50. The footing in the debris-filled canyon is treacherous, and several forks and tributaries can distract you from staying in the main wash. At the end of the route lies a spring marking the Jayhawkers' camp, also a popular stopping place for the native Shoshone. Boulders in the area are marked with petroglyphs depicting bighorn sheep, along with the initials of several pioneers scratched into the rocks. You can stop and turn around here or continue up 3 miles more to the base of Pinto Peak. 4 to 10 miles RT. Moderate. Access: Off Calif. 190, just west of Emigrant Ranger Station.

Telescope Peak Trail ★★★   A grueling 3,000-foot climb ultimately leads to the 11,049-foot summit, where you'll be rewarded with the view described thusly by one pioneer: "You can see so far, it's just like looking through a telescope." Snow-covered in winter, the peak is best climbed from May to November; the trail is snowed in the rest of the year. Consult park rangers for current conditions and detailed advice—and *never attempt this climb alone.* 14 miles RT. Strenuous. Access: Mahogany Flat Campground.

Wildrose Peak Trail ★★   Consisting mostly of steady ascents adding up to more than 2,000 feet en route to the 9,060-foot summit, this trail offers great vistas of the stark Panamint Range, a bird's-eye view of Death Valley, and panoramas of the Sierras on the western horizon. It's unwise to attempt this hike in winter or without obtaining a map from the ranger station. 8.4 miles RT. Strenuous. Access: Wildrose Charcoal Kilns.

WHERE TO STAY

Inside the Park

The Inn at Furnace Creek ★★★   A Great Gatsby-era beaut, this 1927 inn, with its Spanish Mission-inspired architecture, offers one of the most luxurious (and priciest) hostelries in any national park. There are a variety of elegantly appointed guestrooms and suites with a long list of premium amenities (fine linens, Keurig coffeemakers in each rooms, flat screen TVs); some have in-room spas and most offer swell views of the palm-laden property and surrounding mountains. The facilities are first-rate, too, and include two pools, basketball and tennis courts, massage room, and a sauna.

Furnace Creek. ✆ **760/786-2345**, 800/236-7916, or 303/297-2757 for reservations. www.furnace creekresort.com. 66 units. $265–$475 double. Closed mid-May to mid-Oct. **Amenities:** Restaurant; bar; 2 outdoor pools; exercise room; sauna; tennis courts; free Wi-Fi.

Panamint Springs Resort ★   A laid-back, low-price change of pace from the slicker Xanterra-managed properties in the park, Panamint Springs Resort is on the west side of Death Valley at the foot of the Panamint Mountains. Rooms are spartan but well maintained (translation: they're appropriate for folks who simply want a

CAMPING options

My pick for car-camping in Death Valley, **Furnace Creek Campground ★★**, just north of the Furnace Creek Visitor Center. It's the only campground in Death Valley that takes advance reservations (**℃ 877/444-6777;** www.recreation.gov), and it features the best access to civilization (read: air conditioning and swimming pools)—nice in a place that's known to hit 120 degrees Fahrenheit. It offers pay showers nearby (during peak times, there are quotas). Also positioned to access the restaurants, pool, and air-conditioned facilities here is the huge **Sunset Campground ★**, just .25 mile east of the Ranch at Furnace Creek, which has individual sites and nearby showers (fee). **Texas Spring ★**, near Sunset Campground, is a third choice, with 92 sites (so it bustles with activity) and two group sites. The fee for an individual site at these campgrounds ranges from $12 to $18 a night. Even bigger, **Stovepipe Wells Campground ★** has 204 spaces, with 14 RV hookups in two areas, and pay showers; the fee is $12 for a campsite, or $30 if you want an RV utility hookup (**℃ 760/786-2387** for reservations for the latter). The basic, tents-only **Emigrant Campground** is 9 miles southwest of Stovepipe Wells on Calif. 190.

Other campgrounds are known for their off-the-grid solitude. **Thorndike**

Campground ★★, 37 miles south of Stovepipe Wells and 1 mile from Mahogany Flats Campground, off the Trona–Wildrose Road, is accessible only by four-wheel-drive vehicles. It has eight free primitive campsites with pit toilets but no other facilities. **Wildrose Campground ★★**, 30 miles south of Stovepipe Wells off the Trona–Wildrose Road, also has free campsites, pit toilets, drinking water and lots of serenity. For those rugged individualists who really want to get away from it all, **Mahogany Flats Campground ★★**, 38 miles south of Stovepipe Wells, off Trona–Wildrose Road, is the choice, though it can be reached only by four-wheel-drive vehicles. It has pit toilets but no other facilities and is gratis. On the north side of the park, **Mesquite Spring Campground ★** is 5 miles south of Scotty's Castle on Grapevine Road and especially goods for campers planning on a castle tour. The rate is $12 nightly.

The **Panamint Springs Resort ★** (**℃ 775/482-7680;** www.deathvalley.com/psr), 30 miles west of Stovepipe Wells on Calif. 190, operates a commercial campground with RV utility hookups, but the property is not too distinctive in terms of scenery. It charges $30 per night for full RV hookups, $20 for a water-only RV site, and $7.50 for a tent campsite.

decent, cheap place to crash). Even less expensive—and simple—are the tent-cabins for $35 at the campground across the street. Historical trivia: The resort was established in 1937 by Agnes Cody, the cousin of Buffalo Bill.

30 miles west of Stovepipe Wells. **℃ 775/482-7680.** www.deathvalley.com/psr. 14 units, 1 cottage. $79–$108 double; $149 cottage. Pets accepted. ($5/night). **Amenities:** Restaurant; bar; outdoor pool; free Wi-Fi.

The Ranch at Furnace Creek ★★   An off-shoot of the pricier Inn at Furnace Creek, this once was a working ranch and the place still retains a folksy, casual, friendly vibe. Rooms are pleasant (though bathrooms can be small) and all have satellite TV and Wi-Fi—a rarity in national parks! They come in a number of categories from duplex cabins to fairly standard motel rooms with balconies to deluxe rooms with private patios that abut the pool courtyard. This year-round facility is at the center of civilization in the park, offering a golf course, several restaurants, and a pool that is a great escape from the fabled Death Valley heat.

At Furnace Creek. © **760/786-2345;** 800/236-7916 or 303/297-2757 for reservations. www.furnacecreekresort.com. 224 units. $138–$219 double. **Amenities:** Restaurant; bar; outdoor pool; golf course; free Wi-Fi.

Stovepipe Wells Village ★ About 25 miles northwest of Furnace Creek, Stovepipe Wells is a good value, trading scenery for lower rates. Rooms are fairly basic and what you would expect from a well-maintained roadside lodging with subtle Western style, but a good match for those planning on exploring the park during daylight hours. There is a general store and a campground on the property.

23 miles northwest of Furnace Creek. © **760/786-2387.** www.escapetodeathvalley.com. 83 units. $100–$182 double. **Amenities:** Restaurant; bar; outdoor pool; free Wi-Fi.

Near the Park

The money-saving (but inconvenient) option is spending a night in one of the gateway towns. **Lone Pine,** on the west side of the park, is a good choice, with a wide selection of lodgings and great Western views and charm. **Beatty, Nevada,** and **Shoshone** are about an hour's drive from the park's center, and accommodations are limited to basic motels. In Death Valley Junction, the one-of-a-kind **Amargosa Opera House and Hotel** (© 760/852-4441; www.amargosa-opera-house.com; $78–$97 a night) offers 15 rooms about 30 miles from Furnace Creek. A quirky gem, its covered with intricate hand-painted murals by owner Marta Becket, a dancer/chanteuse who also puts on performances in the theater (though her schedule has gotten sporadic in recent years).

WHERE TO EAT

Inside the Park

There are four dining options at the Ranch at **Furnace Creek,** all relatively informal. The best and most economical is the **Forty Niner Cafe,** a diner with better-than-average food and a widely varied menu three meals a day. The adjacent **Wrangler Steakhouse** offers an all-you-can-eat buffet for breakfast and lunch. For dinner, the Wrangler offers table service, grilling steaks, ribs, and other satisfying specialties; the servings are generous, but the dinners are pricey. The most casual option is the **Corkscrew Saloon,** serving pizza, bar fare, and libations at lunch and dinner. At the golf course, the **19th Hole Bar & Grill** serves pub fare from October to May.

At the elegant dining room at the **Inn at Furnace Creek,** the menu highlights several Continental and regional cuisines. The peaceful setting and attentive service can be a welcome (though pricey) treat during exhausting travels through the park. Breakfast, lunch, and dinner are served. The Sunday buffet brunch is truly decadent; reservations are necessary. T-shirts and tank tops are not allowed.

The **Tollroad Restaurant,** the restaurant at Stovepipe Wells, is open daily for breakfast and dinner (lunch is available at the Badwater Saloon). Other choices are a snack bar at Scotty's Castle and a rustic (and affordable) burgers-and-beer cafe at Panamint Springs.

JOSHUA TREE

by Eric Peterson

At Joshua Tree National Park, the trees are merely the starting point for exploring the seemingly barren desert. Viewed from the roadside, the dry land only hints at hidden vitality, but closer examination reveals a giant mosaic of an ecosystem, intensely beautiful and complex. From lush oases teeming with life to rusted-out relics of man's attempts to tame this wilderness, from low plains of tufted cacti to mountains of exposed, gnarled rock, the park is much more than a tableau of the curious tree for which it's named.

The Joshua tree is said to have been given its name by early Mormon settlers (ca. 1850). Its upraised limbs and bearded appearance reminded them of the prophet Joshua leading them to the promised land. It's actually a treelike variety of yucca, a member of the agave family.

At Joshua Tree National Park, the peculiar tree reaches the southernmost boundary of its range. The park straddles two desert environments: The mountainous, Joshua tree–studded Mojave Desert forms the northwestern part of the park, while the hotter, drier, and lower Colorado Desert, characterized by a wide variety of desert flora such as cacti, ocotillo, and native California fan palms, comprises the park's southern and eastern sections. Between them runs the "transition zone," displaying characteristics of each.

The area's geological timeline stretches back almost 2 billion years. Eight million years ago, the Mojave landscape was one of rolling hills and flourishing grasslands; horses, camels, and mastodons abounded, with saber-toothed tigers and wild dogs filling the role of predator. Human presence has been traced back nearly 10,000 years with the discovery of the Pinto culture, and you can see evidence of more recent habitation throughout the park in the form of American Indian rock art. Miners and ranchers began coming in the 1860s, but the boom went bust by the turn of the 20th century.

During the 1920s, a worldwide fascination with the desert emerged. Entrepreneurs hauled truckloads of desert plants into Los Angeles for quick sale or export, and souvenir hunters removed archaeological treasures. In response to the plunder, Pasadena socialite Minerva Hoyt organized the desert conservation movement and successfully lobbied for the establishment of Joshua Tree National Monument in 1936. In 1994, under provisions of the federal California Desert Protection Act, Joshua Tree was "upgraded" to national park status and expanded to nearly 800,000 acres.

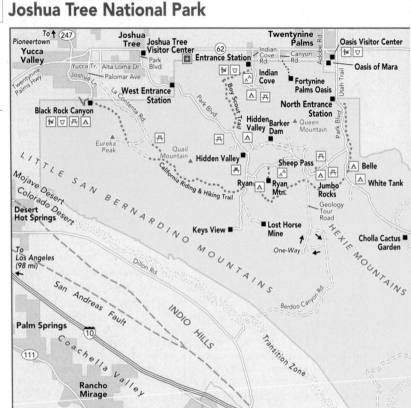

FLORA & FAUNA

The eastern half of the park is typical of the lower Colorado Desert, dominated by the abundant and fragrant **creosote** bush, a drought-resistant survivor that releases secretions into the surrounding soil to inhibit competing seedlings. Adding interest to the arid land are small stands of spidery, tenacious **ocotillo,** a split personality that drops its leaves in times of drought, making it appear dry and spindly. When the rains come, the ocotillo can sprout bushy leaves in a few days, and its flaming blooms atop leafy green branches bear little resemblance to its dormant alter ego.

Most people associate desert plants with **cacti,** which are indeed here in abundance. Most of the park's points of interest lie in the higher, slightly cooler and wetter Mojave Desert, the special habitat of the burly **Joshua tree,** which displays huge white flowers following a good rainy season. Five **fan palm** oases (in both climate zones) flourish in areas where water is forced to the surface along fault lines. The Joshua Tree area has also traditionally been an excellent place to view nature's springtime **wildflower** bonanza, and the lower elevations of the park are hot spots.

From the black-tailed **jackrabbits** abundant at the Oasis of Mara and throughout the park to **bobcats** and the occasional **cougar** prowling around less-traveled areas, the

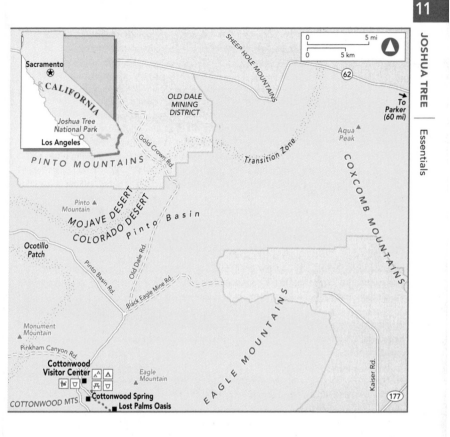

desert teems with animal life, as well. Some other frequently spotted residents: the **roadrunners, coyotes,** and **bighorn sheep,** most often seen atop the rocky hills they ascend with sharp cloven hooves. Perhaps the most unusual animal is the **desert tortoise,** a slow-moving burrow dweller not often seen by casual visitors. The tortoises, which can live more than 50 years, are a protected threatened species, and visitors are prohibited from touching or interfering with them in any way. A poignant exception to this is if one encounters a tortoise on the road in danger of being hit—you're permitted to pick it up gently with two hands and carry it off the road, placing it facing in the same direction in which it was traveling.

ESSENTIALS

Getting There & Gateways

There are three roads into the park. The most commonly used is the **West Entrance Station,** on Park Boulevard in the town of Joshua Tree along Calif. 62. The **North Entrance Station,** at the end of Utah Trail in the town of Twentynine Palms, on Calif. 62, 40 miles north of its junction with I-10, is also a popular gateway to the park. On the southern side of the park is the **Cottonwood Visitor Center,** about 40 miles east of Palm Springs along I-10.

THE NEAREST AIRPORT   The closest airport is the **Palm Springs International Airport** (📞 760/318-3800; www.palmspringsca.gov).

Visitor Centers & Information

Your best sources of information in the park are the Park Service's three visitor centers. The park headquarters and **Oasis Visitor Center,** 74485 National Park Dr. in Twentynine Palms, is on the road to the North Entrance Station. The **Cottonwood Visitor Center,** at the south end of the park, houses a gift shop and bookstore, as well as an interpretive exhibit on the area's wildlife. The **Joshua Tree Visitor Center,** 6554 Park Blvd. in Joshua Tree, is on the road to the West Entrance Station. In addition to providing visitor materials and information, this center has a bookstore and gift shop, a cafe, and an exhibit gallery. Contact **Joshua Tree National Park** (📞 760/367-5500; www. nps.gov/jotr) if you'd like information in advance of your trip. Books and maps can be obtained from the **Joshua Tree National Park Association** (📞 760/367-5525; www. joshuatree.org).

Fees

Admission to the park is $15 per car (valid for 7 days). The nine developed campgrounds charge fees of $10 to $15 for individual sites, more for group sites. Backcountry camping is free, but self-registration is required.

Seasons & Climate

Joshua Tree National Park's 794,000 acres straddle two distinct desert climates. The eastern half of the park is hot, dry Colorado Desert, and most points of interest lie in the higher, slightly cooler and wetter Mojave Desert. The Mojave will occasionally get a dusting of snow in winter, but neither section sees more than 3 to 6 inches of annual rainfall. Winter temperatures are in the comfortable 50s or 60s (lower teens Celsius) during the day and often approach freezing overnight; summer days can blaze past 100°F (38°C) at noon, and even nighttime offers little relief in August and September, when lows are still in the 80s (upper 20s Celsius). At the park's higher elevations the summer climate is much more bearable. Overall, the fall tends to be the best season for hiking.

EXPLORING THE PARK BY CAR

There are two main roads through the park, and by driving them both you'll be able to see virtually every feature that distinguishes Joshua Tree; there are even a couple of easy opportunities to stop and stretch your legs.

Park Boulevard loops through the high northern section between the North Entrance Station in Twentynine Palms and the West Entrance Station in Joshua Tree. Along the drive, which takes about 1 hour one-way, you'll get an eyeful of the rock formations and oddly shaped Joshua trees. Stop at one of the well-marked interpretive trails along the way, but don't miss the detour to **Keys View,** one of the most popular spots in the park. A paved road leads to this mile-high mountain crest, where a series of plaques describe the land below. You'll also have a panoramic view that encompasses both the highest (Mt. San Gorgonio) and the lowest (Salton Sea) points in Southern California.

Pinto Basin Road crosses the park from top to bottom, forking away from Park Boulevard near the North Entrance Station and winding down to the Cottonwood Entrance off I-10. Driving it, you'll pass from the higher Mojave Desert into the lower Colorado Desert, across the "transition zone" snaking through the middle of the park, a fascinating melting pot where the two climates are both represented. Stop to marvel at the Cholla Cactus Garden (or the Ocotillo Patch, where the spidery, tenacious desert shrub sports flaming red blooms following spring rains). At the park's southern end, you can explore the lush Cottonwood Spring or see relics of World War II training maneuvers (see "Park Attractions," below). Driving from end to end takes about an hour.

ORGANIZED TOURS & RANGER PROGRAMS

A multitude of ranger-led seminars and guided hikes are available. They change annually but might include topics such as "Meet the Joshua Tree," "Clever Desert Plants," "Rock of Ages," and "Oasis Walk," as well as guided hikes on many of the park's popular trails and evening campfire talks on weekends. Throughout the wildflower blooming season, and especially during Easter week, special walks visit the most abundantly flowering areas.

The National Park Service also conducts guided tours of the historic **Keys Ranch.** From October to May, tours run twice or thrice daily ($5 adults, $2.50 kids 6–11 and seniors). Daily tours are offered at 10am and 1pm, and sometimes in the evening at 7pm. Make advance reservations by calling ⓒ **760/367-5522.**

Visitors can go more in-depth by enrolling in a workshop with the **Desert Institute** (ⓒ **760/367-5535;** www.joshuatree.org/desert-institute). Their classes range from desert survival and orienteering to poetry and sculpture; workshops typically run one to three daily sessions and cost $30 to $250.

PARK ATTRACTIONS

Miners and ranchers began coming in the 1860s, including the McHaney brothers, who established the Desert Queen Ranch. Later on, Bill Keys acquired it, and he lived with his family on the property, now known as the **Keys Ranch,** until his death in 1969. Many of the ranch structures have been restored to their Keys-era condition, painting a compelling picture of how one hardy family made a home in the unforgiving desert. Admittance is limited to official Park Service tours.

Dehydration is a constant threat in the desert; even in winter, carry plenty of drinking water and drink regularly even if you don't feel thirsty. Recommended minimum supplies are 1 gallon per person per day, or twice that if planning strenuous activity.

Sections of the park (identified on the official map) contain **abandoned mines** and associated structures. Use extreme caution in the vicinity, watching for open shafts and prospect holes. Supervise children closely, and never enter abandoned mines.

Flash flooding is a potential hazard following even brief rain showers, so avoid drainage areas and be especially observant of road conditions at those times.

You can find petroglyphs near **Barker Dam,** where an easy 1.1-mile loop hiking trail leads to a small artificial lake framed by the Wonderland of Rocks. After scrambling a bit to get to the dam, you'll find a sandy path leading to the "Disney Petroglyph" site. Its wry name stems from the fact that a 1950s movie crew retraced the ancient rock carvings to make them more visible to the camera, defacing them forever. If you investigate the cliffs along the remainder of the trail, you're likely to find some untouched drawings depicting animals, humans, and other aspects of desert life as interpreted by long-ago dwellers. You'll see more petroglyphs along the 18-mile **Geology Tour Road,** a sandy, lumpy dirt road accessible only by four-wheel-drive vehicles or hardy mountain bikers.

During World War II, George S. Patton trained over a million soldiers in desert combat at several sites throughout the Mojave and Colorado deserts. Tank tracks are still visible in the desert around the former Camp Young, near Cottonwood Springs. The **Camp Young Memorial** marker is 1 mile east of Cottonwood Springs Road, just before the park entrance; an informational kiosk there gives details of the training maneuvers and daily camp life. To learn more, you can visit the **General Patton Memorial Museum** (© **760/227-3483;** www.generalpattonmuseum.com) in Chiriaco Summit, on I-10 about 4 miles east of the Cottonwood Entrance. The museum contains an assortment of memorabilia from World War II and other military glory days, as well as displays of tanks and artillery; it's open daily from 9:30am to 4:30pm. Admission is $5 for adults, $4.50 for seniors, $1 for children 7 to 12, and free for children under 7.

DAY HIKES

Joshua Tree's natural wonders are accessible to everyone, not just the extreme outdoor adventurer. Nowhere is this more apparent than in the diversity of hiking and nature trails, which range from a half-mile paved nature trail (ideal for even strollers and wheelchairs) to trails of 15-plus miles requiring strenuous hiking and backcountry camping.

Shorter Trails

Cholla Cactus Garden Nature Trail ★★   This trail winds through an unusually dense concentration of Bigelow cholla, one of the desert's more fascinating residents. Often called "teddy bear cactus" for its deceptively fluffy appearance, cholla is also nicknamed "jumping cactus" for the ease with which its barbed spines stick to the clothing and skin of anyone who passes too close. Any ranger can tell you horror stories of people who've tripped into a cholla bush and emerged looking like porcupines and in pain—but please don't let that stop you from enjoying this pretty roadside diversion. .25 mile RT. Easy. Access: Middle of the park, about halfway btw. the north and south entrances.

Cottonwood Springs Nature Trail ★ Trek through rolling desert hills long inhabited by Cahuilla Indians. Signs along the way relate how they used native plants in their everyday lives; the trail culminates at lush Cottonwood Springs. The prolific underground water source supports thick groves of cottonwood and palm trees, plus the birds and animals that make them home. 1 mile RT. Easy. Access: Cottonwood Campground.

Desert Queen Mine ★★ The "trail" meanders and forks through the ruins of a gold mine that yielded several million dollars' worth of ore between 1895 and 1961. Building ruins, steel machinery parts, and sealed mine shafts dot the hillsides and ravine; just up the trail, there's a signboard at the overlook with information about mine operations, and it's 1.6 miles to the mine itself. 1.4–32 miles RT. Easy to moderate. Access: Dirt road leading north from Park Blvd., opposite the Geology Tour Rd.

Fortynine Palms Oasis ★★ This hike begins with a steep, harsh ascent 300 feet up to a ridge fringed with red-spined barrel cacti. Down the other side, a rocky canyon contains the spectacular oasis whose fan palm and cottonwood tree canopy shades clear pools of green water. Plants (especially spring wildflowers), birds, lizards, and other wildlife are abundant in this miniature ecosystem, and the scorched trunks of trees bear witness to past fires that have nourished rather than destroyed the life here. Beware of rattlesnakes in the shaded brush around the oasis. 3 miles RT. Strenuous. Access: End of Canyon Rd. in Twentynine Palms (outside the park, down Canyon Rd.).

Mastodon Peak Trail ★★★ Well worn and scenic, this is the longest loop trail in the park, offering great views of the Eagle Mountains and the nearby Salton Sea. For history buffs, it also passes a long-abandoned gold mine. There is a small amount of elevation gain, about 400 feet on the way to the 3,371-foot summit of Mastodon Peak. 3 miles RT. Moderate. Access: Cottonwood Spring or Cottonwood Campground.

Pine City ★ This path takes you to a cluster of boulder formations and sandy washes. Pinyon trees thrive in the moisture provided by these natural drainage courses; their pine nuts were a food source for early inhabitants. Birds now gather in the trees, and bighorn sheep occasionally appear among the rocks. 3 miles RT. Easy. Access: Dirt road leading from Park Blvd., opposite the Geology Tour Rd.

Ryan Mountain ★★ A steep climb (almost 1,000 ft.) leads to the best panoramic views in the park, encompassing snowcapped mountain peaks, tree-dotted valleys, and volcanic mounds. Ascending through a juniper and pinyon pine woodland, the trail is mostly rocky, well maintained, and easy to follow—you'll likely spot rock climbers to the west of the mountain. 3 miles RT. Strenuous. Access: Marked parking area along Park Blvd.

Skull Rock Nature Trail ★★ Leading to an unusually anthropomorphic rock formation, the trail meanders through boulders, desert washes, and a rocky alleyway. Watch for the "ducks" (small stacks of rocks) that mark the pathway. The official trail ends at the main road, but a primitive trail continues on a mile-long loop across the street. 1.7 miles RT. Easy. Access: Jumbo Rocks Campground (Loop E).

Longer Trails

Lost Horse Mine ★★　　This trail leads to the ruins of the area's most successful mining operation. Well-preserved remnants include the steam engine that powered the machinery, a winch for lowering equipment into the mine, settling tanks, and stone building foundations. The trail, actually an old wagon road, winds gradually up through rolling hills; once there, you can take an additional short, steep hike to the hilltop behind the ruins for a fine view into the heart of the park. Hikers can head back the way they came or continue on a loop trail that is 6.2 miles. 4 miles RT. Moderate. Access: End of a dirt road leading from Keys View Rd., 2.5 miles south of its junction with Park Blvd.

Lost Palms Oasis ★★★　　This long trail leads through sandy washes and rolling hills to the oasis overlook. A steep, rugged, and strenuous trail then continues to the canyon bottom. Whether or not you're up to the entire challenge, the beauty of bird-song and rustling palms echoing through the canyon makes this a special hike. Lost Palms is the park's largest oasis; look closely for elusive bighorn sheep in the remote canyon bottom. 7.2 miles RT. Moderate. Access: Park at Cottonwood Spring, accessible by paved road just beyond the Cottonwood Campground.

OTHER SPORTS & ACTIVITIES

BIKING　　Because most of Joshua Tree National Park is designated wilderness, visitors must take care not to damage the fragile ecosystem. That means bicycles are restricted from hiking trails and allowed only on roads, none of which have bike lanes. This effectively puts biking out of reach for most casual pedalers. If you're into mountain biking and up to a challenge, however, miles of unpaved roads are open to bikers. Distraction from cars is rare, particularly on four-wheel-drive roads such as the 18-mile dirt **Geology Tour Road,** which begins 2 miles west of Jumbo Rocks. Dry lake beds contrast with boulders along this sandy, lumpy downhill road; you can stop to see a Joshua tree woodland, abandoned mines, and petroglyphs.

A short but rewarding ride starts at Covington Flats, accessible only by unpaved (two-wheel-drive okay) La Contentata Road in the town of Joshua Tree. From the picnic area, ride west to **Eureka Peak,** about 4 miles away through lush high desert vegetation such as mammoth Joshua trees, junipers, and pinyons. The road is steep near the end, but your reward is a panoramic view of Palm Springs to the south, the Morongo Basin to the north, and the jagged mountain ranges of the park in between. For other bike-accessible unpaved and four-wheel-drive roads, consult the park map available at all visitor centers. There are no bike rentals available in the park, so you'll have to bring your own. Rentals are widely available in Palm Springs.

ROCK CLIMBING　　During most of the year, visitors to the park can observe rock climbers scurrying up, down, and across the many geological formations in the northwestern quadrant. Joshua Tree is one of the sport's premier destinations, with more than 4,000 individually rated climbs.

Spectacular geological formations have irresistible names such as **Wonderland of Rocks** and **Jumbo Rocks.** Lovers of Stonehenge and Easter Island will delight in bizarre stacks with names such as **Cap Rock** (for the single flat rock perched atop a haphazard pile) and **Skull Rock** (where the elements have worn an almost-human countenance into a boulder arrangement). But human hands had nothing to do with nature's sculptural artistry here; these fantastic formations are made of **monzogranite,** once a molten liquid forced upward that cooled before reaching the surface. Tectonic

DESERT oasis

The Joshua Tree area has long attracted outcasts, misfits, and eccentrics looking for a place where they can let it all hang out. And they've definitely left a mark. Check out the landmarks left by two late desert notables, George Van Tassel and **Noah Purifoy,** in the respective forms of the Integratron near Landers (*ⓒ* **760/ 364-3126;** www.integratron.com), and the **Noah Purifoy Sculpture Park**

Museum in the town of Joshua Tree (*ⓒ* **213/382-7516** for an appointment to visit; www.noahpurifoy.com). The former is an amazing wooden dome built by Van Tassel with unbelievable acoustics and public sound baths ($20) on two weekends a month; and the latter is an free outdoor museum of contemporary art made mostly from media that other artists would have thrown away.

stresses fractured the rocks, and as floods eventually washed away the ground cover and exposed the monzonite, natural erosion wore away the weakened sections, creating the bizarre shapes and piles you see today. Climbers of every skill level travel here from around the world, drawn by the otherworldly splendor of rock piles worn smooth by the elements.

Hidden Valley is another good place to watch enthusiasts from as far away as Europe and Japan scaling sheer rock faces with impossible grace. Climbers sometimes practice bouldering—working on strength and agility on smaller boulders within jumping distance of the ground. You can try some bouldering to sample the high-friction quartz monzogranite; even tennis shoes seem to grip the rock surface.

If you'd like to learn the sport of rock climbing, it's easier than you think—there are 30 climbing guides with permits for the park. The folks at (aptly named) **Uprising** (*ⓒ* **888/254-6266;** www.uprising.com) in Joshua Tree have accredited, experienced guides who'll orchestrate your excursion, starting with detailed instruction on rock-climbing basics. Later the guide will lead each climb, setting up ropes for belay and rappelling, then guiding students every step of the way. All-day excursions are about $150 per person in groups of three or more, $175 each for two people, or $315 for one person.

WHERE TO STAY

Aside from camping, there are no overnight accommodations within the park.

Near the Park

Joshua Tree Highlands Houses ★★ This innovative lodging complex consists of a trio of handsomely renovated homes near the park entrance. We'd say they're the snazziest places to hang your hat in the Joshua Tree area, as all include usable kitchens, hot tubs, outdoor fireplaces and lots of retro-inspired style. There is the one-room Luna Mesa, perfect for couples; the Sky House, a two-bedroom place with a commanding view; and—my favorite—Villa Rocosa, a contemporary remodel of a homesteader's cabin built around boulders in the living room. Yoga and Pilates classes are available, as is massage.

8215 Sunset Rd., Joshua Tree. *ⓒ* **760/366-3636** or 310/562-0511. www.joshuatreehighlandshouse. com. 4 private houses. $200–$300 double with 2-night minimum. Pets accepted ($35 one-time fee). **Amenities:** Free Wi-Fi.

The park has nine developed drive-in campgrounds; individual sites are $10 to $15 nightly. At this writing, you can make reservations for individual sites only at Black Rock Canyon and Indian Cove (© 877/444-6777; www.recreation.gov). You can make group camping reservations (sites accommodate 10–70 people) at the same number and website. **Belle Campground** ★ is on Pinto Basin Road 9 miles south of Twentynine Palms. **Black Rock Campground** ★★ is in the northwest corner, at the head of the 35-mile California Riding and Hiking Trail (to reach it, you have to leave the park boundaries), and is the most developed campground. There is also a visitor center here. **Cottonwood Campground** ★ is in the southern portion of the park, near the Cottonwood Visitor Center. **Hidden Valley Campground** ★, 14 miles south of Joshua Tree, California, is on the main park road. **Indian Cove** ★ is just inside park boundaries west of Twentynine Palms; as at Black Rock,

there are hiking trails leading farther into Joshua Tree, but no roads. **Jumbo Rocks Campground** ★★, named for its—surprise!—jumbo rocks, is 11 miles south of Twentynine Palms. Take Park Boulevard to reach **Ryan Campground** ★★, 16 miles southeast of Joshua Tree, California. **Sheep Pass group camp** ★★, a few miles east of Ryan Campground, has group sites only. **White Tank Campground** ★ is 2 miles beyond the Belle Campground. There are no showers or laundry facilities at any of the campgrounds, and you can make fires only in the fire pits provided at each campsite (bring your own wood).

The park also allows **backcountry camping** in the wilderness areas; regulations include mandatory registration on boards at the trail heads (see the Park Service map for locations). Park staffers recommend backcountry enthusiasts buy a topographic map of the park before embarking on a backpacking trip.

Joshua Tree Inn ★   Best known as the spot where country-rock icon Gram Parsons died in 1973—Room 8 is dedicated to his memory—the 1950s-era motel is more than a morbid asterisk in rock-and-roll history. The roadside motel features a great courtyard pool and adobe style rooms, more than a few of which are named for other musicians who've stayed here (such as Emmylou Harris and Donovan) and feature relevant décor such as rock posters and psychedelic art; even the standard rooms have a bit more personality than your typical chain. The property also manages several cabins and houses in the area.

61259 Twentynine Palms Hwy., Joshua Tree. © **760/366-1188.** www.joshuatreeinn.com. 10 units. $89–$119 double; $119–$159 suite; $174–$360 cabin or house. **Amenities:** Outdoor pool; free Wi-Fi.

Pioneertown Motel ★   In the 1940s and 1950s, Pioneertown served as the location for numerous movies featuring Roy Rogers, Gene Autry, and the Sons of the Pioneers—for whom the town is named. Today movie shoots are few and far between, but the old hotel that housed the stars in the halcyon days is still a fun and funky place to bunk for the night, although it is almost 20 miles from Joshua Tree National Park. Rooms are aptly Western, decorated with handmade quilts and either cowboy art or vintage movie posters.

5040 Curtis Rd., Pioneertown. © **760/365-7001.** www.pioneertown-motel.com. 18 units. $80–$120 double. **Amenities:** Free Wi-Fi.

Spin and Margie's Desert Hide-a-Way ★★ I love this eccentric and eclectic little getaway, tucked away in the desert a few miles east of the town of Joshua Tree. With tiled floors and small, fully equipped kitchens, the rooms are colorful to say the least, decorated with Mexican saddleblankets, beaded curtains, and plenty of oddball touches. The courtyard, outfitted with retro-looking patio furniture, is just the place to kick up your feet after a day on the trails.

Sunkist Rd. and Twentynine Palms Hwy., Joshua Tree. ℂ **760/366-9124** or 760/774-0850. www.deserthideaway.com. 5 units. $135–$175 double; $145 cabin. **Amenities:** Free Wi-Fi.

29 Palms Inn ★★ Dating to the 1920s, this legendary hostelry is located on 70 acres at the Oasis of Mara, just a stone's throw from the primary visitor center for the park. The inn is home to several artesian-fed ponds, not to mention the actual 29 palm trees for which the surrounding town is named. Rooms and guest houses each have their own unique décor and shape. I especially like the Bottle Room, with bottles built into the walls, and Irene's Historic Adobe, a standalone adobe that sleeps up to 4 people. The pool is a perfect respite from the desert heat, and the restaurant is one of the best in the area, sourcing a good deal of produce form gardens onsite.

73950 Inn Ave., Twentynine Palms. ℂ **760/367-3505.** www.29palmsinn.com. 21 units. $120–$190 double; $225–$340 guesthouse. Pets accepted ($35 one-time fee). Lower summer rates. Rates include continental breakfast. **Amenities:** Restaurant; outdoor pool; free Wi-Fi.

WHERE TO EAT

There are no restaurants in the park.

Near the Park

For tasty smoothies, wraps, and other vegetarian specialties, head down the street to **Natural Sisters Cafe,** 61695B Twentynine Palms Hwy. (ℂ **760/366-3600**). Coffee and gourmet takeout fare (including calzones, wraps, and a number of vegan dishes) is available at **Ricochet Gourmet,** 61705 Twentynine Palms Hwy. (ℂ **760/366-1898;** www.ricochetjoshuatree.com) an eclectic store with everything from newspapers, to wine, to fashionable clothing. **Crossroads Cafe,** 61715 Twentynine Palms Hwy. (ℂ **760/366-5414;** www.crossroadscafejtree.com), is a beloved local institution, with creative and healthy breakfasts and lunches and plenty to look at on the walls.

29 Palms Inn ★★ AMERICAN The food may be simple here—grilled meats and fish accompanied by a side dish or two—but with the vegetables grown in the hotel's own garden and meats and fish often locally sourced, you don't need a lot of frills to make the taste of the ingredients shine. The dining room is set behind the Polynesian-esque bar, and live music often accompanies the meals.

73950 Inn Ave., Twentynine Palms. ℂ **760/367-3505.** www.29palmsinn.com. Main courses $10–$22. Mon–Sat 11am–2pm and 5–9:30pm; Sun 9am–2pm.

Pappy and Harriet's Pioneertown Palace ★★★ BARBECUE Pappy and Harriet's is a one-of-a-kind venue and both the music and barbecue verge on transcendent. I like the baby back ribs and barbecue chicken, but there are also burgers, steaks, and Tex-Mex offerings. The stage has played host to everyone from Roy Rogers to Robert Plant, and crowds come all the way from Los Angeles for big shows.

Pioneertown Rd., Pioneertown. ℂ **760/365-5956.** www.pappyandharriets.com. Main courses $6–$30. Mon 5–9:30pm; Thurs–Sun 11am–9:30pm. Bar open later.

REDWOOD

by Eric Peterson

I t's impossible to explain the feeling you get in the old-growth forests of Redwood National and State Parks without resorting to Alice in Wonderland comparisons. Everything is big, misty, and primeval; flowering bushes cover the ground, 10-foot-tall ferns line the creeks, and the smells are rich and musty. Out on the parks' trails, it's impossible not to feel as if you've shrunk, or the rest of the world has grown, or else that you've gone back in time to the Jurassic epoch—dinosaurs would fit in nicely.

When Archibald Menses noted the existence of the coast redwood in 1794, more than 2 million acres of redwood forest carpeted California and Oregon. By 1965, logging had reduced that to 300,000 acres. California created several state parks around individual groves in the 1920s, and in 1968 the federal government created Redwood National Park. In 1994, the National Park Service and the California Department of Parks and Recreation signed an agreement to manage the four redwood parks cooperatively—hence the name Redwood National *and* State Parks.

The modern 131,983-acre park complex offers a lesson in ecology. When the park was created to protect the biggest coast redwoods, logging companies continued to cut much of the surrounding area, sometimes right up to the park boundary. Redwoods in the park began to suffer as the quality of the Redwood Creek drainage declined from upstream logging, so in 1978 the government purchased a major section of the watershed. Although the logging of old-growth redwoods is still a major bone of contention for the government, private landowners, and environmentalists, the trees are thriving. They are living links to the age of dinosaurs and reminders that the era of mankind is but a hiccup in time to the venerable *Sequoia sempervirens.*

FLORA & FAUNA

Below the Redwood canopy, there is a whole host of smaller trees and other plant life, mosses, and wildflowers.

High coastal overlooks such as **Klamath Overlook** and **Crescent Beach Overlook** make great gray-whale-watching outposts during the December–January southern migration and the March–April return migration. The northern sea cliffs also provide valuable nesting sites for marine birds such as auklets, puffins, murres, and cormorants. Birders will also love the park's coastal freshwater lagoons, which are some of the most pristine shorebird and waterfowl habitats left and are chock-full of hundreds of different species.

AVOIDING the crowds

The parks include three major features—the ocean setting, the old-growth forests, and the prairies. Not many people discover the bald hills (called "prairies" here) that offer excellent views over the tops of the redwoods and down to the ocean. And while the coastal environment and the shade of the redwoods can chill a hiker's bones year-round, these treeless spots are warm and sunny sanctuaries in the summertime.

One of the most striking aspects of Prairie Creek Redwoods State Park is its herd of **Roosevelt elk,** usually found in the appropriately named Elk Prairie in the southern end of the park and other spots in the Orick area. These gigantic beasts can weigh up to 1,000 pounds and are most definitely not tame. The bulls carry huge antlers from spring to fall. Elk are also sometimes found at Gold Bluffs Beach—it's an incredible rush to suddenly come upon them out of the fog or after a turn in the trail. Nearly 100 **black bears** also call the park home but are seldom seen. Unlike those in Yosemite, these bears avoid people.

ESSENTIALS
Getting There & Gateways

The parks lie on a narrow strip near the coast in Northern California, about 350 miles north of San Francisco. There are three major routes to the Redwood Coast. **U.S. 101** links San Francisco and Brookings, Oregon, traversing much of the length of the parks. **U.S. 199** takes off from U.S. 101 just north of the parks and heads northeast to Grants Pass, Oregon. The main route to the east is **Calif. 299,** which goes from Redding, California, to meet up with U.S. 101 south of the park.

THE NEAREST AIRPORTS Arcata-Eureka Airport (© 707/839-5401) is in McKinleyville, 28 miles south of the Redwood Information Center near Orick. **McNamara Field** (© 707/464-7288; www.fly-cec.com) is in Crescent City, at the north end of the park.

Visitor Centers & Information

The southern gateway to the Redwood National and State Parks is the dinky town of Orick, on U.S. 101. Just south of town you'll find the **Thomas H. Kuchel Visitor Center** (© 707/465-7765), open daily year-round. About 7 miles farther north on U.S. 101 is the **Prairie Creek Visitor Center** (© 707/488-2171).

The northern gateway to the parks is Crescent City. It's your best bet for a motel, gas, fast food, and outdoor supplies. Before touring the park, stop at the **Crescent City Information Center,** 1111 2nd St. (© 707/465-7335). It's open daily year-round.

If you are arriving on U.S. 199 from Oregon, **Hiouchi Information Center** (© 702/4558-3294) and **Jedediah Smith Visitor Center** (© 707/458-3496) are open daily in the summer.

For pre-trip information, contact **Redwood National and State Parks** (© 707/464-7335; www.nps.gov/redw). Books and maps are available from the **Redwood Parks Association** (© 707/464-9150; www.redwoodparksassociation.org).

Redwood National & State Parks

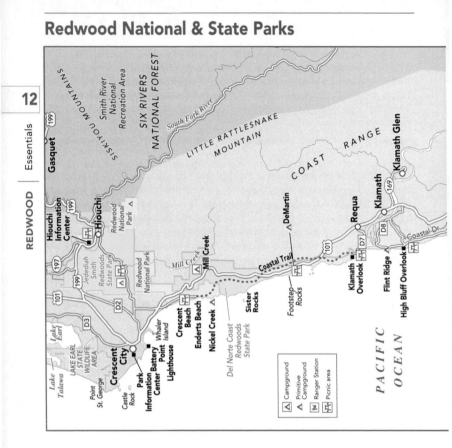

Fees & Permits

Admission to the national park is free, but the state parks (home to some of the best redwood groves) charge a $8 **day-use fee;** federal park passes are valid.

Camping is $35 for drive-in sites. Walk-in sites are free or $5, and a few are $20. Free permits are required for **backcountry camping** along the Redwood Creek Trail.

To travel the **Tall Trees Trail,** you'll have to get a free permit from the Kuchel Visitor Center near Orick.

Seasons & Climate

All those huge trees and ferns wouldn't have survived for 1,000 years if it didn't rain a lot here. Count on cool weather with rain or during your visit, then get ecstatic when the sun comes out—it can happen anytime. **Spring** is the best season for wildflowers. **Summer** is generally foggy along the coast. (It's called "the June gloom," but it can continue into August.) **Fall** is the warmest and (relatively) sunniest time of all, and **winter** isn't bad, though some park facilities are closed.

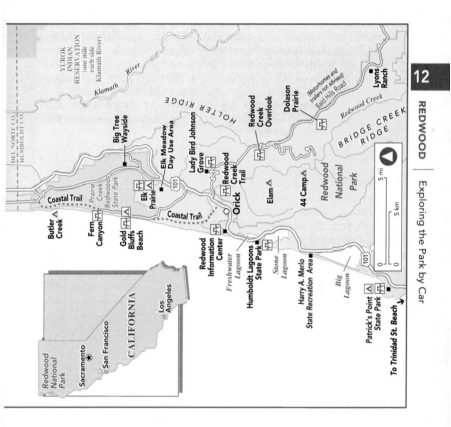

EXPLORING THE PARK BY CAR

A number of scenic drives cut through the park. Steep, windy **Bald Hills Road** (a few miles north of Orick on U.S. 101) will take you back into the Redwood Creek watershed and up to the shoulder of 3,097-foot Schoolhouse Peak. A few miles north is the **Lost Man Creek Trail,** a short, unpaved scenic drive through the redwood forest.

A don't-miss detour along U.S. 101 is the **Newton B. Drury Scenic Parkway,** which passes through redwood groves and elk-filled meadows before returning to the highway 8 miles later. On the way, take the **Cal-Barrel Road** turnoff, a narrow, packed-gravel road off the Newton B. Drury Scenic Parkway that offers a spectacular 3-mile tour through an old-growth redwood forest.

One of the best drives on the Redwood Coast starts at the mouth of the Klamath River and runs 8 miles south toward Prairie Creek Redwoods State Park. The narrow, partially paved **Coastal Drive** winds through stands of redwoods, with spectacular views of the Pacific and numerous pullouts for picture taking (sea lions and pelicans abound) and short hikes. If you're heading south on U.S. 101, take the Alder Camp Road exit just south of the Klamath River Bridge and follow the signs to the Mouth of

Klamath. Northbound travelers should take the Redwood National and State Parks Coastal Drive exit off the Newton B. Drury Scenic Parkway.

The most amazing car-friendly trail in all of the Redwood National and State Parks is the hidden, well-maintained gravel **Howland Hill Road.** It winds for about 10 miles through Jedediah Smith Redwoods State Park, an unforgettable journey through a spectacular old-growth redwood forest. From U.S. 101, keep an eye out for the southernmost traffic light coming into Crescent City, at Elk Valley Road, and head east; Howland Hill Road will be on your right. After driving through the park, you'll end up at U.S. 199 near Hiouchi, where it is a short drive west to get back to U.S. 101. Plan at least 2 to 3 hours for the 30-mile round-trip, or all day if you want to do some hiking.

ORGANIZED TOURS & RANGER PROGRAMS

The parks run interpretive programs on subjects ranging from trees to tide pools, legends to landforms, at the Hiouchi and Kuchel information centers and in the Crescent Beach area during summer months, and year-round at the park headquarters in Crescent City. Park rangers lead campfire programs and numerous other activities throughout the year. Check the free park newspaper or call the **Kuchel Visitor Center** (**© 707/465-7765**) for current schedules.

DAY HIKES

Regardless of the length of your hike, dress warmly and bring plenty of water and sunscreen. The website of Redwood Hikes Press, **www.redwoodhikes.com,** is a great resource, and they also sell printed maps.

Big Tree Trail ★★   For the nonhikers in your group (including those in wheelchairs), this is a short paved trail leading to an impressively large tree. You can return the way you came or make a 2- or 3-mile loop if you continue on other trails here. .25 mile RT. Easy. Access: Big Tree turnoff along Newton B. Drury Scenic Pkwy.

Boy Scout Tree Trail ★★★   After taking this trail through Jedediah Smith Redwoods State Park, you might understand why an activist such as Woody Harrelson would chain himself to the Golden Gate Bridge to protest logging old-growth forests. This is nature primeval, a lush, cool, damp forest brimming with giant ferns and

---

Special Regulations & Warnings

Many of the best scenic drives in these parks are on roads not suitable for motor homes or trailers. If possible, those with RVs should consider towing a car, traveling with a friend who is driving a car, or maybe even renting a car near the parks.

On the beach, be aware of tidal fluctuations. Swimming is hazardous because of cold water, rip currents, and sneaker waves. Don't disturb abandoned baby seals or sea lions on the beach. The mother may be nearby. If a pup appears to be in danger, call the **North Coast Marine Mammal Center** (**© 707/465-6265**).

Additionally, watch for poison oak, particularly in coastal areas; follow park regulations regarding bears and food storage; and treat water from natural sources before drinking. Keep in mind that tree limbs can fall during high winds.

The long, beautiful **Coastal Trail ★★★**, which runs the entire 37-mile length of the parks' coastal section and as near the ocean as possible, can be hiked by the day in small segments. It also makes a great 3- or 4-day trip using backcountry camps on the route. A free permit is required if you overnight at Ossagon Creek or along Redwood Creek.

redwoods. Just being here is truly an emotional experience. 5.6 miles RT. Easy. Access: Off Howland Hill Rd.; ask for directions and map at Jedediah Smith Information Center.

Enderts Beach Trail ★★   This short trail leads down to Enderts Beach. In the summer, free 2½-hour ranger-guided tide pool and seashore walks are offered when the tides are right. You start at the beach parking lot, descend to the beach, and explore rocky tide pools at its southern end. 1.2 miles RT. Easy. Access: End of Enderts Rd. at south end of Crescent City (about 3 miles south on U.S. 101 from downtown).

Fern Canyon Trail ★★★   This short, heavily traveled trail leads to a lush grotto of ferns clinging to 50-foot-high vertical walls divided by a babbling brook. It's only about a 1.5-mile walk from Gold Bluffs Beach, but be prepared to scramble across the creek several times on small footbridges. This short loop connects with a number of trails, including the beautiful Coastal Loop and Friendship Ridge trails, allowing the adventurous hiker to get in a 10-mile hike if he or she desires. 1.5 miles RT. Easy. Access: From U.S. 101, take Davison Rd. exit, which follows Gold Bluffs Beach to Fern Canyon parking lot. Day-use fee $6. No trailers or motor homes over 24 ft. long.

Lady Bird Johnson Grove Loop ★★   Here's a self-guided tour that loops around a lush grove of mature redwoods. It's the site at which Lady Bird Johnson dedicated the national park in 1968. The following year, it was named for her. 1 mile RT. Easy. Access: Lady Bird Johnson Grove. Take Bald Hills Rd. exit off U.S. 101, .5 mile north of Orick.

Tall Trees Trail ★★★   To see the some of the world's tallest trees—about 360 feet tall and more than 600 years old—you'll have to go to the Kuchel Visitor Center near Orick (see "Visitor Centers & Information," earlier in this chapter) to obtain a free **map** and **vehicle permit** to drive to the Tall Trees Grove Trailhead. Once thought to be the world's tallest, these trees lost their title when 378-foot Hyperion was discovered elsewhere in the park in 2006. Hyperion's location is kept secret to protect the surrounding soil. Only 50 permits are issued per day, on a first-come, first-served basis. After a slow, 15-mile one-way drive on a gravel road, you have to walk a steep trail down into the grove, but it's a small price to pay to see some of the tallest trees in the world. Once you figure in the drive and hike to get to the tree, the whole expedition takes at least 4 hours. 3.5 miles RT. Moderate. Access: End of Tall Trees Access Rd., off Bald Hills Rd. Permit required.

OTHER SPORTS & ACTIVITIES

BEACHES   The park's beaches vary from long white-sand strands to cobblestone pocket coves. The water temperature is in the high 40s to low 50s (single digits to 10s Celsius) year-round, and it's often rough out there. Swimmers and surfers should be prepared for adverse conditions. **Crescent Beach** is a long, sandy beach just 2 miles south of Crescent City that's a popular destination for beachcombing, surf fishing, and surfing. Just south of Crescent Beach is **Enderts Beach,** a protected spot with a hike-in campground and tide pools at its southern end.

BICYCLING Most of the hiking trails throughout the national and state parks are off limits to mountain bikers. However, **Prairie Creek Redwoods State Park** has a difficult 19-mile mountain-bike trail through dense forest, elk-filled meadows, and glorious mud holes. Mountain bike rentals are available from **Redwood Adventures** north of Orick (© 866/733-9637; www.redwoodadventures.com) for $50 a day.

FISHING The Redwood Coast's streams are some of the best steelhead trout—and salmon-breeding habitat in California. Park beaches are good for surfcasting, but you should be prepared for heavy wave action. A California **fishing license** (available at local sporting goods stores) is required. Be sure to check with rangers about closures or other restrictions, which seem to change frequently. **Rivers West Outfitters** (© 707/482-5822 or 707/482-7775; www.riverswestoutfitters.com) offers guide service for about $150 per person per day.

HORSEBACK TRAIL RIDES Equestrians can go on a variety of guided trail rides, including lunch and dinner trips, with **Redwood Adventures** (© 866/733-9637; www.redwoodadventures.com).

JET-BOAT TOURS Tours aboard a jet boat take visitors 22 miles up the Klamath River to view bear, birds, otters, and more along the riverbanks. Contact **Klamath River Jet Boat Tours** (© 800/887-5387; www.jetboattours.com).

WHERE TO STAY

The **Crescent City/Del Norte Chamber of Commerce** (www.exploredelnorte.net; © 800/343-8300) is a good resource.

Inside the Park

Elk Meadow Cabins ★ These three-bedroom cabins built in the 1950s and 1960s were originally employee housing for a local logging company, so they have a feel of a fully functional home, not spartan wilderness cabins. In fact, they all have kitchens and plenty of room to spread out. The location is also primo, at the junction of three bike trails in prime elk habitat. The ownership also runs a tour company, **Redwood Adventures,** offering horseback rides to Segway tours.

Located just north of Orick off U.S. 101. © **866/733-9637.** www.redwoodadventures.com. 6 units. $199–$279 double. **Amenities:** Bike rentals; free Wi-Fi.

Near the Park

Curly Redwood Lodge ★ A vintage roadside gem, with a groovy retro vibe, the façade of this motel was created from rare curly redwood, cut from a single ancient tree. They were allowed to do that back in 1957 when the Lodge was built; they also knew their main clientele would be families, so rooms here are oversized, clean, and reliably maintained rooms (the service is friendly, too). A fun trip back in time, especially appropriate for those who are fans of classic motels.

701 U.S. 101 S., Crescent City. © **707/464-2137.** www.curlyredwoodlodge.com. 36 units. $61–$97 double. **Amenities:** Free Wi-Fi.

Historic Requa Inn ★★ Built on a bluff above a steep bank, the Requa has awe-inspiring view of the Klamath River and surrounding redwood forest. Opening in 1914 when Requa was a bustling cannery row, the lodge now has a B&B vibe, but with more privacy—it doesn't have the layout of a private home, so there are larger public spaces

CAMPING options

Most drive-in camping is in the state parks. In the southern part of the complex, Prairie Creek Redwoods State Park, known for its old-growth redwoods and herds of elk, has two drive-in campgrounds. **Elk Prairie Campground ★★,** 5 miles north of Orick on U.S. 101, is near hiking trails, has a nature center, and offers evening campfire talks. Make reservations through **ReserveAmerica (⦿ 800/444-7275;** www.reserveamerica.com). **Gold Bluffs Beach Campground ★★★** is 3 miles north of Orick on U.S. 101, then 5 miles west on Davison Road. It's somewhat more primitive and offers trail and beach access; reservations are not available.

In the northern part of the complex, the campground at **Jedediah Smith Redwoods State Park ★★,** off U.S. 199

at Hiouchi, provides easy access to some of the area's biggest and most spectacular redwoods, as well as campsites along the scenic Smith River. Also in the north is **Mill Creek Campground ★★,** in a beautiful forested setting with good trail access in Del Norte Coast Redwoods State Park, 7 miles south of Crescent City on U.S. 101. Both Jedediah Smith and Mill Creek take **reservations (⦿ 800/444-7275;** www.reserveamerica.com).

There are also **8 small, primitive hike-in campgrounds ★★** in the national park, requiring a walk of .25 to .5 mile. Some are free, others are $5 per person per night, and all have fire rings and toilets. Contact the park office (⦿ **707/464-6101**) for information.

---

and you can come and go unnoticed, if you please. Rooms are individually decorated with lovely antiques, which makes up for the fact that many are rather small; ask for one with a view. Breakfasts are terrific, and the restaurant is open to the public for dinner (see "Where to Eat," below).

451 Requa Rd., Klamath. ⦿ **707/482-1425.** www.requainn.com. 12 units. $119–$179 double. Rates include full breakfast. **Amenities:** Restaurant; hot tub; free Wi-Fi.

WHERE TO EAT

Good Harvest Café ★★ AMERICAN   This local's fave has gotten bigger and better over the years, and does it all: breakfast, lunch, dinner, vegetarian fare, sack lunches for the trail, you name it. That being said, the strengths here, at least at dinner, are the seafood dishes (tuna tacos, salmon with prawns) as well as the darn juicy rib-eye steaks. At breakfast, we order up their fresh-from-the-oven baked goods and lighter than light frittatas.

575 U.S. 101 S., Crescent City. ⦿ **707/465-6028.** Main courses $6–$12 breakfast and lunch; $8–$25 dinner. Mon–Sat 7:30am–9pm; Sun 8am–9pm.

Historic Requa Inn ★★ NEW AMERICAN   The restaurant at the Historic Requa Inn prides itself on showcasing all things local—the salmon is caught 200 yards away in many cases and the chefs often forage for mushrooms and greens. Because the menu is based on what's fresh; it's constantly rotating but don't worry; all the offerings are tantalizing. The four-course dinners are always prix-fixe and family-style, and reservations are required. A hearty, all-you-can-eat hot breakfast is made daily for guests (and included in the room rate), but open to non-guests as well.

451 Requa Rd., Klamath. ⦿ **707/482-1425.** www.requainn.com. All-you-can-eat breakfast $10; prix-fixe dinner $35–$45 . Daily 8am–9:30am (until 9am in winter); one dinner seating at 7pm Mon–Sat.

GRAND CANYON

by Eric Peterson

At 277 river miles long, roughly 4,000 feet deep, and an average of 10 miles across, the Grand Canyon's so big that even the breezes seem to draw a deep breath at the rims. But it's so much more than an enormous gulch. In the past 6 million years, while the river or rivers that eventually became the Colorado River were carving the main canyon, runoff from the rims cut hundreds of side canyons that funnel like capillaries into the larger one. As the side canyons deepened and spread, they gradually isolated buttes and mesas that tower thousands of feet above the canyon floor. Early cartographers and geologists noticed similarities between these rock pinnacles and some of the greatest works of human hands. They called them temples and shrines, and named them after deities such as Brahma, Vishnu, and Shiva.

The canyon not only inspires reverence, but also tells the grandest of stories. Half the earth's history is represented in its rocks. The oldest rock layer, the Vishnu Formation, began forming 2 billion years ago, before aerobic life forms even existed. The layers of sedimentary rock that piled atop the Vishnu Formation tell of landscapes that changed like dreams. They speak of mountains that really did move, eroding into nothingness; of oceans that poured forth across the land before receding; of deserts, swamps, and rivers the size of the Mississippi—all where the canyon now lies. The fossils in these layers illustrate the very evolution of life.

A number of American Indian tribes have lived in or around the canyon, and the Navajo, Havasupai, Kaibab Paiute, Hopi, Zuni, and Hualapai tribes still dwell in this area. The Hopi still regard the canyon as their place of emergence and the place to which their dead return. Their predecessors left behind more than 3,000 archaeological sites and artifacts up to 10,000 years old.

In the 1500s, Spanish missionaries and gold-greedy explorers passed through the area, but it wasn't until the 1800s that Europeans began settling here. Prospectors clambered through the canyon in search of precious minerals, and some of them stayed after their mines, plagued by high overhead costs, shut down. The first tourists followed, and vacationers began flooding the area after the railroad linked Grand Canyon Village to Williams, Arizona, in 1901.

When President Theodore Roosevelt visited in 1903, he was moved to use the Antiquities Act to declare Grand Canyon a national monument in 1908. Congress established Grand Canyon National Park in 1919.

13

GRAND CANYON

Essentials

Although designated a "park," Grand Canyon has a daunting, even ominous side. Visitors, no matter how many times they enter it, must negotiate with it for survival. One look at the clenched jaw of a river guide as he or she rows into Lava Rapids will remind you that the canyon exacts a heavy price for mistakes. The most common mistake is to underestimate it. Try to escape, and it becomes a prison, with walls 4,000 feet high. The canyon's menace reminds us that we still haven't completely conquered nature. It even has its own symbols: the rattlesnake's warning; the elegant symmetry of the black widow; the seductive, lilylike flower of the deadly sacred datura.

Clearly, you can suffer here, but reward is everywhere. It's in the spectrum of colors: The Colorado River, filled with runoff from a recent rain in the Painted Desert, runs blood red beneath slopes of orange Hakatai shale; cactus flowers explode in pink, yellow, and red; and lichens paint rocks orange, green, and gray, creating art more striking than the works in any gallery. It's in the shapes, too—the spires, amphitheaters, temples, ramps, and cliffs—and in the shadows that bend across them before lifting like mist. It's in the myriad organisms and their struggles for survival. Most of all, it's in the constancy of the river, which reminds us that, in time, all things move forward, wash away, and return to the earth.

FLORA & FAUNA

Many of the latest products of evolution—more than 1,500 plant and 400 animal species—survive at the canyon today. If you include the upper reaches of the Kaibab Plateau (on the canyon's North Rim), this small area of northern Arizona includes zones of biological life comparable to ones found as far south as Mexico and as far north as Alaska. The species come in every shape, size, and temperament, ranging from tiny **ant lions** dwelling in the canyon floor to 1,000-pound **elk** roaming the rims. Of the approximately 240 **California condors** in the wild, about 80 live in the canyon country of northern Arizona and southern Utah. And for every species, there is a story within a story. Take the **Douglas fir,** for example. Once part of a forest that covered both rims and much of the canyon, the tree has endured since the last ice age on shady, north-facing slopes beneath the South Rim—long after the sunbaked rim itself became too hot and inhospitable.

ESSENTIALS

Getting There & Gateways

The nearest cities to the South Rim of the Grand Canyon are Flagstaff, Arizona, 78 miles southeast of Grand Canyon Village on U.S. 180; and Williams, Arizona, 59 miles south on Ariz. 64. The closest small town to the park is Tusayan, Arizona, 1 mile south

The Grand Canyon

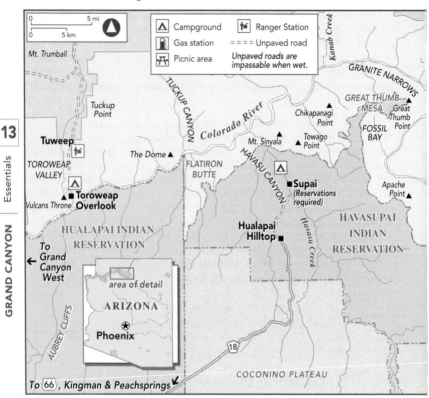

of the south entrance gates on Ariz. 64. The closest substantial town to the North Rim is Kanab, Utah, 78 miles northwest of Grand Canyon National Park on U.S. 89A.

THE NEAREST AIRPORTS   Many travelers fly to **Phoenix Sky Harbor International Airport** (© **602/273-3300;** www.skyharbor.com), 220 miles from the South Rim, or to **Las Vegas McCarran International Airport** (© **702/261-5211;** www. mccarran.com), 263 miles from the North Rim. To land closer to the canyon, consider **Flagstaff Pulliam Airport** (© **928/556-1234**), roughly 80 miles from the park. Closer still is **Grand Canyon National Park Airport** (© **928/638-2446;** www.grandcanyon airport.org) in Tusayan, 5 miles from the park's south entrance. **Grand Canyon Airlines** (© **866/235-9422;** www.grandcanyonairlines.com) and **Vision Air** (© **800/256-8767;** www.visionholidays.com) serve the latter from the Las Vegas area.

BY RAIL   Amtrak (© **800/872-7245;** www.amtrak.com) regularly stops in Flagstaff, as well as Williams, connecting rail service on the historic Grand Canyon Railway is available.

The **Grand Canyon Railway** (© **800/843-8724;** www.thetrain.com) offers daily service linking Williams and Grand Canyon Village. Pulled by historic steam engines

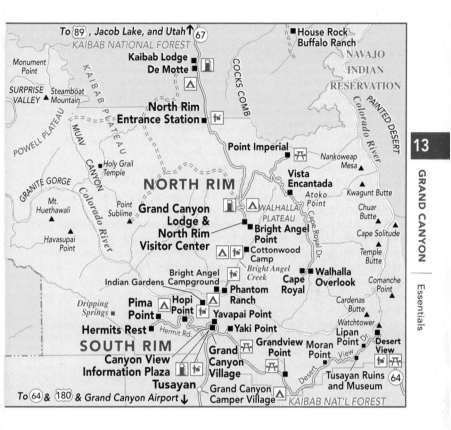

during the summer, the train leaves Williams in the morning and returns in late afternoon. Rates start at $59 for adults and $25 for kids.

BY BUS   **Arizona Shuttle** (© **800/888-2749;** www.arizonashuttle.com) provides bus service between both Flagstaff and Williams and Grand Canyon National Park for $45 each way (prices include entry fee and are discounted if booked online).

Fees & Permits

Admission to Grand Canyon National Park costs $25 per private vehicle and $12 for those on foot, bicycle, or motorcycle. The receipt is good for a week and includes both rims. Campsites are $12 to $35 nightly.

Visitor Centers & Information

The **Grand Canyon Visitor Center,** near Mather Point, has become the first stop for many visitors to the South Rim. The whole complex has the streamlined appearance of a modern mass-transit hub and continues to expand. Various kiosks provide basic information about tours, trails, overlooks, cycling, weather, ranger-guided programs, and other topics. The four large parking lots surrounding the visitor center accommodate

It's illegal to remove any resources from the park. These can be anything from flowers to pottery fragments. Even seemingly useless articles like bits of metal from the canyon's old mines have historical value and are protected by law.

Fires are strictly prohibited except at North Rim, Desert View, and Mather campgrounds. In the backcountry, use a small camp stove for cooking.

Leashed pets are permitted on trails throughout the developed areas of the South Rim, but not below the rim. The only exceptions are service animals.

Discharging weapons, including guns, bows and arrows, crossbows, slingshots, and air pistols, is prohibited, as are all fireworks.

13

Essentials

GRAND CANYON

up to 875 vehicles. Free shuttles connect the Information Plaza with Grand Canyon Village and the Kaibab Trail.

At one end of the visitor center is the Science on a Sphere enclosure presenting "The Canyon World," a short introduction to 1.8 billion years of canyon history projected on the outside of a 6-foot diameter sphere. From the other end of the visitor center you can enter the new theater, which shows the free park film, *Grand Canyon: A Journey of Wonder,* every 20 minutes. Adjacent to the visitor center are restrooms and a large bookstore run by the Grand Canyon Association. The Grand Canyon Visitor Center is open daily 8am to 6pm in summer, and 8am to 5pm during the rest of the year.

The **North Rim Visitor Center** near Grand Canyon Lodge has trail information including water availability and weather conditions, and schedules for ranger programs, as well as a Grand Canyon Association bookstore. It's open daily 8am to 6pm from mid-May to mid-October, and from 9am to 4pm until the first snow closes the road.

Near the east entrance, the **Desert View Visitor Center** is 26 miles east of Grand Canyon Village. It's open daily from 9am to 6pm in summer, and daily from 9am to 5pm the rest of the year.

In Grand Canyon Village, **Verkamp's Visitor Center** features displays depicting the canyon's history as well as a bookstore. It's open daily 8am to 8pm in summer, and 8am to 6pm the rest of the year.

Other park facilities include the **Yavapai Geology Museum,** a half mile west of the Grand Canyon Visitor Center on Yavapai Point; the **Tusayan Ruin & Museum,** 3 miles west of Desert View; and **Kolb Studio** on the rim at the west end of Grand Canyon Village. All three are open daily in the summer season.

Before you head out, contact **Grand Canyon National Park (© 800/638-7888;** www.nps.gov/grca), for a free copy of the *Grand Canyon Trip Planner.* Those who want more in-depth information can buy books, maps, and videos from the **Grand Canyon Association (© 800/858-2808;** www.grandcanyon.org).

Seasons & Climate

The climate at Grand Canyon varies greatly not only from season to season, but from point to point. At over 8,000 feet in elevation, the North Rim is by far the coldest, dampest part of the park. Its temperatures run about 30° cooler than Phantom Ranch at the canyon bottom, and 7° cooler than the South Rim, roughly 1,000 feet below. It averages 25 inches of precipitation per year, compared to just 8 inches at Phantom Ranch and 16 inches on the South Rim.

The North Rim doesn't open until mid-May, so your only choice in early spring is the South Rim, where daily highs average 60° and 70°F (16° and 21°C) in April and May, respectively. Travelers should be prepared for late-winter storms, which occasionally bring snow to the rim. Spring is an ideal time to hike the inner canyon, with highs in April averaging 82°F (28°C).

Summer highs are usually in the 80s (upper 20s Celsius) on the South Rim and in the 70s (low 20s Celsius) on the North Rim. The canyon bottom, on the other hand, can be torrid, with highs in July averaging 106°F (41°C). Thunderstorms frequently drench the park in late July and August, the wettest month of the year, when nearly 2¼ inches of rain fall on the South Rim. On the North Rim, nights can be nippy even during July, when low temperatures average a chilly 46°F (8°C).

After the thunderstorms taper off in mid-September, fall is a great time to be anywhere in the park.

In winter, the North Rim is closed, and drivers to the South Rim should be prepared for icy roads and occasional closures. When the snow isn't falling, the South Rim warms up nicely. Hiking trails remain open but are often snow-packed.

EXPLORING THE PARK BY CAR & SHUTTLE

When the shuttles aren't running in winter, take advantage of the park's **24-hour taxi service** (✆ **928/638-2822**). These taxis do not have meters, as their fares vary according to distance and the number of passengers. The trip from Grand Canyon Village to Tusayan costs $10 for one or two adult passengers, plus $5 for each additional adult.

Hermit Road

This 8-mile road from Grand Canyon Village to Hermits Rest is open to private cars December to February only, when shuttles aren't running. You must ride the park's **free shuttles** here from March 1 through November 30.

Your first stops are at **Trailviews 1 and 2.** Looking north from these view points, you can see straight down the side canyons that formed on either side of the Colorado River along the Bright Angel fault. Below, you may spot lush vegetation growing around a spring. This area is Indian Garden, where Havasupai Indians once farmed.

The next stop, **Maricopa Point,** overlooks the old Orphan Mine, which produced some of the richest uranium ore in the Southwest during the 1950s and 1960s. Below and to the west, you can see the remains of the tramway used to move ore to the rim from 1956 to 1969.

Continue to the **Powell Memorial,** which honors John Wesley Powell, the one-armed Civil War veteran thought to be the first non-native person to float through the canyon. From atop the memorial, you can get an especially fine view 60 miles southeast to the San Francisco peaks, including 12,633-foot Humphreys Peak, the highest point in Arizona.

Because the next stop, **Hopi Point,** projects far into the canyon, its tip is the best place on Hermit Road to watch the sunset. As the sun drops, its light plays across four of the canyon's loveliest temples. The flat mesa almost due north of the point is Shiva Temple. The temple southwest of it is Osiris; the one southeast is Isis. East of Isis is Buddha Temple.

The next stop, **Mohave Point,** is a great place to observe some of the Colorado River's most furious rapids. Farthest downstream (to your left) is Hermit Rapids.

Above it, you can make out the top of the dangerous Granite Rapids. Just above Granite Rapids, you can discern the bottom of Salt Creek Rapids. As you look at Hermit Creek Canyon and the rapids below it, you can visualize how floods washed rocks into the river, forming the natural dam that creates the rapids.

Next you'll come to **The Abyss,** where the steep canyon walls drop 2,600 feet to the base of the Redwall Limestone.

Monument Creek Vista is the subsequent shuttle stop on the way to Hermits Rest that lets you access the greenway trail. Cyclists can bring their bikes on the shuttle to this point and then ride 2.8 miles along the greenway to Hermits Rest.

Three thousand feet below the next stop, **Pima Point,** you'll see some of the foundations and walls from the old Hermit Camp, a tourist destination built in 1912 by the Santa Fe Railroad. Before descending to Hermit Camp, tourists took a break at the final stop, **Hermits Rest.** In this 1914 building, Mary Colter celebrated the "hermit" theme by building what resembled a crude rock shelter.

Desert View Drive

Starting at Grand Canyon Village, the first stop is the Yavapai Geology Museum at **Yavapai Point,** with some of the most expansive views up and down the canyon. The historic observation station has interpretive panels identifying the major landmarks.

People entering the park from the south generally catch their first glimpse of the canyon from the next stop, **Mather Point.** It's a clamorous place with one redeeming feature: a canyon view. (There's no such thing as a bad canyon view.) You can park here and walk to the **Grand Canyon Visitor Center.**

Yaki Point, the first stop off Ariz. 64, is accessible by car only when the shuttles aren't running. It's a great place to see the monuments of the central canyon, including Wotan's Throne, Vishnu Temple, and Zoroaster Temple.

The next stop, 7,406-foot-high **Grandview Point,** is one of the highest spots on the South Rim and aptly named. There are ruins from an old hotel and mining operation in the area, as well as a few trails.

Next you'll come to **Moran Point,** named for landscape painter Thomas Moran. This is the best place from which to view the tilting block of rock known as the **Sinking Ship.** Stand at the end of the point and look southwest at the rocks level with the rim. The "ship" appears to be "submerged" in the horizontal layers of Coronado Butte (in the foreground). It's part of the Grandview Monocline, a place where rocks have bent in a single fold around a fault line.

Keep going and you'll come to the **Tusayan Ruin and Museum**, built in the 12th century by the ancestral Puebloan (sometimes known as Anasazi). Among the 3,500 documented archaeological sites in and around the Grand Canyon, this may have been the last one abandoned. A self-guided tour takes you around the pueblo. The Tusayan Museum delves into the history of the area's tribes.

Don't pass **Lipan Point.** With views far down the canyon to the west, it's a great place to catch the sunset. It also overlooks the Colorado River where the river makes two sweeping curves. Just downstream from the S, the river begins cutting through the 2-billion-year-old Vishnu Formation, and the steep-walled Inner Gorge begins.

Like Lipan Point, the next stop, **Navajo Point,** offers fine views of the Grand Canyon Supergroup, a formation of igneous and sedimentary rocks that have eroded altogether in many other parts of the canyon. The long, thin streaks of maroon, gray, and black, which tilt at an angle of about 20 degrees, are layers of this formation.

The last stop on the Desert View Drive is **Desert View,** where you'll find the Watchtower, a 70-foot-high historic stone building that was modeled after towers found at ancient pueblos such as Mesa Verde and Hovenweep. Atop the Watchtower is an enclosed observation deck, which, at 7,522 feet, is the highest point on the South Rim. The rim at Desert View offers spectacular views of the northeast end of the canyon. There's also a **visitor center,** general store, snack shop, and gas station here.

The Desert View Drive shuttle stops only at Mather, Yavapai, and Yaki points.

North Rim: Cape Royal Drive

Start your driving tour at **Cape Royal,** where a gentle, paved .3-mile (each way) trail passes a natural bridge, Angel's Window, carved into a rock peninsula along the rim. The trail ends at the tip of Cape Royal, with views of the looming butte known as Wotan's Throne.

At **Walhalla Overlook,** you can follow with your eyes the tan line of Unkar Creek as it snakes down toward Unkar Delta. The soil and abundant water at the delta made for excellent farming for the ancestral Puebloan people, who occupied the canyon through about A.D. 1175. Many of these people migrated seasonally to dwellings such as the two small pueblos across the street from this overlook.

The next stop, **Roosevelt Point,** is one of the best places to see the confluence of the gorge of the Little Colorado River with the Grand Canyon. They meet at nearly a right angle, unusual in that most tributaries enter at close to the same direction as the larger rivers.

By starting your driving tour of the Walhalla Plateau early in the day, you can reach the next stop, **Vista Encantada,** in time for a late picnic on one of several tables with canyon views.

From there you can finish your driving tour by taking the 3-mile spur from the Cape Royal Road to Point Imperial, at 8,803 feet, the highest point on the North Rim. It's also the best place on either rim to view the northeastern end of the park.

ORGANIZED TOURS & RANGER PROGRAMS

The park offers a host of free ranger programs. The schedule changes seasonally, but typically includes guided hikes and walks, kids' programs, and discussions of geology, native species, and natural and cultural history. Nightly evening programs run yearround on the South Rim. For a schedule, consult the park newspaper, *The Guide.*

GUIDED HIKES & TRIPS The nonprofit **Grand Canyon Field Institute** (© **866/ 471-4435;** www.grandcanyon.org/fieldinstitute), schedules dozens of multiday classes, backpacking trips, and rafting adventures. Some explore broad subjects such as ecology, cultural or natural history, wilderness studies, and photography and the arts. Fees are typically $100 to $150 per day.

BUS TOURS Of the many private companies that offer bus tours, **Xanterra** presents the largest number of options. Among the tour choices are Desert View Tour (East Rim) and Hermits Rest Tour ($47 and $28, respectively, for adults; free for those 15 and under), sunrise and sunset tours ($21.50), and all-day outings that combine Desert View Drive with any other tour ($60). For advance reservations, call © **888/297-2757** or 928-638-2631 or visit www.grandcanyonlodges.com.

DAY HIKES

There's no better way to enjoy the canyon than by walking down into it, watching the vegetation and rock layers change as you descend. The experience is far more rewarding than looking down from the rims. Unfortunately, hiking below the rims can be dangerous, especially at midday during summer. Changes in temperature and elevation can make hiking difficult even in ideal conditions. The jarring descent can strain your knees; the climb back out will test your lungs and heart. If it's hot out or you aren't up to climbing, consider walking on one of the rim trails.

Wherever you hike, carry plenty of food and water, wear sunscreen, sunglasses, and protective clothing. If you hike into the canyon, allow yourself twice as much time for the trip out as for the descent, and remember that the mileage indicated represents, in large part, vertical distance.

Rim Trail: South Rim

Rim Trail on the South Rim ★★   This walk starts in Grand Canyon Village and goes both east and west along the rim, with the westbound section of the trail spanning 8 miles to Hermits Rest and the eastbound part extending 4.5 miles past Mather Point to the South Kaibab Trailhead. Both sections can be busy, especially near Grand Canyon Village, and both offer stunning canyon views while passing through less-than-pristine rim-top scenery. The eastbound section is paved (from Maricopa Point to Pipe Creek Vista); the westbound part is longer and more rugged, and has lonesome stretches. Much of the westbound section is close to Hermit Road. The **rail of Time** extends 1.3 miles from Verkamp's Visitor Center to Yavapai Point on the eastbound section.

Because 16 miles might be too much for 1 day, I recommend hiking out on this trail from Grand Canyon Village and taking the shuttle back (Mar–Nov). By hiking out, you can avoid revisiting the same overlooks on the shuttle ride back—the shuttles stop at every turnout en route to Hermits Rest, but only at Pima Point, Mohave Point, and Powell Point on their way back to Grand Canyon Village. Up to 10 milestone-way. Easy. Access: Grand Canyon Village.

Rim Trails: North Rim

Ken Patrick Trail ★★   This steeply rolling trail travels through ponderosa pine and spruce-fir forest between the head of Roaring Springs Canyon and Point Imperial. Starting at the North Kaibab end, the first mile of the trail has been pounded into dust by mules. The path becomes very faint about 4 miles in, after passing the trail head for the old Bright Angel Trail. Past the Cape Royal Road, the trail descends into, then climbs out of, a very steep drainage overgrown with thorn-covered New Mexican locust. Although challenging, the 3-mile section between the Cape Royal Road and Point Imperial is also the prettiest stretch, skirting the rim of the canyon above Nankoweap Creek. You'll see plenty of scarlet bugler, identifiable by its tubular red flowers with flared lower petals, as well as a number of Douglas firs interspersed among the ponderosa pines. 10 miles one-way. Strenuous. Access: From south side of parking area for Point Imperial, or from parking area for North Kaibab Trail (on North Rim entrance road, 2 miles north of Grand Canyon Lodge).

The Transept Trail & Bright Angel Point Trail ★★   At the bottom of the stairs behind Grand Canyon Lodge, the Bright Angel Point Trail goes to the left and the Transept Trail goes right.

The paved **Bright Angel Point Trail** travels a quarter-mile to the tip of a narrow peninsula dividing Roaring Springs and Transept canyons. It passes a number of craggy outcroppings of Kaibab limestone, around which the roots of wind-whipped juniper trees cling like arthritic hands. The trail ends at 8,148-foot-high Bright Angel Point.

The **Transept Trail** ventures northeast along the rim of Transept Canyon, connecting the lodge and the North Rim Campground. Passing through old-growth ponderosa pine and quaking aspen, it descends into, then climbs out of, three shallow side drainages, with ascents steep enough to take the breath away from people unaccustomed to the altitude. Bright Angel Point Trail .25 mile each way. Transept Trail 1.5 miles RT. Easy. Access: Behind Grand Canyon Lodge.

Widforss Trail ★★ Named for landscape painter Gunnar Widforss, this trail skirts the head of Transept Canyon before venturing south to Widforss Point. For the first 2 miles, the trail undulates through ponderosa pine and spruce-fir forest, with spruce fir on the shady side of each drainage. Past the head of Transept Canyon, the trail heads south through a stand of old-growth ponderosa, part of which has been singed by forest fires. The trail reaches the rim again at Widforss Point, where you'll have a view of five temples. Near the rim are a picnic table and several good campsites. This is a self-guided hike; obtain brochures at the trail head. 5 miles one-way. Moderate. Access: Dirt road a little more than .25 mile south of Cape Royal Rd. Follow this road about .75 mile to well-marked parking area.

Canyon Trails

Because of the huge elevation changes on the canyon trails, none should be called easy. (More people are rescued off the Bright Angel Trail, generally considered the "easiest" trail into the canyon, than off any other trail.) In general, rating a trail easy, moderate, or difficult oversimplifies the situation; for this reason, I've avoided doing so below.

Bright Angel Trail ★★★ Both American Indians and early settlers recognized this as a choice location for a trail. First, there's an enormous fault line that creates a natural break in the cliffs. Then there's the water—more of it than anywhere else on the South Rim.

On a day hike, follow the switchbacks below Grand Canyon Village to **One-and-a-Half-Mile House** or **Three-Mile House,** each of which has shade, toilets, an emergency phone, and drinking water (seasonally). The Park Service, which responds to hundreds of emergency calls on this trail every year, discourages many day-hikers from going past One-and-a-Half-Mile House.

If you continue on the trail past Three-Mile House, you begin a long descent to the picnic area near the spring at **Indian Garden,** where lush vegetation surrounds you and large cottonwood trees provide shade. At 4.6 miles and more than 3,000 vertical feet from the rim, Indian Garden is dangerously deep for many people. However, a few well-prepared day-hikers may wish to hike an additional 1.5 miles past Indian Garden on the relatively flat (in this area) Tonto and Plateau Point trails. The Plateau Point Trail eventually dead-ends at an overlook of the Colorado River 1,300 feet below. 4.6 miles to Indian Garden, 7.8 miles to Colorado River, 9.3 miles to Bright Angel Campground. Access: Just west of Kolb Studio, near Grand Canyon Village. 6,860 ft. at trail head; 3,800 ft. at Indian Garden; 2,450 ft. at Colorado River. Water sources at One-and-a-Half-Mile House (seasonal), Three-Mile House (seasonal), Indian Garden, Colorado River, Bright Angel Campground.

South Kaibab Trail ★★★ Unlike the Bright Angel Trail, which follows natural routes into the canyon, the South Kaibab was built using dynamite and hard labor. And unlike the Bright Angel Trail, which stays near creek beds for much of the distance to the Colorado River, the South Kaibab Trail travels on ridgelines with expansive views. Because the South Kaibab has no water and little shade, it is best for descending. The Bright Angel Trail is safer for most hikers.

For a good day hike, follow the trail as it makes a series of switchbacks through the upper rock layers, down the west side of Yaki Point. Below the Coconino Sandstone, the trail heads north to Cedar Ridge, a platform that has pit toilets and a hitching post for mules. Shaded by pinyon and juniper trees, it affords expansive views down side canyons to the east and west. This is an excellent place for day-hikers to picnic and rest before hiking the 1.5 miles and 1,500 vertical feet back out. 6.7 miles to Colorado River, 6.8 miles to Bright Angel Campground. Access: Yaki Point (Ariz. 64, East Rim Dr., 5 miles east of Grand Canyon Village). 7,260 ft. at trail head; 2,450 ft. at Colorado River. Water sources at trail head, Colorado River, and Bright Angel Campground.

North Kaibab Trail ★★★   Less crowded than the South Rim corridor trails, this one begins at a parking area off the North Rim entrance road. It starts with a long series of switchbacks through thickly forested terrain at the head of Roaring Springs Canyon. The first major landmark is **Supai Tunnel.** At 2 miles from the trail head, with seasonal water, shade, and restrooms available, this is an excellent turnaround point for day-hikers. Beyond the tunnel, the trail descends in relatively gradual switchbacks through the bright red Supai Formation rocks, then crosses a bridge over a creek bed. Past the bridge, the trail travels along the south wall of Roaring Springs Canyon, on ledges atop cliffs of Redwall limestone. A spire known as **The Needle** marks the point where the trail begins its descent of the Redwall cliffs. A .2-mile spur trail descends to the springs. In the lush vegetation around it, you'll find drinking water (seasonally), shade, and picnic tables. Roughly 5 miles and 3,000 vertical feet below the rim, this is the farthest a day-hiker should go. 2 miles to Supai Tunnel, 4.7 miles to Roaring Springs, 6.8 miles to Cottonwood Campground, 14 miles to the Colorado. Access: North Rim entrance road, 2 miles north of Grand Canyon Lodge. 8,250 ft. at North Kaibab Trail head; 5,200 ft. at Roaring Springs; 4,080 ft. at Cottonwood Campground; 2,400 ft. at Colorado River. Water sources at Roaring Springs (seasonal), Bright Angel Creek, Cottonwood Campground (seasonal), Phantom Ranch, Bright Angel Campground.

OTHER SPORTS & ACTIVITIES

AIR TOURS   The following companies offer air tours originating from Tusayan: **Papillon Grand Canyon Helicopters** (✆ **888/635-7272;** www.papillon.com); **Maverick Helicopters** (✆ **888/261-4414;** www.maverickhelicopter.com); and **Grand Canyon Airlines** (✆ **866/235-9422;** www.grandcanyonairlines.com). Most airplane tours remain airborne for 40 to 50 minutes and cost $125 to $160 per person; most helicopter tours fly for 25 to 50 minutes and range from $200 to $300. The planes cover more ground, crossing the canyon near Hermits Rest and returning along the East Rim, near Desert View, but the helicopters cruise lower—just above the rim.

BIKING   Inside the park on the South Rim, cyclists are allowed on all paved and unpaved roads where motorized vehicles are allowed as well as on the **Greenway Trail,** which now connects Grand Canyon Visitor Center with the South Kaibab Trailhead (2.1 miles) and the gateway community of Tusayan (6.5 miles). Cyclists are not permitted on hiking trails below the rim or pedestrian paths, including the rim trail between Mather Point and Monument Creek Vista. Hermit Road is open to cyclists year-round and makes for a terrific ride, but you'll need to yield to tour buses, shuttles, private vehicles, and people on foot. Bikes are allowed on the **Hermit Road Greenway Trail** from Monument Creek Vista most of the way to Hermits Rest.

Bicycles are available for rent on the South Rim (except in winter) at **Bright Angel Bicycles** (✆ **928/638-3055;** www.bikegrandcanyon.com) at the Grand Canyon Visitor Center. Full-day rentals run about $40.

FISHING There's great trout fishing in the Colorado River just upstream of the national park, between Glen Canyon Dam and Lees Ferry. For advice on fishing this area or a guided trip ($450 for two anglers for a full day), contact **Lees Ferry Anglers Guides and Fly Shop** (✆ **800/962-9755** or 928/355-2261; www.leesferry.com), about 2½ hours north of Flagstaff on U.S. 89A. You'll need an Arizona Fishing Permit, available at Lees Ferry Anglers or at the **market** in Grand Canyon Village. The best trout fishing inside the park is at the eastern end of the canyon, upstream of Phantom Ranch.

MULE RIDES The prospect of descending narrow trails above steep cliffs on animals hardly famous for their intelligence might make you nervous. Once on the trail, however, you'll soon discover that the mules are no more enthralled by the idea of falling than you are. Although the mules walk close to the edges, there has never been a fatal accident. The rides can nonetheless be grueling. Most people's legs aren't used to bending around a mule, and the saddles aren't soft. In addition to the pounding, the canyon can be scorching, and chances for breaks are few. Because the rides are strenuous for both riders and mules, the wranglers strictly adhere to the following requirements: You must weigh less than 200 pounds (everyone is weighed), be at least 4 feet 7 inches tall, not be pregnant, and speak English. Acrophobes are discouraged.

The least expensive ride—the half-day **Canyon Vistas** ride—stays on the rim. The other rides are part of 1- or 2-night packages that include lodging and meals at **Phantom Ranch.** Going down, they follow Bright Angel Trail to the river, then travel east on the River Trail before finally crossing the river via the Kaibab Suspension Bridge. Coming back they use the South Kaibab Trail. The 11-mile descent takes 5½ hours; the 8-mile-long climb out is an hour shorter.

Mule rides are offered on the south rim by **Xanterra** (✆ **888/297-2757** or 303/297-2757; www.grandcanyonlodges.com) and range from about $120 for day rides to $500 to $1,000 for overnights (with Phantom Ranch lodging and meals).

Mule rides on the North Rim are through a small, family-run outfit called **Canyon Trail Rides** (✆ **435/679-8665;** www.canyonrides.com). Several half-day rides, open to ages 7 and up, are offered for $40 to $80; one stays on the rim, following the Ken Patrick and Uncle Jim trails to a canyon viewpoint; another descends 2 miles into the canyon on the North Kaibab Trail, turning back at Supai Tunnel. No one over 200 pounds is allowed on the canyon rides; for the rim rides, the limit is 220. All riders must speak English. Long pants are recommended, and you shouldn't bring anything more than a camera to carry. Water is provided.

RAFTING DAY TRIPS Day trips here don't get anywhere near the heart of the Canyon, but are fun and scenic, and will scratch the paddling itch if you can't spare the time to go on a longer trip. **Colorado River Discovery** (✆ **888/522-6644;** www.raftthecanyon.com) offers half-day guided smooth-water float trips from the base of Glen Canyon Dam to Lees Ferry (where most companies *begin* their overnight trips). The excursions last about 5 hours, cost $85 for adults, $75 for children 12 and under and are offered March 1 through November 30.

One-day guided motorized raft trips through the Grand Canyon's westernmost section are available through **Hualapai RiverRunners** (✆ **888/868-9378;** www.hualapaitourism.com). This is the only 1-day white-water rafting trip on the Colorado River. Riders begin at Diamond Creek's rapids and finish at Grand Canyon West (where a visit to the Skywalk can be added for $71). Time spent on the river is about 5½ hours and includes multiple cluster rapids. These guided trips cost about $350 per person and run from mid-March through October. The Hualapai Indian Reservation is about a 2-hour drive from Grand Canyon Village.

RAFTING OVERNIGHT TRIPS   Guided motorized trips are fastest, often covering the 277 miles from Lees Ferry (above the canyon) to South Cove (in Lake Mead) in 6 to 8 days, compared to as many as 18 days for nonmotorized trips. The motorized trips use wide pontoon boats (known colloquially as "bologna boats") that almost never capsize. Because of the speed, however, there's less time for hiking or resting in camp. If motorized trips are for you, consider using **Moki Mac River Expeditions**(© **800/ 284-7280;** www.mokimac.com) or **Wilderness River Adventures** (© **800/992-8022;** www.riveradventures.com).

For mobile people who want to bask in the canyon's beauty, I strongly recommend guided nonmotorized trips, even if it means seeing half the canyon instead of it all. There are two types of nonmotorized boats: paddleboats and oar boats. Sixteen companies are authorized to provide rafting trips in the Grand Canyon. For a comprehensive list, visit **www.nps.gov/grca** under "River Trips".

Rates typically start around $2,000 for the shortest trips and can exceed $6,000 for the longest trips.

WHERE TO STAY

If you're hoping to spend the night at or near the rim, be sure to reserve well in advance. During busy years, accommodations inside the park and in Tusayan frequently fill up, forcing would-be lodgers to backtrack away from the park.

Inside the Park
SOUTH RIM

Bright Angel Lodge & Cabins ★★   Dating to 1935, Bright Angel Lodge offers a nice balance of historic character and modern conveniences, and is a good mid-priced lodging for visitors looking to stay within park boundaries. The lodge, designed by Grand Canyon hospitality pioneer Mary Jane Colter, remains a prime center of activity on the South Rim, serving as the staging point for the famed mule rides. There are small, spartan rooms in the lodge and more spacious accommodations in the surrounding rustic cabins with colorful window frames and Native American–inspired architecture. Both the lodge rooms and cabins feature mass-produced furnishings. Most units have TVs and one queen bed, but only a few have views—make reservations as early as possible if you want one. The best of the bunch are the two-room Red Horse Cabin, an 1890 cabin that was retrofitted as a lodging in 2012, and the Buckey O'Neill Cabin, with swell views of the canyon and upgraded, Southwestern-tinged furnishings

In Grand Canyon Village. © **888/297-2757** or 928/638-2631. www.grandcanyonlodges.com. 89 units, including 55 cabins. $80–$90 double with shared bathroom; $90–$105 double with bathroom; $120–$130 historic cabin; $150–$200 historic rim-side cabin; $360–$380 rim-side Buckey O'Neill Cabin or Red Horse Cabin. **Amenities:** Restaurant; snack bar; lounge; free Wi-Fi.

El Tovar Hotel ★★★   This iconic hostelry has set the bar for luxury in the park since it opened as the Harvey House in 1905. Architect Charles Whittlesey's iconic design catches the eye from afar, as the limestone-and-pine exterior and mansard roof stand out above the rim for miles. The hotel was originally meant to have a deck jutting out over the rim, but park officials changed their minds and built it 100-feet inland, so there are not as many canyon views as you might expect. In the rooms, the understated décor features blue-hued duvets and drapes, blonde wood, and sun-drenched photographs of the canyon. Deluxe rooms have a bit more space than the standard units, which have notably sizable bathrooms nonetheless, but the four "view suites" are among the best in the Southwest, with original art, unique furnishings, and balconies overlooking the canyon in dramatic fashion. Major renovations are planned for 2014–15, starting with the exterior and moving to the guestrooms.

In Grand Canyon Village. © **888/297-2757** or 928/638-2631. www.grandcanyonlodges.com. 78 units. $180–$240 standard rooms; $280–$310 deluxe rooms; $350–$460 suites. **Amenities:** Restaurant; lounge; concierge; room service; free Wi-Fi.

Maswik Lodge ★ The 1960s-era Maswik Lodge is not nearly as distinctive as Bright Angel Lodge and El Tovar Hotel, but it offers a great value. You're a short walk to the South Rim, so they're aren't any views, and the rooms don't have elaborate amenities, but they are more than functional, especially for visitors who plan on spending their days on the trails. Units in **Maswik South** are smaller and show a bit of age, while the pricier units in **Maswik North** have more square footage, less wear, and open up into the forest. There are also summer-only standalone **cabins** that are similar to the units in Maswik South.

In Grand Canyon Village. © **888/297-2757** or 928/638-2631. www.grandcanyonlodges.com. 278 units. $90–$100 Maswik South; $170–$190 Maswik North; $95–$105 cabin rooms. **Amenities:** Restaurant; lounge; free Wi-Fi.

Thunderbird and Kachina Lodges ★★ The minimalist design of these low-slung, concrete structures was once decried for sullying the South Rim, but these sibling lodges are apt for their setting in that they don't overwhelm the surroundings. Better yet, the canyon-side rooms offer stunning vistas of the Grand Canyon for less than half the price of the renowned view suites next door at El Tovar. The rooms at both lodges were upgraded in 2011–12 with a contemporary style and include black-and-white photos of canyon landscapes, flatscreen TVs, and labyrinth-patterned carpeting. Most rooms have two queen beds, and the cinderblock walls make for a quieter place to sleep than their thin-walled counterparts in other park lodgings.

In Grand Canyon Village. © **888/297-2757** or 928/638-2631. www.grandcanyonlodges.com. 55 units at Thunderbird, 49 at Kachina. $180–$200 Park-side; $190–$220 canyon-side. **Amenities:** Free Wi-Fi

Yavapai Lodge ★ Yavapai Lodge is set in a wooded area with easy access to the South Rim (it's about a mile away), and the combination of open space and reasonable rates makes it a good pick for families. There are two options here: Rooms in **Yavapai East** have plenty of space and one king or two queen beds, and a bit more pizzazz, decorated with earth tones; **Yavapai West**'s units are smaller and more sparsely furnished. This is the largest lodge in Grand Canyon Village, with big parking lots right out front, so expect a bit more activity than the smaller lodgings on the South Rim.

In Grand Canyon Village. © **888/297-2757** or 928/638-2631. www.grandcanyonlodges.com. 358 units. $125–$140 double in Yavapai West; $165–$180 double in Yavapai East. Closed in winter. **Amenities:** Restaurant; free Wi-Fi.

CANYON BOTTOM

Phantom Ranch ★★ This is one of the most remote lodgings on the planet, but its location on the floor of the Grand Canyon hasn't put a dent in its popularity—it routinely sells out the first day reservations are available, 13 months in advance. Locale aside, the ranch's nine air-conditioned cabins are pleasant but ultimately unremarkable, with a concrete floor, as many as 10 bunk beds, and a toilet and a sink, but little else.

However, this is the only place on the bottom of the canyon where you can get a hot shower, a cold beer, and a roof over your head. The setting is like nothing else on Earth—you see the canyon and only the canyon, and have easy access to trails along the Colorado River and to Ribbon Falls—and you'll only get here via a hike, mule ride, or raft trip. Despite the popularity of the ranch, there are often cancellations due to weather or people not making the require 200-pound weight limit for the mule ride; contact the **Bright Angel Transportation Desk** (© **928/638-2631,** ext. 6015) to get on the waiting list when you arrive and you might just get lucky, especially in the colder months.

Bottom of the canyon, .5 mile north of the Colorado River on the North Kaibab Trail. © **888/297-2757** or 928/638-2631. www.grandcanyonlodges.com. 7 4-person cabins, 2 cabins for up to 10 people, 4 10-person dorms. $45–$50 dorm bed; $150–$165 cabin for 4 people. Most cabins are reserved as part of mule-trip overnight packages. Duffel service (baggage service via mule): $65–$70 (each way). **Amenities:** Restaurant.

NORTH RIM

Grand Canyon Lodge ★★　This is among the most iconic of all national-park lodges and a good bet for those looking for solitude when they visit the Grand Canyon. The main lodge, clad in local limestone and timber, sits at Bright Angel Point on the isolated North Rim, a mere 12 miles from the busier South Rim as the crow flies—or 200 miles by car—but a world away. Clustered around the lodge are cabins graded as Western (with two queen beds and a private front porch), Pioneer (with two bedrooms and space for 6), and Frontier (one double and one single, with showers only) as well as annexes containing nondescript rooms with a single queen bed that wouldn't be out of place at a roadside motor inn. Best views are in the rim-side Pioneer cabins; they're $10 extra, but its money well spent.

At North Rim, 214 miles north of South Rim on Hwy. 67. © **877/386-4383** (reservations), 928/638-2611 (main switchboard), or 877/386-4383. www.grandcanyonforever.com. 218 units. $129 Frontier Cabin; $124 double room; $173–$183 Pioneer Cabin; $182 Western Cabin; $187 Rim Cabin. **Amenities:** 3 restaurants; bar.

Outside the Park

NEAR THE NORTH ENTRANCE

Jacob Lake Inn ★　Since 1929, Jacob Lake Inn has served as the prime jumping-off point for the North Rim, and it is one of the best values in the vicinity today. You'll find a wide range of cabins and rooms here, as well as a gas station, old-fashioned restaurant, bakery, and gift shop. Overnight options include new hotel rooms that date from a 2006 expansion alongside woodsy but otherwise unmemorable cabins and rooms that are several decades older. The units are well maintained, but travelers looking for modern comforts would do well to book a newer room, with a balcony, a quilt-clad king or queen bed, and an overall style that nicely balances rustic and modern. However, you are over an hour's drive from the North Rim and about 150 miles from Grand Canyon Village on the South Rim, so for all of its conveniences, the resort isn't exactly close to the big attraction in these parts.

45 miles north of the North Rim, at the junction of Hwy. 67 and 89A, Jacob Lake. © **928/643-7232.** www.jacoblake.com. 63 units. Mid-May–Nov $94–$144 double; Dec–mid-May 13 $70 double. Pets accepted for $10 extra. **Amenities:** Restaurant; free Wi-Fi .

Kaibab Lodge ★　This 1920s-era summer-only cabin resort harks back to a different era, with open meadows where kids can burn off excess energy and a thoroughly Western beer bar that's beloved by their parents. It also boasts a location that's close to the North Rim but far enough away that you don't feel inundated by park traffic.

Clustered around the main lodge are duplex and four-plex cabins of several vintages with two to four units each, and the largest can sleep up to 5 guests. All have private bathrooms but beyond that, they vary considerably. The oldest rooms have just one double bed and not much floor space, and the biggest and best cabins have two queens and a covered porch.

18 miles north of the North Rim on HC 64. © **928/638-2389.** www.kaibablodge.com. 31 units. $90–$185 double. Pets allowed in some rooms. **Amenities:** Restaurant; bar; free Wi-Fi.

TUSAYAN

Grand Hotel ★★   This hotel looks the part of an imposing national park lodge, and features the nicest rooms in Tusayan. The lobby is a gem, with black-and-white photos of Grand Canyon luminaries and notable visitors—get a load of Einstein in a Hopi headdress!—and colorful Native American art. The décor in the rooms would best be described as "New Southwest," and every unit balances regional flair in the form of iron-wrought headboards and striking canyon photos with upscale perks like full-length mirrors, granite countertops, skylights, and in-room safes.

On Ariz. 64, 1.5 miles south of the park entrance, Tusayan. © **888/634-7263** or 928/638-3333. www.grandcanyongrandhotel.com. 121 units. High season $189–$249 standard, $209–$269 balcony; low season $99 standard, $119 balcony. **Amenities:** Restaurant; bar; concierge; exercise room; indoor pool; indoor hot tub; free Wi-Fi.

7-Mile Lodge ★   Arrive at this well-maintained motor inn as early as possible for the best value in the vicinity of the South Rim—rooms are first come, first serve (meaning reservations are not taken), and it's almost always sold out by noon in the peak summer season. The accommodations are nothing fancy, with small bathrooms, wood paneling, and run-of-the-mill furniture; most have two queen beds and a few have one king. But if you are looking for a deal near the South Rim, look no further.

1.5 miles south of Ariz. 64 park entrance, Tusayan. © **928/638-2291.** Reservations not accepted. 20 units. High season (spring to early fall, holidays) $89 double; low season (rest of year) $59–$79 double. **Amenities:** Free Wi-Fi.

WILLIAMS

Budget travelers should consider the rooms, cottages, and train cars converted into overnight lodgings at **Canyon Motel & RV Park ★**, 1900 E. Rodeo Rd. (© **800/482-3955** or 928/635-9371; www.thecanyonmotel.com), with double rates of about $75 to $150, and the no-frills but nicely maintained rooms at **El Rancho Motel ★**, 617 E. Rte. 66 (© **928/635-2552**), with double rates of $80 to $100.

Grand Canyon Railway Hotel ★★   This big, modern hotel is located right next to the depot for the railroad to the South Rim, and specializes in packages that include train tickets. The hotel originally opened in 1901, then closed—along with the railway—in 1969, but reopened in grand fashion 20 years later. Today it does good business when the train runs, housing overnight guests in modern rooms that are slated for a remodel in 2014–15. There are three tiers of rooms (standard, deluxe, and suites), all 300 or more square feet of space (what the décor will be like is anybody's guess as I write this, but if history's any guide, it should be cushy). The 1,000-square-foot **Rail Baron Suite** is, for my money, the nicest room in northern Arizona, with a full kitchen, slick contemporary décor, and a railroad motif. The property also encompasses and RV park and a kennel for dogs whose masters have headed to the pet-unfriendly South Rim for the day.

235 N. Grand Canyon Blvd., Williams. © **800/843-8724** or 928/635-4010. www.thetrain.com. 297 units. $169–$189 double, $219–$349 suite. Lower winter rates. **Amenities:** 2 restaurants; bar; exercise room; indoor pool; indoor hot tub; free Wi-Fi.

CAMPING options

You can make reservations for campsites in the Mather and North Rim campgrounds by calling ℂ **877/444-6777** or visiting www.recreation.gov. Campsites are $12 to $25 nightly, or $35 for RVs in Trailer Village.

Inside the park on the South Rim, 26 miles east of Grand Canyon Village on Ariz. 64, you'll find **Desert View Campground ★★**. The campground offers a break from the summer bustle in a pinyon-juniper woodland at the eastern edge of the park. The only drawback: The nearest showers are 28 miles away. The restrooms here have flush toilets and sinks, but no hot water. During high season, this first-come, first-served campground usually fills up by noon.

Near Grand Canyon Village on the South Rim is **Mather Campground ★★**. Despite having 319 sites in a relatively small area, this is an excellent campground. Pinyon and juniper trees shade the sites, spaced just far enough apart to afford some privacy. But don't stay too near the showers—you'll have hundreds of campers tramping past your site.

For RV drivers on the South Rim, **Trailer Village ★** in Grand Canyon Village (ℂ **888/297-2757** or 928/638-2631 for reservations), offers full hookups. The neighbors are close, the showers half a mile away, and the vegetation sparse.

On the North Rim, the **North Rim Campground ★★★** (ℂ **877/444-6777** for advance reservations) is 44 miles south of Jacob Lake on Ariz. 67. Shaded by old-growth ponderosa pines alongside Transept Canyon (part of Grand Canyon), the most spectacular sites here are the rim sites, which open onto the canyon. They cost an extra $7 but are worth it. Showers, Grand Canyon Lodge, and a store are within walking distance.

BACKCOUNTRY CAMPING

The longest in advance permit requests are accepted (and considered) by the Backcountry Information Center is the first of the month, 4 months before the proposed start month. For example, permits for all of May go on sale on January 1, permits for June go on sale February 1, and so on. To obtain a backcountry permit for the dates and use areas/campsites of your choice, ensure your request arrives on the first day it will be accepted (but not before).

You can pick up the Permit Request Form and instructions in person at the **Backcountry Information Center** (ℂ **928/638-7875;** www.nps.gov/grca) or download them from the website. Once you fill out your form, take it in person to the backcountry offices on the South Rim or North Rim; fax it to ℂ **928/638-2125** or mail it to: Grand Canyon National Park, Permits Office, 1824 S. Thompson St., Suite. 201, Flagstaff, AZ 86001. No requests are taken by phone. Good for up to 11 people, each permit costs $10, plus $5 per person per night.

To increase your odds of receiving a permit, be as flexible as possible. It helps to request three alternative hikes, and more than one starting date. Keeping your group small also helps. Forms must be received at least 2 weeks before the dates requested. Faxing the form will get you a response much faster than mailing it.

If you show up at the park without a permit and find the backcountry booked, you may be able to obtain a permit by putting your name on the waiting list at the backcountry offices on either rim. To stay on the waiting list, you'll have to show back up at 8am every morning until there's an opening.

The Backcountry Information Center takes calls weekdays from 1 to 5pm at ℂ **928/638-7875.** You can visit in person from 8am to noon and 1 to 5pm daily.

The Red Garter Bed & Bakery ★   This former brothel/saloon/opium den has cleaned up nicely into an inn/bakery/gift shop on old Route 66 in downtown Williams. Owner John Holst bought the property in 1979 and painstakingly restored it from shabby to chic. Today the four guestrooms vary in size but have similar style, with custom woodwork by Holst, antiques, and colorful accents. My favorite is **Big Bertha's Room,** with Navajo rugs as duvets on the two queen beds and a clawfoot tub. You can't miss the place—just look for the faux madam with a red feather boa hanging out from the windows on the second floor.

137 W. Railroad Ave., Williams. © **800/328-1484** or 928/635-1484. 4 units. www.redgarter.com. $115–$160 double. Rates include continental breakfast. Usually closed Jan. **Amenities:** Restaurant; free Wi-Fi.

FLAGSTAFF

Hotel Weatherford ★   This 1898 gem is just the place to acclimate yourself to civilization after an expedition in the Grand Canyon. The rooms, with one or two double beds or a single queen, are small and show some age, but the place is full of historic personality, from the antique safe in the lobby to the hand-carved 1870s bar in the **Zane Grey Room,** one of four places to get a drink here. The fact that there are a total of 48 beer tap handles on the premises probably gives you an idea—come here not for the peace and quiet, but for the nightlife that can be a little bit on the raucous side. There's also a good restaurant serving three meals daily in **Charly's,** but no Wi-Fi.

23 N. Leroux, Flagstaff. © **928/779-1919.** www.weatherfordhotel.com. 11 units, 3 with shared bathrooms. $49–$79 double with shared bathroom; $89 double with private bathroom; $139 suite. **Amenities:** Restaurant; 4 bars.

Little America Hotel ★★   One of seven "Little Americas" in the West, this regional chain caters to truckers as well as leisure travelers. The former group tend to gravitate to the truck stop that's next door, but don't let that fool you: The rooms feature elegant European style, complete with granite counters, chandeliers, and reproduction antique furnishings. The bathrooms are enormous, featuring vanities inside and out, and most rooms have small private patios. The best units face away from the interstate for an extra $20, and the surrounding woodland gives the feel that you are farther away from civilization than you really are.

2515 E. Butler (off I-40 exit 198), Flagstaff. © **800/352-4386** or 928/779-7900. http://flagstaff.little america.com. 255 units. High season $149–$189 double; low season $99–$139 double. **Amenities:** Restaurant; lounge; fitness center; outdoor seasonal pool; free Wi-Fi.

KANAB, UTAH

Parry Lodge ★   Kanab is nicknamed "Utah's Hollywood" for the many Western movies shot here over the years, and the Parry Lodge is the best place to connect with that lore—this is where many stars cooled their spurs in between takes. Many rooms are named for the actors who actually once slept in them: John Wayne is unsurprisingly the most popular (and features an in-room Jacuzzi tub), but you can also bunk in the former quarters of Dean Martin, Ronald Reagan, and Barbara Stanwyck, among others. The furnishings are what you'd expect in a mid-priced chain hotel, with two queens in a standard room, but the décor one-ups the norm with old movie posters. The rooms are in wings centered on the **Old Barn,** where classic Western films are screened nightly in summer.

89 E. Center St., Kanab. © **800/748-4104** or 435/644-2601. www.parrylodge.com. 89 units. May 1–Oct 31 $70–$120 double; Nov 1–Apr 30 $49–$69 double. Pets accepted ($10 extra). **Amenities:** Restaurant; outdoor seasonal pool; free Wi-Fi.

Quail Park Lodge ★★ This quirky reinvention of a vintage 1960s motor lodge is my favorite place to stay in Kanab. The rooms are colorful and uniquely decorated, with little touches like lavender-vanilla linen spray on the nightstand, premium amenities in the bathrooms, and eclectic artwork on the walls. There's a touch of intentional kitsch—you might have a lemon-yellow lamp or sculptures of hands making the OK sign—as this blast from the past doesn't take itself too seriously. Up the street and under the same ownership is the summer-only **Canyons Lodge** (www.canyonslodge. com), a woodsy property with log walls, faux taxidermy, and similar rates.

125 N. U.S. 89, Kanab. ⓒ **435/215-1447.** www.quailparklodge.com. 13 units. $129 double; $159 suite. Lower winter rates. Rates include continental breakfast. **Amenities:** Outdoor seasonal pool; complimentary bikes; free Wi-Fi.

WHERE TO EAT

South Rim

Beyond the options listed below, there are **cafeterias** specializing in American and Mexican fare at Maswik Lodge and Yavapai Lodge and a **coffee bar** that becomes an alcohol bar at night in Bright Angel Lodge.

Arizona Room ★★ STEAKHOUSE Less formal than the dining room at El Tovar, this definitively Arizonan eatery is the in-the-know pick for dinner with a canyon view. The Southwestern décor is a good match for the menu, with a focus on steaks, barbecue, and Mexican fare, as well as some eminently sippable margaritas. There's also a nice selection of seafood with regional preparations, like cornmeal-crusted tilapia with spicy rice and blackened salmon with avocado butter. The lunch offerings are primarily sandwiches. Reservations are not accepted, so the wait can be an hour or more in peak summer season.

At Bright Angel Lodge in Grand Canyon Village. ⓒ **928/638-2631.** Lunch $8–$11; dinner $8–$28. Daily 11:30am–3pm and 4:30–10pm. Closed for lunch Nov–Feb, and for lunch and dinner Jan–Feb.

Bright Angel Restaurant ★ AMERICAN This old-fashioned eatery provides value and the kind of casual atmosphere that's a good fit for most Grand Canyon visitors. In a room decorated with oversized vintage postcards and wagon-wheel chandeliers, the servers deliver hearty plates of American fare. Staples include omelets for breakfast and burgers for lunch. The dinner menu includes the salads and sandwiches from lunch as well as salmon and ribs from the Arizona Room plus such specialties as trout, fajitas, and tacos with tofu or shrimp. This is a good pick for families, as it has just enough bustle to muffle noisy toddlers.

At Bright Angel Lodge in Grand Canyon Village. ⓒ **928/638-2631.** Breakfast $6–$13; lunch $8–$11; dinner $8–$24. Daily 6:30am–10pm.

El Tovar Dining Room ★★★ INTERNATIONAL With pine-clad walls, murals of Native American dancers, and more formality than the rest of the South Rim restaurants combined, this is just the spot for a special dinner. The fare matches the atmosphere, influenced by both regional and continental traditions and featuring such winners as a grilled buffalo ribeye, served with fig compote and asiago polenta; and salmon tostada with tequila vinaigrette. The lunch highlight is the Navajo tacos, while breakfast dishes include trout and eggs, and spicy Sonoran eggs with chorizo sausage. This is the only restaurant on the South Rim that accepts reservations, and they're recommended, especially for the few tables that offer an unobstructed canyon view.

At El Tovar Hotel in Grand Canyon Village. ⓒ **928/638-2631,** ext. 6432. Breakfast $9–$17; lunch $10–$16; dinner $17–$33. Daily 6:30–10:45am, 11:15am–2pm, and 4:30–10pm. Dinner starts at 5pm in winter.

INSIDE THE CANYON

Phantom Ranch Canteen ★ AMERICAN   This small stone cabin is the only place to get a hot meal on the canyon floor if you aren't cooking it on a camp stove yourself. Breakfasts are served family-style—you can expect plenty of eggs, bacon, and hotcakes—lunches come in sacks, and there are three dinner options nightly: steak, beef stew, and vegetarian chili. Steaks are served at a 5pm seating and the chili and stew are available at 6:30pm. Because the kitchen's supply chain includes a mule ferrying ingredients a mile downhill, you must have advance reservations to eat here. If you don't, there are a few snacks and beverages (including beer and wine) available for purchase when it is not meal time.

Inside the canyon .5 mile north of the Colorado River on the North Kaibab Trail. To reserve meals more than 1 day in advance, call ℭ **888/297-2757;** to reserve next-day meals, contact the Bright Angel Transportation Desk at ℭ **928/638-2631,** ext. 6015. Steak dinner $44; vegetarian chili or beef stew $28; sack lunch $13; breakfast $21.

NORTH RIM

Beyond the eatery listed below, the North Rim's dining options include Deli in the Pines and the **Roughrider Saloon,** both located in the Grand Canyon Lodge and serving typical American dishes. (The deli offers meals to go.) There's also a **nightly cookout and country-and-western show** every evening from June to September, featuring barbecued beef and roasted chicken.

Grand Canyon Lodge Dining Room ★★ CONTINENTAL   This dining room has better views than any restaurant on the South Rim, with banks of windows overlooking Transept Canyon, an especially scenic segment of the Grand Canyon. The fare is not as creative as what is served at the ritzy El Tovar across the canyon, but there are more vegetarian and healthy options. Dinners range from grilled vegetables and pasta to bison flank steak and grilled salmon with polenta. Breakfast and lunch are fairly traditional American. (Both feature hot buffets as well as a la carte choices.) Reservations are highly recommended for dinner, but not accepted for breakfast or lunch.

At Grand Canyon Lodge. ℭ **928/638-2611.** Breakfast and lunch $7–$15; dinner $12–$33. Daily 6:30–10am, 11:30am–2:30pm, and 4:45–9:45pm.

CAMERON

Cameron Trading Post Restaurant ★ AMERICAN/MEXICAN   Located about 30 miles east of the east entrance to the national park, the trading post has been operating since 1916 and encompasses a sprawling gift shop, motel, and RV park, but the standout operation is the restaurant. With a mix of Victorian (ornate woodwork and a pressed tin ceiling) and Navajo trappings (rugs and art), its an interesting place for the eye, enhanced by the big picture windows affording a view of the seemingly endless red desert. Meals are hearty and feature lots of regional spice, from the French toast stuffed with prickly-pear jelly for breakfast to the French dip on Navajo fry bread at lunch. Dinner adds steak, seafood, and Mexican plates to the mix.

In Cameron Trading Post, 466 U.S. 89, Cameron. ℭ **928/679-2231.** www.camerontradingpost.com. Breakfast and lunch $7–$14; dinner $11–$27. Summer daily 6am–10pm; winter daily 7am–9pm.

TUSAYAN

Canyon Star Restaurant ★ AMERICAN   The best option in touristy Tusayan, breakfast and dinner are served in the wood-clad dining room, featuring Southwestern-tinged variations of American standbys at both meals. Expect chorizo and eggs and breakfast burritos in the morning and juicy steaks and barbecue at night. Lunch is available at **Canyon Star Saloon,** featuring a build-your-own-sandwich option and several regional beers on draft.

In Grand Hotel on Ariz. 64 (1.5 miles from the park's south entrance), Tusayan. © **888/634-7263** or 928/638-3333. Breakfast and lunch $7–$14; dinner $16–$33. Daily 6–10am, noon–4pm, and 5–10pm.

FLAGSTAFF

Head to Charly's Pub & Grill ★ in the historic Hotel Weatherford, 23 N. Leroux St. (© **928/779-1919;** www.weatherfordhotel.com), for Southwestern specialties like posole, Navajo tacos, and huevos rancheros.

Tinderbox Kitchen ★★ AMERICAN   A locals fave, Tinderbox might well be the best restaurant in Flagstaff. The casual dining room, peppered with contemporary photography and décor, is a great canvas for the culinary creativity of the kitchen. Using comfort food as a starting point, the menu changes on a near-weekly basis. When I was there last, highlights included jalapeno tamale pudding, cauliflower fondue, and bacon-wrapped buffalo meatloaf. **The Annex,** a hip cocktail lounge next door (same ownership) offers burgers, chicken wings, and blue-plate specials such as barbecued bologna sandwiches.

34 S. San Francisco St., Flagstaff. © **928/226-8400.** www.tinderboxkitchen.com. Main courses $18–$28. Sun–Thurs 5–9pm; Fri–Sat 5–10pm.

WILLIAMS

Cruisers Cafe 66, 233 W. Rte. 66, (© **928/635-2445;** www.cruisers66.com), is a kid-friendly lunch-and-dinner place bedecked in petroliana and assorted Route 66 memorabilia, playing 1950s music and serving burgers and better-than-average BBQ platters as well as beers from the adjacent Grand Canyon Brewing Company. For hearty American fare or—more importantly—a slice of pie, stop at **Pine Country Restaurant,** 107 N. Grand Canyon Blvd. (© **928/635-9718;** www.pinecountryrestaurant. com) is open for all three meals daily. The kitchen bakes more than 50 varieties of pie, as well as plating up dishes like biscuits and gravy, hoagies, and country-fried steak.

Rod's Steak House ★ STEAKHOUSE   Since 1946, beef has been the specialty of the house at Rod's, and the carnivorous bent means there are no vegetarian options on the menu—don't even ask. But if you are looking for steaks, you've found the right place; The menu also includes trout, fried chicken, and a few other non-beef dishes. The cavernous restaurant, a Route 66 standby during the heyday of "The Mother Road," unsurprisingly sports a cow motif in the décor.

301 E. Rte. 66, Williams. © **928/635-2671.** www.rods-steakhouse.com. $14–$43. Mon–Sat 11am–9:30pm. Closed Sun and first 2 weeks of Jan.

KANAB, UTAH

For affordable Mexican food, Kanab has a pair of standbys in **Nedra's Too ★**, 310 S. 100 E. (© **435/644-2030;** www.nedrascafe.com), and **Escobar's ★**, 373 E. 300 S. (© **435/644-3739**). The former has a notably lengthy vegetarian menu.

Rocking V Café ★★ AMERICAN   In a historic downtown storefront you'll find an art gallery upstairs and the dining room on the main floor, and both are worth a stop. The menu focuses on gourmet comfort food (the owners call it "slow food"); think macaroni and cheese with four cheeses and a bread-crumb crust, pot roast with polenta, and inventive sandwiches. There are also more elaborate and expensive options, often including Western delicacies like buffalo tenderloin and crusted Idaho trout picatta. This is Utah, but tipplers take note: there's a full bar.

97 W. Center St. © **435/644-8001.** www.rockingvcafe.com. Lunch and dinner $10–$27. Summer daily 11:30am–10pm; winter Thurs–Sun noon–8pm. Usually closed for 2 weeks in early Dec.

ARCHES & CANYONLANDS

by Don & Barbara Laine

antastic rock formations, brilliant colors, and some of the most rugged terrain in the continental United States await you in Arches and Canyonlands national parks, sister parks practically across the street from each other in the red rock country of eastern Utah. Your base for exploring both of these parks will be the small, bustling town of Moab, so let's start there.

ESSENTIALS

Getting There & Gateways

To get to Moab from Salt Lake City, about 240 miles away, follow I-15 south to Spanish Fork, take U.S. 6 southeast to I-70, and follow that east to Crescent Junction, where you'll pick up U.S. 191 south. From Grand Junction, Colorado, take I-70 west until you reach Crescent Junction, and then go south on U.S. 191.

The entrance to Arches National Park is 5 miles north of Moab, Utah, on U.S. 191.

There are several sections of Canyonlands National Park. To get to the Island in the Sky Visitor Center from Moab (about 34 miles), take **U.S. 191** (which runs north-south through eastern Utah from Wyoming to Arizona) north to Utah 313, and follow it south into the park. To reach the Needles Visitor Center from Moab, leave U.S. 191 at **Utah 211** south of Moab, and head west into the park. It's about 75 miles. To get to the Maze District from Moab, take U.S. 191 north, then go west for about 11 miles on **I-70** to **Utah 24** and head south. Watch for signs and follow two- and four-wheel-drive dirt roads east into the park.

The Horseshoe Canyon area of Canyonlands is about 120 miles from Island in the Sky. To get there by two-wheel-drive vehicle, follow I-70 west from Green River to U.S. 24, and then go south about 24 miles to the Horseshoe Canyon turnoff (near the WATCH FOR SAND DRIFTS sign), where you turn left. Follow this maintained dirt road for about 30 miles to the canyon's west rim, where you can park. This is the trail head for the hike to the Great Gallery (see "Day Hikes," below).

THE NEAREST AIRPORT   Located 16 miles north of downtown Moab, **Canyonlands Field** (✆ **435/259-4849;** www.moabairport.com) has daily scheduled flights between Moab and Denver and Moab and Prescott, AZ on **Great Lakes Airlines** (✆ **800/554-5111** or 435/259-0566; www. flygreatlakes.com) and car rentals from **Enterprise** (✆ **435/259-8505;**

AVOIDING the crowds

This is a popular park, attracting about one million visitors annually. Expect to find crowded parking areas daily March through October, with the peak month being August. The quietest months are December, January, and February, but it can be cold then. Those wanting to avoid crowds might gamble on Mother Nature and visit in November or late February, when days can be delightfully sunny and just a bit cool, or bitterly cold, windy, and awful. As with most popular parks, avoid visiting during school vacations, if possible.

www.enterprise.com). Shuttle service into Moab is also available from several companies, including **Roadrunner Shuttle** (© **435/259-9402;** www.roadrunnershuttle.com) and **Moab Taxi** (© **435/210-4297;** www.moabtaxicabcom).

The closest major airport is **Grand Junction Regional Airport,** about 112 miles east in Grand Junction, Colorado (© **970/244-9100;** www.gjairport.com). It has direct flights or connections from most major cities. Car rentals are available at the airport from most major rental companies. Another option for air travelers is to fly into **Salt Lake City International Airport** (© **800/595-2442** or 801/575-2400; www.slcairport.com), about 240 miles from Moab, which has service from most major airlines and rental-car companies.

Ground Transportation

Rentals (standard passenger cars, vans, and four-wheel-drive vehicles) are available from **Enterprise** (© **435/259-8505;** www.enterprise.com). For those planning to drive into the backcountry, four-wheel-drive vehicles are available from **Farabee's Jeep Rentals** (© **855/259-7594** or 435/259-7494; www.farabeejeeprentals.com), **Canyonlands Jeep Adventures** (© **866/892-5337** or 435/259-4413; www.canyonlandsjeep.com), and **Cliffhanger Jeep Rental** (© **435/259-0889;** www.cliffhangerjeeprental.com). See p. 189 for more on four-wheeling.

Seasons & Climate

Summer days are hot, often exceeding 100°F (38°C), and winters can be cool or cold, dropping below freezing at night, with snow possible. The best time to visit, especially for hikers, is in the spring or fall, when daytime temperatures are usually between 60° and 80°F (16°–27°C) and nights are cool. Spring winds, although not usually dangerous, can be gusty, so hold on to your hat.

Area Information

Contact the **Moab Area Travel Council,** (© **800/635-6622;** www.discovermoab.com) in advance for information on lodging, restaurants, camping, guides, activities, current weather, and just about anything else.

Then, when you arrive, stop by the **Moab Information Center,** at the corner of Main and Center streets, open Monday through Saturday 8am to 8pm and Sunday from 9am to 7pm from mid-March through October, with shorter hours the rest of the year. This multiagency visitor center has information from the Park Service, Bureau of Land Management, U.S. Forest Service, Grand County Travel Council, and Canyonlands Natural History Association. You can get advice, watch a number of videos on

Southwest attractions, pick up brochures on local businesses and outfitters, and purchase books, videos, and other materials. A board displays current weather conditions and campsite availability.

ARCHES NATIONAL PARK

Natural stone arches and awe-inspiring rock formations, sculpted as if by an artist's hand, are the defining features of this park, and they exist in remarkable numbers and variety. Just as soon as you've seen the most beautiful, most colorful, most gigantic stone arch you can imagine, walk around the next bend and there's another—bigger, better, and more brilliant than the last. It would take forever to see them all, with more than 2,000 officially listed and more being discovered, or "born," every day.

Compared to Canyonlands National Park, Arches is more visitor-friendly, with relatively short, well-maintained trails leading to most of the park's major attractions. It's also a place to let your imagination run wild. Is Delicate Arch really so delicate? Or would its other monikers (Old Maid's Bloomers and Cowboy Chaps) be more appropriate? And what about those tall spires? You might imagine they're castles, giant stone sailing ships, or the petrified skyscrapers of some ancient city.

Some think of arches as bridges, imagining the power of water that literally cuts a hole through solid rock. Actually, to geologists there's a big difference. Natural bridges are formed when a river cuts a channel; the often bizarre and beautiful contours of arches result from the erosive force of rain and snow, freezing and thawing, as it dissolves the "glue" that holds sand grains together and chips away at the stone.

Although arches usually grow slowly—*very* slowly—occasionally something dramatic happens, like that quiet day in 1940 when a sudden crash instantly doubled the opening of Skyline Arch and leaving a huge boulder at its feet. Luckily, no one (that we know of) was standing underneath at the time. The same thing happened to the magnificently delicate Landscape Arch in 1991, when a slab of rock some 60 feet long fell from its underside. Today, it's hard to believe that such a thin ribbon of stone can continue hanging on at all.

Visitor Center & Information

The **Arches National Park Visitor Center,** just inside the entrance gate, offers maps, brochures, and other information, and a museum explains arch formation and other park features. On Christmas Day, the park is open but the visitor center is closed. For info before you get there, contact **Arches National Park,** P.O. Box 907, Moab, UT 84532 (✆ **435/719-2299;** www.nps.gov/arch).

Entrance Fees & Permits

Entry for up to 7 days costs $10 per private vehicle or $5 per person on foot, motorcycle, or bike. Required **backcountry permits** for overnight trips into the backcountry, available at the visitor center, are free.

EXPLORING THE PARK BY CAR

You can see many of the park's most famous rock formations through your car windows along the 18-mile (one-way) **scenic drive,** although we strongly urge you to get out and explore on foot. You have the option of walking short distances to a number of view points or stretching your legs on a variety of longer hikes (see "Day Hikes," below). The main road is easy to navigate, even for RVs, but parking at some view points is limited. Please be considerate and leave trailers at the visitor center parking lot or in a campground.

Along the scenic drive you'll see **Park Avenue,** a solid rock "fin" that reminded early visitors of the New York skyline; **Courthouse Towers,** where monoliths such as Sheep Rock, the Organ, and the Three Gossips dominate the landscape; the **Tower of Babel** on the east (right) side of the road, and **Balanced Rock,** a huge boulder perched on a slowly eroding pedestal. **Panorama Point** offers an expansive view of Salt Valley and the Fiery Furnace, which can really live up to its name at sunset.

A viewpoint provides more views of the **Fiery Furnace,** and ahead is a pullout for **Sand Dune Arch,** down a short path from the road, where you'll find shade and sand along with the arch, a good place for kids to play. Next stop is **Skyline Arch,** and the final stop is the often crowded parking area for the **Devils Garden trail head.** From here you can hike to some of the most unusual arches in the park, including **Landscape Arch,** considered the longest natural rock arch in the world.

ORGANIZED TOURS & RANGER PROGRAMS

From spring through fall, rangers lead 2-mile **guided hikes** into the **Fiery Furnace** ★★★ area daily, by reservation. Cost is $10 per adult, $5 per child from 5 to 12. Children 5 to 12 must be accompanied by an adult, and children under 5 are not permitted. Reservations must be made at least 4 days in advance online at www.recreation.gov. A ranger describes the desert plants, points out hard-to-find arches, and discusses the geology and natural history of the Fiery Furnace. The hike is challenging, but quite exciting. Also from spring through fall, rangers lead daily **nature walks** from various park locations, and present **evening campfire programs,** which cover topics such as rock art, geology, and wildlife.

PARK ATTRACTIONS

Although not many have left their mark in this rugged area, a few intrepid Ute Indians and pioneers have spent time here. Just off the Delicate Arch Trail is a **Ute petroglyph panel** that includes etchings of horses and possibly of bighorn sheep. Also, near the beginning of the trail is **Wolfe Ranch.** Civil War veteran John Wesley Wolfe and his son Fred moved here from Ohio in 1898; John's daughter Flora, her husband, and their two children arrived in 1907. They left in 1910, after which John's cabin was destroyed by a flash flood. The cabin used by Flora's family survived and has been preserved by the Park Service. You'll see the cabin, a root cellar, and a corral.

DAY HIKES

Most trails at Arches are short and relatively easy, although because of the hot summer sun and lack of shade, it's wise to wear a hat and carry plenty of water.

Shorter Trails

Balanced Rock ★ This short, easy walk is perfect for visitors who want to stretch their legs and get a great close-up view of the precariously perched Balanced Rock. The loop takes you around the formation. The trail is wheelchair accessible. .3 mile RT. Easy. Access: Balanced Rock parking area, on east side of main park road.

Broken Arch ★ Fairly level, this hike traverses sand dunes and slickrock to the arch. Watch for the rock cairns, in some places poorly defined, marking the path through the arch. A little farther along is a connecting trail to **Sand Dune Arch,** about .5 mile out and back. At the end of the loop is a .25-mile walk along the paved campground road back to your car. 1.3 mile RT. Easy. Access: End of Devils Garden Campground across from campsite #40 or Sand Dune Arch parking area.

Delicate Arch Viewpoint ★ A very short walk, it provides an ideal location for a photo, preferably with the arch highlighted by a clear blue sky. 100 yards RT. Easy. Access: Delicate Arch Viewpoint Trailhead.

Double Arch ★★ Those who like elephants won't want to miss this trail. It leads to the third-largest arch opening in the park—don't be fooled by how small it looks from the parking area—and along the way passes the delightful **Parade of Elephants** formation off to the left. If you're visiting in spring, look for the **sego lily,** Utah's state flower. It has three lovely cream-colored petals with a reddish-purple spot fading to yellow at the base. 5 mile RT. Easy. Access: Double Arch parking area.

The Windows ★★ This fairly flat hike leads to three massive arches, two of which appear to be almost perfectly round windows. It's a busy trail, but you'll find fewer people if you hike early or late in the day. On your way to **North Window,** take a short side trip to **Turret Arch.** Once you reach North and South Windows, take the loop around back and see for yourself why they are sometimes called Spectacles—the scene looks almost like a sea monster poking its large snout up into the air. 1-mile loop. Easy. Access: Windows parking area.

Longer Trails

Delicate Arch ★★★ Climbing about 480 feet, this hike is considered by many the park's best and most scenic; it's also complicated by slippery slickrock, no shade, and some steep drop-offs along a narrow cliff. The reward for your efforts is a dramatic, spectacular view of **Delicate Arch.** Along the way, you'll see the **John Wesley Wolfe Ranch** and have an opportunity to take a side trip to a **Ute petroglyph panel.** Watch for **collared lizards**—bright-green foot-long creatures with stripes of yellow or rust and black collars. Feeding mostly in the daytime, they particularly enjoy insects and other lizards, and can stand and run on their large hind feet in pursuit of prey. Also watch for **Frame Arch,** off to the right. Its main claim to fame is that numerous photographers have used it to "frame" a photo of Delicate Arch in the distance. Just past Frame Arch, the trail gets a little weird, having been blasted out from the cliff. 3 miles RT. Strenuous. Access: Wolfe Ranch Parking area.

Devils Garden Primitive Loop ★★★ The whole Devils Garden loop is a fairly long, strenuous, and difficult hike, from which you can see 15 to 20 arches and some exciting scenery. Be sure to take plenty of water, and don't hurry. Rangers advise that you not take this trail when the rock is wet. The highlight is **Landscape Arch,** a long (306-ft.), thin ribbon of stone that is one of the most beautiful arches in the park. This is about a 2-mile round-trip trail and is an absolute must-see during a visit to Arches National Park. Geologically speaking, Landscape Arch is quite mature and may collapse any day. 7.2 miles RT. Easy to strenuous. Access: Devils Garden Trailhead.

14

ARCHES & CANYONLANDS | Day Hikes

EXPLORING THE BACKCOUNTRY

There are no designated backcountry trails or campsites, and little of the park is open to overnight camping, but backcountry **hiking** is permitted. Ask park rangers to suggest routes. No fires are allowed, and hikers must carry their own water and practice low-impact hiking and camping techniques. Those planning to be out overnight need free **backcountry permits,** available at the visitor center.

CANYONLANDS NATIONAL PARK

Utah's largest national park, Canyonlands is a rugged high desert of rock, with spectacular formations and gorges carved over the centuries by the park's primary architects, the Colorado and Green rivers. This is a land of extremes, of vast panoramas, deep canyons, steep cliffs, broad mesas, and towering red spires.

The most accessible part of Canyonlands is the Island in the Sky District, in the northern section of the park between the Colorado and Green rivers. A paved road leads to sites such as Grand View Point, overlooking some 10,000 square miles of rugged wilderness. Island in the Sky also has several easy to moderate trails offering sweeping vistas of the park.

The Needles District, in the park's southeast corner, has only a few view points along the paved road, but it offers numerous possibilities for hikers, backpackers, and high-clearance four-wheel-drives. Named for its tall, red-and-white-striped rock pinnacles, this district is home to impressive arches, including the 150-foot-tall Angel Arch, as well as meadows and the confluence of the Green and Colorado rivers.

Most park visitors don't get a close-up view of the Maze District, which lies on the west side of the Green and Colorado rivers, but instead see it off in the distance from Grand View Point at Island in the Sky, or Confluence Overlook in the Needles District. That's because it's inhospitable and practically inaccessible. You'll need a lot of endurance and at least several days to see even a few of its sites. In 1 day, hardy hikers can visit Horseshoe Canyon, where they can see the Great Gallery, an 80-foot-long rock art panel.

The park is also accessible by boat, which is how explorer Maj. John Wesley Powell first saw the canyons in 1869, when he made his first trip down the Green to its confluence with the Colorado, and then traveled farther downstream, eventually to the Grand Canyon. River access is from the towns of Moab and Green River; local companies rent boats and offer boat trips of various durations.

Visitor Centers & Information

Canyonlands National Park operates **Island in the Sky Visitor Center,** in the northern part of the park, and **Needles Visitor Center,** in the southern section. At both, you can get advice from rangers, as well as maps and free brochures on hiking trails. Hours vary by season, and the Needles Visitor Center is closed December through February. The Island in the Sky Visitor Center is closed Christmas and New Year's Day, although the park remains open. Those going into the Maze District can get information at the Hans Flat Ranger Station. Contact **Canyonlands National Park,** 2282 SW Resource Blvd., Moab, UT 84532 (✆ **435/719-2313;** www.nps.gov/cany) for more information.

Entrance Fees & Permits

Entry into the park (for up to 7 days) costs $10 per private vehicle or $5 per person on foot, bike, or motorcycle. **Backcountry permits,** available at either visitor center, are required for all overnight stays in the park, except at the two established campgrounds.

AVOIDING the crowds

Although Canyonlands does not get as crowded as other major national parks—usually about 450,000 visitors annually—the more popular trails can be busy. Spring and fall see the most visitors, but summer has recently become popular, despite scorching temperatures. To avoid humanity, visit from November through February, when the park is practically deserted, though some trails and four-wheel-drives roads may be inaccessible. College spring-break time (usually mid-Mar through Apr) can be especially busy. Hiking in the early morning—often the best time to hike anyway—is a good way to beat the crowds any time of year. One thing that makes the backcountry experience here especially pleasant is that the number of permits for overnight trips is limited (and permits often sell out well in advance). If you hike, bike, or drive far enough, it's almost guaranteed that you won't be sharing the trail or road with a lot of other people.

Permit reservations can be made in advance. Check the park website (www.nps.gov/cany) for deadlines and fees.

EXPLORING THE PARK

No driving tour has yet been designed to show off Canyonlands National Park. The Island in the Sky District has about 20 miles of paved highway, some gravel roads accessible to two-wheel-drive vehicles, and several view points. The Needles District has only 8 miles of paved roads. Many (but not all) of Needles' view points and trail heads are accessible only by high-clearance four-wheel-drive vehicles or on foot. The Maze District has only two main roads, neither of them paved. Both lead to trail heads.

If you happen to have a serious four-wheel-drive vehicle, and if you are equally serious about doing some hard-core four-wheeling, this is the park for you. See "Other Sports & Activities," below. Because of the constantly changing conditions of dirt roads, we strongly suggest that you discuss your plans with rangers before setting out.

ORGANIZED TOURS & RANGER PROGRAMS

A variety of ranger programs are presented from March through October. Several programs are offered daily in the **Island in the Sky District,** including geology presentations at Grand View Point at 10:30 and 11:30am, and talks at the Visitor Center at 2pm. In the **Needles District** there are 1-hour evening programs at Squaw Flat Campground most nights of the week. In the **Maze District,** guided hikes in Horseshoe Canyon are offered most weekends in spring and fall.

PARK ATTRACTIONS

This land was once the domain of prehistoric American Indians, who constructed their buildings out of the region's rock, hunted deer and bighorn sheep, and left numerous drawings on rock walls. Most of the park's archaeological sites are in the Needles District. They include the well-preserved cliff dwelling called **Tower Ruin,** high on a cliff ledge in Horse Canyon, and an easy-to-reach **ancient granary,** near the Needles Visitor Center, that is accessible on the short self-guided Roadside Ruin Trail (see p. 187).

In Horseshoe Canyon, a separate and remote section of the park, you'll find the **Great Gallery,** one of the most incredible rock art panels in the Southwest. More than 80 feet long, the panel contains many red-and-white paintings of what appear to be larger-than-life human figures. The paintings are believed to be at least 2,000 years old.

DAY HIKES

Conditions along these trails can be tough in summer: little shade, no water, and temperatures soaring to over 100°F (38°C). If you plan serious hiking, try to schedule your trip in the spring or fall, when conditions are much more hospitable and follow the safety instructions above (see p. 187).

All hikers should be careful on the trails that cross slickrock, a general term for any bare rock surface. As the name implies, it can be slippery, especially when wet. Also, because some of the trails may be confusing, hikers attempting the longer ones should take good topographical maps, available at visitor centers and at stores in Moab.

The following are some of the park's many hiking possibilities, arranged by district; check with rangers for other suggestions.

Island in the Sky District
SHORTER TRAILS
Grand View Point ★★   At the trail head, read the sign that points out all the prominent features you can see, such as the **Totem Pole** and the confluence of the **Colorado and Green rivers.** Although this is a fairly flat and easy trail, you should watch carefully for the cairns that mark it, because some are on the small side. And stay back from the cliff edge. This trail is especially beautiful at sunset, when the panorama seems to change constantly with the diminishing angle of sunlight. 2 miles RT. Easy. Access: Grand View Point Overlook at south end of paved road.

Mesa Arch ★   This is a pleasant walk through an area of pinyon and juniper trees, mountain mahogany, cactus, and a plant called Mormon Tea, from which Mormon pioneers made hot drinks. The trail's main scenic attraction is the **Mesa Arch,** made of Navajo sandstone. It hangs precariously on the edge of a 500-foot cliff, framing a spectacular view of nearby mountains. Views are especially good at sunrise. .5 mile RT. Easy. Access: Trail head along paved road about 6 miles south of visitor center.

LONGER TRAILS
Neck Spring Trail ★★   This hike follows the paths that animals and early ranchers created to reach water at two springs. You'll see water troughs, hitching posts, and the ruins of an old cabin. Because of the water source, you'll encounter types of vegetation not usually seen in the park, such as maidenhair ferns and Gambel oak. The water also draws wildlife, including mule deer, bighorn sheep, ground squirrels, and hummingbirds. Climbing to the top of the rim, you get a beautiful view of the canyons and even the **Henry Mountains,** some 60 miles away. 5.8 miles RT. Moderate to strenuous. Access: Trail head about .5 mile south of visitor center along paved road.

Syncline Loop Trail ★★   This is a long, hot day hike over one of only three loop trails in the Island in the Sky District. Be sure to start early and carry plenty of water. The trail drops 1,300 feet, and the best approach is clockwise, so you take the steepest part going down into **Upheaval Canyon.** Along the way, you'll follow dry washes, climb small hills and steep canyon sides, cross part of the Syncline Valley, pass

| Special Regulations & Warnings |

Backcountry hikers must pack out all trash, and wood fires are prohibited. Canyonlands National Park is a bad place for pets. Dogs, which must be leashed at all times, are prohibited in public buildings, on all trails, and in the backcountry. This includes four-wheel-drive roads—dogs are not permitted even inside your vehicle.

The main safety problem at Canyonlands is that people underestimate the hazards. It's important that you know your limitations, as well as the limitations of your vehicle and other equipment.

Rangers warn hikers to carry at least 1 gallon of water per person per day, to be careful near cliff edges, to avoid overexposure to the sun, and to carry maps in the backcountry. During lightning storms, avoid lone trees, high ridges, and cliff edges. Four-wheel-drive-vehicle operators should carry extra food and emergency equipment. Also, anyone going into the backcountry should let someone know where they're going and when they'll return. Traveling alone in Canyonlands is really dumb.

Upheaval Dome, traverse some slickrock, and finally hit an area of lush vegetation. 8.3 miles RT. Strenuous. Access: Upheaval Dome Picnic Area, at end of Upheaval Dome Rd.

Needles District

Hiking trails here are generally not too tough, but keep in mind that slickrock can live up to its name and there is generally little shade.

SHORTER TRAILS

Roadside Ruin Trail ★   This self-guided nature walk leads to an ancient granary, probably used by the ancestral Puebloans some 700 to 1,000 years ago to store corn, nuts, and other foods. For 25¢ you can get a brochure at the trail head that discusses the plants along the trail. Although it's flat, this trail can be muddy when wet. .3 mile RT. Easy. Access: Trail head just over .5 mile west of visitor center along paved road.

Slickrock Trail ★★★   View points along this trail show off the stair-step topography of the area, from its colorful canyons and cliffs to its flat mesas and striped needles. Watch for bighorn sheep. 2.4 miles RT. Moderate. Access: Trail head about 6.5 miles from visitor center, almost at end of road.

LONGER TRAILS

Big Spring Canyon to Squaw Canyon Trail ★★   This hike over steep slickrock winds through woodlands of pinyon and juniper, offering views along the way of the Needles rock formations for which the district is named, plus nearby cliffs and mesas as well as distant mountains. Watch for wildflowers from late spring through summer. You can complete this hike in about half a day, but several backcountry campsites make it available to overnighters. 7.5-mile loop. Strenuous. Access: Squaw Flat Campground.

Confluence Overlook Trail ★★★   This hike has steep drop-offs and little shade, but the hard work is worthwhile—it shows off splendidly the many colors of the Needles District and offers excellent views into the Maze District of the park. The climax is a spectacular view overlooking the confluence of the **Green and Colorado rivers** in a 1,000-foot-deep gorge. This excursion can be done as a day hike (allow 4–6 hr.) or quite pleasantly as an overnight hike. 10 miles RT. Moderate to strenuous. Access: Big Spring Canyon Overlook.

Maze District

Getting to the trail heads in the Maze District involves rugged four-wheel-drive roads; rangers can help you with directions.

The 3-mile **Maze Overlook Trail** is not for beginners or those with a fear of heights. It is quite steep in places, requiring the use of your hands. At the trail head, you get a fine view of the narrow canyons that inspired this district's name; the trail then descends 600 feet to the canyon bottom.

The 9-mile **Pictograph Fork to Harvest Scene Loop** is a 7- to 10-hour hike (or an overnight) that leads over slickrock and along canyon washes—watch for the cairns to be sure you don't wander off the trail—to a magnificent example of rock art.

Horseshoe Canyon

This detached section of the park was added to Canyonlands in 1971 mainly because of its **Great Gallery,** an 80-foot-long rock art panel with larger-than-life human figures, which dates from 2000 B.C. to A.D. 500. The Horseshoe Canyon Unit is some 120 miles (one-way) from Island in the Sky, and only one road runs in (see "Getting There & Gateways," above). From the parking area, it's a 6.5-mile round-trip hike to see the rock art. The hike begins with a 1.5-mile section down an 800-foot slope to the canyon floor, where you turn right and go 1.75 miles to the Great Gallery. There is no camping in Horseshoe Canyon, but just outside the park boundary, primitive camping is available on Bureau of Land Management property on the rim.

OTHER SPORTS & ACTIVITIES

If you've come to Utah for mountain biking, backpacking, four-wheeling, or rafting, this is the place. The region holds surprises, too, from ancient American Indian dwellings and rock art to dinosaur bones.

Unlike most national parks, the backcountry at Canyonlands is not only the domain of backpackers. Here rugged four-wheel-drive and mountain-bike roads, as well as rivers navigable by boat, lead to some of the park's most scenic areas. Primitive campsites, strategically located throughout the backcountry, are available. Just be sure to make your backcountry campsite reservations well in advance—up to a year ahead for the more popular areas. You can get reservation forms and detailed information from the park's website (see "Visitor Centers & Information," above).

Outfitters Based in Moab

More than 65 local outfitters, guides, and equipment rental companies offer excursions of all kinds and the equipment to make them, from canoe rides to hair-raising jet-boat and four-wheel-drive adventures. For a chart of the local companies and what they offer go to **www.discovermoab.com,** and under Activities click on Guides & Outfitters. Advance reservations are recommended.

MOUNTAIN BIKING   Although bikes are prohibited on hiking trails and cross-country in the backcountry, they are permitted on designated two- and four-wheel-drive roads, giving mountain bikers numerous opportunities, although they will find themselves sharing dirt roads with motor vehicles and hikers. Also, some spots on four-wheel-drive roads have deep sand that can turn into quicksand when wet—so you may find that mountain biking, while certainly a challenge, is not as much fun as you'd hoped. It's wise to talk with rangers about road conditions before setting out.

Among popular rides are the **Elephant Hill** and **Colorado Overlook roads,** both in the Needles District. The 100-mile **White Rim Road,** in the Island in the Sky District, also makes a great mountain-bike trip (allow at least 4 days), especially for bikers who can arrange for an accompanying four-wheel-drive vehicle to carry water, food, and camping gear.

There are dozens of other mountain biking trails on public lands outside the national parks, check at the Moab Information Center and see "Nearby Attractions," below.

BOATING, CANOEING & RAFTING   After spending hours in the blazing sun looking at mile upon mile of huge red sandstone rock formations, it's easy to get the idea that Canyonlands National Park is a baking, dry, rock-hard desert. Well, it is. But both the Colorado and Green rivers run through the park, and one of the most exciting ways to see the park and surrounding country is from river level.

You can travel into the park in a canoe, kayak, large or small rubber raft (with or without motor), or speedy, solid jet boat. Do-it-yourselfers can rent kayaks, canoes, or rafts, and half- and full-day or multi-day guided river trips are also offered. You might like the thrill of a jet-boat trip, which covers a lot of river in a short amount of time.

One terrific canoe trip is along the Green River. Canoeists usually start in or near the town of Green River (put in at Green River State Park or at Mineral Bottom, just downstream) and spend about 2 days to get to the Green's confluence with the Colorado, where they can be picked up by a local outfitter. For guided trips and canoe and raft rentals, check with **Navtec Expeditions** (*©* **800/833-1278;** www.navtec.com) or **Moab Rafting & Canoe Company** (*©* **435/259-7722;** www.moab-rafting.com).

FOUR-WHEELING   Unlike most national parks, where motor vehicles and mountain bikes must stay on paved roads, Canyonlands has miles of rough four-wheel-drive roads where mechanized transport is king. We're talking serious four-wheeling here; most roads require high-clearance, short-wheelbase vehicles. Many of these roads also require the skill that comes only from experience, so it's usually a good idea to discuss your plans with rangers before putting your vehicle on the line. Four-wheelers must stay on designated four-wheel-drive roads, but here the term *road* can mean anything from a graded, well-marked two-lane gravel byway to a pile of loose rocks with a sign that says THAT-A-WAY. Many of the park's jeep roads are impassable during heavy rains.

The best four-wheel-drive adventure in Canyonlands' Island in the Sky District is the **White Rim Road,** which runs some 100 winding miles and affords spectacular views, from broad panoramas of rock and canyon to close-ups of red and orange towers and buttes. Expect the journey to be slow, lasting 2 to 3 days, although with the appropriate vehicle it isn't really difficult. There are primitive campgrounds along the way. Reservations on this route should be made well in advance.

For a spectacular view of the Colorado River, the **Colorado Overlook Road** in the Needles District can't be beat. This 14-mile round-trip, popular with four-wheelers, backpackers, and bikers, is among the park's easiest four-wheel-drive roads. Starting at the Needles Visitor Center parking lot, it takes you past panoramic vistas to a spectacular 360-degree view of the park and the Colorado River some 1,000 feet below.

You can rent four-by-fours in Moab, and several local companies provide guided trips.

WHERE TO STAY

There are no lodging facilities inside either park, so you will almost certainly stay in Moab, a busy tourist trap where you'll find practically anything you want, at a price.

CAMPING options

INSIDE THE PARKS

At the far end of Arches National Park's 18-mile scenic drive, **Devils Garden Campground ★★** is Arches' only developed campground. Its 50 sites nestle among rocks, with plenty of pinyon and juniper trees. It has no RV hookups, showers, or dump station, but there are toilets and drinking water. Some sites will accommodate RVs up to 30 feet long. The campground is very popular and has reservation-only camping from March through October. **Reservations** must be made 4 days in advance (✆ **877/444-6777**; www.recreation.gov; $9 booking fee). Cost is $20.

Canyonlands National Park has two developed campgrounds, set among rugged rocks. Neither has RV hookups, showers, or a dump station, but there are toilets, and because they're far from the lights of civilization, some of the best night skies you'll ever see. **Willow Flat Campground ★★**, with 12 sites, is in the Island in the Sky District, does not have drinking water, and costs $10.

Squaw Flat Campground ★★, with 26 sites, is in the Needles District, has drinking water, and costs $15. Neither accepts reservations and maximum RV length for most sites is 28 feet.

NEAR THE PARK

Additional camping facilities are available on nearby public lands administered by the Bureau of Land Management and U.S. Forest Service; see "Visitor Center & Information" at the beginning of this chapter.

More than a dozen commercial campgrounds are in and around Moab. We like **Canyonlands Campground ★**, 555 S. Main St. (✆ **800/522-6848** or 435/259-6848; www.canyonlandsrv.com), a surprisingly shady and quiet facility given its in-town location, and popular with both RVers and tenters. RV hookups include cable TV, and there is Wi-Fi throughout the campground. Rates run $26 to $46. There are also six camping cabins ($60–$65 double).

Near the Parks

Most visitors are here for the outdoors and don't plan to spend much time in their rooms. As a result, many book into one of the completely adequate **chain motels,** most of which are located on Moab's Main Street (zip code 84532). A web search of your favorite chain will likely find one in Moab.

Moab's room rates are generally highest from March through October—with the highest rates often in September—and sometimes drop by up to half in winter. High season rates are listed here, and don't expect any bargains at that time. However, call or check websites for off-season discounts.

Cali Cochitta Bed & Breakfast ★★   The willow tree is gone—it finally gave up in the summer of 2013—but its namesake Willow Cottage remains, at this delightful bed and breakfast, Moab's only historic B&B. Located in a quiet, tree-shaded neighborhood a few blocks off Main Street, The Cali Cochitta (Aztec for "House of Dreams") is in a late-1800s Victorian home. There are four large guest rooms and two cottages, all decorated in period furnishings with queen-sized beds, plus modern touches including TVs. All units are smoke-free.

110 S. 200 E., Moab. ✆ **888/429-8112** or 435/259-4961. www.moabdreaminn.com. 6 units. Mar–Oct $140–$180 double. Dogs accepted, $20/night/dog. Rates include full breakfast. **Amenities:** Free Wi-Fi.

The Lazy Lizard International Hostel ★★ Clean, neat, and cheap—that's the Lazy Lizard, and we almost missed it on our latest visit as it is hidden away behind the A-1 Self-Storage units. There are dorm rooms, three private rooms, some cabins that sleep up to six, and space for camping (no hookups). There's also a communal kitchen and living room with TV.

1213 S. U.S. 191, Moab. ☏ **435/259-6057.** www.lazylizardhostel.com. Total capacity about 100 persons. $10 dorm bed; $30 private room double; $34–$36 cabin double; $7 per person camping space. Hostel membership not required. **Amenities:** Coin-op laundry, free Wi-Fi.

Redstone Inn ★ Our favorite (relatively) inexpensive motel in Moab, the only change we discovered during a recent visit was that all the TVs are now flat screens. The log furniture and pine walls give the Redstone a mountain lodge feel, and it has everything you need for your base while exploring the area. Mountain bikes are permitted in the rooms, and although there is no swimming pool, guests can use an outdoor heated pool at another motel across the street.

535 S. Main St., Moab. ☏ **800/772-1972** or 435/259-3500. www.moabredstone.com. 52 units. $105–$110 double. Pets accepted, $5 fee. **Amenities:** Indoor hot tub, coin-op laundry, bike work stand and wash station, free Wi-Fi.

WHERE TO EAT

There are no restaurants inside either park.

Near the Park

The only eateries in the area are in Moab, and you'll find the menus of practically every restaurant in town at **www.moabhappenings.com.** Most of the restaurants here are along Main Street, and most offer basic American food, although there are some Mexican restaurants plus Sabaku Sushi, reviewed below.

Buck's Grill House ★★★ AMERICAN/GAME We wanted to get to Buck's again because it had been a while since we had the opportunity to go out for a really good steak. And the sirloin was excellent—good beef prepared simply and perfectly. But one of the things we like about Buck's (named for owner/chef Tim Buckingham, a Moab native) is that, yes, you can get a great steak for $30, but if that's a bit of a financial stretch you can have one of their burgers, starting at $8.95, or amazingly good buffalo meatloaf, southwest shepherd's pie, or elk stew, all under $20. That makes Buck's one of the best dinner values in town. Décor in the large dining room is unpretentious, with the subtle western look of wood—vigas, tables, and chairs—and local art, with soft country music in the background. Oh, did we mention dessert? The port flan topped with caramel sauce alone is worth the trip to Moab.

1393 N. U.S. 191, about 1.5 miles north of town. ☏ **435/259-5201.** www.bucksgrill house.com. Main courses $9–$39. Daily 5pm–close.

> ### Picnic & Camping Supplies
>
> The best grocery store in town is **City Market,** 425 S. Main St. (☏ **435/259-5181;** www.citymarket.com). You can pick up sandwiches from the deli, assemble your own salad at the salad bar, or choose fresh-baked items from the bakery. The store also sells fishing licenses and has a pharmacy. For camping supplies try **Walker Drug & General Store,** 290 S. Main St. (☏ **435/259-5959).**

Moab Brewery ★ BREWPUB This busy brewpub looks just like a brewpub should, a little funky—it's had a hang glider suspended from the ceiling for years—and serves up great pub food, from burgers to Cajun chicken to steaks and ribs—and all at reasonable prices. There are vegetarian items, such as the hummus wrap and basil pesto linguine, and a few spicy Mexican dishes including a chile verde burrito. Beer is brewed onsite, and we're happy to report that you can now drink full-strength beer in the brewery's restaurant and bar (not to be confused with that 3.2 percent slop Utah state officials mistakenly thought was drinkable and is still all you can buy in grocery stores). We especially recommend the brewery's very hoppy IPA.

686 S. Main St. ℂ **435/259-6333.** www.themoabbrewery.com. Main courses $7–$22. Sun–Thurs 11:30am–10:30pm; Fri–Sat 11:30am–11:30pm.

Moab Diner & Ice Cream Shoppe ★★ AMERICAN/SOUTHWESTERN Our only complaint about this place during our fall 2013 visit, is that after consuming the generous portions of our lunch, we were too full for an ice cream sundae! Decorated in typical diner fashion—red and black vinyl seating at tables and booths, photos and old Coke ads on white walls, and large windows that provide views over the Main Street traffic to the red rocks of Canyonlands. Breakfast is served all day and tasty green chile is offered with omelets, burgers, burritos, and chicken. You can also get other diner food, from plain old ham and eggs to BLTs to liver and onions.

189 S. Main St. ℂ **435/259-4006.** www.moabdiner.com. Main courses $6–$12 breakfast and lunch, $7–$15 dinner. Mon–Sat 6am–10pm. Closed New Year's Day, Thanksgiving, and Christmas.

Sabaku Sushi ★★★ SUSHI Sushi in the middle of the desert might seem a bad idea, but don't fear: all of the fish is flown in daily, much of it from Hawaii, which means you can try some unusual varieties. And not only is it fresh, the sushi is expertly and often creatively prepared. Final reason to pop by: the staff, a group of young, mountain biking enthusiasts, are a delightful bunch. A top choice.

90 E. Center St., just off Main Street. ℂ **435/259-4455.** www.sabakusushi.com. Meals $10–$25. Late spring to early fall, Tues–Sun 5pm-close; rest of year Wed–Sat 5pm-close.

NEARBY ATTRACTIONS

With hundreds and hundreds of miles of trails, a wide variety of terrain, and spectacular scenery, Moab is easily the mountain bike capital of Utah, and possibly of the United States (although the folks in Crested Butte, Colo., might disagree). In addition to the mountain-biking possibilities on four-wheel-drive roads in the national parks, discussed earlier in this chapter, there are abundant trails on Bureau of Land Management and national forest lands.

The area's most famous trail is undoubtedly the **Slickrock Bike Trail ★★★**, a scenic but challenging 9.6-mile loop that crosses a mesa of heavily eroded pale orange Navajo sandstone just a few minutes from downtown Moab. Along the way, the trail offers views that take in the towering La Sal Mountains, the red-rock formations of Arches National Park, a panorama of Canyonlands National Park, and the Colorado River. The trail, open to both mountain bikes and motorcycles, is physically demanding and technically difficult and not recommended for children, novices, or anyone who is out of shape or has medical problems. Allow 4 to 5 hours, and expect to walk your bike in some areas. If you're not sure you're ready for the trail, get started on the 2¼-mile practice loop. To access the trail head from the visitor information center, take

Center Street east to 400 East. Turn south (right) and follow 400 East to Mill Creek Drive. Turn east (left) and follow Mill Creek Drive to Sand Flats Road, which you take 2.3 miles east to the BLM's Sand Flats Recreation Area and the trail head.

Looking for a somewhat less challenging experience? Try the **Gemini Bridges Trail,** a 14-mile one-way trip that shows off the area's colorful rock formations, including the trail's namesake: two natural rock bridges. Considered relatively easy, this trail follows a dirt road mostly downhill, ending at U.S. 191 just under 10 miles from the center of Moab, so it's best to arrange a shuttle (see above). To get to the trail head from the Moab Information Center, drive north along U.S. 191 to Utah 313, turn west (left), and go about 13 miles. Allow a full day, including getting to and from the trail, and be sure to watch for the magnificent view of Arches National Park from a hilltop as you approach U.S. 191 near the end of the ride.

Canyonlands by Night & Day (© **800/394-9978** or 435/259-2628; www.canyon landsbynight.com) offers a variety of excursions in the area, including an evening river trip, operating spring through fall, that combines a 1½-hour sunset jet-boat ride with a Dutch-oven dinner. Cost for the boat trip and dinner is $79 for adults and $69 for children 4 to 12 (minimum age 4), with a family rate of $246 for two adults and two children. A 4-hour daytime jet-boat ride costs $89 for adults and $79 for children 4 to 12 (minimum age 4), with a family rate for two adults and two kids of $279. Reservations are recommended. The office and dock are just north of Moab at the Colorado River Bridge.

ZION

by Don & Barbara Laine

I t's fairly easy to conjure up a single defining image of most national parks, but Zion, a collage of images and secrets, is impossible to pin down. Zion National Park comprises an entire smorgasbord of experiences, sights, sounds, and even smells. Gaze upon Zion's sheer multicolored walls of sandstone, explore its narrow canyons, hunt for hanging gardens of wildflowers, and listen to the roar of the churning, tumbling Virgin River.

Millions of years ago, a shallow sea covered the sand dunes here. It caused minerals, including lime from the shells of sea creatures, to glue sand particles together, forming sandstone. Later, movements in the earth's crust lifted the land, draining away the sea but leaving rivers that gradually carved the soft sandstone into the spectacular shapes we see today.

But where do the marvelous colors of the rocks come from? Essentially, rust. Most of the rocks at Zion are colored by iron or hematite (iron oxide). Although iron often creates red and pink hues, seen in many of Zion's sandstone faces, it can also result in blacks, browns, yellows, and even greens. Sometimes the iron seeps into the rock, coloring it through, but often it just stains the surface in vertical streaks. Rocks are also colored by bacteria that live on their surfaces. The bacteria ingest dust and expel iron, manganese, and other minerals, which stick to the rock and produce a shiny black, brown, or reddish surface called "desert varnish."

Because of its extremes in elevation (3,666–8,726 ft.) and climate, Zion harbors a vast array of flora and fauna. Wildlife here includes pocket gophers, mule deer, mountain lions, and hundreds of birds. As for plants, more than 900 species have been found, including cactus, yucca, and mesquite in the hot, dry desert areas; ponderosa pines on the high plateaus; and cottonwoods and box elders along the rivers and streams. Watch for the red claret cup cactus, which has spectacular blooms in the spring; for wildflowers such as manzanita, with tiny pink blossoms; and for the bright red hummingbird trumpet, sometimes called the "Zion Lily." And don't miss the hanging gardens of plant life clinging to the sides of the sandstone cliffs.

ESSENTIALS

Getting There & Gateways

Zion National Park is in the southwestern corner of Utah, 83 miles southwest of Bryce Canyon National Park and 120 miles northwest of the North Rim of Grand Canyon National Park in northern Arizona. It's 309 miles south of Salt Lake City, 42 miles northwest of Kanab, and 158 miles

AVOIDING the crowds

Try to avoid the peak summer months of June through August, when temperatures are hot and Zion receives almost half its almost three million annual visitors. The quietest time is December through February, but you may have to contend with some snow and ice. Good times to visit, if your schedule permits, are April, May, September, and October, when the weather is pleasant and the park is less crowded than in the summer.

Once in the park, the best way to avoid crowds is to walk away from them, either on the longer and more strenuous hiking trails or on treks into the backcountry. It's sad but true: Most visitors to Zion never bother to venture far from the main view points. Their loss can be your gain. You can also avoid the hordes by spending time in Kolob Canyons, in the far northwest section of the park; it's spectacular and receives surprisingly little use, at least in comparison to Zion Canyon.

northeast of Las Vegas, Nevada. The park consists of two main parts: Zion Canyon, the main section, and Kolob Canyons, in the northwest corner. The closest towns with airports are St. George (46 miles southwest) and Cedar City (60 miles north).

The easiest way to get to the park is to approach from the west on **I-15,** which runs north to Salt Lake City and southwest through Arizona to Nevada. This route is more direct than the eastern approach, avoids possible delays at the Zion–Mount Carmel Tunnel, and delivers you to Springdale, just outside the park's south entrance, where most of the area's lodging and restaurants are located. From I-15, go east on Utah 9 if approaching from the south, or go south on Utah 17 and then east on Utah 9 if approaching from the north; Utah 9 continues east to the park's south entrance.

The eastern approach to the park is less direct but far more beautiful. From the south or the north, take **U.S. 89** to Utah 9 at Mount Carmel, then go west on Utah 9, a spectacularly scenic 24-mile drive. However, be aware that this route into the park drops more than 2,500 feet in elevation, passes through the mile-long Zion–Mount Carmel Tunnel, and winds down six steep switchbacks. Oversize vehicles pay $15 to use the tunnel (see "Special Regulations & Warnings," below).

The Kolob Canyons section, in the park's northwest corner, is accessible on the short Kolob Canyons Road off I-15, exit 40.

Visitor Centers & Information

The park has two visitor centers. The **Zion Canyon Visitor Center,** near the south entrance to the park, has a wide variety of outdoor exhibits. Rangers answer questions and provide backcountry permits, and there's a bookstore. In summer, it's open daily from 8am to 7:30pm, with shorter hours the rest of the year. The **Kolob Canyons Visitor Center,** in the northwest corner of the park, right off I-15, provides information, permits, books, and maps. It is open from 8am to 6pm in summer, with shorter hours the rest of the year. Both visitor centers are closed on Christmas Day.

The **Zion Human History Museum,** located about 1 mile inside the south entrance, offers exhibits, park information, and an orientation program, plus has a bookstore. It's open daily 10am to 5pm; closed December through February.

Zion National Park

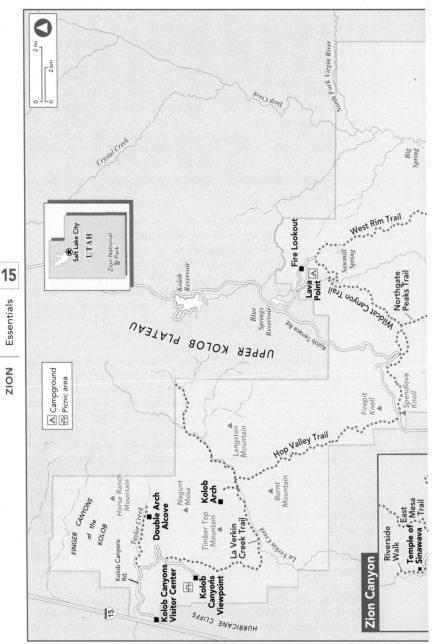

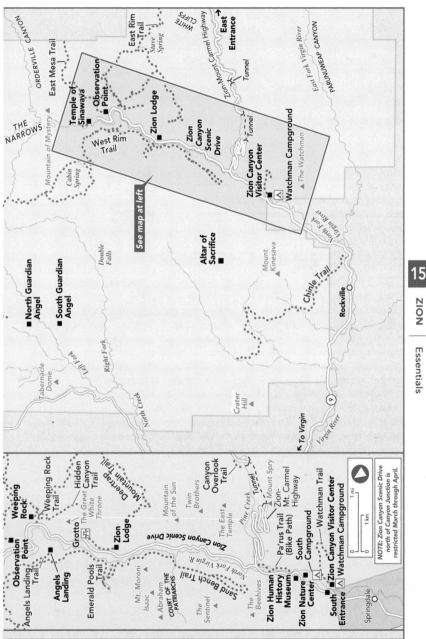

For pre-vacation info, contact **Zion National Park** (✆ **435/772-3256;** www.nps. gov/zion). For information on the gateway town of Springdale check out **www.zion park.com,** website of **Zion Canyon Visitors Bureau** (✆ **888/518-7070**).

Fees

Entry into the park (for up to 7 days), which includes unlimited use of the shuttle bus, costs $25 per private car, pickup truck, van, or RV, or $12 per individual 16 or older on bicycle, foot, or motorcycle; those under 16 admitted free. Oversize vehicles are charged $15 for use of the Zion–Mount Carmel Tunnel on the east side of the park (see "Special Regulations & Warnings," below).

Seasons & Climate

Zion experiences all four seasons, although the winters are fairly mild. The best times to visit the park are spring and fall, when the temperatures range from lows in the 40s (single digits Celsius) to pleasant highs in the 80s (upper 20s Celsius). Remember that summer daytime highs often soar above 100°F (38°C), with lows in the 70s (lower 20s Celsius). During the summer, do your hiking in the early morning to avoid both the heat and the frequent afternoon thunderstorms, which can change a babbling brook into a raging torrent in minutes.

EXPLORING THE PARK

If you enter the park from the east, along the steep **Zion–Mount Carmel Highway,** you'll travel 13 miles to the **Zion Canyon Visitor Center,** passing between the White Cliffs and Checkerboard Mesa, a massive sandstone rock formation covered with horizontal and vertical lines that make it look like a huge fishing net. Continuing, you'll pass through a fairyland of fantastically shaped rocks of red, orange, tan, and white, and you'll encounter the **Great Arch of Zion,** carved high in a stone cliff by the forces of erosion. After driving through the Zion–Mount Carmel Tunnel you'll traverse a number of long switchbacks as you descend to the canyon floor.

A **shuttle bus system** has been implemented in the main section of the park to reduce traffic congestion and the resultant problems of pollution, noise, and damage to the park. The shuttle system consists of **two loops:** one in the town of Springdale and the other along Zion Canyon Scenic Drive. The loops connect at the visitor center just inside the south park entrance. From April through October, access to Zion Canyon Scenic Drive (above Utah 9) is limited to shuttle buses, hikers, and bikers. The only exceptions are overnight Zion Lodge guests and tour buses connected with the lodge— both have access as far as the lodge. Shuttles stop at all the major-use areas in the park, and run frequently (about every 6 min. at peak times). In winter, when visitation is lowest, visitors are permitted to drive the full length of Zion Canyon Scenic Drive in their own vehicles.

ZION CANYON SCENIC DRIVE The park's scenery is impressive, with massive stone reaching straight up to the heavens and the North Fork of the Virgin River threading its way through the maze of rocks. The views in every direction are awe inspiring, and stops along the road provide access to view points and hiking trails.

KOLOB CANYONS ROAD To escape the crowds of Zion Canyon, head to the northwest corner of the park. The Kolob Canyons Road runs 5 miles among spectacular red and orange rocks, ending at a high vista. Be sure to get a copy of the "Kolob Canyons Road Guide" at the Kolob Visitor Center.

RANGER & EDUCATIONAL PROGRAMS

Zion National Park has some of the best **ranger programs** of any national park, and, offered in summer only, they're all free. **Evening programs,** which last about 45 minutes, take place at the Watchman Campground Amphitheater and Zion Lodge Auditorium. They usually include a slide show and cover topics such as the animals or plants of the park, geology, the night sky, or some unique aspect of Zion such as slot canyons. Rangers also give **short talks** on similar subjects during the day at various locations, including the Zion Lodge auditorium and Zion Human History Museum. Ranger-guided **hikes and walks,** which may require reservations, take visitors to little-visited areas of the park, on a trek to see wildflowers, or for night hikes (when the moon is full). The 90-minute **Ride with a Ranger** trip offers an opportunity to see the scenic drive and learn about Zion Canyon from a park ranger's unique perspective. There are also a variety of **youth programs.** Check bulletin boards at the visitor centers, campgrounds, and other locations for the current schedule.

The **Zion Canyon Field Institute,** operated by the nonprofit Zion Natural History Association, Zion National Park (*©* **800/635-3959,** 435/772-3265, or 435/772-3264 for the Field Institute; www.zionpark.org), offers a variety of single and multiday outdoor workshops and classes, covering subjects in the sciences, arts, and humanities. Programs take place year-round with subjects such as bird watching, the hanging gardens of Zion, wasps and ants, and photography. Fees for most of the 1-day programs range from $100 to $200.

PARK ATTRACTIONS

There are no major historic sites in Zion National Park, but there is some evidence of the early peoples who inhabited the area. Just outside the Zion Canyon Visitor Center, the short but steep **Archaeology Trail** (.4 mile round-trip, with an 80-ft. elev. gain) leads to the outlines of small prehistoric storage buildings. The **Zion Human History Museum,** 1 mile from the park's south entrance, includes exhibits on human impacts in the park and an orientation film. The museum is open daily from 10am to 5pm.

DAY HIKES

Zion offers a wide variety of hiking options, ranging from easy half-hour walks on paved paths to grueling overnight hikes over rocky terrain. Hikers with a **fear of heights** should be careful when choosing trails, because many include steep, dizzying, and potentially fatal drop-offs. Carrying water on hikes is essential, and you'll find a **free water fill-up station** near the Castle Rock Café on the north side of Zion Lodge.

Shorter Trails

Canyon Overlook ★★   This self-guided trail takes you to an overlook with a magnificent view of lower Zion Canyon and Pine Creek Canyon. Be aware that there are some steep drop-offs and that the sandy trail can be slippery. 1 mile RT. Moderate. Access: East side of Zion–Mount Carmel Tunnel.

Emerald Pools Trails ★★★   A wonderful trail, especially on a hot day (when you'll enjoy the spray of water from the falls) it can be either an easy 1-hour walk or a moderately strenuous 2-hour hike with steep drop-offs, depending on how much you choose to do. A .6-mile paved path leads from the Emerald Pools parking area, through a forest of oak, maple, fir, and cottonwood, to several waterfalls, a hanging garden, and the picturesque Lower Emerald Pool. From here, a steeper, rocky trail continues to the Middle Emerald Pool, and then climbs past cactus, yucca, and juniper to Upper Emerald Pool, which has another waterfall. Total elevation gain is 69 feet to Lower Emerald Pool and 200 feet to Upper Emerald Pool. Swimming or wading is not permitted in any of the pools. 1.2–2 miles RT. Easy to moderate. Access: Across from Zion Lodge.

Pa'rus Trail ★★   This paved trail (fully accessible to wheelchairs and baby strollers) follows the Virgin River, providing views of the rock formations in lower Zion Canyon. Unlike other park trails, this one is open to bicycles and leashed pets. The elevation gain is only 50 feet. 3.5 miles RT. Easy. Access: Either the entrance to Watchman Campground, near amphitheater parking area, or near the Nature Center at South Campground.

Riverside Walk and the Gateway to the Narrows ★★★   Another paved trail, it follows the Virgin River upstream to the Zion Canyon Narrows, past trailside exhibits and, in spring and summer, hanging wildflowers. Accessible to those in wheelchairs with assistance, the trail has an elevation change of only 57 feet. At the Narrows, the pavement ends and you have to decide whether to turn around or continue upstream into the Narrows itself (yes, you will get wet), where the canyon walls are about 20 feet apart in some areas and more than 1,000 feet high. *Warning:* The bottom of a very narrow slot canyon is definitely not a place you want to be in a rainstorm (common in summer), when flash floods are a serious threat. Before entering the Narrows, check the weather forecast and discuss your plans with park rangers (see The Narrows, below). 2.2 miles RT. Easy. Access: Temple of Sinawava parking lot.

Weeping Rock Trail ★   A self-guiding nature trail, the route leads to a rock alcove with a spring and hanging gardens of ferns and wildflowers. It's among the park's shortest and easiest rambles. Alas, because it is relatively steep (gaining 98 ft.) and slippery, it's not suitable for wheelchairs. .4 mile RT. Easy to moderate. Access: Weeping Rock parking lot.

Longer Trails

Angels Landing Trail ★★   This strenuous 4-hour hike is most certainly not for anyone with even a mild fear of heights. The trail climbs 1,488 feet, with the aid of 21 switchbacks, to a summit that offers spectacular views into Zion Canyon. *But be prepared:* The final half-mile follows a narrow, knife-edge trail along a steep ridge, where footing can be slippery even under the best of circumstances. Support chains have been set along parts of the trail. 5.4 miles RT. Strenuous. Access: Grotto picnic area.

La Verkin Creek/Kolob Arch Trail ★★   Although there are no drop-offs, this backcountry trail is quite strenuous. Descending over 1,000 feet, it follows Timber and La Verkin creeks, ending at Kolob Arch, which is one of the world's largest freestanding arches. Some people choose to camp on this hike. You can camp at La Verkin Creek if you have a permit and have been assigned a campsite at the visitor center. 14 miles RT. Strenuous. Access: Kolob Canyons Rd. at Lee Pass.

The Narrows ★★   The Narrows doesn't really involve hiking a trail at all; it consists of walking or wading in the Virgin River, through a spectacular 1,000-foot-deep chasm that, at a mere 20 feet wide, definitely lives up to its name. Passing sculptured sandstone arches, hanging gardens, and waterfalls, this strenuous hike is recommended for those in good physical condition who are up to fighting currents, which can sometimes be strong. Those who want just a taste of the Narrows can walk and wade in from the end of the Riverside Walk (see above), but more than a short trip will involve a long

The mile-long Zion–Mount Carmel Tunnel was **not built for big vehicles**. It is too narrow for two-way traffic involving anything larger than passenger cars and pickup trucks. Therefore, any vehicle more than 7 feet, 10 inches wide (including mirrors) or 11 feet, 4 inches tall (including luggage racks) must drive down the center of the tunnel after all other traffic has been stopped. The charge is $15, good for two trips through the tunnel during a 7-day period. Drivers pay the fee at the entrance stations in summer but must make advance arrangements in winter.

All vehicles more than 13 feet, 1 inch tall, and certain other particularly large vehicles are prohibited from driving anywhere on the park road between the east entrance and Zion Canyon. **Bicycles** are prohibited in the Zion–Mount Carmel Tunnel, in the backcountry, and on all trails except the Pa'rus Trail.

Backcountry hikers should practice minimum-impact techniques and are prohibited from building fires. A limit on the number of people allowed in various parts of the backcountry may be in force during your visit; prospective backcountry hikers should check with rangers before setting out. You can purchase a backcountry permit at the visitor center, and permits can also be reserved in advance through the park's website (**www.nps.gov/zion**) for a $5 fee.

full- or 2-day trek, which includes arranging a shuttle to the starting point at Chamberlain's Ranch and then transportation from the Temple of Sinawava, where you'll leave the canyon. The Narrows is subject to flash flooding and can be very treacherous, and hikers should definitely check on current water conditions and weather forecasts before setting out. Permits ($5) are required for full-day and overnight hikes, and must be purchased at the visitor center. 16 miles one-way. Strenuous. Access: Chamberlain's Ranch (outside the park). By permit only.

Taylor Creek Trail ★ This is a 4-hour hike along the middle fork of Taylor Creek, and you just might get your feet wet fording the creek. The trail leads past two historic cabins to the colorfully impressive Double Arch Alcove, with an elevation gain of 450 feet. 5 miles RT. Moderate. Access: Kolob Canyons Rd., 2 miles from Kolob Canyons Visitor Center.

EXPLORING THE BACKCOUNTRY

The park offers many backpacking opportunities, and a number of the day hikes discussed above are actually more comfortably done in 2 or more days. In addition to the park's established trails and the famous Narrows, there are a number of off-trail routes for those experienced in using topographical maps—get information at the Backcountry Desk at the Zion Canyon Visitor Center.

Backcountry permits are required for all overnight hikes in the park as well as for slot canyon hikes. You can get permits at either visitor center. They cost $10 for 1 or 2 people, $15 for 3 to 7 people, and $20 for 8 to 12 people. You can purchase a permit the day before or the day of your trip. You can also make reservations for permits in advance through the park's website (**www.nps.gov/zion**), but you must pick them up in person.

OTHER SPORTS & ACTIVITIES

BIKING & MOUNTAIN BIKING   Although bikes are prohibited on almost all trails and are forbidden to travel cross-country within the national park boundaries, Zion is among the West's most bike-friendly parks. The bike-friendly **Pa'rus Trail** runs a little under 2 miles along the Virgin River, from the south park entrance and South Campground to Zion Canyon Scenic Drive. The trail crosses the river and several creeks, and it provides good views of the Watchman, West Temple, the Sentinel, and other lower-canyon formations. This paved trail is open to bicyclists, pedestrians, pets on leashes, strollers, and wheelchairs, but not cars.

From April through October, the **Zion Canyon Scenic Drive,** beyond its intersection with the Zion–Mount Carmel Highway, is closed to most private motor vehicles, but open to hikers and bicyclists as well as shuttle buses. Because shuttle buses are not permitted to pass moving bicycles, cyclists are asked to pull over and stop to allow them to go by. Bicycles can also be ridden on other park roads, though not through the Zion–Mount Carmel Tunnel.

HORSEBACK RIDING   Guided rides in the park are available March through October from **Canyon Trail Rides,** 280 Bryce Way, Tropic (𝄞 **435/679-8665;** www.canyonrides.com), with ticket sales and information near Zion Lodge. A 1-hour ride along the Virgin River costs $40, and a half-day ride on the Sand Beach Trail costs $80. Maximum weight for riders is 220 pounds, and children must be at least 7 years old for the 1-hour ride and 10 for the half-day ride. Reservations are advised.

ROCK CLIMBING   Expert technical rock climbers like the tall sandstone cliffs in Zion Canyon, although rangers warn that much of the rock is loose, or "rotten," and climbing equipment and techniques that are suitable for granite are often less effective (and therefore less safe) on sandstone. Backcountry permits, available at visitor centers, are required for overnight climbs and cost $10 for 1 or 2 people, $15 for 3 to 7, and $20 for 8 to 12. Because some routes may be closed at times, such as during peregrine falcon nesting from early spring through July, climbers should check at the Zion Canyon Visitor Center before setting out. Several local companies offer guided rock climbing trips, as well as instruction. Get details at the Visitor Center.

WILDLIFE VIEWING & BIRD WATCHING   It's a rare visitor to Zion who doesn't spot a critter of some sort, from **mule deer**—often seen along roadways and in campgrounds year-round—to the many varieties of **lizards.** The park's largest lizard, the chuckwalla, can grow to 20 inches. Along the Virgin River you'll see **bank beaver,** so named because they live in burrows instead of dams. The park is also home to coyotes, jackrabbits, cottontails, chipmunks, squirrels, porcupines, and gophers.

The **peregrine falcon,** among the world's fastest birds, sometimes nests in the Weeping Rock area, where you could also see birds such as the American dipper, the canyon wren, and the white-throated swift. Bald eagles sometimes winter in the park, and you might also see golden eagles.

WHERE TO STAY

Inside the Park

Zion Lodge ★★★   Location, location, location. Zion Lodge offers the best lodging while visiting the park mainly because of where it is—inside Zion National Park. There are three choices. If you must have a TV, you'll want one of the

CAMPING options

INSIDE THE PARK

The best places to camp are the **national park campgrounds,** just inside the park's south entrance. Reservations for **Watchman Campground ★★★**, with 164 sites including some with electric hookups, can be made from March through November (℡ **877/444-6777;** www.recreation.gov). Reservations are not accepted for **South Campground ★★**, where all 127 sites, none with hookups, are often claimed by noon in the summer, so get there early to snag one.

Both of Zion's main campgrounds have paved roads, well-spaced sites, some trees, flush toilets, and that national park atmosphere you came here to enjoy. Cost is $16 to $20. **Lava Point ★★**, on the Kolob Terrace, has only six sites. It's more primitive, with vault toilets, no drinking water, and a 19-foot RV limit,

but it is in a delightful wooded setting and camping is free. There are no showers in the national park, but Zion Canyon Campground, discussed below, will let you use their showers for a fee.

NEAR THE PARK

Those who want full RV hookups and onsite showers will likely be staying just outside the park at **Zion Canyon Campground ★★**, 479 Zion Park Blvd., Springdale (www.zioncamp.com; ℡ **435/772-3237**). Although quite crowded in summer, the campground is clean and well maintained, with tree-shaded sites (including big rig sites) and grassy tent areas. Some sites are along the Virgin River, and the campground has a swimming pool, a game room, a playground, and a store. Dogs are permitted at RV sites but not tent sites. Cost is $30 to $39 per night.

nice-but-ordinary motel rooms or pricy, upscale suites. But what do you need a TV for? You're here to see the park, so skip the TV and book one of the historic cabins. No TVs, but they have stone (gas-burning) fireplaces, one queen or two double beds, pine ceilings, and small private porches. Perfect for the national park experience. The motel rooms and suites are okay, too, with all the usual amenities you would expect, and we will give credit for colorful bed coverings, but no rustic charm. The original Zion Lodge, built in 1925, burned down in 1966, but was quickly rebuilt and restored. Ranger programs take place in the lodge auditorium in summer. All units are smoke-free.

In Zion National Park. ℡ **888/297-2757** or 303/297-2757. www.zionlodge.com. 82 units, 40 cabins. Mid-Mar to Nov motel rooms $186 double; $193 cabin double; $227 suite double. Discounts available rest of the year. **Amenities:** 2 restaurants, free Wi-Fi.

Near the Park

For information on lodging choices in Springdale, just outside the park's south entrance, check with the **Zion Canyon Visitors Bureau.** See "Visitor Centers & Information," above.

WHERE TO EAT

Inside the Park

Castle Dome Café ★ SNACK BAR   Pick up your food at the counter, then sit on the patio under an umbrella and watch the world go by. Morning offerings include coffee, cinnamon buns, and the like; and the rest of the day you can get burgers, hot dogs, sandwiches, French fries, and, most importantly, soft-serve ice cream and frozen yogurt. Beer is available at the cafe's Beer Garden cart.

North side of Zion Lodge, Zion National Park. (℃ **435/772-3213.** $3–$9. Summer only, daily 7am–9pm.

Red Rock Grill ★★★ AMERICAN   Rustic wood furnishings—the dining chairs are made of tree branches—plus wood and stone construction, give the park's main restaurant a decidedly mountain lodge atmosphere. Throw in spectacular views of red rocks and forest out the large windows, and you have the perfect spot to enjoy a meal while visiting Zion National Park. The food's good, too. The menu changes periodically, but you'll find a good selection of well-prepared breakfast and lunch offerings, usually including buffets. Dinner entrees might include the excellent Alaskan salmon, prime rib, grilled flatiron steak, and vegetarian dishes. The house-made desserts, such as the bourbon pecan pie, are especially good. There's full liquor service, and the lounge is open continuously from 11:30am to 10pm daily. Dinner reservations are required in summer.

Zion Lodge, Zion National Park. (℃ **435/772-7760.** www.zionlodge.com. Main courses breakfast and lunch $5–$15, dinner $15–$25. Daily 6:30–10:30am, 11:30am–3pm, and 5–10pm.

Near the Park

There are plenty of places to eat in Springdale, just outside the park's south entrance. Check with the **Zion Canyon Visitors Bureau,** which has a restaurant section on its website with links to many restaurant menus. See "Visitor Centers & Information," above.

NEARBY ATTRACTIONS

In Springdale, just outside the south entrance to Zion National Park, the **Zion Canyon Theatre,** 145 Zion Park Blvd. (℃ **888/256-3456** or 435/772-2400; www.zioncanyon theatre.com) boasts a huge screen—some 60 feet high by 82 feet across. Here you can see the dramatic film *Zion Canyon: Treasure of the Gods,* with thrilling scenes of the Zion National Park area, including a hair-raising flash flood through Zion Canyon's Narrows and some dizzying bird's-eye views. The theater also shows a variety of other large-format films. Admission is $8 for adults and $6 for children under 12, and it's open daily from 11am in summer; call for winter hours.

   About 85 miles north of Springdale you'll discover a delightful little park, **Cedar Breaks National Monument,** a wonderful but chilly place to spend a few hours or a few days, gazing down from the rim into the spectacular natural amphitheater, hiking the trails, and camping among the spruce and fir trees. The park forms a natural coliseum more than 2,000 feet deep and over 3 miles across, filled with stone spires, arches, and columns painted in ever-changing reds, purples, and oranges. It reminds us a lot of Bryce Canyon National Park.

The monument is open to those traveling by car, truck, or RV for a short summer season—from after the snow melts, usually in late May, until the first heavy snow, usually in mid-November. However, if you have a snowmobile or a pair of cross-country skis or snowshoes, you can visit throughout the winter.

For advance information, including directions on how to get there, see the monument's website, **www.nps.gov/cebr**, or contact **Cedar Breaks National Monument,** 2390 W. Utah 56, Ste. 11, Cedar City, UT 84720 (✆ **435/586-9451**). At over 10,000 feet elevation, it's always pleasantly cool at Cedar Breaks. In fact, it actually gets downright cold at night, so bring a jacket or sweater.

A 5-mile road through the monument offers easy access to its scenic overlooks and trail heads. Among the trails, the fairly easy 2-mile round-trip **Alpine Pond Nature Trail** loop leads through woodlands of bristlecone pines to a forest glade and a pond surrounded by wildflowers, offering panoramic views of the amphitheater along the way. A more challenging hike, the 4-mile round-trip **Spectra Point/Ramparts Overlook Trail** follows the rim more closely than the Alpine Pond Trail, offering changing views of the colorful rock formations. It also takes you through fields of wildflowers and by bristlecone pines that are more than 1,600 years old.

Because of its relative remoteness, Cedar Breaks is a good place for spotting **wildlife.** You're likely to see mule deer grazing in the meadows along the road early and late in the day. Marmots are often seen along the Spectra Point Trail, and you'll spot ground squirrels, red squirrels, and chipmunks practically everywhere.

Admission for up to 1 week, charged from late May through mid-October, is $4 per person for all those 16 and older, free for under 16. Admission is free the rest of the year. There's a 26-site campground open from mid-June to mid-September. Camping costs $14 per night.

BRYCE CANYON

by Don & Barbara Laine

O f all the national parks we've explored, and there have
been many, Bryce Canyon is our favorite, and we're
pleased to share it with you. This is a magical land, a place
of inspiration and spectacular beauty, where thousands of intricately
shaped hoodoos stir the imagination as they stand in silent watch.
Its often whimsical formations are smaller and on a more human
scale than the impressive rocks at Zion, and Bryce is far easier to
explore than the huge and often intimidating Grand Canyon.

Hoodoos, geologists tell us, are pinnacles of rock, often oddly shaped,
left standing after millions of years of water and wind erosion have carved
away softer or less protected rock. But perhaps the truth really lies in a
Paiute legend. These American Indians, who lived in the area for several
hundred years before being forced out by Anglo pioneers, told of a "Legend People" who lived here in the old days. For their evil ways, the powerful Coyote turned them to stone, and even today they remain frozen in time.

Although the hoodoos grab your attention first, before long you notice
the deep amphitheaters that enfold them, with their cliffs, windows, and
arches—all in shades of red, brown, orange, yellow, and white—that
change and glow with the rising and setting sun. Beyond the rocks and light
are the other faces of the park: three life zones, each with its own unique
vegetation, and a kingdom of animals, from busy ground squirrels to
stately mule deer and their archenemy, the mountain lion.

The park is named for pioneer Ebenezer Bryce and his wife, Mary, who
tried raising cattle here in the late 1800s. They stayed only a few years, but
Bryce left behind his name and his oft-quoted description of the canyon as
"a helluva place to lose a cow."

ESSENTIALS

Getting There & Gateways

Utah 12 crosses the park, which is in the mountains of southern Utah, from
east to west. The bulk of the park, including the visitor center, is accessible
from Utah 63, which turns south off Utah 12. West of the park, **U.S. 89** runs
north to south.

From Salt Lake City, it's about 250 miles to the park. Take **I-15** south
about 200 miles to exit 95 and head east 13 miles on Utah 20, south on U.S.
89 for 17 miles to Utah 12, and east 17 miles to the park entrance road.

From St. George, about 135 miles southwest of the park, travel north on
I-15 10 miles to exit 16, then head east on Utah 9 for 63 miles to U.S. 89,
north 44 miles to Utah 12, and east 17 miles to the park entrance road.

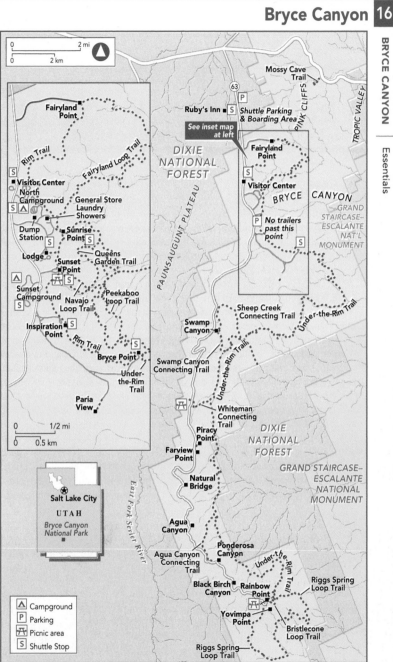

Although Bryce Canyon receives only two-thirds the number of annual visitors that pour into nearby Zion National Park, Bryce can still be crowded, especially from mid-June to mid-September. If you must visit then, try to hike some of the lesser-used trails (ask rangers for recommendations), and get out onto the trails early.

A better time to visit, if your schedule allows, is spring or fall. If you don't mind a bit of cold and snow, the park is practically deserted in the winter—a typical January sees less than 25,000 visitors—and the sight of bright red hoodoos capped with fresh white snow is something you won't soon forget.

Bryce is 83 miles east of Zion National Park, 160 miles north of the North Rim of the Grand Canyon, and 245 miles northeast of Las Vegas, Nevada.

THE NEAREST AIRPORT Bryce Canyon Airport (*©* **435/834-5239;** www. brycecanyonairport.com) is several miles from the park entrance on Utah 12. It has no commercial air service, but charter service is available from **Bryce Canyon Airlines** (*©* **435/834-8060;** www.rubysinn.com/bryce-canyon-airlines.html).

Visitor Center & Information

The visitor center has exhibits on the geology and history of the area. Rangers answer questions, offer advice, and provide backcountry permits. You can also pick up free brochures and buy books, maps, and postcards. There is free Wi-Fi. The visitor center is open daily year-round except Thanksgiving, Christmas, and New Year's Day.

Want advanced info? Officials request that you write for information at least a month before your planned visit. However, you will find everything they will send you and more at the park website **Bryce Canyon National Park,** P.O. Box 640201, Bryce, UT 84764-0201 (*©* **435/834-5322;** www.nps.gov/brca).

For additional information on the area, contact the **Garfield County Office of Tourism** (*©* **800/444-6689** or 435/676-1161; www.brycecanyoncountry.com).

Fees

Entry into the park (for up to 7 days) costs $25 per private vehicle, which includes unlimited use of the park shuttle when it's operating. Those 16 and older entering the park on motorcycle, bike, or foot pay $12 each; those 15 and under are admitted free.

Seasons & Climate

With elevations ranging from 6,620 to 9,115 feet, Bryce Canyon is cooler than southern Utah's lower-elevation parks. From May through October, daytime temperatures are pleasant—usually from the low 60s to the upper 80s (high teens to low 30s Celsius)—but nights are cool, dropping into the 40s (single digits Celsius) even at the height of summer. Afternoon thunderstorms are common in July and August. In winter, days are generally clear and crisp, with high temperatures often reaching the 40s

The Best Time to Make the Scenic Drive

The scenic drive is practically deserted in early **mornings**—anytime before 9am. This is the best time to see deer and the best time to see the hoodoos, when the light on them is at its richest.

(single digits Celsius), and nights are cold, usually in the single digits or teens, and sometimes dipping well below zero. Snow is common in winter, but the roads to the view points are plowed.

EXPLORING THE PARK

By Car

The park's 18-mile (one-way) scenic drive follows the rim of Bryce Canyon, offering easy access to splendid views of the fanciful fairyland of stone below. Trailers are not allowed on the road and must be left at one of several parking lots. Because all over-looks are on your left as you begin, it's safest to drive all the way to the end of the road, turn around, and stop at the overlooks on your return. Allow 1 to 2 hours.

After leaving the visitor center, drive the 18-mile road to **Yovimpa and Rainbow Point overlooks,** which offer expansive views of southern Utah, Arizona, and some-times even New Mexico. From these pink cliffs, you can look down on a platoon of stone soldiers, standing at eternal attention. From here, drive north to **Ponderosa Canyon Overlook,** where you can gaze down from a dense forest of spruce and fir at multicolored hoodoos, and then continue to **Agua Canyon Overlook,** with some of the best color contrasts in the park. Looking almost straight down, watch for a hoodoo known as **The Hunter,** with its hat of green trees.

Continue to **Natural Bridge,** actually an arch carved by rain and wind, spanning 85 feet. Now continue to **Farview Point,** with a panoramic view to the distant horizon and the Grand Canyon's North Rim. Next, pass through **Swamp Canyon** and continue until you hit a turnoff from the main road on the right. This leads to three overlooks. The first is **Paria View,** looking to the south of the White Cliffs, carved into light-colored sandstone by the Paria River. To the north you'll find **Bryce Point,** a splendid stop for seeing **Bryce Amphitheater,** the largest natural amphitheater in the park. From here it's a short drive to **Inspiration Point,** which offers the best view in the park of the **Silent City,** a sleeping metropolis of stone.

Now return to the main road and head north to **Sunset Point,** where you can see practi-cally all of Bryce Amphitheater, including **Thor's Hammer** and the 200-foot-tall cliffs of **Wall Street.** Continue north to a turnoff for **Sunrise Point,** where there's an inspiring view into Bryce Amphitheater. This is the beginning of the **Queen's Garden Trail,** an excellent choice for a walk (even a quick one) below the canyon rim.

By Shuttle

In recent years, congestion has been increasing along the park's only road. To alleviate this, a voluntary free **shuttle service** runs from early May through early October, daily from 8am until 7:40pm (until 5:40pm the last few weeks of the shuttle season). The shuttle stops at various view points, as well as at Ruby's Inn, Ruby's Campground, the

---

Park Attractions

Although American Indians and 19th-century pioneers spent some time here, they left little evidence. The park's main historic site is the sandstone and ponderosa pine **The Lodge at Bryce Canyon,** built by the Union Pacific Rail-road in 1924. Much of it has been faith-fully restored to its 1920s appearance.

visitor center, Sunset Campground, and the Lodge at Bryce Canyon, and you can get on and off as you please. It runs every 12 to 15 minutes and is handicap accessible.

RANGER PROGRAMS

Park rangers present free programs and activities. One-hour **evening programs** take place at the Lodge at Bryce Canyon, the visitor center, and occasionally at the North Campground amphitheater. Topics vary, but could include such subjects as the animals and plants of the park, geology, and the role of humans in the park's early days. Rangers also give half-hour talks several times daily at various locations, and lead hikes and walks, including a **moonlight hike** and a wheelchair-accessible, 1½-hour **canyon rim walk.** Especially popular are the park's **Astronomy Programs,** with telescopes provided. If there's enough snow, **snowshoe hikes** are offered in winter, with snowshoes provided. Check at the visitor center for times and places.

DAY HIKES

One of the wonderful things about Bryce Canyon is that you don't have to be a hardcore backpacker to really get to know the park. But those looking for a challenge won't be disappointed, either.

All trails below the rim have at least some steep grades, so you should wear hiking boots with a traction tread and good ankle support to avoid ankle injuries, the most common accidents in the park. During summer you'll want to hike either early or late in the day, keeping in mind that it gets hotter the deeper you go into the canyon.

Shorter Trails

Bristlecone Loop ★★   An easy walk above the canyon rim, this trail traverses a subalpine fir forest. Here you'll find more bristlecone pines than along the other park trails. It takes just 45 to 60 minutes to complete the loop, which has an elevation change of 150 feet. 1 mile RT. Easy. Access: Rainbow Point parking area at end of scenic drive.

Mossy Cave ★★   This often-overlooked trail outside the main part of the park offers an easy and picturesque 45-minute walk. The trail follows an old irrigation ditch up a short hill to a shallow cave, where seeping water nurtures the cave's moss. Just off the trail, you'll also see a small waterfall. Elevation gain is 200 feet. Hikers will usually get their feet wet; be careful when crossing the ditch. .8 mile RT. Easy. Access: Along Utah 12, about 3.5 miles east of the intersection with Utah 63.

Special Regulations & Warnings

The most common injuries are sprained, twisted, and broken ankles, and rangers strongly recommend that hikers, even those just out for short day hikes, wear sturdy hiking boots with good traction and ankle support.

Another concern in recent years has been **bubonic plague** (treatable with antibiotics if caught early). The bacteria that causes bubonic plague has been found on fleas in prairie dog colonies in the park, so you should avoid contact with wild animals, especially prairie dogs, squirrels, and other rodents.

A great choice for getting down into the canyon and seeing the most with the least amount of sweat is to combine the **Navajo Trail** with the **Queen's Garden Trail.** The total distance is just under 3 miles; allow 2 to 3 hours. It's best to start at the Navajo Trailhead at Sunset Point and leave the canyon on the less steep Queen's Garden Trail, returning to the rim at Sunrise Point, .5 mile north of the Navajo Trailhead.

Navajo ★★★   This trail descends from the canyon rim 550 feet to the canyon floor and back up again. Traversing graveled switchbacks, it affords terrific views of several impressive formations, including the towering skyscrapers of Wall Street and the precariously balanced Thor's Hammer. The round-trip on this trail takes 1 to 2 hours. 1.3 miles RT. Moderate. Access: Trail head at central overlook point at Sunset Point.

Queen's Garden ★★★   A short trail, it drops 320 feet below the rim, takes you down into Bryce Amphitheater, with rest benches near the formation called Queen Victoria. At the beginning of the descent, keep an eye cocked to the distant views so you won't miss Boat Mesa, the Sinking Ship, and Bristlecone Point. As you plunge deeper into the canyon, the trail passes some of the park's most fanciful formations, including "Queen Victoria" herself, plus the Queen's Castle and Gulliver's Castle. The round-trip takes 1 to 2 hours. 1.8 miles RT. Easy to moderate. Access: South side of Sunrise Point.

Longer Trails

Fairyland Loop ★★   From Fairyland Point, this strenuous but little-traveled trail descends into Fairyland Canyon, and then meanders up, down, and around Boat Mesa. It crosses Campbell Canyon, passes Tower Bridge junction—a 200-yard side trail takes you to the base of Tower Bridge—and begins a steady climb to the Chinese Wall. About halfway along the wall, the trail begins the serious ascent back to the top of the canyon, reaching it near Sunrise Point. To complete the loop, follow the Rim Trail back through juniper, manzanita, and Douglas fir to Fairyland Point. The loop has an elevation change of 2,309 feet. 8 miles RT. Strenuous. Access: Fairyland Point Overlook, off park access road north of visitor center; also accessible from Sunrise Point.

Rim ★★★   The Rim Trail, which does not drop into the canyon but offers splendid views from above, meanders along the rim with a total elevation change of up to 1,734 feet if you walk its entire length. This is more a walk than a hike, and includes a half-mile section between two overlooks—Sunrise and Sunset—that is paved, fairly level, suitable for wheelchairs, and open to leashed pets. Overlooking Bryce Amphitheater, the trail offers almost continually excellent views, and is a good choice for an early morning or evening walk, when you can watch the changing light on the rosy rocks below. Some people feel that the best view in the park is from the Rim Trail, south of Inspiration Point, early in the day. 5.5 miles one-way. Easy to moderate. Access: North trail head at Fairyland Point; south trail head at Bryce Point. Also accessible from Sunrise, Sunset, and Inspiration points and numerous locations in between.

EXPLORING THE BACKCOUNTRY

For die-hard hikers who don't mind rough terrain, Bryce has two backcountry trails, usually open in the summer only. The truly ambitious can combine the trails for a weeklong excursion. Permits are required for all overnight trips into the backcountry. Cost is $5 for 1 or 2 people, $10 for 3 to 6 people, and $15 for 7 to 15 people (group sites only). Permits cannot be reserved, but must be obtained at the park during the 48 hours preceding your hike.

Riggs Spring Loop ★★ This hike can be done in 4 or 5 hours, or it can be more comfortably done as a relaxing overnight backpacking trip. The trail goes through a deep forest and also provides breathtaking views of the huge Pink Cliffs at the southern end of the plateau. It has an elevation change of 2,248 feet. 8.5-mile loop. Moderate to strenuous. Access: South side of parking area for Rainbow Point.

Under the Rim Trail ★★ This moderately strenuous trail runs between Bryce and Rainbow points; it offers the full spectrum of views of Bryce Canyon's scenery. Since the trail runs below the rim, it is full of steep inclines and descents, with an overall elevation change of 1,500 feet. Allow 2 to 3 days to hike the entire length. There are five camping areas along the trail, plus a group camp area. 23 miles one-way. Moderate. Access: East side of parking area for Bryce Point Overlook.

OTHER SPORTS & ACTIVITIES

HORSEBACK RIDING To see Bryce Canyon the way the early pioneers did, you need to look down from a horse. **Canyon Trail Rides,** 280 Bryce Way, Tropic, (© **435/679-8665;** www.canyonrides.com), offers a close-up view of Bryce's spectacular rock formations from the relative comfort of a saddle. The company has a desk inside Bryce Lodge. A 2-hour ride to the canyon floor and back costs $60 per person, and a half-day trip farther into the canyon costs $80 per person. Rides are offered April through November. Riders must be at least 7 years old for the 2-hour trip, at least 10 for the half-day ride, and weigh no more than 220 pounds.

WILDLIFE WATCHING The park has a variety of wildlife, ranging from **mule deer,** which seem to be almost everywhere, to the often-seen **golden-mantled ground squirrel** and **Uinta chipmunk.** Occasionally, visitors catch a glimpse of a **mountain lion** and **elk** and **pronghorn** may be seen at higher elevations. Also in the park are **black-tailed jackrabbits, coyotes,** and **striped skunks.**

Many birds live in the park. You're bound to hear the rather obnoxious call of the **Steller's jay.** Other birds often seen include violet-green swallows, common ravens, Clark's nutcrackers, American robins, red-shafted flickers, dark-eyed juncos, and chipping sparrows. Watch for **white-throated swifts** as they perform their exotic acrobatics along cliff faces. The park is also home, at least part of the year, to peregrine falcons, red-tailed hawks, golden eagles, bald eagles, and great horned owls.

WINTER SPORTS & ACTIVITIES Bryce is beautiful in the winter, when snow settles over the red, pink, orange, and brown hoodoos. **Snowshoes** may be used anywhere in the park except on cross-country ski tracks. **Cross-country skiers** will find several marked, ungroomed trails (all above the rim). They include the **Fairyland Loop Trail,** which leads 1 mile through a pine and juniper forest to the Fairyland Point Overlook. From here you can take the 1-mile **Forest Trail** back to the road, or continue along the rim for another 1.2 miles to the park boundary. There are also connections to trails in the adjacent national forest.

WHERE TO STAY

Bryce Canyon is a morning park, where the absolutely best views with the most brilliant colors will be seen just after sunrise. So we suggest strongly that you stay either in the park or as close as possible so you can get to the rim or out on the trail first thing and not miss out.

Inside the Park

The Lodge at Bryce Canyon ★★★   If historic ambiance, the scent of Ponderosa pines, and being close to the action is what you seek, The Lodge at Bryce Canyon is for you. Built in 1924, the stone and wood lodge oozes western charm, and just feels right for a stay in a national park. Rates here aren't cheap, but the facilities are attractive and well maintained, and you can't get any closer to what you want to see in the park. Our first choice here is one of the western cabins, which have been restored to their 1920s appearance, with log beams and rich green roofs. They're a bit small but have two double beds and handsome stone fireplaces (gas-burning). There are also modern motel rooms, with two queen-sized beds or one king, and upscale lodge suites with white wicker furniture. All units are smoke-free.

Bryce Canyon National Park, Bryce. ℭ **877/386-4383** or 435/834-8700. www.brycecanyonforever. com. 114 units (110 in motel rooms and cabins; 3 suites and 1 studio in lodge). $185 double; $210 cabin; $260 lodge suite. Closed mid-Nov to Mar. **Amenities:** 2 restaurants; free Wi-Fi in the lobby.

Near the Park

The following properties are all just outside the park entrance.

Best Western Plus Bryce Canyon Grand Hotel ★★★   The most luxurious lodging for visitors to Bryce Canyon, this facility has absolutely everything you could want, from the most comfortable beds in the area to a hot breakfast included with all room rates. Speaking of which, rates are a bit pricy in summer but an absolute bargain in the off-season. The large rooms have one king or two queen-sized beds, exceptionally good lighting, handsome oak- or dark walnut finished wood furnishings, and big windows. All units are smoke-free.

31 N. 100 East, Bryce Canyon City. ℭ **866/909-8845** or 435/834-5700. www.brycecanyongrand. com. 164 units. Summer $162–$180 double; winter $72–$80. Rates include a hot breakfast. **Amenities:** Restaurant; outdoor pool; fitness center; free Wi-Fi.

Best Western Plus Ruby's Inn ★   Looking for a somewhat upscale but relatively reasonable motel with all the usual amenities? This is it. Rooms are what you would expect at any well-run Best Western, except, of course, that here the artwork on the beige walls depicts scenes of the national park and surrounding area. Furniture is solid wood—mostly with a light oak finish—and most of the spacious rooms have two queen-sized beds or two kings. All units are smoke-free.

26 S. Main St., Bryce Canyon City. ℭ **866/866-6616** or 435/834-5341. www.rubysinn.com. 370 units. Summer $122–$135 double; winter

Picnic & Camping Supplies

A small store inside the national park has groceries, camping supplies, and snacks, all at surprisingly low prices. Just outside the park, the huge **general store** in the Best Western Plus Ruby's Inn (see "Where to Stay," above) offers camping supplies, groceries, Western clothing, and souvenirs.

INSIDE THE PARK

Bryce Canyon's two campgrounds offer plenty of trees with a genuine "forest camping" experience, plus easy access to trails. Both **North ★★★** and **Sunset campgrounds ★★** have sites suitable for tent and RV campers, and there are restrooms but no RV hookups. Sunset Campground is open late spring through early fall only, while a section of North Campground is open year-round. Although we would happily camp at either campground, we prefer North Campground because it's closer to the Rim Trail, making it easier to rush over to catch those amazing sunrise and sunset colors. Cost for both campgrounds is $15 per night. Those without reservations should get to the park early to claim a site (usually by 2pm in the summer). Reservations are available from early May through late September for North Campground and for 20 tent-only sites in Sunset Campground, for an additional nonrefundable booking fee of $10

(www.recreation.gov; ✆ 877/444-6777). There are pay showers at the general store in the park, although it's a healthy walk from either campground. The general store also has a coin-operated laundry and a snack bar. The Park Service maintains an RV dump station ($5 fee) in the summer.

NEAR THE PARK

Those who want a commercial campground with RV hookups won't do better than **Ruby's Inn RV Park & Campground ★★**, 300 S. Main St., Bryce Canyon City, UT 84764 (✆ 866/878-9373 or 435/834-5301; www.rubysinn.com), just north of the park entrance along the shuttle bus route. The RV and tent sites are mostly shady and attractive, and there's an outdoor heated swimming pool, hot tub, barbecue grills, coin-operated laundry, and a store with groceries and RV supplies. The campground is open April through October, with rates of $27 to $43.

$70–$90. Pets accepted, $20 per night fee **Amenities:** 2 restaurants, indoor pool and hot tub; general store; foreign currency exchange; free Wi-Fi.

Bryce View Lodge ★ Nothing special, but the rooms are quiet, clean, and well maintained, and it's a perfectly adequate place to sleep after spending the day exploring the park. White walls decorated with scenes of the area, standard wood motel furnishings, and good beds help make this a good value. Although this motel lacks a swimming pool and other amenities, guests have access to all those across the street at the Best Western Plus Ruby's Inn (see above). All units are smoke-free.

105 E. Center St., Bryce Canyon City. ✆ 888/279-2304 or 435/834-5180. www.bryceviewlodge.com. 160 units. $90–$100 double. Pets accepted, $20 per night fee. Closed in winter (call for specific dates). **Amenities:** Free Wi-Fi.

WHERE TO EAT

Inside the Park

The Lodge at Bryce Canyon Restaurant ★★★ AMERICAN   A big stone fireplace, high ceiling, and lots of rich wood provide a delightful rustic elegance to the best dining in the area, and we suggest that while you're at Bryce Canyon you indulge yourself with at least one meal here. The breakfast menu includes basic American standards and a good buffet, while lunch options range from a variety of entree salads, such as the rib eye beef and bleu cheese on a bed of spinach, to burgers, and bison stew. Also at lunch is a soup, salad, and build-it-yourself sandwich buffet. The dinner menu changes periodically, but may include grilled and oven-roasted rack of Utah lamb, grilled or broiled Alaskan salmon, Utah trout, or prime rib. There are also vegetarian items, and the restaurant serves wine and beer. Also at the Lodge at Bryce Canyon is the **Valhalla Pizzeria & Coffee Shop,** which offers fresh-baked pastries, fruit, espresso, and coffee for breakfast (6–11:30am) and pizza, pasta, and salads for dinner (3–10pm), with prices in the $5 to $15 range.

At The Lodge at Bryce Canyon, Bryce Canyon National Park. ✆ **435/834-8700.** www.bryce canyonforever.com. Main courses $5–$12 breakfast and lunch, $13–$25 dinner. Daily mid-May to mid-Oct 7–10:30am, 11:30am–3pm, and 5:30–10pm.

Near the Park

Cowboy's Buffet and Steak Room ★ STEAK/SEAFOOD   A big family-style restaurant, this eatery plays up its cowboy theme with Western décor and lots of beef. The menu is basic American, offering steak, ribs, seafood (the grilled rainbow trout is good), chicken, and pasta at dinner and burgers, sandwiches, and salads at lunch. During the summer, well-stocked buffets at all meals provide a good variety of items, and if you're in a rush to get into the park the buffet is quicker than ordering off the menu. Full liquor service is available.

At the Best Western Plus Ruby's Inn, 26 S. Main St., Bryce Canyon City. ✆ **435/834-5341.** www. rubysinn.com. Breakfast and lunch $4–$15; dinner main courses and buffets $10–$30. Summer daily 6:30am–9:30pm; winter daily 6:30am–9pm.

Canyon Diner ★ AMERICAN   Burgers, hot dogs, and pizza are the standard fast-food offerings here, but this self-serve plastic palace also has some surprises, including really good bratwurst with sauerkraut and a tasty steak sandwich. They also prepare box lunches for you to take into the park, and make good malts and shakes.

At the Best Western Plus Ruby's Inn, 26 S. Main St., Bryce Canyon City. ✆ **435/834-8030.** www. rubysinn.com. Individual items $4–$8; meals $7–$12. Daily 6:30am–9:30pm. Closed Nov–Apr.

NEARBY ATTRACTIONS

The **Grand Staircase–Escalante National Monument** (www.ut.blm.gov/monument) is a worthwhile side trip, especially for the adventurous who are seeking a rugged, undeveloped area offering practically unlimited opportunities for hiking, mountain biking, four-wheeling, and camping. The monument covers an area almost as large as the states of Delaware and Rhode Island combined, and has quite a few access points. You can get information at several local Bureau of Land Management (BLM) offices but start in the town of Kanab, where your first stop should be the **monument's headquarters** (669 S. U.S. Highway 89A; ✆ **435/644-1200**) to check on current travel and weather conditions—potentially fatal flash floods can catch hikers by surprise.

Outdoor adventures include **canyoneering** through narrow slot canyons (with the aid of ropes). Information on the best areas for canyoneering is at the visitor center, but we cannot emphasize too strongly that this is not a place for beginners, so book a trip with one of the local outfitters, such as **Excursions of Escalante** (✆ **800/839-7567;** www. excursionsofescalante.com). At the **Calf Creek Recreation Area,** along Utah 12 about 15 miles northeast of the town of Escalante, you'll find a small campground and a 5.5-mile round-trip hike to **Lower Calf Creek Falls.** This is the monument's only officially marked and maintained trail, but there are numerous unmarked cross-country routes.

CARLSBAD CAVERNS

by Don & Barbara Laine

f you only explore one cave in your lifetime, the Big Room at Carlsbad Caverns should be the one. It's huge. It's beautiful. And it's so different from anything you've ever seen that its magnificence will stay with you forever.

Formation of the caverns—there are actually more than 100 caves here—began some 250 million years ago, when an inland sea covered the area. A reef formed and when the sea disappeared it was left covered with deposits of salts and gypsum. Eventually, uplifting and erosion brought the reef back to the surface, and then the actual cave creation began.

Rainwater seeped through cracks in the earth's surface, dissolving the limestone and leaving hollows behind, which slowly grew to passageways and even huge rooms. Nature's artistry took over, decorating the rooms with a variety of fanciful formations. Water dripped down through the rock into the caves, dissolving more limestone and absorbing the mineral calcite and other materials on its journey. Each drop of water deposited its tiny load of calcite, gradually creating the cave formations that lure visitors to Carlsbad Caverns each year.

Early settlers were unaware of the cave's existence until they observed sunset flights of bats emerging from the cave opening in the 1880s. A local cowboy named Jim White began exploring the main cave in the early 1900s, and fascinated by the formations, he shared his discovery with others. Word of this magical underground world soon spread.

Carlsbad Cave National Monument was created in October 1923. In 1926, the first electric lights were installed, and in 1930 Carlsbad Caverns gained national park status.

Underground development has been confined to the famous Big Room, with a ceiling 25 stories high and a floor large enough to hold more than six football fields. Visitors can tour parts of it on their own and explore other sections (and several other caves) on guided tours. The cave is also a summer home to more than 400,000 Brazilian (also called Mexican) free-tailed bats, which put on a spectacular show each evening as they leave the cave in search of food, and again in the morning when they return.

ESSENTIALS

Getting There & Gateways

The main section of the park, with the visitor center and entrance to Carlsbad Cavern, is about 30 miles southwest of the city of Carlsbad by way of **U.S. 62/180** and **N. Mex. 7.** From Albuquerque, drive east on I-40 for 59

AVOIDING the crowds

Crowds are thickest in summer and on weekends and holidays year-round; visiting on weekdays between Labor Day and Memorial Day is the best way to avoid them. Visiting during the off season is especially attractive because the temperature in the caves stays the same regardless of the weather above—56°F (13°C). The only downside is that you won't be able to see the bat flights. The bats head to Mexico when the weather starts to get chilly, usually by late October, and don't return until May. The best time to see the park might be September, when you can still see the bat flights but there are fewer visitors than during the peak summer season.

miles to Clines Corners, then turn south on U.S. 285 for 216 miles to the city of Carlsbad. For the caverns, continue southwest 23 miles on U.S. 62/180 to White's City, and go about seven miles on N. Mex. 7, the park access road, to the visitor center. From El Paso, drive east 150 miles on U.S. 62/180 to White's City, then 7 miles on N. Mex. 7 to the visitor center.

THE NEAREST AIRPORT Air travelers can fly to **Cavern City Air Terminal** (www.cityofcarlsbadnm.com/airport.cfm), at the southern edge of the city of Carlsbad, which has commercial service from Albuquerque on **New Mexico Airlines (𝄞 888/ 564-6119;** www.flynma.com), plus **Enterprise** car rentals.

The nearest major airport is **El Paso International (𝄞 915/780-4749;** www.elpaso internationalairport.com), in central El Paso, Texas, just north of I-10, with service from major airlines and car-rental companies.

Visitor Center & Information

The park visitor center is open daily 8am to 7pm from Memorial Day to Labor Day and daily 8am to 5pm the rest of the year, with the exception of December 25. Displays discuss bats and other wildlife and depict the geology and history of the caverns. Ranger programs will also be advertised here. Attached to the visitor center is a restaurant (see "Where to Eat," below), a bookstore, and a souvenir shop.

Contact **Carlsbad Caverns National Park,** 3225 National Parks Hwy., Carlsbad, NM 88220 (𝄞 **575/785-2232;** www.nps.gov/cave) in advance of your trip for full information. Once you get to the city of Carlsbad, you can pick up information at the **National Park Service administration offices,** 727 Carlsbad Caverns Hwy., open weekdays 8am to 4:30pm. Books and maps can be ordered from the **Carlsbad Caverns Guadalupe Mountains Association,** P.O. Box 1417, Carlsbad, NM 88221 (𝄞 **575/785-2484;** www.ccgma.org).

For additional information on area lodging, dining, and other attractions, contact or stop at the **Carlsbad Chamber of Commerce,** 302 S. Canal St., Carlsbad, NM 88220 (𝄞 **866/822-9226** or 575/887-6516; www.carlsbadchamber.com).

Fees & Reservations

Admission to the visitor center and aboveground sections of the park is free. The basic **cavern entry fee,** which is good for 3 days and includes self-guided tours of the Natural Entrance and Big Room, is $6 for adults 16 and older, and free for children under 16. Holders of any America the Beautiful pass, plus up to three adults, are admitted free. An audio tour of the self-guided routes is available for a $5 rental fee.

Reservations are required for all **guided tours** (✆ **877/444-6777** or www.recreation.gov). In addition to tour fees, you will need a general cave admission ticket, except those to Slaughter Canyon Cave and Spider Cave. Holders of the America the Beautiful Senior and Access passes and children under 16 receive a 50% discount on these tours. Children under 16 must be accompanied by an adult 18 or older, and minimum age restrictions for tours also apply.

The King's Palace guided tour costs $8 and tours of Left Hand Tunnel cost $7. Guided tours of Spider Cave, Lower Cave, and Hall of the White Giant cost $20. Slaughter Canyon Cave tours cost $15.

Seasons & Climate

The climate aboveground is warm in the summer, with highs often in the 90s (30s Celsius) and sometimes exceeding 100°F (38°C); evening lows are in the mid-60s (upper teens Celsius). Winters are mild, with highs in the 50s and 60s (10s and mid-teens Celsius) and lows in the 20s and 30s (low negatives Celsius). There may be intense afternoon and evening thunderstorms in summer. Underground it's another story entirely, with a year-round temperature that varies little from its average of 56°F (13°C), making a jacket or sweater a welcome companion.

EXPLORING THE PARK

Most visitors head first to Carlsbad Cavern, which has elevators, a paved walkway, and the Underground Rest Area. A 1-mile section of the Big Room self-guided tour is accessible to those in wheelchairs (no wheelchairs are available at the park), though it's best to have someone along to assist. Pick up an accessibility guide at the visitor center.

Carlsbad Cavern (the park's main cave), Slaughter Canyon Cave, and Spider Cave are open to the public. Experienced cavers with professional-level equipment can request permission to explore some of the park's other caves.

Main Carlsbad Cavern Routes

Most visitors see Carlsbad Cavern by taking the following three trails, all of which are lighted and paved and have handrails. However, the Big Room is the only one of the three that's considered easy.

Big Room Self-Guided Tour ★★★ Considered the one essential of a visit to Carlsbad Caverns National Park, this trail meanders through a massive chamber—it isn't called the Big Room for nothing—where you'll see some of the park's most spectacular formations and likely be overwhelmed by the enormity of it all. Allow about 1½ hours. 1.25-mile loop. Easy.

King's Palace Guided Tour ★★★ This ranger-led 1½-hour walk wanders through some of the cave's most scenic chambers, where you'll see fanciful formations in the King's Palace, Queen's Chamber, and Green Lake Room. Watch for the Bashful

Special Regulations & Warnings

Even touching the formations, walls, or ceilings of the caves can damage them, not only because many of the features are delicate and easily broken, but also because skin oils will discolor the rock and disturb the mineral deposits that are necessary for growth. As you would expect, damaging the cave formations in any way is prohibited.

Strollers are not allowed in the caves, so child backpacks are a good idea, but beware of low ceilings and doorways along the pathways.

Pets are not permitted in the caverns, on unpaved park trails, or in the backcountry. Because of the hot summer temperatures, pets should not be left unattended in vehicles, and pet owners will be issued citations if pets are left in vehicles when air temperatures are 70°F (21°C).or higher. A **kennel** at the visitor center has cages in an air-conditioned room, but no runs, and is primarily used while pet owners are on cave tours. Pets are given water but no food, and there are no overnight facilities. Reservations are not necessary. Cost is $10 per pet.

Elephant formation between the King's Palace and Green Lake Room. Along the way, rangers discuss the geology of the cave and early explorers' experiences. Although the path is paved, the 80-foot elevation change makes this more difficult than the Big Room trail. Children under 4 are not permitted. 1-mile loop. Moderate.

Natural Entrance Route ★★ This moderately strenuous hike takes you into Carlsbad Cavern on the same basic route used by its early explorers. You leave daylight to enter a big hole, then descend more than 750 feet into the cavern on a steep and narrow switchback trail, moving from the "twilight zone" of semidarkness to the depths of the cave, which would be totally black without the electric lights conveniently provided by the Park Service. The self-guided tour takes about 1 hour and ends near the elevators, which can take you back to the visitor center. However, we suggest that from here you proceed on the Big Room Self-Guided Tour, which is described above, if you have not already been there. 1.25 miles. Moderate to strenuous.

Caving Tour Programs in Carlsbad Cavern

Ranger-led tours to these less developed sections of Carlsbad Cavern provide more of the experience of exploration and genuine caving than the above routes, which follow well-trodden trails. Caving tours vary in difficulty, but all include a period of absolute darkness or "blackout," which can make some people uncomfortable. Because some tours involve walking or crawling through tight spaces, people who suffer from claustrophobia or who have other health concerns should discuss specifics with rangers before purchasing tickets. Tours can book up weeks in advance, so reserve early. To make reservations, go to www.recreation.gov or call ℂ **877/444-6777.**

Hall of the White Giant ★★ If you want a strenuous 4-hour trip during which you crawl through narrow, dirty passageways and climb slippery rocks, this tour is for you. The highlight is the huge formation called the White Giant. Only those in excellent condition should consider this half-mile one-way tour; children must be at least 12. Four AA batteries for the provided headlamp, sturdy hiking boots, kneepads, gloves, and long pants are required.

Left Hand Tunnel ★★ The easiest of the caving tours, this one allows you to actually walk—rather than crawl—the entire time! Hand-carried lanterns (provided by the Park Service) light the way, and the trail is dirt but relatively level. You'll see a variety of formations, fossils from Permian times, and pools of water on this half-mile one-way walk. Children must be at least six. The tour takes about 2 hours.

Lower Cave ★ This 3-hour trek involves descending or climbing over 50 feet of ladders, and an optional crawl. It takes you through an area that was explored by a National Geographic Society expedition in the 1920s, and you'll see artifacts from that and other excursions. In addition, you'll encounter a variety of formations, including cave pearls, which look a lot like the pearls created by oysters and can be as big as golf balls. Participants must be at least 12 for this 1-mile round-trip moderate hike. Four AA batteries are required for the provided headlamp. Hiking boots or good sneakers and gloves are also required.

Exploring By Car & Foot

No, you can't take your car into the caves, but it won't be totally useless, either. For a close-up as well as panoramic view of the Chihuahuan Desert, head out on the **Walnut Canyon Desert Drive,** a 9.5-mile loop. You'll want to drive slowly on the one-way gravel road, both for safety and to appreciate thoroughly the dramatic scenery. Passenger cars can easily handle the tight turns and narrow passage, but the road is not recommended for motor homes or cars pulling trailers. Pick up an interpretive brochure for the drive at the visitor center, and allow about 1 hour.

HIKING Most of the hiking here is done underground, but there are opportunities on the earth's surface as well. The park's busiest trail is the **Nature Trail** ★, a fairly easy, 1-mile paved loop that begins just outside the visitor center and has interpretive signs describing the various desert plants. About a half-dozen other trails wander through the park's 30,000 acres of wilderness. Again, info will be at the information center.

Other Caving Tours

It takes some hiking to reach the other caves in the park, so carry drinking water, especially on hot summer days. Tours are popular and are frequently fully booked; call a few months ahead for reservations.

Slaughter Canyon Cave ★★★ Discovered in 1937, this cave was commercially mined for bat guano (used as fertilizer) until the 1950s. It consists of a corridor 1,140 feet long with many side passageways. The tour lasts about 5 hours, plus another half-hour to hike up the steep trail to the cave entrance. No crawling is involved, although the smooth flowstone and old bat guano on the floor can be slippery. You'll see wonderful cave formations, including the crystal-decorated Christmas Tree, the 89-foot-high Monarch, and the menacing Klansman. Children must be at least 8. Participants must take strong flashlights with fresh batteries, drinking water, and good hiking boots. 1.25 miles RT (plus .5-mile hike to and from cave entrance). Moderate. Access: Meet at the visitor center and carpool to the cave entrance.

Spider Cave ★★ Very strenuous, this tour is for those who want to experience a rugged caving adventure, as well as some great underground scenery. Highlights include climbing down a 15-foot ladder, squeezing through tight passageways, and climbing on slippery surfaces—all this after a steep half-mile hike to the cave entrance. But it's worth it. The cave has numerous beautiful formations—most much smaller than those in the Big Room—and picturesque pools of water. Allow 4 hours. Participants must be at least 12, you will need four AA batteries for the provided headlamps and should have good hiking boots, kneepads, gloves, long pants, and water. 1-mile loop (plus .5-mile hike to and from cave). Strenuous. Access: Visitor center; follow ranger to cave.

> **Bat Talks**
>
> In addition to cave tours, rangers give a **sunset bat talk** each evening from mid-May through mid-October at the Bat Flight Amphitheater at the cavern's Natural Entrance. Rangers also offer other programs on various subjects, including a night sky program with provided telescopes. Check at the visitor center for the current schedule.

WHERE TO STAY

There are no accommodations within the park. Although the closest lodging to the national park is in White's City, which has a **Rodeway Inn** (www.rodewayinn.com), we recommend that you stay in the city of Carlsbad, which offers more and better lodging and dining choices. In addition to the Trinity Hotel (see below), options in Carlsbad include the usual chain motels, including the **Best Western Stevens Inn ★** (www.bestwestern.com), with discounted rates of $130 to $140 double; the **Days Inn** (www.daysinn.com), where you'll pay about $125 double; **Econolodge** (www.econolodge.com), where you'll pay $75 to $80 double; and **Motel 6** (www.motel6.com), with rates for two of about $60. These and several other motels are on the main road through town, Canal Street, which becomes National Parks Highway as it heads south to the caverns. Check their websites for more information.

The Trinity Hotel ★★ This boutique hotel is a class act, and as far as we're concerned the only lodging in Carlsbad that is more than just a place to sleep. The handsome brick building was constructed in 1892 as the First National Bank, and over the years served various purposes. It had fallen into disrepair and demolition was being considered when in 2007 three local businessmen began a 2-year project to restore the structure and convert it to a small upscale hotel and restaurant. The result was this genuinely historic building that houses a boutique hotel with all the latest amenities and one of the best restaurants in southern New Mexico. It's decorated in the style of the late 1800s, with dark wood, light walls, and period-style furnishings, but also boasts queen- and king-sized beds, large bathrooms—some with whirlpool tubs and others with glassed-in showers—flat-screen TVs, and of course, iPod docking stations. *Note:* There are only two rooms on the ground floor and access to the seven second-floor units is by stairs only.

201 S. Canal St., at the corner of Fox St. ℂ **575/234-9891.** www.thetrinityhotel.com. 9 units. $169–$219 double. **Amenities:** Restaurant, free Wi-Fi.

CAMPING options

There are no developed campgrounds or vehicle camping of any kind inside the national park. Backcountry camping, however, is permitted in some areas. Pick up free permits at the visitor center.

NEAR THE PARK

The best campground in the area is the **Carlsbad KOA ★★**, 2 Manthei Road (✆ **800/562-9109** or 575-457-2000; www.carlsbadkoa.com), just off U.S. 285. But why did they have to put it 15 miles north of the city of Carlsbad, when we all want to go to the caverns, which is south of the city? No matter, the KOA is worth the drive. This top-rated RV park is nicely landscaped with grass and trees and boasts large (40 × 75-ft.) sites that can accommodate the really big rigs with slideouts. All RV sites have full hookups, including cable TV and Wi-Fi, and there is an outdoor heated pool, playground, coin-op laundry, and fenced pet park where dogs can be off-leash. Some tent sites have water and electric available, and there are two meticulously maintained bathhouses. It has 132 sites, is open year-round, and has rates of $27 to $64.

A good choice for those looking for more rugged camping is **Brantley Lake State Park ★**, 33 E. Brantley Lake Rd.

(✆ **575/457-2384;** www.nmparks.com). Located 14 miles north of the city of Carlsbad (take U.S. 285, then north-east on Eddy C.R. 30), this quiet and relaxing park is just under 40 miles from the Carlsbad Caverns Visitor Center. Activities include boating, swimming, and fishing on the 3,000-acre lake, as well as bird watching. There are 51 developed RV campsites (48 with water and electric hookups, three that also have sewer), plus prim-itive camping along the lake. Primitive camping costs $8; developed sites cost $14 to $18.

The closest camping to the national park that we recommend is **Carlsbad RV Park & Campground ★**, 4301 National Parks Hwy., Carlsbad, NM 88220 (✆ **888/878-7275** or 575/885-6333; www.carlsbadrvpark.com). This tree-filled campground on the southern edge of the city of Carlsbad offers pull-through sites large enough to accommodate big rigs, plus tent sites and sites for every-thing in between. All sites have free Wi-Fi. There are clean bathhouses, an indoor heated pool, game room, play-ground, and fenced pet areas. Rates are $23 to $41.

WHERE TO EAT
Inside the Park

The only eateries in the park are two not-very-enticing concessionaire-operated restau-rants, whose hours coincide with visitor center and cave hours. A cafeteria-style res-taurant at the **visitor center** serves three fast-food meals daily, with an emphasis on Mexican food and prices from $5 to $9. The **Underground Rest Area,** inside the cavern 750 feet belowground, has a snack bar that offers a limited menu of mostly pre-packaged items in the $4-to-$8 range.

Near the Park

The best area dining is in the city of Carlsbad, and you'll find most of it along Canal Street, the city's main drag. A lot of the restaurants here are Mom and Pop places, and we guess they want some time off, so check days and hours as quite a few restaurants are closed weekends or at least Sundays. In addition to the restaurants discussed below, we like **The Flume** ★ in the Best Western Hotel Stevens, 1829 S. Canal St. (© **575/887-2851**), where you'll find a good selection of American favorites with prices mostly from $8 to $24. It serves three meals Monday through Saturday, and Sunday until 2pm, and offers a good breakfast buffet 6 to 9am daily.

> ### Picnic & Camping Supplies
>
> You'll find a good variety of stores in the city of Carlsbad, including a 24-hour **Walmart Supercenter**, 2401 S. Canal St. (© **575/885-0727**; www.walmart.com).

Trinity Hotel Restaurant ★★★ AMERICAN/ITALIAN   Quietly elegant as well as comfortable and inviting, this is the best restaurant in Carlsbad. It's located in an historic building, constructed as a bank in 1892 and now an excellent hotel (see "Where to Stay," above). There's lots of wood, large windows, and dazzling chandeliers, and the service is friendly and efficient. The dinner menu includes plenty of pasta—from hearty beef lasagna to chicken marsala (our favorite)—to an excellent grilled Norwegian salmon and equally delicious black Angus filet mignon. The lunch menu offers top sirloin burgers, sandwiches, grilled salmon, and salads.

At the Trinity Hotel, 201 S. Canal St., Carlsbad. © **575/234-9891.** www.trinityhotel.com. Main courses $8–$12 lunch, $10–$34 dinner. Mon–Sat 7am–2pm; 5–9pm.

Pecos River Cafe ★ AMERICAN   Want to rub elbows with the locals? Pecos River Cafe is the place. A very busy, noisy diner, this breakfast and lunch joint has a simple décor—rough white plaster walls, wood trim, large windows, booths along the walls and tables in the middle of the room. The menu includes the usual breakfast offerings of eggs, pancakes, French toast, plus a few really good but spicy Mexican items, such as the Burrito Pronto (an egg, bacon, and potato burrito, smothered in green or red chile—we like green). At lunch you can get sandwiches, burgers, burritos, and tacos. *Tip:* The breakfasts are great and you can get them anytime, but they cost an extra $1 after 11am.

409 S. Canal St., Carlsbad. © **575/887-8882.** Most items $5–$10. Mon–Fri 6am–2pm.

NEARBY ATTRACTIONS

Many visitors to Carlsbad Caverns also spend time at nearby **Guadalupe Mountains National Park** (www.nps.gov/gumo), 55 miles south of the city of Carlsbad just over the border into Texas. This is a hikers' paradise of rugged wilderness where you'll find the tallest peak in Texas, numerous hiking trails, panoramic vistas, and the famed McKittrick Canyon, an oasis known for its brilliant fall colors produced by maples, oaks, and other hardwoods.

We also recommend spending a few hours at **Living Desert Zoo & Gardens State Park,** located on the northwest edge of the city of Carlsbad off U.S. 285 (© **575/887-5516;** www.nmparks.com), where you'll get a close-up look at the plants and animals of the Chihuahuan Desert. Admission costs $5 adults, $3 children 7 to 12, and is free for children under 7. The park is open 8am to 5pm from Memorial Day to Labor Day and 9am to 5pm the rest of the year, although the last entry into the zoo is 3:30pm year-round.

OLYMPIC

by Eric Peterson

G et ready for sensory overload. Olympic National Park is an area of such variety in climate and terrain that it's hard to believe it's just one park. Here you can view white, chilled alpine glaciers; wander through a green, sopping-wet rainforest; or soothe your muscles with a soak in a hot springs pool. Or perhaps you'd prefer to ponder the setting sun from the sandy Pacific coastline, or disappear from the outside world altogether in the deep green forests of largely untouched mountains.

In the Olympic Mountains, remnants survive of 20,000-year-old glaciers that continue to grind and sculpt the mountains now as they did then, albeit on a smaller scale—the glaciers have been shrinking rapidly in the past half-century. Farther down in some of the peninsula's west-facing valleys are some of the best remaining examples of temperate rainforests in the contiguous United States. In addition, Olympic National Park contains one of the longest stretches of uninterrupted coastal wilderness in the country, 73 miles in all.

Water is serious business here. Precipitation in the peninsula's rainforests is measured in feet, not inches, with some areas receiving over 12 feet each year. Contrast this with some parts of the drier northeastern section of the peninsula, which receive a comparatively paltry 15 to 20 inches on average. Again, variety is the rule. If the crystalline, jade waters of the glacier-fed lakes feel a little too cold for comfort, you have the opportunity to warm your bones in hot springs in the northern section of the park.

Despite its inherent ruggedness, rainy, and mysterious nature, the interior of the park has long been known to native peoples, as well as white settlers since the mid- to late 1800s. Unbridled curiosity and the inevitable desire for timber, mineral, and tourism dollars played a part in its recent exploration. Homesteads had been established by westward-moving pioneers on the periphery of the peninsula as early as the mid-1800s. However, the first documented exploration of the interior by white settlers didn't occur until 1885, and it was no easy feat. One group of explorers spent a grueling month hacking through dense brush to get from Port Angeles to Hurricane Ridge. Today the trip takes about an hour by car.

In 1909, just before leaving office, President Theodore Roosevelt, an avid hunter, established Mount Olympus National Monument. It was set aside to preserve the summer range and breeding grounds of dwindling herds of Roosevelt elk (flatteringly named for the president himself in a brilliant piece of prelegislative public relations). In 1938, President Franklin Roosevelt signed the bill that turned the national monument into a national park, and in 1953 the coastal strip was added. In 1981, the park was declared a World Heritage Park, and in 1988, 95% of the 922,000-acre park was designated a wilderness area.

FLORA & FAUNA

By a fortunate stroke of planning or a fortunate lack of money, no roads divide the interior of the park. Consequently, large sanctuaries exist here for **elk, deer, eagles, bear, cougars,** and other inhabitants and visitors to its interior. There are numerous species of **marine mammals** and **fish** who inhabit the coastal waters here, and numerous tidepools on the beaches teeming with crabs, starfish, and other life.

The plant life of Olympic is just as impressive. Many of the largest trees for their species are here—such as **the world's largest silver fir.** There are a wide range of **mosses, ferns,** and **flowering plants** in the forests as well.

ESSENTIALS

Getting There & Gateways

The main travel artery for all visitors to Olympic National Park is **U.S. 101.** This northernmost point of the famous coastal highway encircles and only briefly enters the park. Most of the traffic into and out of the park is on the northeastern side, from Vancouver and Seattle.

If you're departing from **Seattle,** you can take either of the ferries that run regularly every day from the same downtown Seattle dock. No reservations are available for most of the ferries, which cost about $10 to $15 one-way for a standard passenger vehicle. The **Seattle–Bainbridge Island Ferry** takes you for a half-hour ride across the Puget Sound before arriving in Bainbridge Island. From there, take Wash. 305 north through Poulsbo to the Hood Canal floating bridge, and then Wash. 104 across to U.S. 101. The **Seattle–Bremerton Ferry** arrives in Bremerton after a 60-minute ride. From Bremerton, take Wash. 3 north to the Hood Canal floating bridge. The **Edmonds–Kingston Ferry** is a 30-minute ride to Kingston, where you take Wash. 104 24 miles to U.S. 101. In addition, the **Coupeville Ferry** shuttles between Whidbey Island and Port Townsend, but it's smaller and runs less frequently; reservations, available for this ferry only, are recommended.

For all ferry **schedules and rates,** contact **Washington State Ferries (© 888/808-7977** or 206/464-6400 local and out of state; www.wsdot.wa.gov/ferries).

If you'd rather drive your car over dry land only, head west from **Tacoma** on Wash. 16 over the Tacoma Narrows Bridge, which connects with the eastern shore of the Kitsap Peninsula just south of Gig Harbor. Drive north on Wash. 16 to Port Orchard and Bremerton. From Bremerton, take Wash. 3 to the Hood Canal floating bridge and across to U.S. 101.

To reach the park from the south, take I-5 to **Olympia,** where you can connect with U.S. 101 North, or with Wash. 8 West to the other side of the U.S. 101 loop, to enter the Pacific Ocean section of the park.

THE NEAREST AIRPORT   Seattle–Tacoma International Airport (© **206/787-5388;** www.portseattle.org/seatac) is 15 miles south of Seattle on I-5. It's served by most major airlines and car-rental companies.

Visitor Centers & Information

There are three visitor centers in the park, offering exhibits, maps, guides, and information. Smaller ranger and information stations at popular trail heads are open only in summer. For pre-trip info, contact **Olympic National Park (© 360/565-3130,** or 360/565-3131 for a road and weather hotline; www.nps.gov/olym).

Olympic National Park

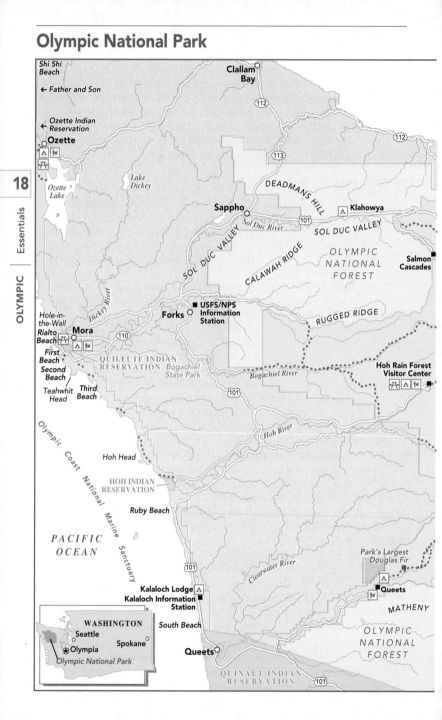

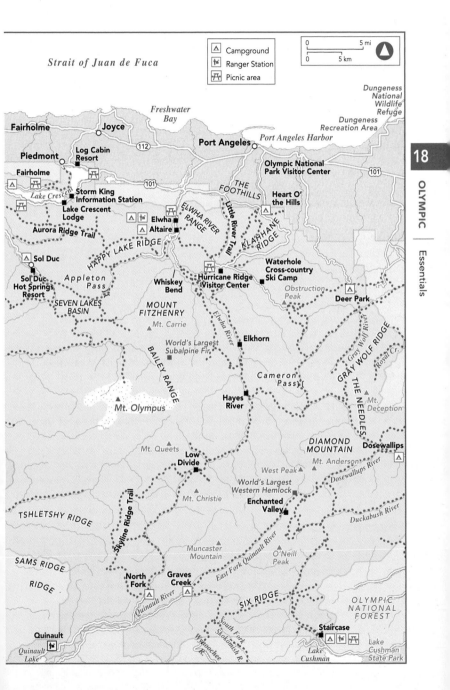

Strait of Juan de Fuca

Freshwater
Bay

Dungeness
National
Wildlife
Refuge

Dungeness
Recreation
Area

Fairholme

Joyce

Port Angeles

Port Angeles Harbor

Piedmont

Log Cabin
Resort

Olympic National
Park Visitor Center

Fairholme

Lake Crescent

Storm King
Information Station

THE
FOOTHILLS

Heart O'
the Hills

Lake Crescent
Lodge

Elwha

ELWHA RIVER RANGE

Little River Trail

Altaire

Aurora Ridge Trail

HAPPY LAKE RIDGE

KLAHHANE RIDGE

Sol Duc

Appleton
Pass

Whiskey
Bend

Hurricane Ridge
Visitor Center

Waterhole
Cross-country
Ski Camp

Sol Duc
Hot Springs
Resort

SEVEN LAKES
BASIN

MOUNT
FITZHENRY

Obstruction
Peak

Deer Park

Mt. Carrie

Elkhorn

Gray Wolf River

GRAY WOLF RIDGE

Royal Cr.

World's Largest
Subalpine Fir

BAILEY RANGE

Cameron
Pass

THE NEEDLES

Mt.
Deception

Mt. Olympus

Hayes
River

Mt. Queets

Low
Divide

West Peak

DIAMOND
MOUNTAIN

Mt. Anderson

Dosewallips

Dosewallips River

Skyline Ridge Trail

Mt. Christie

World's Largest
Western Hemlock

Enchanted
Valley

Duckabush River

TSHLETSHY RIDGE

SAMS RIDGE

RIDGE

Muncaster
Mountain

East Fork Quinault River

O'Neill
Peak

North
Fork

Graves
Creek

SIX RIDGE

OLYMPIC
NATIONAL
FOREST

Quinault River

South Fork Skokomish R.

Staircase

Lake
Cushman
State Park

Quinault

Quinault
Lake

Wynoochee R.

Lake
Cushman

Campground
Ranger Station
Picnic area

0   5 mi
0   5 km

AVOIDING the crowds

Avoiding the crowds in Olympic National Park is not as simple as you may think. With easy access from both Seattle and Victoria, BC, the park is a magnet for visitors from around the world.

The easiest solution is to go in the off season, especially in the fall. **September** is a great time to visit for the fall colors and visible wildlife. However, starting in mid-October, the west side of the park is often deluged with rain.

You might also try driving in from the southwest via Aberdeen. If you choose this route, you can see everything the peninsula offers in a nutshell. Instead of going to the Hoh, try the less visited **Queets Rain Forest.**

If you absolutely have to come in the summer and don't want to miss the most popular views, such as those on **Hurricane Ridge,** try heading up in the late afternoon when everyone else is on his or her way down.

The **Olympic National Park Visitor Center** (© 360/565-3130), on the northern end of the park near Port Angeles, is a good jumping-off station before heading into the northwest part of the park. It's a 45-minute drive from there to one of the most popular spots in the park, the **Hurricane Ridge Visitor Center,** where you'll find beautiful views of the Olympic Mountains and alpine meadows blooming with wildflowers each summer. It also has a snack bar, interpretive exhibits, and trails.

The **Hoh Rain Forest Visitor Center,** on the west side of the main part of the park, is some 15 miles off a turnoff from U.S. 101. This is an excellent spot for those who want to experience a temperate rainforest without spending a couple of days hiking in the elements. There are several interpretive trails and the beautiful **Hall of Mosses** nearby, as well as longer trails into the heart of the rainforest.

Smaller centers include the **Storm King Information Station,** on Lake Crescent in the northern section of the park, and the **Kalaloch Information Station,** on the western coastal section of the park. You can get food and some supplies near the **Sol Duc Ranger Station** at the Sol Duc Hot Springs Resort.

Fees & Permits

Entrance to the park for up to a week costs $15 per vehicle, or $5 per individual on foot, bicycle, or motorcycle. Camping in the park campgrounds costs $10 to $18 a night. Wilderness camping costs $5 plus $2 per person per night.

Seasons & Climate

The climate of the entire peninsula is best described as varied, of the marine type. In the winter, the temperatures stay in the 30s and 40s (single digits Celsius) during the day, and 20s and 30s (negative single digits Celsius) at night. The lower elevations, near the water, rarely receive more than 6 inches of accumulated snow per season, and it melts quickly. However, on the upper slopes, the snowfall can become quite heavy.

Spring is the late half of the rainy season, mostly wet, mild, and windy. Temperatures range from 35° to 60°F (2°–16°C), with lingering snow flurries in the mountains.

Summer temperatures range from a low of 45°F (7°C) in the evening to 75°F (24°C) and up to 80°F (27°C) or higher during the afternoons. In the latter half of the summer and early fall, fog and cloud banks often drift into the valleys and remain until midday, burn off, and sometimes return in the evening. Thunderstorms may occur in the evening in the upper elevations.

The fall is moderately cold and blustery; it ushers in the rainy season, which usually begins in mid- to late October. Snow begins to fall in the mountains as soon as early autumn. Temperatures range from 30° to 65°F (–1° to 18°C).

Rainfall varies throughout the Olympic Peninsula, but about three-quarters of the precipitation falls during the 6-month period from October through March, primarily on the Pacific side of the peninsula.

EXPLORING THE PARK BY CAR
The Rainforests & the Coast

If the rainforests are your destination, your best bet is to drive west and north from Olympia (or, if you're coming from Seattle on a ferry, west and south from Port Angeles or Port Townsend) along the western side of the peninsula. The first opportunity to see a bit of the rainforest is near the north shore of **Lake Quinault,** at the southern end of the main part of the park. If you plan to stay the night, this area has a number of lodges, motels, and campgrounds. From the ranger station on the south shore, there are several interpretive hikes along the lake; those who want to delve into the rainforest should start on the north side of the lake. The view of the mountains from Lake Quinault is quite spectacular on a sunny day, but the area serves as a good hors d'oeuvre more than anything else.

Drive north on U.S. 101. You should be able to get to the **Queets River Valley** if the road is open (it washes out frequently); the valley is home to some of the most beautiful (and remote) rainforests on the peninsula. Or you can keep driving northwest on U.S. 101 to the **Kalaloch Information Station,** where you can enjoy views of the Pacific from Kalaloch to Ruby Beach. Of the two options, it's a tough call. You might get to see elk in some of the former homestead meadows in the early morning or late afternoon on the 3-mile **Sams River Loop Trail** in the Queets, but understand that it's the least accessible of the rainforests. Watch for seasonal closures during the winter and late fall.

After leaving the coastal area at Ruby Beach, continue your northward drive on U.S. 101 to the turnoff for the **Hoh Rain Forest Visitor Center.** It's a 19-mile drive from U.S. 101 to the center, with excellent views of the Hoh River along the way. You could also spend a day (or more) hiking on the **Hoh River Trail**—it is 9 miles up to the **Olympus Guard Station** and 17 miles to the **Mount Olympus summit.** In just a few hours, this hike goes from temperate rainforest to alpine meadows with stunning views of Mount Olympus. If you're not feeling so ambitious, take the short **Hall of Mosses** or **Spruce Nature trail,** and get ready to head north again, to Sol Duc.

The last leg of our excursion takes you to one of the most commercially developed areas in the park, **Sol Duc** and the **Sol Duc Hot Springs Resort.** It might be a nice idea, before you head back down the coast to Olympia, or to sleep in your campsite or hotel room, to have a dip in these famous hot springs (open from late spring to early fall). The hot springs experience costs $12.25 to enter ($9.25 for kids); packages, including a sauna and a massage, are available. There's a resort here, and the springs can be crowded. Still, if you're into a relaxing soak after a long day of hiking, it may be just the thing.

The area has more than hot springs. Try taking the 1.5-mile round-trip hike from the springs through some wonderfully dense forest to **Sol Duc Falls.** Or take the **Mink Lake Trail** through 2.5 miles of uphill grade and forest to get a look at one of the many higher-altitude lakes that dot the Sol Duc region.

Wilderness use permits, available at the Wilderness Information Center (just behind the main visitor center in Port Angeles) and at all ranger stations, are required for overnight stays in the back-country. During the summer, you may also need reservations for certain areas. Call the **Wilderness Information Center**

((✆ **360/565-3100**) for details.

When hiking, be prepared for sudden and extreme weather. Also, in October 2010, a hiker was killed by a mountain goat near Klahane Ridge—be sure to maintain a safe distance if you encounter any wildlife.

The East Side of the Park

Seen the rainforests? You could do a lot worse than spending a day seeing the glaciers and the alpine meadows of the east side of the park. This time, the jumping-off point is probably **Port Angeles.** First, visit the **Olympic National Park Visitor Center,** to get acquainted with what you're about to see.

As in the rainforest tour, this trip starts with a choice: Head back through Port Angeles for the **Elwha/Altair area,** or from the visitor center to **Hurricane Ridge.** Either way, you're in for a variety of Olympic experiences.

The Elwha area has a small ranger station and, farther up the road, the site of Lake Mills, which is undergoing dam removal (the largest in U.S. history) until fall 2014, likely interfering with travel until the project is completed. Several trails will be closed for the duration of the project.

Along the way to Hurricane Ridge from Port Angeles, pass the **Heart O' the Hills Campground.** At Hurricane Ridge, one of the most popular spots in the park, there are a number of short interpretive trails, very good for seeing wildflowers during times of big blooms. Many larger trails intersect here as well. The visitor center has numerous interpretive exhibits and a snack bar.

Leaving Hurricane Ridge, Port Angeles, or the Elwha area, drive a little farther southeast. Off a turnoff from U.S. 101 is the less crowded **Deer Park Ranger Station,** where you get the same sort of views as at Hurricane Ridge without jostling for position. The road to Deer Park is steep and graveled. It's not suitable for RVs and trailers, and be prepared to deal with steep inclines, turns, and potholes. The road is closed in winter.

Outside Olympic National Park, consider visiting other locations along U.S. 101, such as the community of **Dungeness** and **Sequim Bay State Park** on the northeastern tip of the peninsula, with their beautiful shorelines and views of the strait. As you travel farther south, the **Hood Canal** will appear on your left. There are numerous places here to see seals on the rocks, especially at **Seal Point.**

ORGANIZED TOURS & RANGER PROGRAMS

Olympic National Park offers a variety of programs, including **campfire talks** and **beach walks.** You'll find **rainforest tours** originating from the Hoh and Quinault ranger stations, **alpine wildflower walks** from the Hurricane Ridge area, and **waterfall walks** from the Storm King Ranger Station. Check the park newspaper, *The Bugler,* for a current schedule.

DAY HIKES

The park has a vast number of trails, and they all seem to connect somewhere. Consequently, it's possible to tie several trails together to create your own route. It's also easy to get lost—make sure to carry a map (and tide tables for coastal hikes), a compass, and water at all times. Maps are available at visitor centers.

The following is a partial, though representative, list of some of the many wonderful trails in the park. **Backcountry permits** are required for overnight trips. They're available at the **Wilderness Information Center,** behind the main visitor center in Port Angeles (*C* **360/565-3100**), and at all ranger stations. During the summer, you may also need reservations for certain areas. You'll pay a $5 fee for wilderness camping for groups of up to 12 people, plus $2 per person per night. Call the Wilderness Information Center for information.

Coastal Area

Cape Alava/Sand Point Loop ★★★   This loop begins with a stroll over a cedar-plank boardwalk through teeming coastal marsh and grasslands. (Careful! Boards are slippery when wet, which is most of the time.) The trail connects to its second leg on a wilderness beach strip of the Pacific shoreline, the westernmost point in the Lower 48. Camping is permitted on the beach, but it's a popular spot in the summer and reservations are required. Continue south 1 mile past the petroglyphs that can be seen from the rocks along the shore next to the high-tide line. Two miles south of this area, the trail connects to the Sand Point leg, which is an easy stroll back to the Ozette Ranger Station. A permit and reservation are required here. Call the Wilderness Information Center. 9 miles RT. Easy. Access: Ozette Ranger Station.

Sand Point to Rialto Beach ★★★   This is a coastline famous for its shipwrecks, the memorials of which dot the beach at many points, along with an abandoned mine. Other than that, there are few signs of human activity. Enjoy the sand and the mist, take in the forests that come down to land's end, and get ready for the storms that visit here regularly. Up to 20 miles one-way. Easy to strenuous. Access: Ozette Ranger Station from the north or Rialto Beach from the south.

Third Beach to Hoh River ★★   This trail is not a leisurely stroll. You'll do a bit of inland skirting along old oil company roads to avoid some of the more wicked headlands, and there are some sand ladders (contraptions constructed of cables and wooden slats) just beyond Taylor Point. In addition, a slightly treacherous crossing is farther south at Goodman Creek. So what's the reward for the intrepid hiker? Toleak Point is 5 miles down the beach, where there is a sheltered campsite that's famous for its wildlife. The entire area is well known for its shipwrecks, wildlife, coastal headlands, and sea stacks (vertical rock formations just off the coast). The trail ends at Oil City, north of the Hoh Indian Reservation. 17 miles one-way. Moderate to strenuous. Access: Third Beach parking area, 3 miles beyond La Push Rd. left fork.

Western Parklands & Rainforests

Bogachiel River ★★★   This hike, an equally beautiful cousin to the often-crowded Hoh River Trail, is as long or short as you want to make it. The beginning, outside of the national park boundary, has been harvested, but once you enter Olympic proper, you'll enter a rainforest extravaganza—huge Douglas firs, spruce, cedar, and big-leaf maples, including the world's largest silver fir, some 8 miles from the trailhead. Approximately 6 miles into the trail is the Bogachiel Shelter, and 8 miles in is

Flapjack Camp, both good backcountry campsites. This is pretty much the end of the flatland; farther up, the trail begins to get steep. Length varies. Easy to moderate in the lowlands, more strenuous farther inland. Access: 5 miles south of Forks, turn left across from Bogachiel State Park onto Undie Rd., and continue 5 miles to the trail head.

Hoh River Valley ★★★   This is one of the most heavily traveled trails in the park, at least in the lower elevations, and it won't take you long to figure out why. Huge Sitka spruces, hung with moss, shelter the Roosevelt elk that wander among its lowlands. The first 13 miles, through the massive rainforests and tall grass meadows along the Hoh River Valley bottomlands, are relatively flat. The number of fellow walkers drops off after the first few miles. Happy Four Camp (6 miles in) and Olympus Guard Station (9 miles in) provide excellent camp or turnaround sites. The trail continues climbing east for the remaining 4 or 5 miles. You can eventually find yourself at the edge of the famous Blue Glacier on Mount Olympus, elevation 7,965 feet. Be careful. After July, hiking near the park's glaciers can be dangerous because of snowmelt. Up to 17 miles one-way. Easy to moderate in the lowlands, more strenuous farther inland. Access: Hoh Rain Forest Visitor Center.

Lake Quinault Loop ★★   Inside the Olympic National Forest, not the park, this trail is easily accessible, is well maintained, and offers beautiful views. Consequently, it's quite crowded in the summer. Elevation changes are gentle, making this an excellent walk for kids. The trail wanders about the shore of Lake Quinault, past historic Lake Quinault Lodge as well as the adjacent campgrounds and other lakeside attractions, before heading into its most popular section, the Big Tree Grove. Here you can wander among the huge trunks of 500-year-old Douglas firs. Watch for the interpretive signs. In addition, the Big Tree Grove is accessible on a 1-mile loop trail that originates from the Rain Forest Nature Trail parking lot. 4 miles RT. Easy. Access: Trail heads at various spots along the loop, including South Shore Rd., Quinault Lodge, Willaby Campground, Quinault Ranger Station, and Falls Creek Campground. All access originates from south shore of Lake Quinault.

North Fork of the Quinault ★★   The North Fork Trail could conceivably take you 47 miles, all the way through the park to the Elwha Valley on the north side—if you make the right connections and are maniacal enough. The trail is relatively benign for the first dozen miles as it winds inward along the river toward its source near Mount Seattle. Wilderness camping areas are available at Wolf Bar (2.5 miles in), at Halfway House (5.3 miles in), and in a gorge in Elip Creek (6.5 miles in). Next, the trail climbs steeply toward Low Divide, Lake Mary, and Lake Margaret, where you can get beautiful views of Mount Seattle, at an elevation of 6,246 feet. Snow can remain at this elevation until midsummer, so be ready. There's a summer ranger station at Low Divide, and high-elevation campsites here as well. Up to 17 miles one-way. Moderate. Access: End of North Fork Rd.

Queets River Trail ★★   This is the trail for the serious rainforest and wilderness lover. Part of its appeal is that the average hiker must exert a bit of an effort to reach the trail's solitude and quietly majestic scenery. Within 50 yards of your car, you'll be crossing the Queets River—without a bridge. Even on this first of several trips across the river, the water can be treacherous. It's best to visit during the dry season in late summer. An option is to cross the Sams River to the right of the Queets, connecting and crossing the Queets River farther up. At 2.5 miles, gape at one of the largest Douglas firs in the park. After 5 miles of hiking through elk and giant fern territory, you'll arrive at Spruce Bottom, which is a common haunt for steelhead anglers and has several good campsites. The trail ends at Pelton Creek, where more campsites are available. Up to 16 miles one-way. Moderate to strenuous. Access: Queets River Campground.

Sam's River Loop Trail ★★ This short loop parallels both the Sams River and the Queets River, providing a view of some old homestead meadows, beautiful spruce trees, and perhaps an elk or two in the meadows in the evening. 2.8 miles RT. Easy to moderate. Access: Queets River Ranger Station.

Northern Park Regions

Elwha River Trails ★★★ The serious backpacker arranges a pickup car at the Dosewallips or North Fork trail heads and heads for a week or so along the trail that was blazed by the famed 1889 Press Expedition, the first Anglo excursion across the Olympic Mountains. For a good distance, the trail follows the blue-green of the Elwha River to its source on the sometimes snow-slushy peak at Low Divide (elev. 3,600 ft.), which is also the head of the Quinault River. You can follow the trail downhill to the North Fork of the Quinault.

What can you expect on such a monumental trip? Old-growth forests, moist valley flatlands, and gently sloping hills appear around you as you explore the Elwha Valley before you begin your ascent toward the sometimes calf-busting Low Divide. Roosevelt elk, black bears, mountain lions, marmots, or a grouse or two might show up. At Low Divide, you're treated to spectacular views of Mount Seattle to the north and Mount Christie to the south. From here, you begin your descent from alpine heights to the rainforests along the Quinault.

As with any overnight wilderness trip, be sure to check in at the park's **Wilderness Information Center** (© **360/565-3100**) beforehand. Also, the Elwha River restoration will entail some road closures through September of 2014 or beyond. Up to 50 miles one-way. Difficulty varies. Access: Drive just beyond Elwha Ranger Station to Whiskey Bend Rd. Go past Glines Canyon Dam, 1.5 miles up the road. At road's end is Whiskey Bend trail head, just beyond Upper Lake Mills trail head.

Geyser Valley Loop ★★ From the Whiskey Bend trail head, hike down the trail to the Eagles Nest Overlook for a view of the meadows that stretch from valley to valley. You may see an elk or black bear if you're lucky. Head back to the trail and proceed a half-mile to the Rica Canyon Trail for a view of Goblin's Gate, a rock formation in the Canyon Gorge that might look like a bunch of goblins' heads staring at you, if you stare back hard enough. The trail to Goblin's Gate drops 325 feet on the half-mile walk to the viewing area. At this point, you can follow a riverside trail for another half-mile to some prime fishing spots, or continue to the Krause Bottom and Humes Ranch area; you can get a glimpse into the park's homesteading history. At any one of these points, you can return to the Whiskey Bend Trail or continue northeast past Michael's Cabin, another old homestead. 6 miles RT. Moderate. Access: Whiskey Bend Rd.

Marymere Falls ★★★ This is one of the most popular hikes in the park. It's well maintained, sits close to U.S. 101, and has a definite goal: beautiful Marymere Falls. It's a popular trail for kids, but the littlest ones will have trouble with the steep ascent to the viewing platform. Start out on the Barnes Creek Trail, which leads .7 mile through beautiful maples and conifers to the Marymere Trail turnoff. Continue up to the falls, where silvery water drops from a moss-covered outcropping some 100 feet to the basin below. 1.8 miles RT. Easy. Access: Storm King Ranger Station.

North Fork of the Sol Duc ★★ On this trail, you climb the ridge between the main and north forks of the river before descending into the North Fork Valley. The trail passes through old-growth forests before arriving at the deep-green pools of the river. The curious can venture upriver for several more miles. 2.4 miles RT. Moderate. Access: North Fork trail head, 3.75 miles down Sol Duc Rd. away from the resort.

Sol Duc Falls ★★★   One of the more popular spots on the peninsula, Sol Duc Falls is viewed from a bridge that spans the canyon just below the falls. On the way, check out the huge hemlocks and Douglas firs, some of which are 300 years old. This trail is wide, graveled, and level, making it great for kids. 1.7 miles RT. Easy. Access: Sol Duc Ranger Station.

Spruce Railroad ★★   This is the trail you want to take for a leisurely stroll on a hot summer afternoon. The flat, wide trail wanders around the unbelievably blue-green waters of Lake Crescent, along an old stretch of abandoned railroad, with excellent views of Mount Storm King. There are two abandoned railroad tunnels (don't go in!) and a much-photographed arch bridge at Devil's Punchbowl. 8 miles RT. Easy. Access: End of North Shore Rd. along Lake Crescent, or from east end near Log Cabin Resort.

Hurricane Ridge Area

Cirque Rim Trail & Big Meadow Loops ★★   These trails provide a wonderful little taste of subalpine meadows, deer, and the summer displays of wildflowers, along with excellent views of Port Angeles, the Strait of Juan de Fuca, and the Olympic Mountains. .5 mile and .25 mile RT. Easy. Access: Hurricane Ridge Visitor Center parking lot.

Grand Ridge (Obstruction Point to Green Mountain) ★★   This is the highest section of trail in the park, a fact you might notice as you gaze out to Victoria, BC, and the Strait of Juan de Fuca to the north, or to the south, toward the Grand Valley with its string of lakes and the numerous snow-clad peaks of the Olympic interior. There is a shortage of both trees and water on this hike. From the parking lot, follow the trail to the left. (The right goes to Grand Valley.) In 2 miles you'll find yourself at the breathtaking top of Elk Mountain. Over the next 5.5 miles, you will pass through Roaring Winds Camp (not misnamed) on your way up to Maiden Peak. This is a good turnaround point, unless you want to descend to Deer Park. 11 miles RT. Moderate. Access: From Hurricane Ridge, turn right onto dirt road to Obstruction Point, and continue 8.5 miles to end of road.

High Ridge, Alpine Hill to Klahhane Ridge ★★★   You can take the short, paved 1-mile High Ridge Route (which is chock-full of interpretive exhibits) and then return to the parking lot. Or you can proceed along the unpaved portion to Sunrise Ridge, a rocky little backbone of a view point off the High Ridge Trail, providing excellent panoramas of the Olympic Mountains, the Strait of Juan de Fuca, Port Angeles, and numerous beautiful alpine glaciers and wildflowers. The rest of the 3.3-mile, somewhat strenuous walk climbs to the top of Klahhane Ridge. As numerous signs warn, do not feed or approach the deer and marmots here. 1–8 miles RT. Easy to moderate. Access: Hurricane Ridge Visitor Center.

Hurricane Hill ★★   This is a popular trail in the summertime. The broad, paved trail climbs along an abandoned work road up to brilliant alpine meadows, with fantastic views of the Strait of Juan de Fuca and Port Angeles to the north and glacier-crowned Mount Olympus to the south. 3.2 miles RT. Moderate. Access: 1.5 miles from Hurricane Ridge Visitor Center.

Eastern & Southeastern Section

Note: At press time, Dosewallips Road was washed out and no timeline was set for repair (the U.S. Forest Service has prepared a **Draft Environmental Impact Statement** to address the future of this road, but it doesn't look like the road will be rebuilt or reopened any time soon). Hikers and stock can still explore the area, but the new trek to the trail head adds about 5.5 miles (one-way) to the hikes below. The bright side? Fewer people venture here with the closure, so solitude is easy to find.

Main Fork Dosewallips/Constance Pass ★★   Take the Main Fork Dosewallips to the north, and you'll find yourself on a moderate climb through old-growth forest for 7.5 miles before the trail flattens out at Constance Pass. Fields of wildflowers skirt the edge of Mount Constance. The trail ends in another 3.4 miles at Boulder Shelter in Olympic National Forest. You can also catch the Upper Big Quilcene Trail or the Upper Dungeness Trail here. 11 miles one-way. Moderate. Access: Dosewallips trail head.

Main Fork of the Dosewallips ★★   This is a versatile trail. You can catch a lot more of the inland trails from here, including Constance Pass Trail, the Gray Wolf Trail, and the Elwha River Trail. The Dosewallips side of the park sometimes seems like the neglected side—it's not as flashy as a glacial meadow or a rainforest. But the Dosewallips is one of the most beautiful rivers in the country, its jade-green water crashing down among narrow cliffs. And you might skirt some of the crowds. 31 miles RT. Moderate. Access: Dosewallips trail head.

OTHER SPORTS & ACTIVITIES

BIKING   Almost all trails in the park are closed to mountain bikes. The only exception is the **Spruce Railroad Trail,** which was once a railroad grade that ran along the shore of the lake. It is quite flat and easy for its 4-mile length; an additional 1.5-mile stretch of road extends past the North Shore Picnic Area. The highlight of the trail is a much-photographed arched bridge across a rocky cove. A few **dirt roads** for mountain bikers extend from paved roads; they include the section from Hurricane Ridge to Obstruction Peak.

For road bikers, U.S. 101 can be treacherous, with eager motorists rubbernecking and all. But if you get through that, you can find some pleasant rides on any of the roads that poke into the park.

KAYAKING & CANOEING   Although large and often windy, glacier-carved **Lake Crescent** is a beautiful place to do a little paddling. Lush, green forests rise straight up from the shores of the 624-foot-deep lake, giving the waters a fjordlike quality unmatched on the peninsula. Boat ramps are on U.S. 101 at Storm King (near the middle of the lake) and at Fairholme (at the west end of the lake). On East Beach Road, on the lake's northeast shore, there is a private boat ramp at the Log Cabin Resort.

If you launch at Storm King, you can explore around Barnes Point, away from U.S. 101 traffic noise (but in view of the Lake Crescent Lodge). From Fairholme, you can paddle along the north shore. From the Log Cabin Resort, you can explore the bay that feeds the Lyre River, the lake's outlet stream. When winds blow down this lake, as they often do, the waters can be dangerous for small boats.

Fairholm Store & Marina, at the west end of the lake (© **360/928-3020**), rents canoes, kayaks, and rowboats. Boats are also available for rent at the **Log Cabin Resort** (© **360/928-3325;** www.olympicnationalparks.com), on the lake's northeast shore (see p. 237).

Lake Ozette, surprisingly deep and nearly 10 miles long, is the third-largest natural lake in Washington and a fascinating place to explore by sea kayak or canoe. Only a mile from the Pacific Ocean, the lake is indented by numerous coves and bays, and surrounds three small islands. Campsites along the shore include the boat-in sites at Erickson's Bay.

The **Swan Bay boat launch,** one of two on the large lake, is probably the best choice for paddlers. For a leisurely half-day paddle, just explore the shores of the convoluted bay, in the middle of which is Garden Island. For a daylong trip, try paddling down the lake to Tivoli Island. For an overnighter, head to the lake's western shore and the campsites at Erickson's Bay. From here, you can explore up and down the west shore.

Both Lake Crescent and Lake Ozette are big lakes subject to quick changes of weather and wind. Whitecaps can come up suddenly, and cold waters can cause hypothermia. Check the weather forecast before leaving, and keep an eye on the sky.

SNOWSHOEING & CROSS-COUNTRY SKIING Any of the roads leading into the mountains will offer a satisfying winter trek; check with park rangers about avalanche hazards before you go. If you seek views, head to **Hurricane Ridge** with the rest of the winter crowd and set out on any of the area's trails. Rent skis and other gear in Port Angeles.

WHITE-WATER KAYAKING & RAFTING White-water rafting, scenic floats, and sea kayaking are options in and around Olympic National Park. Guided trips last approximately half a day. Canoe and kayak rentals are available from **Olympic Raft & Kayak,** 123 Lake Aldwell Rd., Port Angeles (✆ **360/452-1443;** www.raftandkayak.com); prices start at $50 per day. Rates for guided trips start at $54 for adults and $44 for kids 5 to 11. The company also offers classes.

WHERE TO STAY

Inside the Park

Kalaloch Lodge ★★ Located on the bluffs above the drop-dead gorgeous, tide-pool-rich beach of the same name, cedar-shingled Kalaloch Lodge is a picture-perfect lodging for Olympic visitors who want to get close to the coastal wilderness without sacrificing comfort. But plan your trip long before you go: Prime dates are sometimes sold out a year in advance. You have a wide choice of lodgings from comfortable, modern rooms in the main lodge and motel annex (a few with fireplaces, for you romantics, even more spacious suites, and an assortment of one- and two-bedroom cabins (try and get one directly on the bluff for the views). Décor is quaint and woodsy, with a subtle marine theme; some cabins have cooking facilities. This is also a place that almost forces guests to truly unplug (a good thing): The rooms lack phones, Wi-Fi, and there are TVs in only a pair of suites.

157151 U.S. 101, Forks. ✆ **866/662-9928.** www.thekalalochlodge.com. 64 units. Summer $132–$314 lodge or motel room double; $274–$338 suite; $162–$338 cabin. Lower rates rest of year. Pets accepted in cabins ($25 one-time fee). **Amenities:** 2 restaurants; bar.

Lake Crescent Lodge ★★ Since 1916, this classic national-park lodge on scenic Lake Crescent has been one of the most posh hostelries on the Olympic Peninsula. The property feels like a world unto itself, nestled in the trees along the south side of the lake, and it is a romantic destination that rivals the Kalaloch Lodge on the coast. The plush Roosevelt Cabins are my favorite here, with a lakeside location, fireplaces, and superlative views. In the lodge are the smallest and oldest rooms, sharing a communal bathroom, and good for travelers on a budget. There are also some simple one- and two-bedroom cottages and newer, larger rooms in a pair of two-story structures.

416 Lake Crescent Rd., Port Angeles. (C) **888/723-7127** or 360/928-3211. www.olympicparks.com $100–$120 double with shared bathroom; $165–$280 double with private bathroom; $230–$350 cabin or cottage. Closed Jan–Apr. Children 17 and under not accepted in main building. Pets accepted in cottages ($25 one-time fee). **Amenities:** Restaurant; bar; boat rentals.

Log Cabin Resort ★   Dating back to the 1890s, this longstanding cabin complex on the north shore of Lake Crescent is much less formal than Lake Crescent Lodge on the opposite shore, making it a better pick for families. The out-of-the-way location, off of the main park road is darn nice, and the ability to hike, boat, and eat without driving anywhere is another big plus. However, it is pretty rustic, and many of the 80-year-old cabins are showing their age. Some of the cabins have kitchens and bathrooms, and others share a communal bathhouse, and there are also lodge rooms and more upscale chalets, the nicest and largest units with waterfront locations and unobstructed mountain views. Onsite also: a small grocery store, laundry machines, and a campground with RV hookups.

3183 E. Beach Rd., Port Angeles. (C) **888/896-3818** or 360/928-3325. www.olympicnationalparks. com. 24 cabins, 8 with bathroom; 4 motel units; 2 chalet units. $60–$80 cabin for 2 without bathroom; $95–$125 cabin for 2 with bathroom; $120–$140 double lodge unit; $160–$200 chalet. Closed Nov–Mar. Pets accepted in cabins ($12 per pet). **Amenities:** Restaurant; boat rentals.

Sol Duc Hot Springs Resort ★★   Located south of Lake Crescent at the foot of the Olympic Mountains, this collection of cabins is one of my favorites in park boundaries. This is in large part due to the onsite hot springs pools (perfect for a soothing soak after a day on the trails), as well as a location that's much more remote than the other park lodges, near the end of the road in the Sol Duc Valley about 12 miles from busy U.S. 101. The location is ideal for day hikers, with trails emanating from a peaceful spot along the Sol Duc River leading to waterfalls and beyond, deep into the park's interior. Sleeping up to four guests, the cabins are relatively modern by national-park standards and many have kitchens, but the décor is spare and the furnishings are a bit dated. The exception is the deluxe three-bedroom River Suite, one of the nicest rooms in the park, with hardwood floors and much more style. The soaking pool is open to the public ($12.25 adults, $9.25 children 4–12, free for kids under 4); room rates include unlimited pool access for resort guests.

At the end of Sol Duc Rd., off U.S. 101. (C) **866/476-5382.** www.olympicnationalparks.com. 32 cabins. $163–$232 double; $412 suite. Rates include full breakfast and pool access. Closed late Sept to early Mar. Pets accepted ($25 one-time fee). **Amenities:** 2 restaurant; outdoor pool.

Near the Park

Red Lion Hotel Port Angeles ★★   Location, location, location—this full-service hotel in downtown Port Angeles has it. You are right on the ferry dock, downtown is steps away, and Hollywood Beach is just steps away from the door. The rooms are what you'd expect from a larger chain hotel, but with microwaves and fridges as nice extra amenities. In fact, there are far more amenities and comforts here than at any of the park lodges. This is a great base to recuperate for the night after a hiking-heavy excursion at Olympic National Park.

221 N. Lincoln St., Port Angeles. (C) **360/452-9215.** www.redlion.com/portangeles. 186 units. $129–$159 double; $239–$319 suite. Lower rates off season. **Amenities:** Outdoor pool; exercise room; free Wi-Fi.

CAMPING options

Many campgrounds here open seasonally, and their exact schedules are subject to change. But as a rule of thumb, campgrounds at higher elevations are often snow-covered (and closed) from early November to late June; seasonal campgrounds at lower elevations may open earlier. Camping in the park campgrounds costs $10 to $18 a night.

There are no showers or laundry facilities inside the park; the Log Cabin Resort, on the north shore of Lake Crescent at the northern edge of the park, has both.

NORTH- & EAST-SIDE CAMPGROUNDS

The six campgrounds on the northern edge of the park are some of the busiest in the park, due to their proximity to U.S. 101. **Deer Park ★★** is the easternmost of these campgrounds (to get there, take Deer Park Rd. from U.S. 101 east of Port Angeles); at 5,400 feet, it's also the only high-elevation campground in the park. The winding one-way gravel road to the campground will have you wondering how you're ever going to get back down the mountain. (RVs and trailers are prohibited.) Deer frequent the campground, and hiking trails head out from here.

Because of its proximity to Hurricane Ridge, **Heart O' the Hills ★★** is especially popular. It's on Hurricane Ridge Road, 5 miles south of the Olympic National Park Visitor Center. Several trails start at or near the campground.

Two campgrounds are on Olympic Hot Springs Road, up the Elwha River, which is popular with kayakers and anglers. **Elwha ★★** is the trail head for a trail leading up to Hurricane Ridge. **Altair ★★** has a boat ramp often used by rafters and kayakers. And, yes, there are undeveloped hot springs pools, just a 2.5-mile hike away, a very nice perk.

The only national park campground on Lake Crescent is **Fairholme ★**, at the west end of the lake. This campground is popular with power boaters and can be rather noisy. South of this area, nearby **Sol Duc ★** sits amid impressive stands of old-growth trees near the Sol Duc Hot Springs (and the resort there) and is one of just two park campgrounds that accept RVs. Not surprisingly, it is often crowded.

You'll find RV sites with full hookups at the **Log Cabin Resort ★** on the north shore of Lake Crescent ((C) **360/928-3325;** www.olympicnationalparks.com). Because there are no hookups at any of the national park campgrounds, this is a good choice for RVers.

In the Forks Area

Manitou Lodge Bed & Breakfast ★★ Touting itself as the westernmost B&B in the lower 48, the Manitou Lodge is my favorite lodging on the entire Olympic Peninsula. It doesn't feel quite like your typical inn, but instead has the vibe of a wilderness resort—apt for the setting. There are five colorful guestrooms in the main house and another two in a detached cottage (expect Native American art, not doilies and Victorian frills in all seven; the cottage rooms are notably woodsier). There is also a pair of dinky camping cabins (with bathrooms but no tubs or showers) and two pre-pitched tents for those who want to rough it without going too far. Breakfasts are in baskets in your room when you check in, and each unit has a fridge and microwave. You are just 3 miles from Rialto Beach, one of the park's best, and there are trails to other beaches accessible only by hiking just a few more miles away.

SOUTHEAST-SIDE CAMPGROUNDS

Along the Dosewallips River, you'll find the walk-in-only **Dosewallips Campground ★★** in a forested setting. The campground is a 5.5-mile hike from the road; a landslide closed the road for cars.

The remote **Staircase Campground ★★** is inland from the Hood Canal and is a good base for day hikes or as a starting point for a longer backpacking trip. It's up the Skokomish River from Lake Cushman on F.S. 24 and is the trail head for the Six Ridge, Flapjack Lakes, and Anderson Pass trails.

SOUTH- & SOUTHWEST-SIDE CAMPGROUNDS

If you want to say you've camped in the wettest rainforest in the Lower 48, head for **Hoh ★★★**, a busy campground near the Hoh Rain Forest Visitor Center, 31 miles from U.S. 101. Camping here means you wake up right in the middle of this fascinating ecosystem, rather than driving an hour to get here, and can hike the popular Hoh River Trail (see p. 229) first thing in the morning. If you just have one night to camp, pitch your tent here.

East of Lake Quinault, **North Fork ★★** and **Graves Creek ★★**, reached only by unpaved roads that are prone to washouts and not recommended for RVs, provide access to several long-distance hiking trails.

Queets ★★ is a beautiful and uncrowded rainforest setting that rivals the Hoh. The road often washes out; call for the latest information.

COASTAL CAMPGROUNDS

Along the peninsula's west side are several beach campgrounds. Busy **Kalaloch ★★★**, at the southernmost portion of the park's coastal strip, is the only Olympic National Park campground that accepts reservations, and only for the period from mid-June through early September (www.recreation.gov; ✆ **877/444-6777**).

Up the coast is **Mora ★★**, along the Quillayute River about 2 miles from beautiful Rialto Beach. About 3 miles in from the coast is the remote **Ozette ★★**, on the north shore of Lake Ozette. It's a good choice for kayakers and canoeists, as well as people wanting to day-hike to the beaches on either side of Cape Alava. Like Hoh, this campground is far from U.S. 101 (22 miles) and that means staying here gives you a head start on hikers driving in from other areas. This campground may be closed during periods of heavy rain because of flooding.

813 Kilmer Rd., about 10 miles northwest of Forks. ✆ **360/374-6295**. www.manitoulodge.com. 9 units. $99–$179 double; primitive cabins (May–Oct only) $65–$99 double; luxury campsite $49 double. Rates include full breakfast. Pets accepted in several units ($10 nightly fee). **Amenities:** Free Wi-Fi.

Quillayute River Resort ★   This small resort fronts the river of its name and is convenient to Rialto Beach and other Olympic park beaches. Each of the five two-story units is large, functional, and smacks of the 1950s, the decade the resort opened—but in a good way. Another plus: Every unit has a full kitchen and river views, and the property is 7 acres, so there is plenty of room to spread out.

473 Mora Rd., about 10 miles northwest of Forks. ✆ **360/374-7447**. www.qriverresort.com. 5 units. Mid-May to Sept $185 double; Oct to mid-May $115–$150 double. **Amenities:** Free Wi-Fi.

South of the Park

Lake Quinault Lodge ★★ Just outside the park on Lake Quinault, this stately lodge, on the southwesterly side of the park, is a great option for people looking for a high degree of civilization in an out-of-the-way setting. Originally built in 1926, Quinault offers guest quarters that sport a more contemporary look than its peers inside park boundaries, but subtly so, and many rooms have fireplaces. There are several more rustic units in the Boathouse annex, along with the most upscale suite on the premises, which occupies the entire second floor of the structure.

345 S. Shore Rd., Quinault. ✆ **800/562-6672** or 360/288-2900. www.olympicnationalparks.com. 91 units. Summer $119–$239 double, $284 suite. Lower winter rates. Pets accepted ($25 one-time fee). **Amenities:** Restaurant; bar; indoor pool; boat rentals; sauna; free Wi-Fi.

WHERE TO EAT

Inside the Park

Restaurant choices inside the park are slim. On the north side, on the shore of Lake Crescent, the dining room at **Lake Crescent Lodge** serves Continental and Northwestern cuisine with an emphasis on local seafood. Also along the lakeshore, the **Log Cabin Resort** offers a Northwestern menu, specializing in organic and natural fare. Both restaurants are open for the summer season only. On Lake Quinault, try the dining room at **Lake Quinault Lodge**. The restaurant at **Sol Duc Hot Springs Resort** is open for the summer season only. It offers traditional American breakfasts and Northwest cuisine at dinner. Also on the premises is a deli that serves lunch. The restaurant at the **Kalaloch Lodge** serves three meals a day year-round.

In Port Angeles

Bella Italia ★★ ITALIAN   For a nice dinner on your way in or out of the park, Bella Italia is a solid option in downtown Port Angeles. The cuisine is Italian, often prepared with local seafood, on a menu that ranges from sausage pizza to clam linguine. Vampire junkies take note: This was the place Edward took Bella on their first date in *Twilight*.

118 E. 1st St. ✆ **360/457-5442.** www.bellaitaliapa.com. Main courses $9–$32. Daily 4–10pm (until 9pm fall–spring). Closed major holidays.

SoHo Asian Bistro ★★ CHINESE/THAI   In a historic building on the Port Angeles waterfront, SoHo Asian Bistro boasts a long and varied menu and a choice of bar or table seating. Many entrees are Chinese and Thai standards, but the menu extends far beyond mere kung pao and pad thai. There are several dishes that incorporate local ingredients, like the Salmon Hot Mok with a Thai coconut-curry sauce, a personal favorite.

134 W. Front St. ✆ **360/417-8966.** www.sohoasianbistro.com. Main courses $9–$13 lunch, $10–$27 dinner. Daily 11am–9pm.

MOUNT RAINIER

by Eric Peterson

O n summer weekends, when "the mountain is out," as the
locals say, busloads of noisy tourists descend on Mount
Rainier, cameras at hand. But for anyone willing to expend
a little bit of energy to get away from the crowds, this mountain,
which dominates the Puget Sound and western Washington skyline
for miles, has many secrets to share: mountain goats and marmots,
streaming waterfalls, ominous walls of ice deep in the rainforest,
and thousand-year-old trees set against subalpine meadows teeming with summer wildflowers.

19

Should you visit on a wet, dreary October day, you may theorize that
Mount Rainier was named for the weather. In fact, Capt. George Vancouver
named it in 1792 for his friend Rear Adm. Peter Rainier (who never saw
it). The region's native people had been calling it Tahoma, or other variations, for centuries, however, and the name remains contentious to some to
this day.

Although the early pioneers saw most of the mountains in the West as
obstacles, 14,411-foot Mount Rainier so captivated the settlers that as early
as the 1850s, less than a decade after Seattle was founded, mountaineers
were heading for its snowcapped slopes. In 1857, an army lieutenant,
August Valentine Kautz, climbed to within 400 feet of the summit. In 1870,
Gen. Hazard Stevens and Philemon Van Trump made the first recorded
complete ascent. (Trapped near the summit at dark, they survived the night
huddled in ice caves formed by sulfurous steam vents, with the steam providing enough heat to keep them from freezing.) In 1884, James and Vir-
inda Longmire opened the mountain's first hotel, at a spot that now bears
their name. In 1899, Mount Rainier became the nation's fifth national park,
and by 1916, the system now known as the Wonderland Trail was completed, forming a loop nearly 100 miles long around the mountain.

Because of its massive network of glaciers and unpredictable weather,
Mount Rainier is an unforgiving peak. Dozens of climbers have died on its
slopes, yet each year about 10,000 people set out for the summit of the
dozing volcano. Only about half reach the top, however. The rest are turned
back by bad weather, altitude sickness, exhaustion, and hazardous glacial
crossings. This is not a mountain to be treated lightly. Although the mountain is a magnet for climbers, the adventurers make up only a fraction of
the 2 million visitors who arrive each year. This mountain is really all about
hiking through subalpine meadows.

Scenic idylls through flower-strewn meadows aside, the Cascades are
not dead—they're just sleeping. The eruption of Mount St. Helens in 1980
drove that fact home. But what of Mount Rainier? Snow and glaciers not-
withstanding, Rainier has a heart of fire. Steam vents at the mountain's

summit are evidence of that. Though the volcanic peak has not erupted for more than 150 years, it could erupt again at any time. Some scientists believe that Rainier's volcanic activity occurs in 3,000-year cycles; if this holds true, it'll be another 500 years (give or take) before another big eruption. So go ahead and plan that trip. In all likelihood, only the scenery will blow you away.

FLORA & FAUNA

Cougars, black bears, deer, elk, and **mountain goats** all live in park boundaries. Perhaps the most entertaining and enviable of the park's wild residents are its **marmots.** These largest members of the squirrel family spend their days nibbling wildflowers in subalpine meadows and stretching out on rocks to bask in the sun. Marmots share these subalpine zones with **pikas,** tiny relatives of rabbits that are more often heard than seen.

Monkeyflowers, elephant's heads, parrot's beaks, bear grass: They represent just a small fraction of the variety of **wildflowers** on the slopes of Mount Rainier. This mountain's subalpine meadows are among the most celebrated in the Northwest and the world.

In the northwest corner of the park, the **Carbon River Valley** opens out to the Puget Sound and channels moisture-laden air into its valleys. As a result, this valley is a rainforest where tree limbs are draped with moss and lichen, and where Douglas fir and western red cedar grow to enormous proportions. In the southeast corner of the park, in the **Grove of the Patriarchs** near the Stevens Canyon Entrance, stand some of the oldest trees—Douglas firs more than 1,000 years old and western red cedars more than 25 feet in circumference.

ESSENTIALS

Getting There & Gateways

Unlike its cousin across the Puget Sound, Olympic National Park, Rainier does not lie within a circle of roads; the northwest corner of the park, for example, is accessible only through one entrance.

The **Nisqually Entrance** (also known as the Nisqually–Longmire Rd.), in the southwest corner of the park, is the park's main access point. Just to the west on Wash. 706 is **Ashford,** where most of the area's accommodations and services are. A few miles farther west is **Elbe,** with a few more choices.

At the park's northeast corner, the **White River Entrance,** off Wash. 410, provides easier access from Seattle and points north if your goal is the Sunrise area. The town closest to this entrance is **Greenwater,** which has some overnight options.

In the northwest corner, the **Carbon River Entrance** is off Wash. 165 but is closed to vehicular traffic inside the park because of flooding; a reconstruction will soon allow vehicles 1.25 miles into the park and convert the remainder of the road into an improved trail. **Enumclaw** offers motels, restaurants, and fuel.

At the southeast corner, the **Stevens Canyon Entrance,** off Wash. 123 from U.S. 12, provides access from Yakima. **Packwood** and **Randle,** both south of the park on U.S. 12, are two of the larger towns in the nearby area. You'll find some accommodations in Packwood.

During the summer, it is also possible to enter the park from the east on **Wash. 410,** which also leads to Yakima by way of Chinook Pass. Entering this way gives you the

Mount Rainier National Park

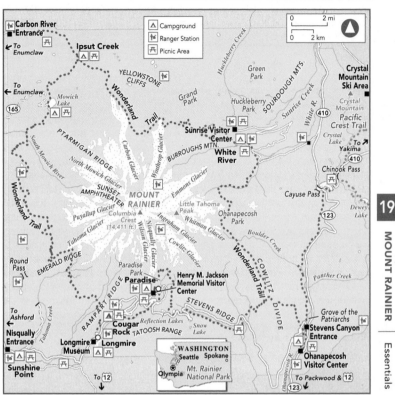

option of heading north to the White River Entrance and Sunrise, or south to Stevens Canyon.

In winter, only the Nisqually Entrance is open. Severe winter road damage often closes roads during summer; contact the park for current information.

THE NEAREST AIRPORT   The **Seattle–Tacoma International Airport** (© 206/787-5388; www.portseattle.org/seatac) is 70 miles northwest of the park. Allow about 2 hours for the drive on I-5, Wash. 7, and Wash. 706 to the Nisqually Entrance. The airport is served by practically all major airlines and car-rental companies.

Visitor Centers & Information

When you arrive, stop at one of the park's four visitor centers. The year-round **Long-mire Museum** (© 360/569-6575) is inside the park beyond the Nisqually Entrance and is the welcoming center for the park. The **Henry M. Jackson Visitor Center,** near Paradise Meadows, is the park's main visitor center, open year-round. The **Ohana-pecosh Visitor Center,** off Wash. 123 in the southeast corner of the park, is near the Stevens Canyon Entrance. It's open in summer only. The **Sunrise Visitor Center,** off

AVOIDING the crowds

On a sunny summer weekend, it is sometimes necessary to park more than a mile from Paradise and walk on forest trails and the road to the meadows. You can avoid the crowds by **visiting in the spring or fall.** Keep in mind that, in May, Paradise and Sunrise will still be snow-covered and most park roads will be closed; weather may still be unsettled. Even in June, Paradise may remain snow-covered and some park roads may be closed. Also, the rainy season starts in mid- to late October and continues until early summer.

Perhaps the best tip, if you're traveling in busy months, is to **visit on** **weekdays** rather than weekends. You might also consider avoiding the Sunrise and Paradise areas altogether, heading instead to the **more remote sections** of the park, such as the Carbon River area in the northwest section, or the Denman Falls/Gobblers Knob area in the southwest. Both are accessible, at least part of the way, by car, and they provide the same sorts of stunning vistas you get at Sunrise and Paradise. Carbon River Road and Westside Road, which leads to the Denman Falls area (open summer only), are often closed due to floods. Be sure to check at the ranger station for the latest info.

Wash. 410, past the White River Entrance, is in the northeast section of the park. It's also open in summer only.

Need more info? Contact **Mount Rainier National Park** (*©* **360/569-6575 or** 605/569-2211; www.nps.gov/mora). The park publishes a free newspaper, *The Tahoma News,* available at visitor centers with information about park activities.

Fees

Entry to the park for up to 7 days costs $15 per vehicle, $5 for individuals on foot, bike, or motorcycle. Camping costs $12 to $15 per night, depending on the campground and season.

Seasons & Climate

Summer is the warmest and driest time of the year, with frequent fog banks rolling in late and early in the day, and temperatures ranging from the upper 40s to the low 80s (10s to mid-20s Celsius). Spring and fall are cool and drizzly, with occasional days of warm weather late in the spring and early in the fall. The greatest rainfall comes in January and December, with daytime temperatures in the 40s (10s Celsius). Weather generally gets colder and nastier the higher up you go, and there is lots of snow in the higher elevations. This snow can linger well into the summer, even at popular Paradise.

It's important that you dress in layers for a day visit, when you may encounter any type of weather. It can go from warm to cool very quickly as you climb in altitude. Rain can come in suddenly, so rain gear is a good precaution.

EXPLORING THE PARK

Longmire, just inside the Nisqually Entrance, is the park's oldest developed area and the site of the historic hotel, which opened in 1899. Here you'll find the old Mount Rainier National Park Headquarters, now the National Park Inn, a year-round lodge and restaurant. There's also a museum, a general store, a wilderness information center, and a post office. Although it sounds as if this must be a small city, it is actually quite compact and rarely very crowded. Other important features of the area are the Trail of the Shadows, Historic District Walking Trail, and a Transportation Exhibit.

Paradise, in the south-central portion of the park, is a subalpine meadow and one of the most popular areas for visitors. Nearby you'll find the Jackson Visitor Center, the park's main visitor center, a gracefully curving stone and concrete structure that houses a snack bar and the only public showers in the park. Interesting exhibits on geology, glaciers, and the local flora and fauna are here. Paradise is also the site of the Paradise Inn, a historic mountain lodge. On busy days in the summer, there is a free shuttle from Ashford to Paradise; check the website for the current schedule.

Ohanapecosh, off Wash. 123 in the park's southeast corner, offers scenic views of the Ohanapecosh River near a visitor center. Inside, look for exhibits focused primarily on the old-growth forest ecosystem that surrounds this area. The 188-site Ohanapecosh Campground is here, as are several good, short hikes.

At 6,400 feet, **Sunrise,** in the northeast part, is the highest point to which you can drive in the park. This is the second most popular spot in the park. You'll find displays and naturalist-led walks, a snack bar and restaurant, and interpretive programs on the subalpine and alpine ecosystems. You can look at the glaciers up close with free telescopes. The visitor center is open daily from July through mid-September, when the roadway is open.

The **Carbon River area,** in the northwest corner, provides access to the most heavily forested area in the park. The jury is still out as to whether the terrain is actually lowland forest or temperate rainforest. The road here is currently closed to vehicle traffic until a reconstruction opens a small segment (most of it will become a hiking route), but trails lead into the backcountry and connect with the **Wonderland Trail.** A separate road (Wash. 165) reaches the Mowich Lake area, open to the lake in summer only.

ORGANIZED TOURS & RANGER PROGRAMS

Ranger-led tours, discussions, and seminars take place or begin at visitor centers. At **Longmire,** short talks take place daily in summer. There are evening programs at Cougar Rock Campground. At **Ohanapecosh,** there are ranger-led hikes and walks along popular trails weekend afternoons, as well as evening programs during June and July devoted to natural and cultural history and resources. From **Paradise,** there are daily walks to view wildflowers and glaciers. Park naturalists also roam the area answering questions. Daily ranger led walks also originate in the **Sunrise** area. During July and August, evening campfire programs take place at White River Campground on Thursday through Saturday night. Programs change each year and season. Check at a visitor center or the free park newspaper for specific programs and times during your visit.

DAY HIKES

Some trails, especially those near Sunrise and Paradise, are packed throughout the summer. However, many forest trails offer solitude. Trails in the northwest corner, near the Carbon River Entrance, are relatively quiet but now require a 4-mile hike along the destroyed roadway to get to the former trail head. Mowich Lake sees more weekend foot traffic, since the road is open in the summer. There is a free shuttle between Longmire and Paradise that stops at numerous trail heads.

The main thing to remember in the heavily visited spots in the subalpine portions of the park is to stay on the trails and stay off the wildflowers. Off-trail trampling erodes the thin loam topsoil that supports the fragile vegetation.

Be sure to boil any water taken from the park's rivers, as it has been known to carry *Giardia,* the little bug that causes mighty intestinal disorder. Don't even think about heading for a day climb anywhere near the upper altitudes of Rainier without checking in at a ranger station or employing a guide. Steep snowfields can become slippery in the sun or contain unstable ice bridges. Remember, people die in the high altitudes every year. Additionally, the National Park Service wants visitors to be aware of some other risks: Mud flows, glacial outburst floods, and falling rocks are hazards that may be encountered here.

19

For current information on trail availability or closures, call the **Longmire Wilderness Information Center** (© **360/569-6650**) in summer, or the Longmire Museum (© **360/569-6575**) year-round.

All the Way Around Mount Rainier

Wonderland Trail ★★★   With varying degrees of difficulty, this 93-mile loop is the mother of all trails in the park. It circles Mount Rainier, with numerous connecting trail heads. To some, making this loop through some of the most stunning vistas in the continental United States is a Northwest rite of passage. Think hard and plan ahead before you try to take it all at once. You'll want to leave yourself about 2 weeks' time to make the whole loop; campsite reservations are required and hard to get in midsummer.

There are more things to see on this trail than you can name. But expect to find yourself traveling through subalpine meadows, glacial streams, mountain passes, valley forests, and an ultimate summit point of 6,500 feet at Panhandle Gap. Many backcountry camping spots along the way provide water in the summer, but be sure to purify every drop. In the interest of planning shorter trips, keep in mind that you can connect with this trail from any of the spokelike trails that crisscross and touch the trail throughout the park, allowing you to set up a hiking mileage and time schedule all your own. It's possible for 1 day's elevation gain to be as much as 7,000 feet. 93 miles RT. Allow 10–14 days. Strenuous. Access: Start from Longmire, Paradise, Sunrise, Mowich Lake, or Carbon River.

Longmire Area

Carter Falls Trail ★★   This trail passes a wooden pipeline that once carried water, which generated electricity for Longmire. Go past Carter Falls about 50 yards for a look at the second waterfall, the zany Madcap Falls. This trail is part of the Wonderland Trail, between Paradise to the east and Indian Henry's to the west. 2.2 miles RT. Moderate. Access: 100 yards downhill from Cougar Park Campground, on the road to Paradise.

Rampart Ridge Trail ★★   This is a somewhat steep trail at first (the elev. gain is 1,339 ft.), before you arrive at the top of an ancient lava flow called the Ramparts, which offers panoramic views of the Nisqually Valley to the south, Mount Rainier to the north, and, to the west, the site of the massive Kautz Creek Mudflow of 1947. It's also your connection with many of the other trails in the area, including the Van Trump, Comet, and Christine Falls trails. 4.6 miles RT. Moderate. Access: Across road from Longmire Museum.

Van Trump Park & Comet Falls Trail ★★★   This steep trail (total elev. gain of 2,200 ft.) leads 1.9 miles through old-growth forest to Comet Falls, the second-highest falls in the park at 320 feet. Hiking another mile uphill takes you to beautiful views of the Nisqually, Van Trump, and Kautz glaciers. This is a popular trail in the summer, but it can be dangerous in early summer due to trail damage and steep, icy slopes; stop at the ranger station and ask for information on trail conditions before going. Up to 5.8 miles RT. Moderate. Access: Below Christine Falls Bridge on road to Paradise.

Paradise Area

Alta Vista ★★   This popular day hike meanders through subalpine meadows along a trail that leads to the top of an overlook with views of Paradise Meadows, Mount Adams, and Mount St. Helens to the south. There's a 600-foot elevation gain. 1.75 miles RT. Easy. Access: Jackson Visitor Center parking lot.

Skyline Trail ★★★   A good choice for high-elevation hiking, without going all the way to the top of Mount Rainier, Skyline is a sort of extended versions of all the trails that surround Paradise, offering lots of beautiful subalpine meadows and close-up views of the Nisqually Glacier, one of the most visible and beautiful glaciers in the park. At Panorama Point, there is a pit toilet for a quick stop before the trail begins to loop back around to the southeast. At the top of this loop, you may have to traverse some snow. There's a 1,700-foot elevation gain. On the way back, check out the views of Mount Adams and Mount St. Helens. 5 miles RT. Moderate. Access: Left of Paradise Ranger Station, next to restrooms.

Sunrise & Northeastern Areas

Glacier Basin Trail ★★   Watch for rusting machinery on this journey through a part of the park that wasn't always so protected. You'll see remnants of a mining operation from the late 1800s in this glacial valley. Follow an old road up past the headwaters of the White River. After 1 mile, veer to the left for beautiful views of the Emmons Glacier. Beyond the junction of the trail with the Burroughs Mountain Trail, you'll arrive at Glacier Basin Camp. Look for climbers making the ascent to the summit here, along a secondary route. Elevation gain is about 1,300 feet. 7 miles RT. Moderate to strenuous. Access: Past White River Entrance, in upper area of White River Campground.

Sourdough Ridge/Dege Peak Trail ★★   From the trail head, climb to a ridge top and turn east beneath the gaze of Antler Peak, after which you'll cruise along the ridge for wonderful views of Rainier to the south and the brilliant greens of the Yakima parklands below. At the top of Dege Peak, look south for close-up views of the Cowlitz Chimneys and farther-off views of snowcapped Mount Adams. 4.2 miles RT. Easy to moderate. Access: Sunrise Visitor Center.

Summerland Trail ★★   Hundreds of hikers can flock to this trail on a peak summer day, so beware. And stay on the trails to avoid trampling the wildflowers. It's a 3.5-mile graded walk through mature forests before entering the Frying Pan Creek area, where the scenery opens up into the brushy upper Frying Pan Valley. From there it's a steep .5-mile climb to the spectacular Summerland Meadows. The total elevation gain is 1,500 feet. 8.5 miles RT. Easy to moderate. Access: Past White River Entrance, on the way to Sunrise or White River area.

Sunrise Rim Trail ★★★ This is a nature trail with many interpretive signs to tell you what to look for as you gaze up at Mount Rainier, to the north. About 1.5 miles into the trail, you'll arrive at Shadow Lake and, just beyond, the walk-in Sunrise Campground. With a little more effort, you can hike south to the glacier overlook and be awed by the blue-white overhangs of Emmons Glacier and on to the first Burroughs Mountain. Total elevation gain is 900 feet. 4.8 miles RT. Easy to moderate. Access: Sunrise Visitor Center.

Ohanapecosh Area

Silver Falls Trail ★★ Popular with families, as its fairly level, the trail winds its way through old-growth forests and over a bridge above the pristine waters of the Ohanapecosh River facing the falls that give the area its name. The misty falls themselves drop 75 feet. Across the bridge below the falls is the return trail to the Ohanapecosh Campground. 2.4 miles RT. Easy. Access: Ohanapecosh Visitor Center; start at far end of "B" Loop of Ohanapecosh Campground.

Northwestern Rainier

Carbon Glacier & Moraine Park Trails ★★★ After hiking in the first 4.5 miles on the Carbon River Road, you begin this hike toward Moraine Park on the Wonderland Trail, the first 3 miles of which are a gentle uphill grade as they parallel the beautiful glacial waters of the Carbon River. Subsequently, the trail crosses the river on a suspension bridge just below the lower edge of the Carbon Glacier. Take a right turn on the Wonderland Trail at its junction with the Northern Loop, and the trail will lead you to the edge of this, the lowest and seemingly most monstrous glacier in the Lower 48. The trail then becomes a series of steep switchbacks that lead you through the neighboring forest to Moraine Park. Along the way, you'll pass several campsites (Carbon River, Dick Creek, and, farther along, Mystic Lake). The elevation gain is 1,200 to 3,300 feet, depending on the route you take. 17–21 miles RT. Moderate to strenuous. Access: Carbon River Entrance Station.

Tolmie Peak ★★ This is a hugely popular day hike, with lots of traffic from weekenders and kids, but you can't really go that wrong anywhere around here. The trail proceeds gently through 1.25 miles of forested woodland to the junction at Ipsut Pass (elev. 5,100 ft.). Stay left and proceed uphill another 1.75 miles to the subalpine meadows at Eunice Lake for a look at how far you're going to have to climb to Tolmie Peak. The entire hike has a 1,010-foot elevation gain. 6.5 miles RT. Moderate. Access: End of Mowich Lake Rd. on left side of lake.

OTHER SUMMER SPORTS & ACTIVITIES

BIKING No trails are open to mountain bikes in Mount Rainier National Park. A gravel road for great biking is Westside Road, which you can reach through the Nisqually Entrance of Mount Rainier National Park. It is completely closed to motorized vehicles after 3 miles. One of the best reasons to ride this road is the chance to get on some of the little-used west-side hiking trails (closed to bikes). Try strapping some hiking boots on your bike; this is a great way to get away from the crowds and see some of the rare, less crowded areas of the park. Another option is Carbon River Road, open to only bikes and pedestrians en route to the Ipsut Creek Campground and myriad trail heads.

BOATING & CANOEING Located in the northwest corner of the park, Mowich Lake is a pristine little lake with a peekaboo view of the mountain from its west side. The water is incredibly clear, and it's fun to paddle around gazing down into the deep at the large logs and boulders lying on the bottom. Early morning and late afternoon are particularly good times. You might catch a glimpse of an otter, and in the evening, deer often feed in the meadows by the lake's edge. A walk-in campground beside the lake makes this a great spot for a weekend camping and paddling trip. There are no facilities at the lake other than the campground and a ranger station, so you will need to bring your own boat.

MOUNTAINEERING Each year, more than 10,000 people set out to climb the 14,411-foot summit of Mount Rainier. That only slightly more than half make it to the top is a testament to how difficult the climb is. Although the ascent does not require rock-climbing skills, the glacier crossings require basic mountaineering knowledge, and the 9,000-foot climb from Paradise is physically demanding. This is not a mountain to be attempted by the unprepared or the untrained; over the years, dozens of people have died attempting the summit.

The easiest and most popular route starts at Paradise, at 5,400 feet, and climbs to the stone climbers' shelter at 10,188-foot Camp Muir. From here, climbers, roped together for safety, set out in the middle of the night to reach Columbia Crest, the mountain's highest point at 14,411 feet. From the summit on a clear day, seemingly all of Washington and much of Oregon stretches below.

The best way for most of us to climb Mount Rainier is with somebody who knows what he or she is doing, and that means **Rainier Mountaineering, Inc.,** (© **888/892-5462;** www.rmiguides.com); **International Mountain Guides** (© **360/569-2609;** www.mountainguides.com); or **Alpine Ascents** (© **206/378-1927;** www.alpineascents.com). Each offers a variety of mountaineering classes, as well as guided summer climbs. A class combined with the 2- or 3-day summit climb runs about $1,000 to $2,000.

WINTER SPORTS & ACTIVITIES

CROSS-COUNTRY & DOWNHILL SKIING There are several ungroomed cross-country trails around the Paradise and Longmire areas. Perhaps equally satisfying in winter is the absence of crowds and cars that haunt these regions during the summer months. Peace and quiet abound when snow covers the landscape, although there is often a threat of avalanches (check at the Jackson Visitor Center or Paradise Ranger Station). The slopes above the Paradise Inn usually stay covered with snow well into June. You can rent cross-country skis at **Longmire** at the National Park Inn (© **360/569-2411;** www.mtrainierguestservices.com). Skis, poles, and shoes will cost you about $20 per day.

Outside the northeast entrance of the park, downhill resort **Crystal Mountain ski area** (© **360/663-2265;** www.crystalmountainresort.com) offers 57 runs on 2,600 acres served by 11 lifts.

SNOWMOBILING Snowmobiles are permitted on designated roadways, and only when snow closes the roadways to normal traffic. Do not attempt to travel cross-country on trails or on undesignated roads. Obtain a copy of the park's snowmobile regulations.

SNOWSHOEING If you've never tried snowshoeing and want to, visit Mount Rainier National Park when free, ranger-led **snowshoe walks** lasting about 90 minutes are offered, on winter weekends and holidays from late December to early April. You can rent snowshoes at **Longmire** at the National Park Inn (© **360/569-2411;** www. mtrainierguestservices.com) for about $15 a day.

WHERE TO STAY

Inside the Park

National Park Inn ★ Not far from the Nisqually Entrance in the southwest part of the park, this 1920 lodge is the only year-round lodging on Mount Rainier. But even if it weren't, it would make a solid base for exploring the mountain, as the inn has easy access to hiking trails in summer and cross-country and snowshoeing routes in the wintertime (rentals available onsite). Guestrooms can be quite small (they vary), but have homey furnishings and boast spectacular views of the summit of Mount Rainier. Which is lucky as there's nothing else to look at once you're there—there's no Internet access or in-room phones or TVs.

At the Longmire Entrance. © **360/569-2275.** www.mtrainierguestservices.com. 25 units, 18 with bathroom. $116–$152 double without bathroom; $172–$244 double with bathroom. **Amenities:** Restaurant.

Paradise Inn ★★ With Mount Rainier looming above, this historic hotel sits next to numerous trail heads in Paradise, eliminating the rush for the parking lot in the morning—you can be the first one on the trails without a fuss. The stately inn, built in 1916 and significantly renovated in 2008, is the only lodging deep inside park boundaries. The original rooms are pretty dinky and share bathrooms down the hall (they have in-room sinks), but never fear, the units in a slightly newer annex have more space and private bathrooms. Some of the latter have two bedrooms and can accommodate four people in three beds. There are no TVs, phones, Wi-Fi in the rooms here, which seems appropriate in these rustic surroundings.

At Paradise. © **360/569-2275.** www.mtrainierguestservices.com. 121 units, 92 with bathroom. $119–$155 double without bathroom; $178–$297 double with bathroom. Closed mid-Oct to late May. **Amenities:** 2 restaurants.

Outside the Southwest Entrance (Ashford)

Budget travelers might want to look into the hostel-style accommodations at **Whittaker's Bunkhouse,** 30205 Wash. 706 E., Ashford (© **360/569-2439;** www.whittakers bunkhouse.com), with bunks for $35 and private rooms for $90 to $130 double. Private room rates are lower in winter, however bunks aren't available then.

Deep Forest Cabins ★★ These lovingly restored, downright glam 1940s cabins offer a sense of isolation in two forested settings near the entrance to Mount Rainier National Park. Looking for a honeymoon-esque getaway? Ask for a cabin with a soaking tub inside and a hot tub on the deck. The majority of the cabins have rustic architecture, but a few have eye-catching contemporary designs in blond wood; and almost all have such luxuries as full kitchens, flat screen TVs, I-Pod docks, and outdoor gas grills. Many are big enough for families or large groups. If you want a place with unique and stylish furnishings, and a distinctive sense of place, you've found it at this cabin group.

33823 Wash. 706, Ashford. © **866/553-9373** or 360/569-2954. www.deepforestcabins.com. 7 cabins. July–Aug $125–$325 double; Sept–May $110–$275 double. **Amenities:** Free Wi-Fi.

Stormking Spa Retreat ★★★ My favorite getaway in the area, this romantic lodging started out as a day spa. The beautiful setting outside Mount Rainier's

CAMPING options

Mount Rainier has more than 400 campsites in three drive-in campgrounds. None of the campgrounds in the park have RV utility hookups, nor are there laundry or shower facilities. Nightly fees are $12 to $15.

You should definitely make reservations at Cougar Rock and Ohanapecosh campgrounds between the last Friday in June and Labor Day; call ℂ **877/444-6777** or visit www.recreation.gov. Other campgrounds are on a first-come, first-served basis.

Cougar Rock Campground ★, a little more than 2.25 miles northwest of Longmire, has an amphitheater for ranger programs. I like it for its easy access to trails, but at 3,100 feet in elevation it can be a bit colder than **Ohanapecosh Campground ★**, 11 miles north of Packwood, Washington, on Wash. 123, which also has an amphitheater. **White River Campground ★★** is 5 miles west of the White River Entrance. It might be the prettiest of the three and has a spot right on the Wonderland Trail, but at 4,232 feet in elevation, it is also the chilliest. **Sunshine Point Campground** was closed in 2006 due to flood damage.

There are two walk-in campgrounds that often have spaces available, even on weekends. **Mowich Lake Campground ★★** is the nicer of the two, in the northwest corner of the park, at the end of unpaved S.R. 165, and the sites are only 100 yards from a parking lot.

A **permit** is required for all overnight stays in the wilderness. **Backcountry camping** is free with a permit obtained at any of the ranger stations, although the first-come, first-served permits are grabbed up quickly. Reservations ($20 per permit) can be made by mail or fax beginning in mid-March for the period from May through September. For information, call ℂ **360/569-6550.**

Nisqually Entrance begged for overnight accommodations, so the proprietors started building some here in the late 1990s. They have since put in five of the most chic cabins in the Northwest, in the form of four circular yurts and one square cabin, each with dazzling woodwork, river-rock showers, a private hot tub, and a gas fireplace. They are nicely spread out on the densely forested property, offering a sense of isolation but easy access to Ashford and the park.

37311 Wash. 706 E., Ashford. ℂ **360/569-2964.** www.stormkingspa.com. 5 cabins. Cabin $160–$220 double (2-night minimum). **Amenities:** Spa; free Wi-Fi.

Outside the Northeast (White River) Entrance

Alta Crystal Resort at Mount Rainier ★★ Alta Crystal Resort is known primarily as a lodge for skiers at nearby Crystal Mountain, but it's a fine choice for a summer visit to Mount Rainier, as well. Rooms here are one-bedroom suites that can accommodate a family of four, and loft units that sleep up to 6; all have a kitchen, fireplace or wood stove, and TV with DVD player (the resort has a library of about 700 movies). The romantic honeymoon cabin sleeps two adults, and is a masterwork of log architecture and interior woodworking. The resort offers a long list of recreational activities, including nightly activities in peak summer and winter seasons. A number of trails begin on the property.

68317 Wash. 410 E., Greenwater. ℂ **800/277-6475** or 360/663-2500. www.altacrystalresort.com. 24 units. $179–$269 1-bedroom suites; $249–$329 loft suites and honeymoon cabins. **Amenities:** Outdoor pool; outdoor hot tub; bike rentals ($35/day); free Wi-Fi.

WHERE TO EAT

Inside the Park

The dining rooms at the **Paradise Inn** and the **National Park Inn** (see "Where to Stay," p. 250) serve American and regional dishes, including salmon, chicken, steak, and pasta at dinner, with creative sandwiches and burgers at lunch. Lunch prices are mostly in the $10 to $16 range; dinners run $12 to $27. Specialties include a venison sloppy joe sandwich for lunch and bourbon buffalo meatloaf at dinner. The restaurants do not accept reservations, and because they are the only formal dining options within the park, you may have to wait a bit for a table. For quick meals, there is fast food at the **Jackson Visitor Center, Paradise Inn,** and **Sunrise Lodge.**

Near the Park

For a quick, casual meal in Ashford, try the **BaseCamp Grill** at Whittaker Mountaineering (© **360/569-2727;** www.basecampgrill.com); it serves burgers and sandwiches ($6–$11) as well as pizzas (about $20) and draft beer at lunch and dinner.

Copper Creek Inn ★★ In the mood for superb blackberry pie? The Copper Creek Inn bakes them up daily, along with an excellent grilled salmon fillet with blackberry vinaigrette (are you seeing a pattern?). Cuisine is American Northwest here, with burgers, sandwiches, and lots of salads on the lunch menu with the dinner menu expanding to include well-prepared steak, chicken, pasta, and fish. It's one of the closest restaurants to the park's southwest (Nisqually) entrance. The inn also offers lodging in cabins and historic suites.

35707 Wash. 706 E., Ashford. © **360/569-2326.** www.coppercreekinn.com; Main courses $6–$25. Open daily year-round, serving three meals in summer, and lunch and dinner the rest of the year. $6–$25.

Alexander's ★★ AMERICAN Located at a bed-and-breakfast inn with a landmark turret and waterwheel out front, this is a good pick for a fancy dinner in the Ashford area. The menu changes regularly, but you can always expect fresh salmon and trout sourced from the icy pond on the premises, as well as an assortment of lamb, beef, and poultry dishes. Burgers and vegetarian dishes are also available. Desserts are memorable, most of all the standout blackberry pie.

37515 Wash. 706 E., Ashford. © **360/569-2300.** www.alexanderscountryinn.com. Main courses $6–$12 breakfast and lunch, $10–$26 dinner. Summer daily 8:30–10:30am and 11:30am–8pm. No lunch and weekends only in winter.